S0-EVA-277

A COMMENTARY

ON

ACTS OF APOSTLES,

WITH A

REVISED VERSION OF THE TEXT.

BY

J. W. McGARVEY.

TENTH EDITION

Guardian of Truth Foundation
P.O. Box 9670
Bowling Green, Kentucky 42102

INTRODUCTION.

IT is necessary to the successful study of any literary production, that the exact design of the author should be known and kept constantly in view. It would be doing great injustice to the author of Acts, to suppose that he undertook this work without having before him some one leading object, which should serve as the connecting thread of the narrative, and according to which all the historic details should take place and form.

The conjectures of commentators as to what this leading object is are various and somewhat conflicting. "The writer's object," says Dr. Hackett, "if we are to judge of it from what he has performed, must have been to furnish a summary history of the origin, gradual increase, and extension of the Christian Church, through the instrumentality, chiefly, of the Apostles Peter and Paul."* This is rather a statement of *what* he has performed than of the *object* for which he performed it. The same defect attaches to Dr. Alexander's conjecture. He says: "The book before us is a special history of the planting and extension of the Church, both among Jews and Gentiles, by the gradual establishment of radiating centers, as sources of influence, at certain salient points throughout a large part of the empire, beginning at Jerusalem and ending at Rome."† That the history does exhibit these facts is certainly true, but that there is behind this a design for the accomplishment of which these facts are stated, must be equally true.

The author's design is equally misunderstood by Bloomfield, and others with him, who say that it was "to give an authentic account of the communication of the Holy Spirit, and of the miraculous powers and supernatural gifts bestowed by the Spirit," and "to establish the full claim of the Gentiles to be admitted into the Church of Christ."‡ It is true that the history establishes the claim of the Gentiles to admission into the Church, and also contains an account of the descent and work of the Holy Spirit, yet neither of these can be regarded as the leading thought around which the contents of the volume adjust themselves.

Mr. Barnes, in the midst of some detached statements upon this subject, has approached the true idea in the following characteristic remark: "This book is an inspired account of the character

*Com. on Acts, Int., p. 19. †Com. on Acts, Int., p. 13.
‡Greek Testament, with English notes, Int. to Acts.

(3)

4   INTRODUCTION.

of *true revivals of religion.*"* But the true idea is still more nearly approached by a writer in Kitto's Encyclopedia, who says: "Perhaps we should come still closer to the truth if we were to say that the design of Luke, in writing Acts, was to supply, by select and suitable instances, an illustration of the power and working of that religion which Jesus had died to establish."†

It is correctly assumed by Dr. Hackett, in the words above quoted, that we are to judge of a writer's design by what he has performed. Bearing in mind the distinction between the *work done* and the *design* for which it is done, a slight glance at the contents of this book will reveal to us a design which has escaped the notice of all the above-named writers.

Much the greater part of Acts may be resolved into a detailed history of cases of conversion, and of unsuccessful attempts at the conversion of sinners. If we extract from it all cases of this kind, with the facts and incidents preparatory to each and immediately consequent upon it, we will have exhausted almost the entire contents of the narrative. All other matters are merely incidental. The events of the first chapter were designed to prepare the apostles for the work of converting men; the gift of the Holy Spirit to them and to others was to qualify them for it; the admission of the Gentiles was an incident connected with the conversion of Cornelius, and others after him; the conference, in the fifteenth chapter, grew out of these conversions; and the long account of Paul's imprisonment in Jerusalem, Cesarea, and Rome, with his sea-voyage and shipwreck, constitute but the connected history of his preaching to the mob in Jerusalem, to the Sanhedrim, to Felix, to Festus, to Agrippa, and to the Jews and Gentiles in Rome. The episode in the twelfth chapter, concerning the persecutions by Herod, and his death, is designed to show that, even under such circumstances, "the word of God grew and multiplied." All the remainder of the history consists, unmistakably, in detailed accounts of conversions.

Such being the work performed by the author, we may readily determine his design by inquiring, Why should any cases of conversion be put upon record? Evidently, it was that men might know how conversions were effected, and in what they consisted. The cases which are recorded represent all the different grades of human society; all the different degrees of intellectual and religious culture; all the common occupations in life, and all the different countries and languages of the then known world. The design of this variety is to show the adaptation of the one gospel scheme to the conversion of all classes of men.

The history of a case of conversion necessarily embraces two distinct classes of facts: *First,* the agencies and instrumentalities employed in effecting it; *second,* the changes effected in the individual who is the subject of it. In the pursuit of his main design, therefore, the author was led to designate specifically all these agencies, instrumentalities, and changes. He does so in order that his readers may know what agents are employed, and how they work; what instrumentalities must be used, and how they are

*Notes on Acts, Int.   † Article, Acts.

applied; and what changes must take place, in order to the Scriptural conversion of a sinner.

The chief agent employed in the conversion of men is the Holy Spirit. It is this fact which led the author to detail so minutely the descent of the Holy Spirit, and the various gifts and influences by which his work was accomplished. He thus teaches the reader what part this divine agent performed in the conversion of sinners, and how he performed it.

Another important agency employed was the personal labor of the apostles and inspired evangelists. The manner in which their part of the work was performed is carefully described, in order that men of every age and country, whose business it is to perform the part corresponding to theirs, may learn, from their example, how to perform it Scripturally. But Peter and Paul were the chief laborers of that generation, and for this reason their names occupy the prominent position assigned them.

It is well known that the recital by men of the process of their conversion is well calculated both to teach sinners the process through which they must struggle in order to conversion, and to stimulate them to undertake it. Men are taught more successfully and influenced more powerfully by example than by precept. Many religious teachers of the present day, having discovered the practical workings of this principle in human nature, depend much more, in their efforts to convert sinners, upon well-told experiences than upon the direct preaching of the Word. The success which has attended this policy should admonish us that these experiences of conversion recorded in Acts are by no means to be lightly esteemed as instrumentalities for the conversion of the world. They possess, indeed, this advantage: that, in contrast with all the conversions of the present day, they were guided by infallible teaching, and were selected by infallible wisdom from among thousands of others which had occurred, because of their peculiar fitness for a place in the inspired record. They have, we may say, twice passed the scrutiny of infinite wisdom; for, *first*, all the conversions which occurred under the preaching of inspired men were directed by the Holy Spirit; and, *second*, if any difference existed between those put on record and the others, the Holy Spirit, by selecting these few, decided in their favor as the best models for subsequent generations. If a sinner seek salvation according to the model of modern conversions, he may be misled; for his model is fallible at best, and may be erroneous; but if he imitate these inspired models, it is impossible for him to be misled, unless the Holy Spirit itself can mislead him. Moreover, in so far as any man's supposed conversion does not *accord* with these, it *must* be wrong; in so far as it does accord with them, it *must* be right.

If it be asked why we may not as well take for our model the cases of conversion which occurred under the former dispensation, or during the life of Jesus, the answer is obvious. We do not live under the law of Moses, or the personal ministry of Jesus, but under the ministry of the Holy Spirit. Jesus, just previous to his ascension, committed the affairs of his kingdom on earth into the hands of twelve men, to be guided by the Holy Spirit, who descended shortly after he ascended; and now all that we can know of present terms of pardon must be learned through the teaching and example of these men. If, then, the conditions of pardon under any preceding dispensation be found to differ from those propounded in Acts, in all the points of difference the latter, and not the former, must be our guide. These are the last, and certainly the most elaborately detailed communications of the Divine will upon the subject, and belong peculiarly to the new covenant under which we live. If God has made them to differ, in any respect, from those under the old covenant, he teaches us, by this very difference, that he has thus far set aside the old through preference for the new. In the following pages it is made a leading object to ascertain the exact terms of pardon as taught by the apostles, and the precise elements which constitute real conversion to Christ.

The present is pre-eminently a missionary period of the Church. None has been more so, except the age of the apostles. Especially is it distinguished by success in the conversion of sinners in professedly Christian lands. Hence, it is a demand of the age that the true method of evangelizing the world should be known and read of all men. But the true method can be found only in the labors of inspired apostles and evangelists, and the record of these labors is found only in the book of Acts. A failure to understand and to appreciate this book has been, and still is, a most prolific source of confusion and error in the popular presentation of the gospel. By failing to discover its chief design, sinners are far more frequently directed to the Psalms of David for instruction upon the subject of conversion than to this book, which was written for this express purpose. There is, therefore, no one book in all the Bible to which the present generation of Bible readers so much need to have their attention specially directed. We have endeavored, in this volume, to set forth the labors of these inspired preachers as the true and infallible guide of the modern evangelist.

Another peculiarity of the present age is, the unlimited range given to speculations concerning the agency of the Holy Spirit in human redemption. A subject into which investigation should never have been pushed beyond the simple facts and statements of revelation, has thus become a most fruitful source of philosophical vagaries and of unbridled fanaticism. Whatever differences may appear among the many erroneous theories upon the subject, they all agree in the conception of a direct impact of the Spirit of God upon the spirit of man, by which the latter is enlightened and sanctified. This conception is not only common to them all, but it is the fundamental conception in each one of them. Under the influence of it, the more contemplative theorist receives new revelations, or "speaks as he is moved by the Holy Ghost;" the more enthusiastic calls for outpourings of the "Holy Spirit and of fire," dances, shouts, and falls in spasms; while the transcendentalist, receiving still further measures of the Spirit, points out mistakes made by the inspired apostles, and exposes defects in the character of Jesus.

INTRODUCTION. 7

Among the prevailing Protestant sects, a common theory of spiritual influence serves almost as a bond of union. It sometimes makes them almost forget the conflicts of past ages, melts down the cold barrier of separating creeds, and brings hereditary enemies together, to worship, for a time, at a common shrine. It is made the standard of orthodoxy; and to him who devoutly swears by it, it serves, like charity, to cover a multitude of sins, while to him who calls it in question, and contents himself with the very words of Scripture, it is a ban of excommunication. A difference on all other subjects is tolerated, if there is agreement on this; an agreement on all other subjects can be no bond of union, if there is a difference on this. In public discourse all other topics are made subordinate, and even the preaching of Christ, which was *the* work of the apostles, has been supplanted by *preaching the Holy Spirit.*

Various as are the conclusions of these theorists, they all have a common tendency to disparage the Word of God. Precisely as a man learns to depend upon internal admonitions for his religious guidance will he feel less dependence upon the written Word. Hence it is that the masses of the people, who are under the influence of these teachings, are so deplorably ignorant of the Bible. To call back the mind of the reader from all such vagaries to the revealed facts and simple apostolic statements upon this important subject, is another leading object of the following work. We will find that the book of Acts presents, in living form and unmistakable simplicity, the work of the Holy Spirit.

Some sixteen of the twenty-eight chapters of Acts are devoted almost exclusively to the labors of the Apostle Paul. Whatever can be known of this most heroic and successful of all the apostles must not only be interesting to every reader, but also highly instructive, as an example of faith in Christ in its higher development. Some of the most interesting facts in his history, and those which throw the greatest light upon his inner life, are not recorded by Luke, but may be gathered from incidental remarks in his own epistles. In this obscure position, they must ever escape the notice of ordinary readers. It is proposed, in this volume, to give them their chronological place in the narrative, thus filling up the blanks which Luke's design caused him to leave, and rounding out to some fullness and symmetry the portraiture of this noblest of all human subjects of Scripture biography.

We have already assumed, in accordance with the universal judgment of competent critics, that Luke is the author of Acts. For the evidences on which this judgment is based, I refer the reader to works devoted to this department of Scripture study. It appears, from his being distinguished by Paul, in Gal. iv: 11–14, from those "of the circumcision," that he was a Gentile, but of what country is not certainly known. He was a physician by profession, and is styled by Paul "the *beloved* physician."* This encomium, together with the fact that he shared with Paul many of the labors of his life, was his ever-present companion in his imprisonment, even his only companion in the closing scenes of his

* Col. iv: 14.

life;* and that we detect his presence or absence in the scenes of the narrative only as he uses the pronoun *we* or *they* to describe the party, are circumstances which indicate a character marked by great courage and endurance, yet softened by extreme modesty and warm affections. That he was a most enthusiastic admirer of Paul is evident both from the devotion with which he clung to his side, and from the vividness with which every peculiar expression of countenance and gesture of the apostle impressed his memory. He frequently records the sweeping motion of the hand with which Paul arrested the attention of an audience, and the glance with which he fixed his eyes upon the enemies of the truth. Yet, notwithstanding this personal admiration, so just is his sense of propriety that he never pauses for a moment to express his admiration for the wonderful developments of character which he portrays. In this, however, he but imitates a distinguishing peculiarity of all the inspired writers.

The book of Acts embraces a period of about thirty years—from the ascension of Christ, A. D. 33, to the end of the second year of Paul's imprisonment at Rome, A. D. 63. In the latter part of the year 63, or the beginning of 64, while Luke was still with Paul in Rome, it is most likely that the work was published. For the historical connection and chronology of particular events described in the work, the reader is referred to the body of the Commentary.

It was no part of my original design to undertake a revision of the English text of Acts, but I hoped that, ere this time, an improved version of the whole New Testament would be put into the hands of the public by the American Bible Union. No final revision of Acts, however, having appeared from that Society, or from any other source, up to this writing, I am constrained to content myself with such a revision of the text as I have been able to prepare during the progress of the work. I have aimed to preserve, in general, the language of the common version. Where the propriety of a change would be obvious to the reader of the Greek, or depends merely upon taste, no notes are given to justify it. In cases where a defense seemed to be needed, the reader will find it, either in the body of the work or in foot-notes. I beg the critical reader, however, to remember that the revision is designed not for general adoption, but simply for the purpose to which it is applied in this Commentary, and that, even here, it is a secondary part of the undertaking.

In the execution of the work, I have aimed to make not merely a book of reference, but a volume to be read consecutively through, with the interest which belongs to the narrative. In order to this end, I have aimed to make prominent the author's connection of thought throughout; and, in order to render it the more instructive, wherever the text presents important issues connected with the great religious questions of the day, I have taken time to elaborate the argument as freely as the space which I had allotted myself would admit.

* 2 Tim. iv: 11.

COMMENTARY.

ACTS I: 1, 2.

1, 2. A NARRATIVE of Jesus of Nazareth, designed to convince men that he is the Christ, would most naturally begin with his birth, and terminate with his ascension to heaven. Such was the "former narrative" which Luke had addressed to Theophilus, and he alludes to it as such, in introducing his present work: (1) "*The former narrative I composed, O Theophilus, concerning all that Jesus began both to do and to teach,* (2) *until the day in which, having given commandment through the Holy Spirit to the apostles whom he had chosen, he was taken up.*"

This reference to his former narrative is most appropriate in its place, inasmuch as the one now undertaken is based entirely upon it. The specific reference to "the day in which, having given commandment through the Holy Spirit to the apostles whom he had chosen, he was taken up," is still more in point, from the fact that all the authority which the apostles had for the labors Luke is about to narrate was derived from the commandment given on that day. The history of that day furnishes but one commandment then given, which was the apostolic commission. In this commission, then, Luke locates the starting point of his present narrative.

If we would appreciate the narrative thus briefly introduced to us, we must begin, with the author, by a proper understanding of this commission.

During the personal ministry of Jesus, he authorized no human being to announce his Messiahship. On the contrary, whenever he discovered a disposition to do so, he uniformly forbade it, and this not only to various recipients of his healing power, but to the apostles themselves. When Peter made the memorable confession, "Thou art the Christ, the son of the living God," we are told that, at the close of the conversation, "he charged his disciples that they should tell no man that he was Jesus the Christ."* Such was his uniform injunction on similar occasions. Even when Peter, James, and John had witnessed his transfiguration, and heard God himself proclaim him his Son, as they came down from the mount, "Jesus charged them, saying, Tell the vision to no man, until the Son of man is risen from the dead."†

* Matt. xvi: 20. † Matt. xvii: 9.

(9)

This stern prohibition, quite surprising to most readers of the New Testament, may be accounted for, in part, by a desire to avoid that political ferment, which, in the existing state of the public mind, might have resulted from a general belief among the Jews that he was their Messiah. But there is a much more imperative reason for it, found in the mental and moral condition of the disciples themselves. Their crude conceptions of the Messiahship, their gross misconception of the nature of the expected Kingdom, their misunderstanding of much that he had taught them, and their imperfect remembrance of that which they had understood, rendered them incapable of presenting his claims truthfully, not to say infallibly, to the world. Moreover, their faith had not, as yet, acquired the strength necessary to the endurance of privations and persecutions. While laboring under these defects, they were most wisely prohibited from preaching that he was the Christ.

During the last night he spent on earth, Jesus at length informed them that this restriction would soon be removed, and they should receive the qualifications necessary to be his witnesses. He says: "The Advocate, the Holy Spirit, whom the Father will send in my name, he shall *teach you all things*, and bring all things to your remembrance, whatsoever I have said to you."* "I have many things to say to you, but you can not bear them now; howbeit when he, the Spirit of truth, is come, he will *guide you into all the truth*."† "He shall testify of me, and *you* also shall *testify*, because you have been with me from the beginning."‡ In these words they have a promise that they shall testify of Jesus, with the Holy Spirit for their guide; but the promise looks to the future for its fulfillment.

Finally, "on the day in which he was taken up," he gives them the commandment which is to unseal their lips, and authorizes them to preach the glad tidings to every creature. Without this commandment, they could not have dared to tell any man that he was the Christ; with it, they are authorized to begin the labors which our historian is about to narrate. But even yet there is one restriction laid upon them; for they have not yet received the promised qualifications. "He commanded them that they should not depart from Jerusalem; but await the promise of the Father, which you have heard from me."∥

Such was the necessity for the commandment in question, and for the limitation which attended it when given. The items of which it is composed are not fully stated by either one of the historians, but must be collected from the partial statements of Matthew, Mark, and Luke. Matthew presents three of them, as follows: "Go *disciple* all nations, *immersing* them into the name of the Father, and of the Son, and of the Holy Spirit, *teaching* them to observe and do all whatsoever I have commanded you."§ Mark presents five items in these words: "Go *preach the gospel* to every creature; he who *believes* and is *immersed* shall be *saved;* he who *believes not shall be condemned*."¶ Luke simply states that Jesus said, "Thus it behoved

---

* John xiv: 26. † John xvi: 12, 13. ‡ John xv: 26, 27.
∥ Verse 4, below. § Matt. xxviii: 19, 20. ¶ Mark xvi: 15, 16.

the Christ to suffer, and to rise from the dead the third day, and that *repentance* and *remission of sins* should be preached in his name among all nations, beginning at Jerusalem."* If we combine these items, by arranging them in their natural order of succession, we will have the commission fully stated.

The command quoted by Mark, "Preach the gospel to every creature," necessarily comes first. The command, "Disciple all nations," is next in order; for it is by means of preaching that they were to make disciples. But when a man is made a disciple he becomes a *believer;* and Matthew and Mark agree in the statement that he who *believes*, or, in Matthew's style, he who is discipled, is then to be *immersed.* Luke, however, says that *repentance* must be preached, and as repentance precedes obedience, we are compelled to unite it with faith, as antecedent to immersion. Next after immersion comes Mark's statement, "he shall be saved." But salvation may be either that which the pardoned sinner now enjoys, or that to be enjoyed after the resurrection from the dead: hence this term would be ambiguous but for Luke's version of it, who quotes that "*remission of sins*" is to be preached. This limits the meaning of the promise to that salvation which consists in remission of sins. Next after this comes the command, "teaching them to observe and do" what I have commanded you. Finally, they were to proclaim that they who believed not, and, consequently, complied not with the terms of the commission, should be condemned. In brief, they were commanded to go into all the world, and make disciples of all nations by preaching the gospel to every creature; to immerse all penitent believers into the name of the Father, and of the Son, and of the Holy Spirit, promising such the remission of their sins; then teaching them all their duties and privileges, as disciples of Jesus. In the mean time, all were to be assured that he who believed not should be condemned.

Making this commission the starting point of his narrative, Luke proceeds, after a few more preliminary observations, to relate the manner in which it was executed. This is the key to the whole narrative. We will find the apostles adhering strictly to its guidance. Their actions will furnish a complete counterpart to the items of their commission, and the best exposition of its meaning. For the strongest confirmation of the brief exposition just given, we refer to the course of the narrative as set forth in the following pages.

3. As our author is about to present the apostles testifying to the resurrection of Jesus, he sees proper, in his introduction, to state briefly the ground of their qualifications for this testimony. He does this in the remainder of the paragraph of which we have already quoted a part: (3) "*To whom, also, he presented himself alive, after his suffering, by many infallible proofs, being seen by them during forty days, and speaking the things pertaining to the kingdom of God.*" From the concluding chapters of the former narratives, we learn more particularly the nature and number of these infallible proofs. These, having been fully stated by himself and others, are not here

* Luke xxiv: 46, 47.

repeated. We learn here, however, a fact not there related: that the space from the resurrection to the ascension was forty days.

4, 5. To account for the delay of the apostles in Jerusalem after receiving their commission, and to prepare the reader for the scenes of the coming Pentecost, the historian next relates a part of the conversation which had taken place on the day of the ascension: (4) *"And being assembled with them, he commanded them not to depart from Jerusalem, but to await the promise of the Father, which you have heard from me. (5) For John, indeed, immersed in water; but you shall be immersed in the Holy Spirit, not many days hence."* The command not to depart from Jerusalem is mistaken, by some commentators, for the commandment mentioned above, as being given on the day he was taken up. But, in truth, as we have already seen, the commission constituted that commandment, while this is merely a limitation of the commission, in reference to the time and place of beginning. The *"promise* of the Father" which they were to await, is the promise of the Holy Spirit, which they had heard from him on the night of the betrayal, and which, they now learn, is to be fulfilled by their immersion in the Spirit. On this use of the term *immersion* see the Commentary, 2: 16–18.

6–8. We are informed by Matthew that Jesus prefaced the commission by announcing, "All authority in heaven and on earth is given to me." It was, probably, this announcement that led to the inquiry which Luke next repeats. Being informed that all authority was now given to him, the disciples expected to see him begin to exercise it in the way they had long anticipated. (6) *"Now when they were come together, they asked him, saying, Lord, wilt thou at this time restore the kingdom to Israel?* (7) *But he said to them, It is not for you to know the times or seasons which the Father has appointed in his own authority.* (8) *But you shall receive power, when the Holy Spirit comes upon you, and you shall be witnesses for me in Jerusalem, and in all Judea, and Samaria, and to the uttermost part of the earth."*

The question, "Lord, wilt thou at this time restore the kingdom to Israel?" indicates two interesting facts: *First*, that the apostles still misconceived the nature of Christ's kingdom; *second*, that the kingdom was not yet established. Both these facts deserve some attention at our hands, especially the latter.

Their misconception consisted in the expectation that Christ would re-establish the earthly kingdom of Israel, and restore it to its ancient glory, under his own personal reign. In his reply, the Savior does not undertake to correct this misconception, but leaves it as a part of that work of enlightenment yet to be effected by the Holy Spirit.

The time at which the kingdom of Christ was inaugurated is the point of transition from the preparatory dispensation, many elements of which were but temporary, into the present everlasting dispensation, which is to know no change, either of principles or of ordinances, in the course of time. It is necessary to determine this point, in order to know what laws and ordinances of the Bible belong to the present dispensation. All things enjoined subsequent to this period are binding upon us as citizens of the kingdom of Christ; but nothing enjoined as duty or granted as a privilege, under former dispensations, is applicable to us, unless it is specifically extended to us. It requires no less divine authority to extend into the kingdom of Christ the institutions of the Jewish kingdom than it did to establish them at first. This proposition is self-evident. To fix, therefore, most definitely this period is a matter of transcendent importance, and must here have all the space that it requires. It is a question of fact, to be determined by positive Scripture statements.

The expression "kingdom of heaven" is used only by Matthew. In the connections where he uses this expression, the other three historians uniformly say "kingdom of God." This fact shows that the two expressions are equivalent. Explaining the former by the latter, we conclude that the "kingdom of heaven" is not *heaven*, but simply a kingdom of God, without regard to locality. This kingdom is also called by Christ his own, as the Son of man; for he says, "There are some standing here who shall not taste of death till they see the *Son of man* coming in *his kingdom.*"* The Apostle Paul also speaks of the "kingdom of God's dear Son,"† and says, "He must *reign* till he has put all enemies under his feet."‡

Of the kingdom of God, then, Jesus is the king: hence the time at which he became a king is the time at which "the kingdom of Christ and of God"|| began. Furthermore, as it was *Jesus*, the *Son of man*, who was made king, it is evident that the kingdom could not have commenced till after he *became* the Son of man. This consideration at once refutes the theory which dates the beginning of the kingdom in the days of Abraham.

But it is not only Jesus the *Son* of *man*, but Jesus who *died*, that was made king. "We see Jesus," says Paul, "who was made a little lower than the angels, on account of the *suffering of death*, *crowned* with glory and honor."§ It was after his death, and not during his natural life, that he was made a king. It is necessary, therefore, to reject the other theory, which locates the beginning of the kingdom in the days of John the Immerser.

Finally, it was after his resurrection and his ascension to heaven that he was made a king. For Paul says, "Being found in fashion as a man, he humbled himself, and became obedient unto death, even the death of the cross; wherefore, God hath *highly exalted* him, and given him a name that is *above every name*, that at the name of Jesus *every knee should bow*, of things in heaven, and things in earth, and things under the earth, and that every tongue should confess that Jesus Christ is *Lord*, to the glory of God the Father."¶ It is here we are to locate that glorious scene described by David and by Paul, in which God said to him, "Sit thou on my right hand, till I make thine enemies thy footstool."** He "sat down on the right hand of the throne of God,"†† and the Father said, "Let all the angels of God worship him."‡‡ At this

* Matt. xvi: 28. † Col. i: 13. ‡ 1 Cor. xv: 25. | Eph. v: 5. § Heb. ii: 9.
¶ Phil. ii: 8, 11. ** Ps. cx: 1; Heb. i: 13. †† Heb. xii: 2. ‡‡ Heb. i: 6.

word, among the gathering and circling hosts of heaven, every knee was bowed and every tongue confessed that Jesus is "Lord of lords and King of kings." It was then that the kingdom of God was inaugurated in heaven; and it was in immediate anticipation of it, with all things in readiness and waiting, that Jesus said to his disciples, as he was about to ascend on high, "All authority, in heaven and on earth, is given to me"

Having now fixed the time at which the kingdom was inaugurated in heaven, we are prepared to inquire when it began to be administered on earth. It began, of course, with the first administrative act on earth, and this was the sending of the Holy Spirit upon the apostles on the day of Pentecost. On that occasion, Peter says, "This Jesus has God raised up, whereof we are witnesses. Therefore, being *to the right hand of God exalted*, and having received from the Father the promise of the Holy Spirit, he has *shed forth this* which you now *see* and *hear*." "Therefore, let all the house of Israel know assuredly, that God has made that same Jesus whom you have crucified, both *Lord* and *Christ*."* This event is here assumed as the proof of his exaltation, and the history shows it to be the first act of the newly-crowned King which took effect on earth. These facts are consistent with no other conclusion than that the kingdom of Christ was inaugurated on earth on the first Pentecost after his ascension.

We might assume that the above argument is conclusive, and here dismiss the subject, but for some passages of Scripture which are supposed to favor a different conclusion. It was said by Jesus, "The law and the prophets were until John; since that time the kingdom of God is preached, and every man presses into it."† Again: "Woe unto you, Scribes and Pharisees, hypocrites! for you shut up the kingdom of heaven against men; for you neither go in yourselves, nor will you suffer those who are entering, to go in."‡ And again: "If I cast out demons by the Spirit of God, then is the kingdom of God come to you."‖ It is argued, from these and kindred passages, that the law and the prophets ceased, as authority, with the beginning of John's ministry; that the kingdom of heaven then began, and men were pressing into it, while Scribes and Pharisees were striving to keep them from entering it; and that Jesus recognizes it as an existing institution, in the remark, "Then is the kingdom of God *come to you.*"

But there are other passages in the gospels which appear to conflict with these, and are inconsistent with this conclusion. The constant preaching of John, of Jesus, and of the Seventy, was, "The kingdom of heaven is *at hand;*" ἤγγικε, "*is near.*" Jesus exclaims, "Among them who are born of women there hath not arisen a greater than John the Immerser; notwithstanding, he that is *least* in the kingdom of heaven is *greater* than he."§ Again: "There are some standing here who shall not taste of death *till* they *see* the kingdom of God."¶ And, finally, the question we are now considering, "Lord, wilt thou at this time restore the kingdom

---

*Acts ii: 32–36. †Luke xvi: 16. ‡Matt. xxiii: 13. ‖Matt. xii: 28.
§Matt. xi: 11. ¶Luke ix: 27.

to Israel?" It is evident, from these passages, *first*, that John was not in the kingdom, for otherwise the *least* in the kingdom could not be greater than he; *second*, that the generation then living were *yet* to see the kingdom of God; *third*, that the disciples themselves were still looking for it *in the future*. If it be urged, in reference to the first of these conclusions, that the kingdom, of which John was not a citizen, is the kingdom in its future glory, the assumption is refuted by the very next verse in the context: "From the days of John the Immerser till now the kingdom of heaven suffers violence, and the violent take it by force."* Whatever may be the true interpretation of these rather obscure words, they certainly can not refer to the kingdom of glory.

Now, no hypothesis upon this subject can be accepted which does not provide for a complete reconciliation of these apparently conflicting passages of Scripture. The hypothesis that the kingdom was inaugurated by John can not do so; for, in that case, it is inconceivable that John himself was not a member of it, and equally so that he should constantly preach, "The kingdom of heaven *is near*." Again: if it was inaugurated during the personal ministry of Jesus, it is unaccountable that he should state, as a startling fact, that some of those present with him should live to see it, or that the disciples themselves should be ignorant of its existence. This hypothesis, therefore, is incapable of reconciling the various statements on the subject, and must, for this reason, be dismissed.

On the other hand, if we admit, according to the irresistible force of the facts first adduced in this inquiry, that the kingdom was inaugurated in heaven when Jesus was coronated, and that it began to be formally administered on earth on the next succeeding Pentecost, there is no difficulty in fully reconciling all the passages quoted above. It was necessary to the existence of the kingdom on earth not only that the king should be upon his throne, but that he should have earthly subjects. In order, however, that men should acknowledge themselves his subjects the moment that he became their king, it was necessary that they should be previously prepared for allegiance. This preparation could be made in no other way than by inducing men, in advance, to adopt the principles involved in the government, and to acknowledge the right of the proposed ruler to become their king. This was the work of John and of Jesus. When men began, under the influence of their teaching, to undergo this preparation, they were, with all propriety of speech, said to be *pressing* into the kingdom of God. Those who opposed them were striving to keep them from entering the kingdom; and to both parties it could be said, "The kingdom of God is *come to you*." It had come to them in the influence of its principles. "From the days of John the Immerser the kingdom of heaven was preached," not as an *existing* institution, but in its elementary principles, and by asserting the pretensions of the prospective king. Thus, we find that the various statements in the gospels upon this subject, when harmonized in the only way of which they are capa-

* Matt. xi: 12.

ble, lead us back to our former conclusion, with increased confidence in its correctness.

We may pursue the same inquiry in an indirect method, by determining when the previous kingdom of God among the Jews terminated. As they both, with their conflicting peculiarities, could not be in formal existence among the same people at the same time, the new one could not begin till the old one terminated. That the law and prophets were until John, Jesus declares; but he does not declare that they continued no longer. On the contrary, he was himself "a minister of the circumcision,"* and kept the law till his death. The law and the prophets were, until John, the *only* revelation from God. Since then the gospel of the coming kingdom was preached in *addition* to it, and was designed to fulfill the law and the prophets by preparing the people for a "better covenant." Even the sacrifices of the altar, however, continued, with the sanction of Jesus, up to the very moment that he expired on the cross. Then "the vail of the temple was rent in two from the top to the bottom," indicating the end of that dispensation. All the sacrifices being then fulfilled in him, and a new and living way being consecrated for us, not *under* the vail, as the high priest had gone, but *through* the vail—that is to say, his flesh†—he put an end to the priesthood of Aaron,‡ and took out of the way the handwriting of ordinances, nailing it to his cross.‖ At the death of Christ, therefore, the old kingdom came to its legal end, and on the next Pentecost the new kingdom began.

Regarding this, now, as a settled conclusion, we proceed to consider, briefly, the Savior's answer to the question which has detained us so long. He said to them, "It is not for you to know the times or the seasons which God has appointed in his own authority." By the expression "in his own authority," I suppose he intended to indicate that the times and seasons of God's purposes are reserved more specially under his own sovereign control, and kept back more carefully from the knowledge of men, than the purposes themselves. It is characteristic of prophesy that it deals much more in facts and the succession of events than in definite dates and periods. The apostles were to be agents in inaugurating the kingdom, but, as proper preparation for their work did not depend upon a foreknowledge of the time, it was not important to reveal it to them.

But it was all-important that they should receive the necessary *power:* hence Jesus adds, "But you shall receive power, when the Holy Spirit comes upon you." The power here promised is not *authority*, for this he had given them in the commission; but it is that miraculous power to know all the truth, and work miracles in proof of their mission, which he had promised them before his death. He says to them, virtually, It is not for you to know the time at which I will establish my kingdom, but you shall receive power to inaugurate it on earth when the Holy Spirit comes upon you. This is an additional proof that the kingdom was inaugurated on the day of Pentecost.

While promising them the requisite power, Jesus takes occasion

* Rom. xv: 8. † Heb. x: 20. ‡ Heb. vii: 11, 12. ‖ Col. ii: 14.

to mark out their successive fields of labor: first "in Jerusalem," next, "in all Judea," then "in Samaria," and finally, "to the uttermost part of the earth." It is not to be imagined that this arrangement of their labors was dictated by partiality for the Jews, or was merely designed to fulfill prophesy. It was rather foretold through the prophets, because there were good reasons why it should be so. One reason, suggested by the commentators generally, for beginning in Jerusalem, was the propriety of first vindicating the claims of Jesus in the same city in which he was condemned. But the controlling reason was doubtless this: the most devout portion of the Jewish people, that portion who had been most influenced by the preparatory preaching of John and of Jesus, were always collected at the great annual festivals, and hence the most *successful* beginning could there be made. Next to these, the inhabitants of the rural districts of Judea were best prepared, by the same influences, for the gospel; then the Samaritans, who had seen some of the miracles of Jesus; and, last of all, the Gentiles. Thus the rule of *success* was made their guide from place to place, and it became the custom of the apostles, even in heathen lands, to preach the gospel "first to the Jew" and "then to the Gentile." The result fully justified the rule; for the most signal triumph of the gospel was in Judea, and the most successful approach to the Gentiles of every region was through the Jewish synagogue.

9. Having now completed his brief notice of the last interview between Jesus and the disciples, Luke says, (9) "*And when he had spoken these things, while they were beholding, he was taken up, and a cloud received him out of their sight.*" We learn, from Luke's former narrative, that it was while Jesus was in the act of blessing them, with uplifted hands, that he was parted from them and borne aloft into heaven.* The cloud which floated above formed a background, to render the outline of his person more distinct while in view, and to suddenly shut him off from view as he entered its bosom. Thus all the circumstances of this most fitting departure were calculated to preclude the suspicion of deception or of optical illusion.

It has been urged by some skeptical writers, that the silence of Matthew and John, in reference to the ascension, who were eye-witnesses of the scene, if it really occurred, while it is mentioned only by Luke and Mark, who were not present, is ground for suspicion that the latter derived their information from impure sources. Even Olshausen acknowledges that, at one time, he was disquieted on this point, because he could not account for this peculiar difference in the course of the four historians.† That the testimony of Mark and Luke, however, is credible, is made apparent to all who believe in the *resurrection* of Jesus, by simply inquiring, what *became* of his body after it was raised? It was certainly raised immortal and incorruptible. There is nothing in his resurrection to distinguish it from that of Lazarus, or the widow's son of Nain, so that he should be called "the first fruits of them who slept,"‡ but the fact that he rose to die no more. But when he was about to leave

* Luke xxiv: 50, 51.   † Com. *in loco.*   ‡ 1 Cor. xv: 20.

the earth, there was only this alternative, that his body should return again to the grave, or ascend up into heaven. So far, therefore, is the account of the ascension from being incredible, that even if none of the historians had mentioned it, we would still be constrained to conclude that, at some time, and in some manner, it did take place.

We may further observe, that though Matthew and John do not mention the ascension, the latter reports a conversation with Mary the Magdalene at the sepulcher, in which Jesus clearly intimated that it would take place. He said to her, "*Touch* me not; for I am not yet *ascended* to my Father."* And that his ascension would be visible, he had intimated to the disciples, when he said, "Doth this offend you? What if you shall *see* the Son of Man *ascend up* where he was before?"†

But still the question recurs, why should Matthew and John omit an account of this remarkable event, and why should Luke and Mark, who were not eye-witnesses, make mention of it? It would be sufficient to answer, For a similar reason, no doubt, to that which led each of these writers to omit some interesting facts which are mentioned by others.

But we may find a still more definite answer by examining the last chapter of each of the four gospels. It will be observed, that John saw fit to close his narrative with the fishing scene which occurred on the shore of Galilee, making no mention at all of the last day's interview. Of course, it would have required a departure from this plan to have mentioned the ascension. Matthew brings his narrative to a close with the scene on a *mountain in Galilee*, whereas the ascension took place from Mount Olivet, near Jerusalem. There was nothing in his closing remarks to suggest mention of the ascension, unless it be his account of the commission; but the commission was really first given to them at that time,‡ though finally repeated on the day of the ascension.‖ On the other hand, Mark and Luke both choose, for their concluding paragraphs, such a series of events as leads them to speak of the last day's interview; and as the ascension was the closing event of the day, it would have been most unnatural for them not to mention it. Still further, in the introduction to the book of Acts, the leading events of which are to have constant reference to an ascended and glorified Redeemer, Luke felt still greater necessity for giving a formal account of the ascension.

10, 11. Not only the ascension of Jesus to heaven, but his future coming to judgment, is to be a prominent topic in the coming narrative, hence the introduction here of another fact, which not even Luke had mentioned before. (10) "*And while they were gazing into heaven, as he went away, behold, two men stood by them in white apparel*, (11) *who also said, Men of Galilee, why stand ye gazing up into heaven? This same Jesus, who was taken up from you into heaven, shall so come, in the same manner that you have seen him going into heaven.*" These "two men in white apparel" were, undoubtedly, angels in human form. This is the natural conclusion from the words they utter, and

* John xx: 17.   † John vi: 62.   ‡ Matt. xxviii: 16-18.   ‖ Mark xvi: 14-19.

ACTS I: 12-14.

is confirmed by the fact that two others who appeared at the sepulcher, and are called "men in shining garments" by Luke,* are called "two angels in white" by John.† Luke speaks of them according to their appearance; John, according to the reality.

It should be observed that the angels stated not merely that Jesus would *come* again, but that he would come *in like manner* as they had seen him go; that is, visibly and in his glorified humanity. It is a positive announcement of a literal and visible second coming.

12. At the rebuke of the angel, the disciples withdrew their longing gaze from the cloud into which Jesus had entered, and, cheered by the promise of his return, (12) "*Then they returned into Jerusalem from the Mount called Olivet, which is near Jerusalem, distant a Sabbath-day's journey.*" The ascension took place near Bethany,‡ which was nearly two miles from Jerusalem,‖ and on the further side of Mount Olivet. It was the nearer side of the Mount, which was distant a Sabbath-day's journey, or seven-eighths of a mile. We learn, from Luke's former narrative, that they returned to Jerusalem "with great joy."§ Their sorrow at parting from the Lord was turned into joy at the hope of seeing him again.

13. "*And when they were come in, they went up into an upper room, where were abiding Peter, and James, and John, and Andrew, Philip and Thomas, Bartholomew and Matthew, James son of Alpheus, and Simon Zelotes, and Judas brother of James.*" This enumeration of the apostles very appropriately finds place here, showing that all of those to whom the commission was given were at their post, ready to begin their work, and waiting for the promised power from on high.

14. The manner in which these men spent the time of their waiting, which was an interval of ten days, was such as we would expect: (14) "*These all continued with one accord in prayer and supplication, with the women, and Mary the mother of Jesus, and with his brothers.*" The chief scene of this worship was not the upper room where the eleven were abiding, but the temple; for we learn, from Luke's former narrative, that they "were continually in the temple, praising and blessing God."¶

The mother of Jesus is here mentioned for the last time in New Testament history. The fact that she still remained with the disciples, instead of returning to Nazareth, indicates that John was faithful to the dying request of Jesus, and continued to treat her as his own mother.** Though the prominence here given to her name shows that she was regarded with great respect by the apostles, the manner in which Luke speaks of her shows that he had not dreamed of the worship which was yet to be offered to her by an idolatrous church.

Whether those here called the "brothers" of Jesus were the sons of Mary, or more distant relatives of Jesus, is not easily determined, from the fact that the Greek word is ambiguous. The Catholic dogma of the perpetual virginity of Mary is dependent upon the solution of this question, but it properly belongs to commentaries

---

* Luke xxiv: 4. † John xx: 12. ‡ Luke xxiv: 50. ‖ John xi: 18.
§ Luke xxiv: 52. ¶ Luke xxiv: 53. ** John xix: 26, 27.

on the gospels, and to these the reader is referred for the arguments, *pro* and *con.*

15–18. We next have an account of the selection of an apostle to fill the place of Judas. There is no intimation that Jesus had authorized this procedure; on the contrary, it would be presumed that, as he himself had selected the original twelve, he would, in like manner, fill the vacancy, if he intended that it should be filled. Neither had the apostles yet received that power from on high which would enable them to act infallibly in a matter of this kind. From these considerations, it has been supposed by some that the whole procedure was both unauthorized and invalid. But the fact that Matthias was afterward "*numbered with* the eleven apostles,"* and that the whole body were from that time called "the twelve,"† shows that the transaction was sanctioned by the apostles even after they were fully inspired. This gave it the *sanction* of inspired authority, whatever may have been its origin. Moreover, Jesus had promised them that they should sit upon twelve thrones judging the twelve tribes of Israel,‡ and the fulfillment of this promise required that the number should be filled up. The Apostle Paul was not reckoned among "the twelve." He distinguishes himself from them in 1 Cor. xv: 5, 8: "He was seen by Cephas, then by the *twelve*," and "he was seen by *me* also, as by one born out of due time."

The particular time within the ten days, at which this selection was made, is not designated. The incident is introduced in these terms: (15) "*And in those days, Peter stood up in the midst of the disciples, and said, (the number of the names together was about one hundred and twenty,)* (16) *Brethren, this scripture must needs have been fulfilled which the Holy Spirit, through the mouth of David, spoke before concerning Judas, who was guide to them that seized Jesus.* (17) *For he was numbered with us, and had obtained part of this ministry.* (18) *Now this man purchased a field with the reward of iniquity, and falling headlong, he burst asunder in the midst, and all his bowels gushed out.*"

The parenthetical statement that the number of names together were about one hundred and twenty is not to be understood as including all who then believed on Jesus, but only those who were then and there assembled. Paul states that Jesus was seen, after his resurrection, by "above five hundred brethren at once."‖ The hundred and twenty were, perhaps, all who were then in the city of Jerusalem.

The statement in reference to the fate of Judas is supposed by most commentators to be part of a parenthesis thrown in by Luke, though some contend that it is part of Peter's speech.§ If the latter supposition is true, there was no ambiguity in it to the original hearers, for they all well knew that the field referred to was purchased by the Sanhedrim with money which Judas forced upon them, and which was invested in this way because they could find no other suitable use for it.¶ Knowing this, they could but understand Peter as meaning that Judas had indirectly *caused* the field

* Acts i: 26. † Acts vi: 2. ‡ Matt. xix; 28.
‖ 1 Cor. xv: 6. § Alexander *in loco.* ¶ Matt. xxvii: 3–8.

to be purchased. But whether the words are Peter's or Luke's, it must be admitted that a reader unacquainted with the facts in the case would be misled by them. Luke, however, presumed upon the information of his first readers, and that knowledge of the facts which they possessed has been transmitted to us by Matthew, so that we have as little difficulty as they did in discovering the true meaning of the remark.

As respects the manner of the death of Judas, the common method of reconciling Luke's account with that of Matthew is undoubtedly correct. We must suppose them both to be true, and combine the separate statements. The whole affair stands thus: "He went out and hanged himself;"* and, by the breaking of either the limb on which he hung, or the cord, "falling headlong, he burst asunder in the midst, and all his bowels gushed out."

19. The next statement, (19) "*And it was known to all the dwellers in Jerusalem, so that that field is called, in their proper tongue, Aceldama, that is to say, the field of blood,*" is undoubtedly a parenthesis by Luke. Peter was addressing the very people in whose proper tongue the place was called Aceldama, and would not, of course, *translate* it to them. Hence, we can not attribute these words to him. But Luke was writing in Greek, and felt called upon to translate Hebrew words which he might use into Greek, and the fact that this is done here prove the words to be his.

20. The historian now resumes the report of Peter's speech, which he had interrupted by the parenthesis. In the remarks already quoted, Peter bases the action which he proposes, not upon any commandment of Jesus, but upon a prophesy uttered by David. He also states, as the ground for the application of that prophesy which he is about to make, the fact that Judas had been numbered with them, and had "obtained part of this ministry." He now quotes the prophesy alluded to: (20) "*For it is written in the book of Psalms, Let his habitation be desolate, and let no man dwell therein.*† *His office let another take.*"‡

These two passages from the Psalms, when read in their original context, seem to apply to the wicked in general, and there is not the slightest indication that David had Judas in prophetic view when he uttered them. This is an instance, therefore, of the particular application of a general prophetic sentiment. If it be proper that the habitation of a wicked man should become desolate, and that whatever office he held should be given to another, then it was pre-eminently proper that such a crime as that of Judas should be thus punished, and that so important an *office* as that of Judas should be filled by a worthy successor.

21, 22. It is of some moment to observe here that the question on which Peter is discoursing has not reference to the original appointment of an apostle, but to the selection of a *successor* to an apostle. The qualifications, therefore, which are found necessary to an election, must always be possessed by one who proposes to be a successor to an apostle. He states these qualifications in the next sentence: (21) "*Wherefore, of these men who have accompanied us all the*

*Matt. xxvii: 5.   †Ps. lxix: 25.   ‡Ps. cix: 8.

time that the Lord Jesus went in and out among us, (22) *beginning from the immersion of John till the day he was taken up from us, must one be made a witness with us of his resurrection."* There being no other instance in the New Testament of the selection of a successor to an apostle, this is our only scriptural guide upon the subject, and, therefore, it is unscriptural for any man to lay claim to the office who has not been a companion of Jesus, and a witness of his resurrection. The reason for confining the selection to those who had accompanied Jesus from the beginning, is because such would be the most reliable witnesses to his identity after the resurrection. One less familiar with his person would, *ceteris paribus,* be less perfectly guarded against imposition. Peter, here, like Paul in 1 Cor. xv, makes the whole value of apostolic testimony depend upon ability to prove the resurrection of Jesus.

23–26. *"Then they appointed two, Joseph, called Barsabas, who was surnamed Justus, and Matthias.* (24) *And they prayed, and said, Thou Lord, who knowest the hearts of all men, show which one of these two thou hast chosen* (25) *to receive the lot of this ministry and apostleship, from which Judas, by transgression, fell, that he might go to his own place.* (26) *And they gave forth their lots, and the lot fell upon Matthias, and he was numbered together with the eleven apostles."* It will be observed that the brethren did not themselves select Matthias; but, having first appointed two persons between whom the choice should be made, they prayed the Lord to show which one *he* had chosen, and then cast lots, understanding that the one upon whom the lot fell was the Lord's choice. The reason that they did not make the selection themselves was evidently because they thought proper that the Lord, who had chosen Judas, should also choose his successor. If it be inquired why, then, they ventured to confine the Lord's choice to these two, the most plausible answer is that suggested by Dr. Alexander, that, after a careful examination of the parties present, these were the only two who possessed all the qualifications named by Peter. Whether the selection of these two was made by the whole body of the disciples, or by the apostles alone, it is unimportant to determine. The case does not, as many have supposed, furnish a precedent on the subject of popular election of church officers; for the selection of the two persons between whom an election was to be made, was not the election itself; and when the election took place, it was made by the Lord, and not by the disciples or the apostles. One of them cast or drew the lots, but the Lord determined on whom the lot should fall.

The prayer offered by the apostles on this occasion is a model of its kind. They had a single object for which they bowed before the Lord, and to the proper presentation of this they confine their words. They do not repeat a single thought, neither do they elaborate one beyond the point of perspicuity. The question having reference to the spiritual as well as the historical characteristics of the two individuals, most appropriately do they address the Lord as καρδιογνωστα *the heart-knower.* They do not pray, Show which thou *wilt* choose, or *dost* choose, as though there was need of reflection with the Lord before the choice; but, "show which one of these two thou *hast* chosen." They describe the office they desire the Lord to fill, as the "ministry and apostleship from which Judas, by transgression, fell, that he might *go to his own place."* He had been in a place of which he had proved himself unworthy, and they have no hesitation in referring to the fact that he had now gone to his *own* place. That place is, of course, the place to which hypocrites go after death. Here is a simple address to the Lord, beautifully appropriate to the petition they are about to present; then the petition itself concisely expressed, and the prayer is concluded. So brief a prayer, on any occasion in this voluble age, would scarcely be recognized as a prayer at all, so prone are men to the delusion that they will be heard for their much speaking.

II: 1. Thus far our author has been engaged in preliminary statements, which were necessary to the proper introduction of his main theme. He has furnished us a list of the eleven apostles, and the appointment of the twelfth; rehearsed briefly their qualifications as witnesses of the resurrection; informed us that they were in Jerusalem, dwelling in an upper room, but spending the most of their time in the temple, and waiting for the promised power to inaugurate on earth the kingdom of Christ. He now proceeds to give an account of the descent of the Holy Spirit, and enters upon the main theme of his narrative, (1) " *When the day of Pentecost was fully come, they were all with one accord in one place."*

The day of Pentecost was the fiftieth day after the Passover. It was celebrated, according to the law of Moses, by offering the first fruits of the wheat harvest, in the form of two loaves made of fine flour.* On account of the seven weeks intervening between it and the Passover, it is styled, in the Old Testament, "the feast of weeks." But the fact that it occurred on the fiftieth day, gave it, in later ages, under the prevalence of the Greek language, the name of *Pentecost*, which is a Greek adjective, meaning *fiftieth*.

This is one of the three annual festivals at which the law required every male Jew of the whole nation to be present.† The condemnation and death of Jesus had occurred during one of these feasts, and now, the next universal gathering of the devout Jews is most wisely chosen as the occasion for the vindication of his character and the beginning of his kingdom. It is the day on which the law was given on Mount Sinai, and henceforth it is to commemorate the giving of a better law, founded on better promises. It is remarkable that the day of giving the law was celebrated throughout the Jewish ages, without one word in the Old Testament to indicate that it was designed to commemorate that event. In like manner, the day of the week on which the Holy Spirit descended has been celebrated from that time till this, though no formal reason is given in the New Testament for its observance. The absence of inspired explanations, however, has not left the world in doubt upon the latter subject; for the two grand events which occurred on that day—the resurrection of Jesus and the descent of the Holy Spirit—are of such transcendent importance, that all minds at once agree in attributing to them, and especially to the former, the celebration of the day.

* Lev. xxiii: 15-17. † Ex. xxiii: 14-17.

That we are right in assuming that this Pentecost occurred on the first day of the week, there is no room to doubt, though Dr. Hackett advocates a different hypothesis. After stating that the Lord was crucified on Friday, he says, "The fiftieth day, or Pentecost, (beginning, of course, with the evening of Friday, the second day of the Passover,) would occur on the Jewish Sabbath." He seems to have forgotten, for the moment, that Friday was "preparation day,"* and that Saturday was, therefore, the first day of unleavened bread.† According to the law, the count began on "the morrow after" this day, which was Sunday.‡ Counting seven full weeks and one day from that time, would throw the fiftieth day, or Pentecost, on Sunday, beginning at six o'clock Saturday evening, and closing at the same hour Sunday evening. As certainly as Jesus arose on Sunday, he died on Friday; and as certainly as this Friday was the preparation day of the Passover, so certainly did the Pentecost occur on Sunday.

Why Luke uses the expression, "When the day of Pentecost was *fully* come," is best explained in this way. The day began with sunset, and the first part of it was night, which was unsuited for the purpose of these events. The *day* was not *fully* come until *daylight*.

It is important to determine who are the parties declared by Luke to be "all with one accord in one place;" for upon this depends the question whether the whole hundred and twenty disciples, or only the twelve apostles, were filled with the Holy Spirit. The words are almost uniformly referred, by commentators, to the hundred and twenty. Any one who will read the first four verses of this chapter, noticing the connection of the pronoun "they," which occurs in each of them, will see, at a glance, that it has, throughout, the same antecedent, and, therefore, all the parties said in the first verse to be together in one place, are said in the fourth to be filled with the Holy Spirit, and to speak in other tongues. The question, then, Who were filled with the Holy Spirit? depends upon the reference of the pronoun "they" in the statement "*They* were all together in one place." Those who suppose that the whole hundred and twenty are referred to, have to go back to the fifteenth verse of the preceding chapter to find the antecedent. But, if we obliterate the unfortunate separation between the first and second chapters, and take the last verse of the former into its connection with the latter, we will find the true and obvious antecedent much nearer at hand. It would read thus: "The lot fell upon Matthias, and he was numbered together with the eleven *apostles*. And when the day of Pentecost was fully come, *they* were all with one accord in one place." It is indisputable that the antecedent to *they* is the term *apostles;* and it is merely the division of the text into chapters, severing the close grammatical connection of the words, which has hid this most obvious fact from commentators and readers. The apostles alone, therefore, are said to have been filled with the Holy Spirit. This conclusion is not only evident from the context, but it is required by the very terms of the promise concerning the Holy Spirit. It

---

* John xix: 31. † Lev. xxiii: 5–7. ‡ Lev. xxiii: 15.

was to the apostles alone, on the night of the betrayal, that Jesus had promised the miraculous aid of the Spirit, and to them alone he had said, on the day of ascension, "You shall be immersed in the Holy Spirit." It involves both a perversion of the text, and a misconception of the design of the event,* to suppose that the immersion in the Holy Spirit was shared by the whole hundred and twenty.

2. It was the apostles, then, and they alone, who were assembled together; (2) "*And suddenly there came a sound out of heaven, as of a rushing mighty wind, and it filled all the house where they were sitting.*" What house this was has been variously conjectured; but the supposition of Olshausen, that it was one of the thirty spacious rooms around the temple court, described by Josephus and called οἶκοι, *houses,* is most agreeable to all the facts. Wherever it was, the crowd described below gathered about them, and this required more space than any private house would afford, especially the upper room where the apostles had been lodging.

3, 4. Simultaneous with the sound, (3) "*There appeared to them tongues, distributed, as of fire, and it sat upon each one of them.* (4) *And they were all filled with the Holy Spirit, and began to speak in other tongues, as the Spirit gave them utterance.*" This is the immersion in the Holy Spirit which had been promised by Jesus, and for which the apostles had been waiting since his ascension. It is highly important that we should understand in what it consisted, and the necessity for its occurrence.

There is not, in the New Testament, a *definition* of the immersion in the Holy Spirit, but we have here what is possibly better, a living instance of its occurrence. The historian gives us a distinct view of men in the act of being immersed in the Spirit, so that, in order to understand it, we have but to look on, and tell what we see and hear. We see, then, flaming tongues, like flames of fire, distributed so that one rests upon each of the twelve apostles. In the clause, "it sat upon each of them," the singular pronoun *it* is used after the plural *tongues,* to indicate that not all, but only one of the tongues sat upon each apostle, the term *distributed* having already suggested the contemplation of them singly. We *see* this, and we *hear* all the twelve at once speaking in languages to them unknown. We see a divine power present with these men, for to no other power can we attribute those tongues. We hear the unmistakable effects of a divine power acting upon their minds; for no other power could give them an instantaneous knowledge of languages which they had never studied. The immersion, therefore, consists in their being so filled with the Holy Spirit as to be attended by a miraculous physical power, and to exercise a miraculous intellectual power. If there is any other endowment conferred upon them, the historian is silent in reference to it, and we have no right to assume it. Their ability to *speak* in other languages is not an effect upon their tongues directly, but merely a result of the *knowledge* imparted to them. Neither are we to regard the nature of the sentiments uttered by them as proof of any miraculous *moral* endow-

* See below, on verses 3, 4.

ment; for pious sentiments are the only kind which the Spirit of God would dictate, and they are such as these men, who had been for some time "continually in the temple, praising and blessing God,"* and "continuing with one consent in prayer and supplication,"† would be expected to utter, if they spoke in public at all.

We have already said something of the necessity for this event;‡ but, at the risk of some repetition, we must here advert to the subject again. What the apostles needed, at this point in their history, was not moral courage, or devoutness of spirit; for they had already recovered from the alarm produced by the crucifixion, and were now boldly entering the temple together every day, and spending their whole time in devout worship. Their defects were such as no degree of courage or of piety could supply. It was *power* that they wanted—power to remember all that Jesus had taught them; to understand the full meaning of all his words; of his death; of his resurrection; to pierce the heavens, and declare with certainty things which had transpired there; and to know the whole truth concerning the will of God and the duty of men. There is only one source from which this power could be derived, and this the Savior had promised them, when he said, "You shall receive *power* ($\delta \acute{v} v a \mu \iota v$,) when the Holy Spirit comes upon you."‖ This power they now received, and upon the exercise of it depends the entire authority of apostolic teaching.

But power to establish the kingdom and to proselyte the world involved not merely the possession of the miraculous mental power above named, but the ability to prove that they did possess it. This could best be done by an indisputable exercise of it. To exercise it, however, by merely beginning to speak the truth infallibly, would not answer the purpose, for men would inquire, How can you assure us that this which you speak is the truth? To answer this question satisfactorily, they gave such an exhibition of the superhuman knowledge which they possessed as could be tested by their hearers. They might have done this by penetrating the minds of the auditors, and declaring to them their secret thoughts or past history; but this would have addressed itself to only one individual at a time. Or they might, like the prophets of old, have foretold some future event, the occurrence of which would prove their inspiration; but this would have required some considerable lapse of time, and would not, therefore, have answered the purpose of immediate conviction. There is, indeed, but one method conceivable, by which they could exhibit this power to the immediate conviction of a multitude, and that is the method adopted on this occasion, *speaking in other tongues*, as the Spirit gave them utterance. If any man doubts this, let him imagine and state, if he can, some other method. True, they might have wrought miracles of healing, but this would have been no *exhibition* of miraculous mental endowments. If wrought in confirmation of the claim that they were inspired, it would have proved it; still, the proof would have been indirect, requiring the minds of the audience to pass through a course of reasoning before reaching the conclusion. The proof, in this case, is direct, being an

* Luke xxiv: 53.   † Acts i: 14.   ‡ Com. i: 2.   ‖ Acts i: 8.

ACTS II: 5–13.

exhibition of the power which they claimed. By the only method, then, of which we can conceive, the apostles, as soon as they became possessed of the promised power, exhibited to the multitude an indisputable exercise of it. It should be observed, that this exhibition could be available to its purpose only when individuals were present who understood the languages spoken. Otherwise, they would have no means of testing the reality of the miracle. Hence, to serve the purpose of proof where this circumstance did not exist, the apostles were supplied with the power of working physical miracles; and inasmuch as this circumstance did not often exist in the course of their ministry, they had resort almost uniformly to the indirect method of proof by a display of miraculous physical power.

5. The circumstances of the present occasion were happily suited to this wonderful display of divine power, the like of which had never been witnessed, even in the astonishing miracles of Moses and of Jesus. (5) "*Now there were dwelling in Jerusalem, Jews, devout men, from every nation under heaven.*" The native tongues of these Jews were those of the nations in which they were born, but they had also been instructed by their parents in the dialect of Judea. This enabled them to understand the tongues which were spoken by the apostles, and to test the reality of the miracle.

6–12. "*And when this sound occurred, the multitude came together, and were confounded, because each one heard them speaking in his own dialect.*" The historian seems here to exhaust his vocabulary of terms to express the confusion of the multitude upon witnessing this scene. Not content with saying they were *confounded*, he adds, (7) "*And all were amazed, and marveled, saying to one another, Behold, are not all these who are speaking, Galileans? (8) And how do we hear, each one in our own dialect in which we were born? (9) Parthians, and Medes, and Elamites, and those inhabiting Mesopotamia, Judea and Cappadocia, Pontus and Asia, (10) Phrygia and Pamphylia, Egypt and the parts of Lybia about Cyrene; and Roman strangers, both Jews and proselytes, (11) Cretes and Arabians; we hear them speaking in our own tongues the wonderful works of God.*" Not yet satisfied with his attempts to express their feelings, Luke adds, (12) "*And they were all amazed, and perplexed, saying one to another, What does this mean?*"

13. We have in this last sentence an instance of the peculiar use of the term *all* in the New Testament, to signify the great mass; for, after saying that "*all*" were amazed," etc., Luke immediately adds, (13) "*But others, mocking, said, These men are full of sweet wine.*" The wine was not *new*, as rendered in the common version; for *new* wine was not intoxicating; but it was old, and very intoxicating, though by a peculiar process it had been kept sweet.*

In order that we may discriminate accurately concerning the effects of this phenomenon, we must observe that the only effects thus far produced upon the multitude, are perplexity and amazement among the greater part, and merriment among the few. It was impossible that any of them, without an explanation, could un-

* See Hackett.

derstand the phenomenon; and without being understood, it could have no *moral* or *religious* effect upon them. It was, indeed, quite natural, that some of the audience, to whom most of the languages spoken at first sounded like mere *gibberish*, and who were of too trivial a disposition to inquire further into the matter, should exclaim that the apostles were *drunk*. This being true of the phenomenon while unexplained, it is evident that all the moral power which it is to exert upon the multitude must reach their minds and hearts *through* the *words* in which the explanation is given. To this explanation our attention is now directed.

14, 15. "*Then Peter, standing up with the eleven, lifted up his voice and said to them, Men of Judea, and all you who dwell in Jerusalem, be this known to you, and hearken to my words:* (15) *for these men are not drunk as you suppose, seeing it is but the third hour of the day.*" After all that has been said of this defense against the charge of drunkenness, it must be admitted that it is not conclusive; for men might be drunk, as they often were and are, at any hour of either day or night. Still, the fact that men are not *often* found drunk so early in the day, rendered the defense sufficiently plausible to ward off the present effect of a charge which had been preferred in mere levity, while Peter relies upon the speech he is about to make for a perfect refutation of the charge, and for an impression upon the multitude, of which they little dreamed. He proceeds to speak in such a way as only a sober man could speak, and this is the best way to refute a charge of drunkenness.

16–18. Peter continues: (16) "*But this is that which was spoken through the prophet Joel;* (17) *And it shall come to pass in the last days, says God, I will pour out from my Spirit upon all flesh; and your sons and your daughters shall prophesy, and your young men shall see visions, and your old men shall dream dreams:* (18) *And on my men-servants and on my maid-servants, in those days, I will pour out from my Spirit, and they shall prophesy.*"

From this passage it is evident that the immediate effects of the outpouring of the Spirit, so far as the recipients are concerned, are mental, and not moral effects. The prophesy contemplates, not a miraculous elevation of the moral nature, but an inspiration of the mind, by which prophesy, and prophetic dreams and visions would be experienced. If the entrance of the Holy Spirit into men, to operate by an abstract exertion of divine power, which is certainly the nature of the operation here contemplated, was designed to take effect immediately upon the heart, it is certainly most unaccountable, that neither by the prophet foretelling the event, nor by Luke describing it, is one word said in reference to such an effect. On the contrary, the only effects foretold by the prophet are dreams, visions, and prophesy, and the only one described by the historian is that species of prophesy which consists in speaking in unknown tongues. We desire to note such observations as this, wherever the text suggests them, in order to correct prevailing errors upon this subject. It will be found the uniform testimony of recorded facts, that the power of the Holy Spirit took immediate effect upon the intellectual faculties, leaving the moral nature of inspired men to the effect of the

·deas revealed, in precisely the same manner that the hearts of their hearers were affected by the same ideas when uttered by inspired lips.*

It is quite common with pedobaptist writers and speakers to make use of the expression, "I will *pour out* from my Spirit," to prove that *pouring* may be the action of baptism. The substance of the argument, as stated by Dr. Alexander,† is as follows: "The extraordinary influences of the Holy Spirit are repeatedly described, both in the language and the types of the Old Testament, as *poured* on the recipient. . . . This effusion is the very thing for which they (the apostles) are here told to wait; and therefore, when they heard it called a baptism, whatever may have been the primary usage of the word, they must have seen its Christian sense to be compatible with such an application." That the apostles must have expected something to occur, in their reception of the Holy Spirit, to which the term baptism would properly apply, is undoubtedly true, for Jesus had promised that they should be *baptized* in the Holy Spirit. But, in the event itself, there are two facts clearly distinguishable, and capable of separate consideration: 1st. The coming of the Holy Spirit upon them, called an *outpouring*. 2d. The *effect* which followed this coming. It is important to inquire to which of these the term *baptism* is applied. Dr. Alexander, and those who argue with him, assume that it is applied to the former. He says, "This *effusion* is the very thing" which they had "heard called a baptism." If this assumption is true, then the conclusion follows, that the baptism consisted in that movement of the Spirit expressed by the word *pour:* otherwise there would be no ground for the assumption that the word *pour* is used as an equivalent for the word *baptize*. If the act of *pouring*, then, was the baptism, most undoubtedly the thing *poured* was the thing *baptized;* but it was the Holy Spirit that was *poured*, and not the apostles; hence, the *Holy Spirit*, and not the *apostles*, was baptized.

The absurdity of this conclusion drives us back to search for the baptism in the *effect* of the outpouring, rather than in the outpouring itself. This, indeed, the language of the Savior unquestionably requires; for he says, "You shall *be* baptized." These words express an *effect* of which they were to be the subjects. This effect can not be expressed by the term *pour*, for the apostles were not and could not be *poured.* The effect was to *depend* upon the coming or pouring; for Jesus explains the promise, "You shall be baptized in the Spirit," by saying, "You shall receive power when the Holy Spirit *comes upon* you." This is still further proof that it is an effect which the outpouring of the Spirit produced, that is called a baptism. But if it be said, that, at any rate, we have here a baptism *effected* by pouring, we reply that this very fact proves the baptism and the pouring to be two different things; and that an *immersion* may be effected by *pouring*.

We further remark, that there was no literal pouring in the case; for the Holy Spirit is not a liquid, that it might be literally poured. The term *pour*, here, is used metaphorically. In our vague concep-

*See further on this subject, Com. x: 9, 16. †Com. i: 5.

tion of the nature of Spirit, there is such an analogy between it and a subtile fluid, that the action, which, in the plain style of the Savior, is called a *coming* of the Spirit, may, in the highly figurative style of the prophet Joel, be properly styled an *outpouring* of the Spirit. The analogy, therefore, which justifies the use of the word *pour*, is not that between baptism and the act of pouring, but that between a subtile fluid and our inadequate conceptions of spirit.

We now proceed to consider the propriety of styling the effect in question an immersion. When Jesus said, "John baptized in water, but you shall be baptized in the Holy Spirit," his words suggested an analogy between John's baptism and that of the Spirit. But they could not have so far mistaken this analogy as to suppose that their *bodies* were to be subjects of the Spirit baptism, for this is forbidden by the very nature of the case. But they would naturally expect that their *spirits* would be the subjects of the baptism in the Spirit, as their *bodies* had been of the baptism in water. The event corresponded to this expectation; for they were "*filled* with the Holy Spirit;" he pervaded and possessed all their mental powers, so that, as Jesus had promised, it was not they that spoke, but the Spirit of their Father that spoke in them.* Their spirits were as *literally* and completely *immersed* in the Holy Spirit, as their bodies had been in the waters of Jordan.

19, 20. So much of Peter's quotation from Joel as we have now considered was in process of fulfillment at the time he was speaking, and is of quite easy interpretation; but not so with the remaining portion; (19) "*And I will show wonders in heaven above, and signs on the earth below, blood, and fire, and smoky vapor.* (20) *The sun shall be turned into darkness, and the moon into blood, before that great and illustrious day of the Lord come.* (21) *And it shall come to pass that every one who will call on the name of the Lord shall be saved.*"

It is quite evident that there was nothing transpiring at the time of Peter's speech to which the multitude could look as the fulfillment of these words; hence the remark with which he introduces the quotation, "*This* is that which was spoken by the prophet Joel," is to be understood only of the manifestation of the Holy Spirit. The remainder of the prediction must have still looked to the future for its fulfillment. How far in the future is not indicated, except that the events mentioned were to take place "*before* that great and illustrious day of the Lord." This day of the Lord is certainly spoken of as a day of terror and danger; and no doubt the salvation contemplated in the words, "every one who will call on the name of the Lord shall be saved," is salvation from the dangers of "that great and illustrious day." The interpretation of the whole passage, therefore, depends upon determining what is meant by that day. Is it the day of the destruction of Jerusalem, or of the final judgment? The best way to settle this question is to examine the use of the phrase, "day of the Lord," in both Old Testament and New.

In the first eleven verses of the second chapter of Joel, the phrase

* Matt. x: 20.

"day of the Lord" occurs three times, and designates a time when the land should be desolated by locusts, insects, and drought. But with the passage now under consideration, in the latter part of the same chapter, the prophet begins a new theme, and therefore speaks of some other great and terrible day. Throughout the prophecies of Joel, and of all the Old Testament prophets, this phrase is used invariably to designate a day of disaster. Isaiah calls the time in which Babylon was to be destroyed, "the day of the Lord," and says of it, "The stars of heaven, and the constellations thereof, shall not give their light; the sun shall be darkened in its going forth, and the moon shall not cause her light to shine."* Ezekiel, in like manner, foretelling the desolation of Egypt, says, "The day of the Lord is near; a cloudy day; it shall be the time of the heathen."† Obadiah uses the same phrase in reference to the destruction of Edom;‡ Amos, in reference to the captivity of Israel;‖ and Zechariah, in reference to the final siege of Jerusalem.§ An induction of these passages establishes the conclusion that "the day of the Lord," with the prophets, is always a day of calamity, the precise nature of which is to be determined in each case by the context. In some cases the context is so obscure as not to determine the reference with certainty. The text before us possesses some of this obscurity, yet with the aid of the above remarks, and the use made of the passage by Peter, we may determine the reference with no small degree of certainty.

It is evident, from Peter's application of the first part of the quotation to the advent of the Spirit, that the latter part, which is contemplated as still future, was to be fulfilled after the scene then transpiring. Now, if the dangers of the day, as indicated by the words employed, were such as concerned the Jews alone, there would be good ground to suppose that reference was had to the destruction of Jerusalem. But the parties contemplated in the prophesy are "*all flesh;*" therefore, all classes of men are embraced in the prophetic view, and the "day of the Lord" must, according to Old Testament usage, be a day of terror in which all are interested. But in the destruction of Jerusalem the Jews alone had any thing to dread; hence this can not be the reference. It must, then, be the day of judgment; for this is the only day of pre-eminent terror yet awaiting all mankind.

This conclusion is confirmed by the invariable usage of New Testament writers. The apostolic writings afford little ground indeed for the prominence that has been given by commentators to the destruction of Jerusalem, in their interpretations of prophesy. There was another and far different day, in their future, to which they gave the appellation, "the day of the Lord." Paul says, "Deliver such a one to Satan for the destruction of the flesh, that the spirit may be saved in the *day of the Lord Jesus.*"¶ "We are your rejoicing, even as ye also are ours, in the *day of the Lord Jesus.*"** "Yourselves know perfectly that the *day of the Lord* so comes as a thief in the night."†† "But the *day of the Lord* will come as a thief

---
*Isa. xiii: 9–11.   †Ezek. xxx : 3.   ‡Ob. 15.   ‖Amos v : 18.   §Zech. xiv : 1.
¶1 Cor. v : 5.   **2 Cor. i : 14.   ††1 Thess. v : 2.

in the night."* These are all the occurrences of this expression in the New Testament, and they show conclusively that "the day of the Lord," with the apostles, was the day of judgment.

The great and illustrious day must not be confounded with the *signs and wonders,*" mentioned by the prophet; for these are to occur *before* that day. Whatever may be the exact symbolic meaning of the "blood and fire, and smoky vapor," and the darkening of the sun and moon, they represent events which are to take place *before* the day of judgment.

Having now determined the reference of the day in question, we can at once decide what salvation is contemplated in the declaration, "Every one who will call on the name of the Lord shall be saved." The only salvation connected with the day of judgment is the salvation from *sin* and *death.* The reference, therefore, is to this, and not to salvation from the destruction of Jerusalem.

This salvation is made to depend upon *calling on the name of the Lord,* an expression equivalent to prayer. It is, of course, acceptable prayer which is intended, and it therefore implies the existence of that disposition and conduct necessary to acceptable worship. Certainly no one calling upon the name of the Lord while persisting in disobedience can be included in this promise.

Thus far, in his discourse, Peter has directed his attention to the single object of proving the inspiration of himself and his associates. This was logically necessary previous to the utterance of a single word by authority, and most logically has he conducted his argument. The amazement of the people, upon beholding the miraculous scene, was a tacit acknowledgment of their inability to account for it. They were well prepared, therefore, to hear Peter's explanation. But if even he had attributed the effects which they witnessed to any less than divine power, they must have rejected his explanation as unsatisfactory. The question with them, indeed, was not, whether this was a divine or human manifestation, but, admitting its divinity, they asked one another, "What does this *mean?*" When, therefore, Peter simply declares, that this is a fulfillment of Joel's prophesy concerning the outpouring of the Spirit of God, they had no alternative but to receive his explanation, while the fact that it was a fulfillment of prophesy gave to it additional solemnity.

If Peter had closed his discourse at this point, the multitude would have gone away convinced of his inspiration, but not one of them would have been converted. All that has yet been said and done is preparatory; a necessary preparation for what is to follow. We are yet to search for the exact influence which turned their minds and hearts toward Jesus Christ.

22–24. It is impossible, at this distance of space and time, to realize, even in a faint degree, the effect upon minds so wrought up and possessed of such facts, produced by the announcement next made by Peter. (22) *"Men of Israel, hear these words. Jesus of Nazareth, a man approved by God among you, by miracles and wonders and signs, which God did by him, in the midst of you, as you yourselves also know;* (23) *him, delivered by the determined purpose*

*2 Peter iii : 10.

ACTS II: 24.

and foreknowledge of God, you have taken, and by wicked hands have crucified and slain: (24) *whom God has raised up, having loosed the pains of death, because it was not possible that he should be held under it.*" Filled with amazement, as they were already, by a visible and audible manifestation of the Spirit of God, they now see that the whole of this amazing phenomenon is subservient to the name of that Nazarene whom they had despised and crucified. This conviction is brought home to them, too, in a sentence so replete with overwhelming facts, as to make them reel and stagger under a succession of fearful blows rapidly repeated. In one breath they have heard no less than seven startling propositions: 1st. That Jesus had been approved by God among them, by miracles and wonders and signs, which God had done by him. 2d. That they, themselves, *knew* this to be so. 3d. That it was not from impotence on his part, but in accordance with the purpose and foreknowledge of God, that he was yielded up to them. 4th. That when thus yielded up they had put him to death by the torture of crucifixion. 5th. That they had done this with wicked hands. 6th. That God had raised him from the dead. 7th. That it was not possible that death should hold him.

Here is a complete epitome of the four gospels, condensed into one short sentence. The name "Jesus of Nazareth" brought vividly before their minds a well-known personage, and all his illustrious history flashes across their memory. The first assertion concerning him is an appeal to his miracles as a demonstration that he was from God. There is no need of argument to make this demonstration clear; nor of evidence to prove the reality of the miracles; for they were done "in your midst, as you yourselves also *know.*" The fearfulness of the murder is magnified by the thought, that he had been voluntarily delivered to them, in accordance with a deliberate purpose of God long ago declared by the prophets. The manner of his death makes it more fearful still. They had nailed him to a cross, and compelled him to die like a felon. These things being so, how penetrating the appeal to their consciences, "with *wicked* hands you have crucified and slain him!" This was no time for nice distinctions between what a man does himself, and what he does by another. The "wicked hands" are not, as some suppose, the hands of Roman soldiers, who had performed the actual work of his execution, but the hands of wicked Jews. Here, before him, were the very persons who had been assembled but fifty days before at the Passover, and had *taken a hand* in the proceedings of that awful day. He appeals to their individual consciousness of guilt; and this gives an intensity to the effect of his discourse upon their hearts, which it could not otherwise have possessed. Conscious of fearful guilt in having thus cruelly murdered the attested servant of God; and suddenly revealed to themselves as actors in the darkest scene of prophetic vision, how shall they endure the additional thought, that God has raised the crucified from the dead? Never did mortal lips pronounce, in so brief a space, so many thoughts of so terrific import to the hearers. We might challenge the world to find a parallel to it in the speeches of all her orators, or the songs of all her poets. There is not, indeed, such a thunderbolt in the burdens of all the prophets of Israel, nor among the mighty voices which echo through the pages of the Apocalypse. It is the first announcement to the world of a risen and glorified Redeemer.

25–28. There are two points in this announcement which required proof, and to the presentation of this Peter immediately proceeds. Having stated that Jesus was delivered according to the determined purpose of God, he now quotes that purpose as expressed by David in the 16th Psalm. (25) *"For David says concerning him, I foresaw the Lord always before my face; for he is on my right hand, that I should not be moved. (26) Therefore did my heart rejoice, and my tongue was glad. Moreover, my flesh shall rest in hope; (27) because thou wilt not leave my soul in hades, neither wilt thou suffer. thy Holy One to see corruption. (28) Thou hast made known to me the ways of life; thou wilt make me full of joy with thy countenance."* Only so much of this quotation as refers to the resurrection suits the special purpose of the speaker, the preceding portion serving only to connectedly introduce it.

The words, "Thou shalt make known to me the ways of life," constitute the affirmative assertion of a restoration to life, which had been negatively expressed in the statement, "Thou wilt not leave my soul in hades, neither wilt thou suffer thy Holy One to see corruption." The words, "Thou wilt make me full of joy with thy countenance," no doubt refer to that joy set before Jesus, for which "he endured the cross, despising the shame, and is now set down at the right hand of the throne of God."*

It is commonly agreed among interpreters, that in the sentence, "Thou wilt not leave my soul in hades, neither wilt thou suffer thy Holy One to see corruption," there is no distinction intended between the condition of the soul and that of the body; but that the whole is merely equivalent to the statement, Thou wilt not leave *me* among the *dead*. I am constrained, however, to adopt the opinion advanced, but not defended, by Olshausen, that the apostle does intend to fix our attention upon the body and soul of Jesus separately. The most obvious reason for this opinion is the fact that his body and soul are spoken of separately, and with separate reference to their respective places of abode during the period of death. The soul can not see corruption, neither can the body go into hades; but when men die, ordinarily, their bodies see corruption, and their souls enter, not the grave, but hades. The words in question declare, in reference to both the soul and body of Jesus, that which must have occurred in his resurrection, that the one was not left in hades, neither did the other see corruption. The apostle, in commenting upon them, makes the distinction still more marked, by saying, (verse 31, below), "He spoke of the resurrection of Christ, that his *soul* should not be left in hades, nor his *flesh* see corruption." Why do both the prophet and the apostle so carefully make the distinction, unless they wish to fix attention upon it?

The term *hades* designates the place of disembodied spirits. It is, as its etymology indicates, (*a* privative ἰδεῖν *to see*) *the unseen*. The

* Heb. xii: 2.

Greeks were good at giving names to things. When they watched a friend sinking into the arms of death, they could see, by the motion of the frame and the light of the eye, the continued presence of the soul, until at last, the muscles were all motionless, and the eye fixed and leaden. They could still see the body, and after it had been deposited in the grave they could revisit it and see it again. But where is the soul? You see it no longer. There are no signs of its presence. It is gone; and its invisible abode they call *hades*, the *unseen*. That the soul of Jesus entered hades is undeniable. That it returned again to the body at the resurrection is asserted by Peter; and it is this return which was predicted by the prophet, and which caused the exultation both of himself and the apostle.

The resurrection of Jesus is not appreciated by the religious world now, as it was by the apostles. As respects the return of his soul from hades, Protestant writers have fled so far from the justly-abhorred purgatory of the Catholic, and the gloomy soul-sleeping of the Materialist, that they have passed beyond the Scripture doctrine, and either ignore altogether the existence of an intermediate state, or deny that the souls of the righteous are short of ultimate happiness during this period. On the other hand, they have so great a tendency to absolute spiritualism in their conceptions of the future state, that they fail to appreciate the necessity for the resurrection of the body of Jesus, or to exult, as the apostles did, in anticipation of the resurrection of their own bodies. As long as men entertain the idea that their spirits enter into final bliss and glory immediately after death, they can never be made to regard the resurrection of the body as a matter of importance. This idea has even produced a general skepticism among the masses, in reference to a resurrection of the body; for men are very apt to doubt the certainty of future events for which they see no necessity. As respects the resurrection of the body of Jesus, the most popular conception of its necessity is no doubt this, that it was merely to comply with the predictions of the prophets and of Jesus himself. It would be far more rational to suppose that it was made a subject of prophesy, because there was some grand necessity that it should occur.

It would occupy too much space, in a work of this kind, to fully develop this subject, we must, therefore, content ourselves with only a few observations, tne complete vindication of the correctness of which we must forego.

When the eternal Word became flesh, he assumed all the limitations and dependencies which belong to men; "for it behooved him to be made in all things like his brethren."* One of these limitations was the inability to work without a body; hence, to him, as well as to his brethren, there was a night coming in which he could not work. He says, "I must work the works of him who sent me while it is day; the night is coming when no man can work."† This night can not be the period after the resurrection, for then he did work. It must, then, be the period of death, while his soul was absent from his body During this period, he himself asserts, he could do no work, and certainly neither history nor prophesy refer

* Heb. ii: 17. † John ix: 4.

to any work which he then did. It was the Jewish Sabbath among the living, and he observed it with absolute stillness in hades. If he had appeared to his disciples, as angels appear to men, convincing them that he was still alive, and could then have gone to heaven in his mere spiritual nature, who could say there was any necessity for a resurrection of that body in which all his sufferings were endured, and through which all temptations had reached him? But this could not be. Hades was to him a night of inactivity, as it is to all his disciples, though to neither is it a state of unconsciousness. If it had continued forever, then the further work of redemption, which could only be effected by a mediator in heaven, a Christ on the throne, sending down the Holy Spirit, directing the labors of men and angels, and finally raising the dead to judgment, would have remained undone forever. It was this thought which caused the exultation of the apostles, in view of the recovery of his soul from the inactivity of hades, and its reunion with the uncorrupted and now incorruptible body. "He was delivered for our offenses," but "was *raised* again for our justification."* His death was the atonement, enabling God to be just in justifying those who believe on Jesus; but his resurrection enabled him to enter heaven with his own blood, securing eternal redemption for us. The resurrection was, therefore, an imperious necessity in his case, and it will be in ours; for not till he comes again will we enter the mansions he is preparing for us, and receive the crown of righteousness which he will give to all them who love his appearing.†

29–31. Having exhibited, in the quotation from David, "the determined purpose and foreknowledge of God," in reference to the resurrection of Jesus, the apostle, never overlooking the logical necessities of his argument, next considers the only objection which his hearers would be likely to urge against his prophetic proof. In the words quoted, David speaks in the first person, and this might lead some to object, that he was speaking of himself, and not of the Messiah. If, however, it be proved that he did not speak of himself, they would readily admit that he spoke in the name of the Christ. Peter proves this, in these words: (29) "*Brethren, let me freely speak to you of the patriarch David, that he is both dead and buried, and his sepulcher is with us to this day.* (30) *Being a prophet, then, and knowing that God had sworn to him, that from the fruit of his loins he would raise up the Christ, according to the flesh, to sit on his throne;* (31) *foreseeing this, he spoke of the resurrection of the Christ, that his soul was not left in hades, neither did his flesh see corruption.*" David's own flesh having seen corruption, as they themselves admitted, and his soul being still in hades, there was no alternative but to admit that he spoke of the Messiah. This brief argument not only refuted the supposed objection, but opened the minds of his hearers to an entirely new conception of the prophetic throne of David, and of the Messiah who was to occupy it; showing, that instead of being the ruler of an earthly kingdom, however glorious, he was to sit upon the throne of the whole universe.

32, 33. Thus far in his argument, the speaker has proved that the

* Rom. iv: 25.   † John xiv: 2, 3; 2 Tim. iv: 8.

ACTS II: 32-36.

Messiah must rise from the dead to ascend his throne; but he has yet to prove that *Jesus* was thus raised, and was, therefore, the Messiah of whom David had spoken. He proves the resurrection by the testimony of himself and the eleven other witnesses standing with him: (32) "*This Jesus has God raised up, of which we are all witnesses.*" Here were twelve unimpeached witnesses testifying to a sensible fact, and presenting their testimony with all the authority belonging to miraculously attested messengers from God. This was sufficient, as to the resurrection. But it must also be proved that after he arose he ascended to heaven and sat down upon his throne. It would be unavailing, for this purpose, to urge the fact that the twelve had seen him ascend; for their eyes had followed him no further than the cloud which received him out of sight. But he presents, in proof, this immersion in the Holy Spirit, which the multitude were witnessing, and which could be effected by no one beneath the throne of God. (33) "*Therefore, being to the right hand of God exalted, and having received from the Father the promise of the Holy Spirit, he has shed forth this which you now see and hear.*" What they then saw and heard was both the proof that he who sent it down had ascended the throne of heaven, and the assurance that Peter spoke by divine authority in declaring this fact.

34, 35. One more point established, not so much in proof of the exaltation of Christ, as to show that it also was a subject of prophesy, and this inimitable argument will be complete. (34) "*For David has not ascended into the heavens, but he himself says, The Lord said to my Lord, Sit thou at my right hand,* (35) *until I make thy foes thy footstool.*" The Pharisees themselves admitted that in this passage David referred to the Messiah, and had been much puzzled by the admission in a memorable conversation with Jesus;* but Peter, unwilling to take any thing as granted, which might afterward be made a ground of objection, carefully guards the application, as he had done that of the previous quotation from David, by the remark that David himself had not ascended to heaven; hence he could not, in these words, be speaking of himself. This admitted, it must be granted that he spoke of the Messiah, for certainly David would call no other his Lord.

36. The progressive advances of his argument being now complete, those of them which needed proof being sustained by conclusive evidence, and the remainder consisting in facts well known to his audience, he announces his final conclusion in these bold and confident terms: (36) "*Therefore, let all the house of Israel know assuredly, that God has made that same Jesus whom you have crucified both Lord and Christ.*"

37. It has already been observed, that up to the moment in which Peter arose to address the audience, although the immersion in the Holy Spirit had occurred, and its effects had been fully witnessed by the people, no change had taken place in their minds in reference to Jesus Christ, neither did they experience any emotion, except confusion and amazement at a phenomenon which they could not comprehend. This fact proves, conclusively, that there was no power in the

*Matt. xxii: 42-6.

miraculous manifestation of the Spirit, which they witnessed, in itself alone, to produce in them the desired change. All the power which belonged to this event must have come short of the desired effect, but for a medium distinct from itself, through which it reached the minds and hearts of the people. That medium was the *words* of Peter. He spoke; and when he had announced the conclusion of his argument, Luke says: (37) "*Now when they heard this, they were pierced to the heart, and said to Peter and the other apostles, Brethren, what shall we do?*" In this exclamation there is a manifest confession that they *believe* what Peter has preached to them; and Luke's declaration that they were pierced to the heart shows that they felt intensely the power of the facts which they now believed. Since Peter began to speak, therefore, a change has taken place both in their convictions and their feelings. They are convinced that Jesus is the Christ, and they are pierced to the heart with anguish at the thought of having murdered him. In the mean time, not a word is said of any influence at work upon them, except that of the words spoken by Peter; hence we conclude that the change in their minds and hearts has been effected *through* those words. This conclusion was also drawn by Luke himself; for in saying "when they *heard* this, they were pierced to the heart and cried out," he evidently attributes their emotion and their outcry to what they *heard*, as the cause of both.

If Luke had regarded the change effected as one which could be produced only by the direct agency of the Holy Spirit, he could not have expressed himself in these words, for his language not only entirely ignores such an influence, but attributes the effect to a different instrumentality. We understand him, therefore, to teach that the whole change thus far effected in these men was produced through the word of truth which they heard from Peter.

Let it be observed, however, that what they had heard concerning Christ, they had heard not as the words of the mere man Peter; for, previous to introducing the name of Jesus, he had clearly demonstrated the *inspiration* of himself and the other apostles. This being established beyond the possibility of a rational doubt, from the moment that he began to speak of Jesus they were listening to him as an inspired man. But the Jews had long since learned to ascribe to the words of inspired men all the authority of the Spirit who spoke through them; hence this audience realized that all the power to convince and to move, that the authority of God himself could impart to words, belonged to the words of Peter. If they could believe God, they must believe the oracles of God which find utterance through Peter's lips. They do believe, and they believe because the words they hear are recognized as the words of God. Faith, then, comes by hearing the word of God; and he who hears the admitted word of God, must believe, or deny that God speaks the truth. This is true, whether the word is heard from the lips of the inspired men who originally gave it utterance, or is received through other authentic channels. The power by which the word of God produces faith is all derived from the fact that it *is* the word of *God*.

No words, whether of men or of God, can effect moral changes in the feelings of the hearer, unless they are believed; nor can they when believed, unless they announce truths or facts calculated to produce such change. In the present instance, the facts announced placed the hearers in the awful attitude of murderers of the Son of God, who was now not only alive again, but seated on the throne of God, with all power in his hands, both on earth and in heaven. The belief of these facts necessarily filled them with the most intense realization of guilt, and the most fearful anticipation of punishment. The former of these emotions is expressed by the words of Luke, " They were *pierced to the heart;*" the latter, in their own words, " Brethren, *what shall we do?*" They had just heard Peter, in the language of Joel, speak of a possible salvation; and the question, What shall we do? unquestionably means, What shall we do to be saved?

38. This is the first time, under the reign of Jesus Christ, that this most important of all questions was ever propounded; and the first time, of course, that it was ever answered. Whatever may have been the true answer under any previous dispensation, or on any previous day in the world's history, the answer given by Peter on this day of Pentecost, in which the reign of Christ on earth began, is the true and infallible answer for all the subjects of his authority in all subsequent time. It deserves our most profound attention; for it announces the conditions of pardon for all men who may be found in the same state of mind with these inquirers. It is expressed as follows: (38) "*Then Peter said to them, Repent and be immersed, every one of you, in the name of Jesus Christ, for the remission of sins, and you shall receive the gift of the Holy Spirit.*"

That the offer of pardon, made to the world through Jesus Christ, is conditional, is denied only by the fatalist. We will not argue this point, except as it is involved in the inquiry as to what the conditions of pardon are. When we ascertain the prescribed conditions of pardon, both questions will be settled in settling one.

Pardon is the chief want of the human soul, in its most favorable earthly circumstances. The rebel against God's government, though he lay down his arms and become a loyal subject, can have no hope of happiness without pardon for the past; while the pardoned penitent, humbly struggling in the service of God, knows himself still guilty of shortcomings, by which he must fail of the final reward, unless pardoned again and again. The question as to what are the conditions of pardon, therefore, necessarily divides itself into two; one having reference to the hitherto-unpardoned sinner, the other to the saint who may have fallen into sin. It is the former class who propounded the question to Peter, and it is to them alone that the answer under consideration was given. We will confine ourselves, in our present remarks, to this branch of the subject, and discuss it only in the light of the passage before us.

If we regard the question of the multitude, What shall we do? as simply a question of duty under their peculiar circumstances, without special reference to final results, we learn from the answer that there were two things for them to do—*Repent*, and *be immersed*. If Peter had stopped with these two words, his answer would have been satisfactory, in this view of the subject, and it would have been the conclusion of the world, that the duty of a sinner, "pierced to the heart" by a sense of guilt, is to *repent* and *be immersed.*

But if we regard their question as having definite reference to the *salvation* of which Peter had already spoken, (verse 21,) and their meaning, What shall we do to be *saved?* then the answer is equally definite: it teaches that what a sinner thus affected is to do to be saved, is to *repent* and *be immersed.*

From these two observations, the reader perceives, that so far as the conditions of salvation from past sins are concerned, the duty of the sinner is most definitely taught by the first two words of the answer, taken in connection with their question, without entering upon the controversy concerning the remainder of the answer. If it had been Peter's design merely to give an answer in concise terms, without explanation, no doubt he would have confined it to these two words, for they contain the only commands which he gives.

But he saw fit to accompany the two commands with suitable explanations. He qualifies the command to be immersed by the clause, "in the name of Jesus Christ," to show that it is under his authority that they were to be immersed, and not merely under that of the Father, whose authority alone was recognized in John's immersion. That we are right in referring the limiting clause, "in the name of Jesus Christ," to the command *be immersed,* and not to the command *repent,* is evident from the fact that it would be incongruous to say, "*Repent in* the name of Jesus Christ."

Peter further explains the two commands, by stating their specific *design;* by which term we mean the specific blessing which was to be expected as the consequence of obedience. It is "*for the remission of sins.*" To convince an unbiased mind that this clause depends upon both the preceding commands, and expresses their design, it would only be necessary to repeat the words, "Repent and be immersed in the name of Jesus Christ *for* the remission of sins." But, inasmuch as it has suited the purpose of some controversialists to dispute this proposition, we here give the opinions of two recent representative commentators, who can not be suspected of undue bias in its favor.

Dr. Alexander (Presbyterian) says, "The whole phrase, *to* (or toward) *remission of sins,* describes this as the end to which the multitude had reference, and which, therefore, must be contemplated in the answer." Again: "The beneficial end to which *all* this led was the *remission of sins.*"

Dr. Hackett (Baptist) expresses himself still more satisfactorily: "ἐις ἀφεσιν ἀμαρτιων, in order to *the forgiveness of sins,* (Matt. xxvi: 28; Luke iii: 3,) we connect, naturally, with both the preceding verbs. This clause states the motive or object which should induce them to repent and be baptized. It enforces the entire exhortation, not one part of it to the exclusion of the other."

The connection contended for can not be made more apparent by argument; it needs only that attention be called to it, in order to be perceived by every unbiased mind. It is possible that some doubt might arise in reference to the connection of the clause with the term *repent*, but one would imagine that its connection with the command *be immersed* could not be doubted, but for the fact that it has been disputed. Indeed, some controversialists have felt so great necessity for denying the last-named connection, as to assume that the clause "for the remission of sins" depends exclusively upon the term *repent*, and that the connection of thought is this: "Repent for the remission of sins, and be immersed in the name of Jesus Christ." It is a sufficient refutation of this assumption to remark, that, if Peter had intended to say this, he would most certainly have done so: but he has said something entirely different; and this shows that he meant something entirely different. If men are permitted, after this style, to entirely reconstruct the sentences of inspired apostles, then there is no statement in the Word of God which may not be perverted. We dismiss this baseless assumption with the remark, that it has not been dignified by the indorsement of any writer of respectable attainments, known to the author, and it would not be noticed here, but for the frequency of its appearance in the pulpit, in the columns of denominational newspapers, and on the pages of partisan tracts.

The dependence of the clause, "for the remission of sins," upon both the verbs *repent* and *be immersed*, being established, it would seem undeniable that remission of sins is the blessing in order to the enjoyment of which they were commanded to repent and be immersed. This is universally admitted so far as the term *repent* is concerned, but by many denied in reference to the command *be immersed;* hence the proposition that immersion is for the remission of sins is rejected by the Protestant sects in general. Assuming that remission of sins *precedes* immersion, and that, so far as adults are concerned, the only proper subjects for this ordinance are those whose sins are already pardoned, it is urged that *for* in this clause means "*an account of*" or "*because of.*" Hence, Peter is understood to command, "Repent and be immersed *on account of* remission of sins *already enjoyed.*" But this interpretation is subject to two insuperable objections. 1st. To command men to repent and be immersed because their sins were already remitted, is to require them not only to be *immersed* on this account, but to *repent* because they were already pardoned. There is no possibility of extricating the interpretation from this absurdity. 2d. It contradicts an obvious fact of the case. It makes Peter command the inquirers to be immersed because their sins were *already* remitted, whereas it is an indisputable fact that their sins were *not* yet remitted. On the contrary, they were still pierced to the heart with a sense of guilt, and by the question they propounded were seeking how they might obtain the very pardon which this interpretation assumes that they already enjoyed. Certainly no sane man would assume a position involving such absurdity, and so contradictory to an obvious fact, were he not driven to it by the inexorable demands of a theory which could not be otherwise sustained.

We observe, further, in reference to this interpretation, that even if we admit the propriety of supplanting the preposition *for* by the phrase *on account of*, the substitute will not answer the purpose for which it is employed. The meaning of this phrase varies, according as its object is *past* or *future*. "*On account of*" some past event may mean *because it has taken place;* but *on account of* an event yet in the future, would, in the same connection, mean *in order that it might* take place. The same is true of the equivalent phrase "because of." If, then, the parties addressed by Peter were already pardoned, "*on account of* the remission of sins" would mean, because their sins had been remitted. But as it is an indisputable fact that the parties addressed were yet unpardoned, what they are commanded to do *on account of* remission of sins must mean, *in order that their sins may be remitted.* Such a rendering, therefore, would not even render the obvious meaning of the passage less perspicuous than it already is.

It will be found that any other substitute for the preposition *for*, designed to force upon the passage a meaning different from that which it obviously bears, will as signally fail to suit the purpose of its author. If, with Dr. Alexander, we render, Repent and be immersed "*to* (or *toward*) remission of sins," we still have remission beyond both repentance and immersion, and depending upon them as preparatory conditions. Indeed, this rendering would leave it uncertain whether repentance and immersion would bring them *to* remission of sins, or only *toward* it, leaving an indefinite space yet to pass before obtaining it.

If, with others still—for every effort that ingenuity could suggest has been made to find another meaning for this passage—we render it, Repent and be immersed *unto* or *into* remission of sins, the attempt is fruitless; for remission of sins is still the blessing *unto* which or *into* which repentance and immersion are to lead the inquirers.

Sometimes the advocates of these various renderings, when disheartened by the failure of their attempts at argument and criticism, resort to raillery, and assert that the whole doctrine of immersion for the remission of sins depends upon the one little word *for* in the command, "be immersed *for* the remission of sins." If this were true, it would be no humiliation; for a doctrine based upon *a word of God*, however small, has an eternal and immutable foundation. But it is not true. On the contrary, you may draw a pencil-mark over the whole clause, "for the remission of sins," erasing it, with all the remainder of Peter's answer, and still the meaning will remain unchanged. The connection would then read thus: "Brethren, what shall we do? Then Peter said to them, Repent, and be immersed every one of you in the name of the Lord Jesus." Remembering now that these parties were pierced to the heart with a sense of guilt, and that their question means, What shall we do to be *saved from our sins?* the answer must be understood as the answer to that question. But the answer is, *Repent and be immersed;* therefore, to *repent* and to *be immersed* are the two things which they must do in order to be *saved from their sins.*

The reader now perceives, that, in this first announcement to sinners of the terms of pardon, so guardedly has Peter expressed himself, and so skillfully has Luke interwoven with his words the historic facts, that whatever rendering men have forced upon the leading term, the meaning of the whole remains unchanged; and even when you strike this term and its dependent words out of the text, that same meaning still stares you in the face. This fact is suggestive of more than human wisdom. It reminds us that Peter spoke, and Luke wrote, as they were moved by the Holy Spirit. That infinite wisdom which was dictating a record for all time to come is displayed here, providing for future controversies which no human being could anticipate. Like the sun in the heavens, which may be temporarily obscured by clouds, but will still break forth again, and shine upon all but those who hide from his beams, the light of truth which God has suspended in this passage may be dimmed for a moment by the mists of partisan criticism, but to those who are willing to see it, it will still send out its beams, and guide the trembling sinner unerringly to pardon and peace.

If there were any real ground for doubt as to the proper translation and real meaning of the words εἰς ἄφεσιν ἁμαρτιῶν, *for the remission of sins*, when connected with the term immersion, a candid inquirer would resort to its usage when disconnected from this term, and seek thus to determine its exact import. It happens to occur only once in a connection suitable to this purpose, but no number of occurrences could more definitely fix its meaning. When instituting the supper, Jesus says, "This is my blood of the new covenant, shed for many *for the remission of sins*, εἰς ἄφεσιν ἁμαρτιῶν. It is impossible to doubt that the clause here means *in order to* the remission of sins. In this case it expresses the object for which something is to be done; in the passage we are discussing, it expresses the object for which something is *commanded* to be done: the grammatical and logical construction is the same in both cases, and, therefore, the meaning is the same. Men are to repent and be immersed in order to the attainment of the same blessing for which the blood of Jesus was shed. The propitiation through his blood was in order to the *offer* of pardon, while repentance and immersion are enjoined by Peter upon his hearers, in order to the attainment of pardon.

The careful reader will have observed that in stating the conditions of remission of sins to the multitude, Peter says nothing about the necessity of faith. This omission is not sufficiently accounted for by the fact that faith is implied in the command to repent and be immersed; for the parties now addressed were listening to the terms for the first time, and might fail to perceive this implication. But the fact is, that they did already believe, and it was a result of their faith, that they were pierced to the heart, and made to cry out, What shall we do? This Peter perceived, and therefore it would nave been but little less than mockery to command them to believe. It will be observed, throughout the course of apostolic preaching, that they never commanded men to do what they had already done, but took them as they found them, and enjoined upon them only that which they yet lacked of complete obedience. In the case before us, Peter was not laying down a complete formula of the conditions of pardon; but was simply informing the parties before him what *they* must do in order to the remission of *their* sins. Being believers already, they must add to their faith repentance and immersion.

Before dismissing this topic, we must remark that the doctrine of immersion for the remission of sins does not assume that immersion is the only condition of remission, but simply that, it is *one* among *three* conditions, and the *last* of the three. Administered previous to faith and repentance, as in the case of infants, it is not only absolutely worthless, but intensely sinful.

The exact meaning of the term *repent* will be considered below, under iii: 19.

After commanding the inquirers to repent and be immersed for the remission of sins, Peter adds the promise, "and you shall receive the gift of the Holy Spirit." The *gift* of the Holy Spirit should not be confounded with the Holy Spirit's *gifts*, nor with the *fruits* of the Spirit. The *fruits* of the Holy Spirit are religious traits of character, and they result from the *gift* of the Holy Spirit. The latter expression means, *the Holy Spirit as a gift*. It is analogous to the expression, "promise of the Holy Spirit," in verse 33, above, where Peter says, "having received from the Father the *promise of the Holy Spirit*, he has shed forth this which you now see and hear." The *gifts* of the Holy Spirit were various miraculous powers, intellectual and physical. These were conferred only upon a few individuals, while the *gift* of the Spirit is promised to all who repent and are immersed.

39. Peter does not limit the promise of the Holy Spirit to his present audience; but adds, (39) "*For the promise is to you and to your children, and to all that are afar off, even as many as the Lord our God shall call.*" That we are right in referring the word *promise*, in this sentence, to the promise of the Holy Spirit just made by Peter, is evident from the fact that this is the only promise made in the immediate context.

Some pedobaptist commentators have affected to find in the words, "The promise is to you and your *children*," a show of authority for infant membership in the Church of Christ.* But Mr. Barnes, though of that school himself, has the candor to say of this expression, "It does not refer to children *as children*, and should not be adduced to establish the propriety of infant baptism, or as applicable particularly to infants. It is a promise, indeed, to parents, that the blessings of salvation shall not be confined to parents, but shall be extended also to their posterity." That this is the true conception of the apostle's meaning is demonstrated by the fact that the promise in question is based upon the conditions of repentance and immersion, with which infants could not possibly comply.

The extension of this promise "to all who are afar off," is not to be limited to all the *Jews* who were afar off; but it is properly qualified by the additional words "even as many as the Lord our God shall call." It included, therefore, every individual who should, at any future time, be a subject of the gospel call, and guarantees to us, of the present generation, the gift of the Holy Spirit upon the same terms on which it was offered to Peter's hearers on the day of Pentecost.

* Alex.

ACTS II: 40, 41.

40. The historian has now concluded his report of Peter's discourse, but informs us that he has given only an epitome of it. (40) "*And with many other words did he testify and exhort, saying, Save yourselves from this untoward generation.*" The term *testify* refers to the argumentative portion of his discourse; and the term *exhort* to the hortatory portion. The latter naturally and logically followed his statement of the conditions of pardon, and the substance of it is compressed by Luke into the words, "*Save* yourselves from this untoward generation." The command to *save themselves* must sound quite strange in the ears of such modern theorists as affirm that men have no ability to do, or say, or think any thing tending to their own salvation. But this only shows how far they have departed from apostolic speech and thought. Peter had proposed conditions of pardon which they could comply with, and now their salvation depended upon their compliance with these conditions. When they complied with them, they saved themselves. To be saved *from* that untoward *generation* was not, as the conceit of Universalists would have it, to *escape the siege of Jerusalem;* for the great mass of them escaped that, by dying a natural death before it took place. It was to escape the fate which the mass of that generation were destined to meet in eternity, on account of their sins. We will more fully discuss the exact import of the term *saved* in this and similar connections under verse 47, below.

41. The multitude, who had been so pierced to the heart by Peter's discourse, as to cry out, "Brethren, what shall we do?" were happily surprised to find the terms of pardon so easy. (41) "*Then they gladly received his word, and were immersed; and the same day there were added about three thousand souls.*" The pronoun *they* identifies the parties immersed with those who had cried out, What shall we do? It shows that they promptly complied with the command which Peter had given them. The word which they gladly received can not be the main part of Peter's speech, for this had pierced them to the heart; but it is the word of his answer, which gave their feelings great relief by opening to them so easy a method of escape from the doom which they dreaded, and which they so richly deserved.

Times without number the objection has been urged, and as often refuted, that three thousand men could not have been immersed in so short a time, and with the inadequate supply of water afforded in Jerusalem. As to the quantity of available water, Dr. J. T. Barclay, in his work entitled "The City of the Great King," written during a residence of three years and a half in Jerusalem, as a missionary, shows that Jerusalem was anciently better supplied with water than any other city known to history not permeated by living streams. Even to the present day, though most of the public reservoirs are now dry, such as the supposed pool of Bethesda, 365 feet long by 131 in breadth, and the lower pool of Gihon, 600 feet long by 260 in breadth, there are still in existence bodies of water, such as the pool of Siloam, and the pool of Hezekiah, affording most ample facilities for immersing any number of persons.

As to the want of *time* for the immersion of so many, any one who will make the mathematical calculation, without which it is folly to offer the objection, will find that there was the greatest abundance of time. Allowing that Peter's speech commenced at nine o'clock, as he himself states in verse 15, and that the exercises at the temple closed at noon, we have left six hours till sunset. To immerse sixty men in an hour would be very deliberate work for one administrator. But there were *twelve* administrators, hence, each hour there were not less than *seven hundred and twenty* persons immersed. At this rate, in less than four and one-fourth hours the whole multitude would be immersed, leaving the sun nearly two hours high when the last candidate emerged from the water. In view of this simple calculation, which a child could make, it is truly astonishing that so many grave critics and preachers should urge this objection. It strikingly illustrates the blinding effects of partisan zeal.

Now that the three thousand are added to the Church, we may glance back over the history of the day, and learn upon what preparation they were received to the fellowship of the disciples. To accomplish this, we must first consider their state of mind before Peter spoke to them, and then observe the changes through which they passed. Being Jews, then, they were already believers in the true God, and in the inspiration of the Old Testament scriptures. Luke declares, also, that they were "devout men." * They were, however, unbelievers in reference to Jesus Christ, and they were guilty of participating in his crucifixion.† At the moment that Peter arose to speak, they were full of amazement at witnessing the immersion of the twelve in the Holy Spirit, but their religious character remained unchanged. Peter speaks; and, at the conclusion of his argument, there is an evident change in their convictions. But they believe now nothing additional to what they did at first, except what Peter has proved to them. He has attempted to prove, however, only two propositions: *first*, That he and the eleven were inspired; *second*, That Jesus of Nazareth was now both Lord and Christ. The first, moreover, was established only as a means of proving the second. Several other subordinate facts were also proved for the same purpose, so that the whole speech is properly resolved into an attempt to prove the single proposition with which it concludes, that "God has made that same Jesus whom you have crucified both Lord and Christ." This, then, is what the three thousand believed, and this is all that distinguished their faith when immersed, from what it was before they heard the gospel from Peter's lips.

But another change had occurred within them. Under the influence of their new faith, they were pierced to the heart with a sense of guilt. This is the "godly sorrow" which "works repentance," ‡ and it prepared them to promptly obey Peter's command, "Repent, and be immersed." They repented, and were immersed. Their conversion, therefore, consisted in believing that Jesus is the Christ, repenting of their sins, and being immersed. This entitled them to membership in the Church, and so it does every human being who does likewise.

42. Having been immersed simply upon their faith in Jesus Christ, these young disciples had many subordinate objects of faith to become

* Verse 5.　　† Verse 23.　　‡ 2 Cor. vii: 10.

acquainted with, and many duties yet unknown, in which to be instructed. In giving an account of these matters, Luke is far more brief, adhering strictly to the chief purpose of his narrative, which is to give the process and means of conversion, rather than a history of the edification and instruction of the converted. He closes this section of the history with a brief notice of the order established in the new Church, first describing their order of worship. (42) "*And they continued steadfastly in the apostles' teaching, and in fellowship, and in breaking the loaf, and in prayers.*"

The apostles were as yet the only teachers of the Church, and in this work they were executing the second part of their commission, which required them to teach those whom they immersed all things that Jesus had commanded. The same command which made it their duty to teach, made it also the duty of the disciples to learn from them, and to abide by their instruction. This duty the first disciples faithfully complied with, though it has been grievously neglected by their brethren of later ages.

For the purpose of being taught by the apostles, they must have assembled together, and this was the occasion for manifesting their *fellowship*, which term expresses their common participation in religious privileges. It has been urged by some writers, that the term κοινωνία should here be rendered *contribution*, instead of *fellowship*, and that it refers to contributions which were regularly made in the public assemblies, for the poor. That the term is used in this limited sense in at least two places in the New Testament must be admitted, viz.: in Rom. xv: 16, "It hath pleased them of Macedonia to make a certain *contribution* for the poor of the saints in Jerusalem;" and in 2 Cor. ix: 13, where Paul says the saints "glorify God for your liberal *contribution* to them and to all men." But such is not, by any means, its common usage. It usually occurs in such connections as the following: "You were called into the *fellowship* of his Son Jesus Christ."* "The favor of our Lord Jesus Christ, the love of God, and the *fellowship* of the Holy Spirit be with you."† "And truly our *fellowship* is with the Father and with his Son Jesus Christ."‡ "We have *fellowship* with one another."‖

The radical idea in this term is that of *participation in common*. We have fellowship with God, because we are made *partakers* of the divine nature, as we escape the corruption which is in the world through lust. We have fellowship with the Son, because of the common sympathies which his life and sufferings have established between himself and us; and with the Spirit, because we partake of the strengthening and enlightening influences of his teachings, and because he dwells in us. We have fellowship with one another, because of the mutual participation in each other's affection and good offices. The term is also used in reference to the Lord's supper. "The cup of blessing which we bless, is it not the *fellowship* of the blood of Christ? The loaf which we break, is it not the *fellowship* of the body of Christ?"§ We *partake in common* of the benefits of his broken body and shed blood, which are symbolized in the cup and the loaf.

* 1 Cor. i: 9.   † 2 Cor. xiii: 14.   ‡ 1 John i: 3.   ‖ 1 John i: 7.   § 1 Cor. x: 16.

From the meaning of the term, as thus exemplified, originates its use in the sense of *contribution;* for in the act of contributing to the necessities of others, we allow them to participate in the blessings which we enjoy. We are not authorized, however, by the rules of criticism, to give it this limited signification, except where the context clearly requires it. Seeing that Christians enjoy fellowship with so many sources of happiness, the term unrestricted must embrace them all. In the present instance the context imposes no limitation upon its meaning, and it would be quite arbitrary to restrict it to the sense of contribution. The use of the article before κοινωνία can not be pleaded as a ground for such restriction; for it only indicates the notoriety of that which the term designates. Still, the idea of contributing to the wants of poor brethren is involved in the fellowship of Christians, and by the statement that they continued steadfastly in the fellowship, we understand that they continued in the common participation of religious enjoyments, *including* contributions for the poor. Whether these contributions were made at every meeting or not, we are not informed; but they were certainly made when circumstances required.

Together with the apostles' teaching and the fellowship, Luke enumerates "breaking the loaf and prayers," as part of the exercises in which the disciples continued. The frequency with which the loaf was broken is not intimated here. It will be discussed under chapter xx: 7. This brief statement shows merely that this institution, according to the Savior's command, was observed from the very beginning of the Church.

The prayers mentioned are those that were offered in public. The number of prayers offered on any occasion, or the order in which the prayers, the instruction, breaking the loaf, and the other acts of fellowship followed each other, is not intimated. Luke's silence in reference to these particulars may have arisen from the fact that there was no invariable order of exercises; or may have been intended to prevent the order in the Jerusalem Church from being regarded as an authoritative precedent. It shows clearly the intention of the Holy Spirit that the assemblies of the saints should be left to the exercise of their own discretion in matters of this kind, and furnishes a most singular rebuke to the hundreds of party leaders who have since attempted to impose authoritative rituals upon the congregations. If the example of the Church in Jerusalem, in this respect, though its exercises were directed by the whole body of the apostles, was not binding upon other Churches, what body of uninspired men shall have the presumption to bind what God has purposely left free?

43. Next to this brief notice of the exercises of the Church, we have a glance at the effect of the scenes just described, upon the surrounding community. (43) *"And fear came upon every soul, and many wonders and signs were done by the apostles."* This fear was not that which partakes of aversion, for we learn below, (47) that many were daily added to the Church; but it was that silent awe which miracles naturally inspired, mingled with respectful deference to a people of such holiness.

44, 45. We are next introduced to a striking instance of the fellow ship previously mentioned. (44) "*Now all who believed were together, and had all things common,* (45) *and sold their possessions and goods, and distributed them to all, as any one had need.*" This was not a community of goods, by which all were placed on a pecuniary level; for distribution was made only as any one had *need.* It was only such a liberality to the poor as should characterize the congregations of the Lord in every age and country. Poor brethren must not be allowed to suffer for the necessaries of life, though it require us to divide with them the last loaf in our possession. "He who has this world's goods and sees his brother have need, and shuts up his compassion from him, how dwells the love of God in him?"* We will, hereafter, see that the Church in Jerusalem was not the only one which engaged in this species of benevolence.† This conduct was in marked contrast with the neglect of the poor which was then common among the Jews, even in violation of their own law, and which was universal among the Gentiles. Nothing of this kind had ever been seen on earth before. We will refer to the subject again, under iv: 32, below.

46, 47. The further history of the Church, for a short time, is condensed into this brief statement: (46) "*And they, continuing daily with one accord in the temple, and breaking bread from house to house, received their food with gladness and singleness of heart,* (47) *praising God, and having favor with all the people. And the Lord added those saved every day to the Church.*"

Whether the disciples continued to offer sacrifices or not—on which question see Com. xxi: 18–26—that they should "continue daily with one accord in the temple," was most natural. The temple had been, to them and their fathers, for many generations, the house of God and the place of prayer. The apostles had been led to its sacred precincts by the Savior himself, and here it was that the Holy Spirit had come upon them. Their most holy local associations were connected with it, and it would have been doing great violence to their feelings to require them at once to abandon it. This natural reverence for the place continued till its destruction by Titus; and even to this day, the hill where the temple once stood has a peculiarly sacred place in the hearts of Christians. The "breaking bread," κλῶντές ἄρτον, mentioned in this sentence, is not the "breaking of the loaf," ἡ κλάσις τοῦ ἄρτου, of verse 42; but refers to common meals of which they partook "from house to house." This is evident from the connection: "breaking bread from house to house, they *received their food* with gladness and singleness of heart." It was that breaking of bread in which they "received their food," which was not done in partaking of the emblematic loaf. There is no evidence that the emblematic loaf was ever broken in mere social gatherings. It belongs exclusively to the Lord's day.‡

By the expression "singleness of heart" is meant the concentration of their affections and desires upon a single subject. This devotion and concentration of thought could but result, as it did, in giving the disciples "favor with all the people," and causing **daily additions** to the Church.

* 1 John iii: 17.   † See Com. xi: 27–30. xx: 2–3.   ‡ See xx: 7.

Those added to the Church daily were not "such as should be saved," as rendered in the common version, but τοὺς σωζομένους, *the saved*. In what sense they were saved, is a question of some importance. Dr. Hackett says: "The doctrine is that those who embrace the gospel adopt the infallible means of being saved." This is, undoubtedly, true doctrine; but it is not what is taught in the passage; for Luke speaks not of those who daily *embraced the means of salvation*, but of those who were *saved*. The view expressed by Alexander, that "men are said to be saved, not only in reference to the final consummation, but to the inception of the saving work," is a nearer approach to the true conception, but still falls short of it. It is not an *inception* of the saving work, of which Luke speaks, but the salvation referred to is complete; the parties spoken of being called "the *saved*." Both these learned commentators, by keeping their minds fixed upon a future state as offering the only fulfillment of the word "*saved*," have failed to discover the exact sense in which it is here used by the historian. Primarily, the term *save* means simply to *make safe*. In the religious sense, it means to make safe from the consequences of sin. If men had never sinned, they could not be *saved*, seeing they would be already *safe*. But having sinned, they are *saved* when they are *made safe* from the consequences of their sins. This is done when their sins are forgiven. At the moment a penitent sinner obtains pardon, he is, so far as the past is concerned, *completely saved*. It is in this sense that the parties in this case added to the Church are called "*the saved*." Paul uses the term in the same sense when he says of God, "According to his mercy he *saved* us, by the laver of regeneration, and the renewing of the Holy Spirit."*

The fact that the Lord added the *saved*, or *pardoned*, to the Church, justifies two conclusions; *first*, That men are entitled to membership in the Church the moment they are pardoned; *second*, That men should join the Church, not as a means of obtaining pardon, but because they have already obtained it. The former conclusion shows that it is unscriptural to admit, as some parties do, that certain persons are pardoned, and yet refuse them Church-fellowship. The latter condemns the practice observed by others, of receiving persons to membership "as a *means of grace;*" i. e., as a means of obtaining pardon.

III. 1–10. Thus far, the labors of the apostles had met with uninterrupted and most astonishing success. Luke is now about to introduce us to a series of conflicts, in which success and temporary defeat alternate in the history of the Jerusalem Church.

(1) "*Now Peter and John were going up together into the temple at the hour of prayer, the ninth hour.* (2) *And a certain man, lame from his birth, was carried thither, whom they laid every day at the gate of the temple which is called Beautiful, to ask alms of those entering into the temple:* (2) *who, seeing Peter and John about to go into the temple, asked alms.* (4) *And Peter, earnestly looking on him, with John, said, Look on us.* (5) *And he gave heed to them, expecting to receive something from them.* (6) *But Peter said, Silver and gold I have not; but*

---

* Titus iii: 5.   See also 2 Tim. i: 9; 1 Cor. i: 18.

what I have, this I give you. In the name of Jesus Christ of Nazareth, rise up and walk. (7) *And seizing him by the right hand, he lifted him up, and immediately his feet and ankles received strength; (8) and leaping forth, he stood and walked, and entered with them into the temple, walking, and leaping, and praising God. (9) And all the people saw him walking and praising God, (10) and recognized him, that it was he who sat for alms at the Beautiful gate of the temple. And they were filled with wonder and amazement at that which had happened to him.*"

This is by no means the first miracle which had been wrought by the apostles since the day of Pentecost; for we have seen, in chapter ii: 43, that many signs and wonders had been wrought, by which the people were filled with awe. But the circumstances attending this miracle were calculated to awaken, as it did, an unusual excitement. The Beautiful gate of the temple, so called because of its magnificent folding doors, fifty feet high and forty wide, covered with gold and Corinthian brass, was the favorite pass-way into the temple. The subject of this cure, being laid every day at this gate to beg, was well known to all who frequented the temple. From the natural curiosity of the benevolent in reference to the afflictions of those to whom they minister, it was probably known to all that he had been a cripple from his birth. Besides this, the time of the cure was when a multitude of pious people were entering the temple for evening prayer; and their attention was unexpectedly arrested by the leaping and shouting of the man who was healed. As they witnessed his ecstasy, and saw him clinging to Peter and John, no one asked the meaning of the scene, for all saw at once that the cripple had been healed by the apostles, and they stood gazing in amazement upon Peter and John.

11–15. The apostles took a position in one of the open colonnades which faced the inner side of the temple wall, called Solomon's Portico. (11) "*And while the lame man who was healed was holding fast Peter and John, all the people ran together to them on the portico called Solomon's, greatly wondering.*" The admiration of the multitude was directed toward Peter and John; and was understood by Peter to indicate that they attributed the cure rather to the singular holiness of himself and John, than to the power of their master. He determined to take advantage of the circumstances, by turning their excited thoughts into the proper channel. (12) "*Then Peter, seeing this, answered to the people, Men of Israel, why do you wonder at this, or why do you look so earnestly on us, as though by our own power or piety we had caused this man to walk? (13) The God of Abraham, and of Isaac, and of Jacob, the God of our fathers, has glorified his son Jesus, whom you delivered up, and rejected in the presence of Pilate, when he had determined to let him go. (14) But you rejected the holy and just, and desired a murderer to be granted to you; (15) and you killed the author of life, whom God has raised from the dead, of which we are witnesses.*"

In this passage the apostle makes the same statement, in substance, with which he introduced the main theme of his former discourse. The antithetical style adopted on this occasion gave to it a force scarcely excelled by his former discourse, while it was even more penetrating to the consciences of his hearers. The fact that the God of their fathers had *glorified* Jesus, is contrasted with the fact that they had delivered him up to die; their refusal to let him be released, with the cruel Pilate's determination to let him go; their rejection of one holy and just, with their demand that a murderer should be released to them; and their murder of him, with his authorship of all life. These four points of antithesis form the four steps of a grand climax. Whom the God of your fathers glorified, you have delivered up to die. Your criminality is hightened by the fact, that when even a heathen judge declared him innocent, and desired to release him to you, you rejected him. Even this does not express the enormity of your guilt, for you yourselves knew him whom you rejected to be holy and just, and preferred the release of one whom you knew to be a murderer. But, above all, in murdering him, you *put to death the author of life*, who has *arisen* from the dead. We might challenge the pages of all the classics for a climax more thrilling in its effect upon the audience, or for a happier combination of climax and antithesis. The effect upon the multitude was overwhelming.* The facts declared were undeniable, except the resurrection, and of this the men who had just healed the cripple were the witnesses.

16. But Peter does not stop short with this climax, terminating in the resurrection from the dead. He proceeds to prove his present power and glory by the facts which were then filling them with amazement. (16) "*And his name, through faith in his name, has made this man strong, whom you see and know. Even the faith which is through him, has given him this perfect soundness in the presence of you all.*" In this verse, there is one of those repetitions common with extemporaneous speakers, and designed to express more guardedly a thought already uttered. Perhaps the formula employed by Peter in the act of healing, "*In the name* of Jesus of Nazareth, rise up and walk," suggested to him the phraseology, "his *name*, through faith in his name, has made this man strong." But lest the superstitious audience might imagine that there was some *charm* in the mere *name* of Jesus, a mistake which was afterwards made by certain Jews in Ephesus,† he adds, "The *faith* which is *through* him has given him this perfect soundness." The faith was not that of the cripple; for it is clear, from the description, that he had no faith. When Peter said to him, "Look on us," the man looked up, expecting to receive alms. And even when Peter told him, in the name of Jesus, to rise up and walk, he did not attempt to move till Peter "took him by the right hand, and lifted him up." He exhibited no faith, either in Jesus, or in Peter's healing power, till after he found himself able to stand and walk. We must locate the faith, therefore, in the apostles; and in this we are sustained by the fact that the exercise of miraculous power, by those in possession of spiritual gifts, was always dependent upon their faith; Peter was empowered to walk upon the water; but, when his faith wavered, he began to sink, and Jesus said, "O thou of *little* faith, wherefore didst thou doubt?" Nine of the apostles, once, having failed to cast out a demon, asked Jesus, "Why could

*See below, on verse 17. † Acts xix: 13.

we not cast him out?" He replied, "Because of your unbelief."* In answer to their prayers, also, many miracles were wrought, but it was only "the prayer of *faith*" which could heal the sick.†

It must be here observed that faith was necessary to the *exercise* of spiritual gifts, already *imparted*, and that no faith, however strong, ever enabled the *uninspired* to work miracles. The notion, therefore, which has existed in some minds, from time to time, ever since the apostolic period, that if our faith were strong enough, we, too, could work miracles, has as little foundation in scripture as it has in experiment.

17–18. At this point in the discourse there is a marked change in Peter's tone and manner, which we can attribute to nothing else than some visible indication of the intense pain produced by what he had already said. He had made a most terrific onslaught upon them, and exposed their criminality in unsparing terms; but now, induced by some perceptible change in their countenances, he softens his style and extenuates their fault. (17) "*And now, brethren, I know that you did it in ignorance, as did also your rulers.* (18) *But those things which God had before announced through the mouth of all his prophets, that the Christ should suffer, he hath thus fulfilled.*" That they acted in ignorance of the real character of Jesus was an extenuation of their crime, but it did not render them innocent; for the preceding remarks were intended to convict them of crime, and in his preceding discourse he charged that with *wicked hands* they had crucified and slain him. Peter assumes, what none of them could honestly deny, that it was by *wicked motives* they were impelled to the fatal deed.

In connection with this assertion of their criminality, he states another fact hard to be reconciled with it in the philosophy of man, that, in the commission of this crime, God was fulfilling what he had declared through his prophets should be done. Once before, in speaking of this same event, Peter had brought these two apparently conflicting facts, the sovereignty of God, and the free agency of man, into juxtaposition, when he said, "Him, being delivered by the *determined purpose* and *foreknowledge* of God, you have taken, and with *wicked hands* have crucified and slain." That God had predetermined the death of Jesus can not be denied without contradicting both the prophets and the apostles; and that they acted wickedly in doing what God had determined should be done, Peter affirms, and three thousand of them on Pentecost, with many more on this occasion, admitted it. If any man can frame a theory by which to philosophically reconcile these two facts, we will assent to it, if we can understand it; but unless both facts, unaltered, have a place in the theory, we must reject it. We reject every man who denies either of the facts; but while he admits them both, we will not dispute with him about the theory upon which he attempts to reconcile them. This much, fidelity to the word of God on the one hand, and brotherly kindness on the other, demand of us. In the mean time, it is better to follow Peter's example. He lays the two facts side by side, appealing to the prophets for the proof of one, and to the consciences

* Matt. xvii: 14. † James v: 15.

of men for the proof of the other, and there he leaves them, seeming not to realize that he had involved himself in the slightest difficulty. It is folly to attempt to climb where we are certain of a fall.

19–21. Having now fully demonstrated the Messiahship of Jesus, and exposed the criminality of those who had condemned him, the apostle next presents to his hearers the conditions of pardon. (19) *"Repent, therefore, and turn, that your sins may be blotted out, and that seasons of refreshing may come from the presence of the Lord, (20) and he may send Jesus Christ, who has before preached to you, (21) whom heaven must retain* until the time of the restoration of all things which God has spoken, through the mouth of all his holy prophets, since the world began.*

Here, as in his former statement of the conditions of pardon, the apostle makes no mention of faith. But, having labored, from the beginning of his discourse, to convince his hearers, they necessarily understood that his command, based as it was, upon what he had said, implied the assumption that they believed it. A command based upon an argument, or upon testimony, always implies the sufficiency of the proof, and assumes that the hearer is convinced. Moreover, Peter knew very well that none would repent at his command who did not believe what he had said; hence, in every view of the case, he proceeded, naturally and safely, in omitting the mention of faith.

In the command "Repent and turn," the word "turn" expresses something to be done subsequent to repentance. There is no way to avoid this conclusion, unless we suppose that *turn* is *equivalent to repent;* but this is inadmissible, because there could be no propriety in adding the command *turn*, if what it means had been already expressed in the command *repent.* We may observe, that the term *reform*, which some critics would employ instead of *repent*, would involve the passage in a repetition not less objectionable. To *reform* and to *turn to the Lord* are equivalent expressions, hence it would be a useless repetition to command men, Reform, *and turn.*

In order to a proper understanding of this passage, it is necessary to determine the exact scriptural import of the term *repent*. The most popular conception of its meaning is "godly sorrow for sin." But, according to Paul, "godly sorrow *works* repentance in order to salvation."† Instead of being identical with repentance, therefore, it is the immediate cause which *leads* to repentance. Paul says to the Corinthians, in the same connection, "Now I rejoice, not that you were made sorry, but that you *sorrowed to* repentance." This remark shows that it is sorrow which brings men to repentance, and also implies that there may be sorrow for sin without repentance. That there is a distinction between these two states of mind, and that sorrow for sin may exist without repentance, is also implied in commanding those on Pentecost who were already *pierced to the heart*, to *repent*. It is also evident from the case of Judas, who experienced the most intense sorrow for sin, but was not brought to repentance. His feeling is expressed by a different term in the original, which is

---

* Receive (common version) is the literal meaning of the original δέξασθαι, but it is certainly used here in the sense of *retain*. Heaven had already *received* him; it was yet to *retain* him. † 2 Cor. vii: 10.

never used to express the change which the gospel requires, and is equivalent to *regret*, though sometimes, as in his case, it expresses the idea of *remorse*. In thus tracing the distinction between "godly sorrow" and repentance, we have ascertained the fact that repentance is produced by sorrow for sin, and this must constitute one element in the definition of the term. Whatever it is, it is produced by sorrow for sin. Is it not, then, reformation? Reformation is certainly produced by sorrow for sin; but, as we have already observed, *turning*, which is equivalent to *reforming*, is distinguished, in the text before us, from *repenting*. The same distinction is elsewhere apparent. John the Immerser, in requiring the people to "bring forth *fruits meet* for repentance," clearly distinguishes between repentance and those deeds of a reformed life which he styles fruits *meet* for repentance. With him, reformation is the *fruit* of repentance, not its equivalent. The distinction is that between fruit and the tree which bears it. When Jesus speaks of repenting *seven times a day*,* he certainly means something different from reformation; for that would require more time. Likewise, when Peter required those on Pentecost to *repent* and be immersed, if by the term *repent* he had meant *reform*, he would certainly have given them time to reform before they were immersed, instead of immersing them immediately. Finally, the original term is sometimes used in connection with such prepositions as are not suitable to the idea of reformation. As a general rule it is followed by απο, or εκ, which are suitable to either idea; but in 2 Cor. xii: 21, it is followed by επι with the dative: "Many have not repented, επι *of* the uncleanness, and fornication, and lasciviousness which they have committed." Now men do not reform *of* their evil deeds, neither will the preposition, in this case, bear a rendering which would suit the term *reform*.† *Reform*, then, does not express the same idea as repent, but, as we have seen above, reformation is the *fruit* or *result* of repentance.

Seeing now that repentance is produced by sorrow for sin, and results in reformation, we can have no further difficulty in ascertaining exactly what it is; for the only result of sorrow for sin which leads to reformation, is a *change of the will* in reference to sin. The etymological meaning of μετανοια is a *change of mind;* but the particular element of the mind which undergoes this change is the *will*. Strictly defined, therefore, repentance is *a change of the will, produced by sorrow for sin, and leading to reformation*. If the change of will is not produced by sorrow for sin, it is not *repentance*, in the religious sense, though it may be μετανοια, in the classic sense. Thus, Esau "found no place for μετανοιας, *a change of mind*, though he sought it carefully with tears."‡ Here the word designates a change in the mind of Isaac in reference to the blessing which he had already given to Jacob; but this change did not depend upon sorrow for sin, hence it was not repentance, and should not be so translated. Again, if the change of will, though produced by sorrow for sin, is one which does not lead to reformation, it is not *repentance;* for there was a change

* 1 Luke xvii: 4.
† For the suggestion of this criticism, I am indebted to my friend and brother, H. T. Anderson. ‡ Heb. xii: 17.

in the will of Judas, produced by sorrow for sin, yet Judas did not *repent*. The change in his case led to *suicide*, not to *reformation;* it is, therefore, not expressed by μετανοέω, but by μεταμέλομαι. Our definition, therefore, is complete, without redundancy.*

We can now perceive, still more clearly than before, that in the command, "Repent and turn," the terms *repent*, and *turn*, express two distinct changes, which take place in the order of the words. Their relative meaning is well expressed by Dr. Bloomfield, who says that the former denotes "a change of *mind*," the latter "a change of *conduct.*" Mr. Barnes also well and truly remarks: ".This expression ('*be converted,*') conveys an idea not at all to be found in the original. It conveys the idea of *passivity*—BE *converted*, as if they were to yield to some foreign influence that they were now resisting. But the idea of being *passive* in this is not conveyed by the original word. The word properly means to *turn*—to return to a path from which one has gone astray; and then to turn away from sins, or to forsake them." That *turn*, rather than *be converted*, is the correct rendering of the term, is not disputed by any competent authority; we shall assume, therefore, that it is correct, and proceed to inquire what Peter intended to designate by this term.

As already observed, it designates a change in the conduct. A change of conduct, however, must, from the very necessity of the case, have a beginning; and that beginning consists in the first act of the better life. The command to *turn* is obeyed when this first act is performed. Previous to that, the man has not turned; subsequent to it he *has* turned; and the act itself is the *turning* act. If, in turning to the Lord, any one of a number of actions might be the first that the penitent performed, the command to *turn* would not specially designate any one of these, but might be obeyed by the performance of either. But the fact is that one single act was uniformly enjoined upon the penitent, as the first overt act of obedience to Christ, and that was, to *be immersed*. This Peter's present hearers understood. They had heard him say to parties like themselves, "Repent and be immersed;" and the first act they saw performed by those who signified their repentance, was to be immersed. When, now, he commands them to repent and *turn*, they could but understand that they were to turn as their predecessors had done, by being *immersed*. The commands *turn*, and *be immersed*, are equivalent, not because the words have the same meaning, but because the command "Turn to the Lord" was uniformly obeyed by the specific act of being immersed. Previous to immersion, men *repented*, but did not *turn;* after immersion, they had *turned*, and immersion was the *turning act.*

We may reach the same conclusion by another course of reasoning. The command *Turn* occupies the same position between repentance and the remission of sins, in this discourse, that the command *Be immersed* had occupied in Peter's former discourse. He then said, "Repent and *be immersed* for the remission of sins;" he now says, "Repent and *turn* that your sins may be blotted out." Now, when his present hearers heard him command them to *turn* in order to the

* In perfecting this definition, I am indebted to Prof. W. K. Pendleton, of Bethany College, for valuable suggestions.

same blessing for which he had formerly commanded them to be immersed, they could but understand that the generic word *turn* was used with specific reference to immersion, and that the substitution is founded on the fact that a penitent sinner *turns* to God by *being immersed.*

This interpretation was first advanced, in modern times, by Alexander Campbell, about thirty years ago, and it excited against him then an opposition which still rages. The real ground of this opposition is not the interpretation itself, but a perversion of it. The word *conversion* being used in popular terminology in the sense of a *change of heart*, when Mr. Campbell announced that the word incorrectly rendered in this passage, *be converted*, means to *turn* to the Lord by *immersion*, the conclusion was seized by his opponents that he rejected all change of heart, and substituted immersion in its stead. He has reiterated, again and again, the sense in which he employed the term *convert*, and that the heart must be changed by faith and repentance *previous* to the *conversion* or *turning* here commanded by Peter; yet those who are determined upon doing him injustice still keep up the wicked and senseless clamor of thirty years ago. The *odium theologicum*, like the scent of musk, is not soon nor easily dissipated. There are always those to whose nostrils the odor is grateful.

There are several facts connected with the use of the original term, ἐπιστρέφω, in the New Testament, worthy of notice. It occurs *thirty-nine* times, in *eighteen* of which it is used for the mere physical act of *turning* or *returning*. Nineteen times it expresses a change from evil to good, and twice* *from good to evil.* If the term *convert*, therefore, were retained as the rendering, a man could, in the scriptural sense, be converted to *Satan* as well as to *God.* But *be converted* can never truly represent the original, though it is so rendered six times in the common version. The original is invariably in the active voice, and it is making a false and pernicious impression on the English reader to render it by the passive voice. If we render it truthfully by the term convert, we would have such readings as these: "Repent and *convert;*" "lest they should see with their eyes, and hear with their ears, and understand with their hearts, and should *convert*, and I should heal them," etc. The absurdity of such a rendering shows the necessity for some other term. In a correct version of the New Testament, the expression *be converted* could not possibly occur; for there is nothing in the original to justify it.

Not less worthy of observation is the fact, that while the change called *conversion* is popularly attributed to a divine power, as the only power capable of effecting it, and it is considered scarcely less than blasphemy to speak of a man converting another, or converting himself, yet the original word never does refer either to God, or Christ, or the Holy Spirit, as its agent. On the contrary, in *five* of its nineteen occurrences in the sense of a change from evil to good, it is employed of a human agent, as of John the Immerser, Paul, or some brother in the Church;† and in the remaining *fourteen* instances, the agent is the *person who is the subject of the change.* Thus, men may be properly said to *turn* their fellows, yet the subjects of this act are

---

* Gal. iv: 9; 2 Peter ii: 21.   † Luke i: 16, 17; Acts xxvi: 18; James v: 19, 20.

never said to *be* turned, but to *turn* to the Lord. The term invariably expresses something that the sinner is *to do*. These observations show how immeasurably the term *convert* has departed, in popular usage, from the sense of the original which it so falsely represents, and how imperious the necessity for displacing it from our English Bibles. The word *turn* corresponds to the original in meaning, in usage, in inflections, and translates it unambiguously in every instance.*

Peter commands his hearers to repent and turn, in order to three distinct objects: *first*, "That your sins may be blotted out;" *second*, "That seasons of refreshing may come from the presence of the Lord;" *third*, "That he may send Jesus Christ who was before preached to you." It is supposed, by the commentators generally, that the last two events are contemplated by Peter as cotemporaneous, so that the "seasons of refreshing" spoken of are those which will take place at the second coming of Christ. That there will be seasons of refreshing then, is true; but there are others more immediately dependent upon the obedience here enjoined by Peter, to which the reference is more natural. The pardon of sins and the gift of the Holy Spirit, which were immediately consequent upon repentance and immersion, certainly bring "seasons of refreshing," which might well be made the subject of promise to hearers supposed to be trembling with guilty apprehension. The reference of these words is, doubtless, to the gift of the Spirit; for they occupy the same place here that the gift of the Spirit did in the former discourse. Then, after repentance, immersion, and the remission of sins, came the promise of the Holy Spirit; now, after the same three, somewhat differently expressed—*i. e.*, repentance, turning to the Lord, and blotting out of sins—comes the promise of "seasons of refreshing from the presence of the Lord." They are, then, the fresh and cheering enjoyments of him whose sins are forgiven, and who is taught to believe that the presence of the approving Spirit of God is with him.

The third promise, that God would send Jesus Christ, who was before preached to them, was dependent upon their obedience only in so far as they would thus contribute to the object for which he will come, to raise from the dead, and receive into glory, all who are his. It is qualified by the remark, "whom heaven must retain until the times of the restoration of all things of which God has spoken by the mouth of all his holy prophets since the world began." It is difficult to determine the exact force of the term *restoration* in this connection. It is commonly referred to a state of primeval order, purity, and happiness, which, it is supposed, will exist just previous to the second coming of Christ†. But the apostle speaks of a restoration of all things of which God has spoken by the mouth of *all* his holy prophets. Now, there are many things spoken of by the prophets besides those which refer to the final triumphs of the truth, and *all* these are included in the expression. Some of these things will not consist, individually considered, in *restoration*, but in *destruction*. Still, the prevailing object of all the things of which the prophets

---

* It is gratifying to observe that the incipient version of the American Bible Union corresponds to the views here expressed. † Hackett.

have spoken, even the destruction of wicked nations and apostate Churches, is to finally *restore* that moral sway which God originally exercised over the whole earth. It is doubtless this thought which suggested the term *restoration*, though reference is had to the fulfillment of all the prophesies which are to be fulfilled on earth. Not till all are fulfilled will Christ come again.

22, 23. For the twofold purpose of giving confirmation to the claims of Jesus, and warning his hearers as to the consequences of rejecting him, the apostle next introduces a well-known prophesy of Moses.* (22) "*For Moses, indeed, said to the fathers, A prophet shall the Lord your God raise up for you, from among your brethren, like me: him shall ye hear in all things, whatever he shall say to you.* (23) *And it shall come to pass that every soul who will not hear that prophet shall be destroyed from among the people.*" Whether Peter was right in applying this prophesy to Christ depends upon the likeness between him and Moses. This likeness may be traced in many subordinate incidents of his history, but lies chiefly in that which distinguishes both Moses and Christ from all other prophets. Moses was a deliverer of his people, and an original lawgiver. No prophet had been like him in these two particulars. The chief mission of the other prophets, so far as their cotemporaries were concerned, was to enforce the law of Moses. But Christ had now come, speaking by his own authority, offering a more glorious deliverance to the people than that from Egypt, and issuing new laws for the government of men. This proved that he, and he alone, was the prophet spoken of by Moses, and Peter's hearers now perceive that the authority of Moses himself binds them to the authority of Jesus, and that they must hear him, on the penalty of destruction if they refuse.

24. Not content with bringing to bear the testimony of Moses, Peter adds to it the combined voices of all the prophets: (24) "*And, indeed, all the prophets, from Samuel and those following in order, as many as have spoken, have also foretold these days.*" This declaration is to be understood only of those prophets whose predictions are recorded in the Old Testament, for to these alone could Peter appeal in proof of his proposition. It was conceded by the Jews, that all the prophets had spoken of the days of the Messiah, and it was already proved, by Peter's preceding remarks, that Jesus was the Messiah; hence the argument is now complete.

25, 26. Having completed his argument, in which the Messiahship of Jesus was demonstrated by the miraculous cure they had witnessed, and by the testimony of all the prophets, from Moses and Samuel down to Malachi, Peter next makes a powerful appeal to his hearers, based upon their veneration for the fathers of their nation, and for the covenant which God had made with them. (25) "*You are the sons of the prophets, and of the covenant which God made with our fathers, saying to Abraham, And in thy seed shall all the kingdoms of the earth be blessed.* (26) *Unto you first, God, having raised up his son Jesus, has sent him to bless you, in turning away each one of you from his iniquities.*" This was a tender appeal to their national sympathies, made more effective by the statement that to them *first*, because of their

* Deut. xviii: 15–19.

relation to the prophets and to Abraham, God had sent his risen Son to bless them, before visiting the rest of the world.

The use here made of the promise to Abraham shows the true interpretation of it. It is to be fulfilled, according to Peter, in turning living men away from their iniquities. Those only, therefore, who, under the influence of the gospel, turn away from their iniquities, can lay claim to the blessings contemplated in this promise. That all the kindreds of the earth were to be blessed does not affect this conclusion, except to extend its application to those of all nations who should, at any period of time, turn from their iniquities. The Universalian view of this promise is contradicted by all the apostolic comments upon it; for they all unite in denying the blessing to any but those who in this life believe and turn to the Lord.*

IV: 1–3. Just at this point in Peter's discourse: "*And while they were yet speaking to the people, the priests, and the captain of the temple, and the Saducees came upon them,* (2) *being indignant that they taught the people, and preached, through Jesus, the resurrection from the dead.* (3) *And they laid hands on them, and put them in prison until the next day; for it was already evening.*" This sudden disturbance of the interested audience, by a body of armed men rushing through their midst and seizing Peter and John, is the beginning of a series of persecutions with which Luke is about to follow the account of the first peaceful triumphs of the apostles.

We would naturally, at first thought, expect to find the parties to this violent proceeding identical with the chief persecutors of Jesus, supposing that the same motives which had excited opposition to him would perpetuate it against his disciples. But the *Pharisees* were *his* most bitter enemies, the Saducees being comparatively indifferent to his pretensions, while here we see the Saducees leading the attack upon the apostles, and we will soon see the leader of the Pharisees interfering to save them from threatened death.† In order to appreciate this unexpected change in the aspect of parties, we must note a little more carefully the ground of opposition in each case.

The supposition sometimes entertained that Jesus was hated by men simply because there is in human nature an innate aversion to truth and holiness, is not less false to the facts of history than to the nature of fallen man. It is disproved by the fact that it was not the mass of his cotemporaries who hated him, as the supposition would require, but chiefly, and almost exclusively, the Pharisees. That portion of the people who were most depraved, according to external appearances, heard him gladly, and delighted to praise him, while the Pharisees, who were most of all noted for their piety, were the men who hated him most. Neither were they actuated simply by an aversion to his holiness; for they had a more substantial, if not a better reason for hating him. If he had been content merely to go about doing good, and teaching righteousness, "letting other people alone," he might have passed his days in peace. But such was not his sense of duty. He knew that his teaching could not have proper effect unless the erroneous doctrines of the Pharisees, who were then the chief teachers of Israel, were dislodged from the public mind, and

* See Gal. iii: 7–9, *et al.*   † V: 34, below.

ACTS IV: 4–6.

the mask of hypocrisy, which had secured them their great reputation for piety, were stripped off. He undertook, therefore, an offensive warfare upon their doctrinal tenets and their religious pretensions. The twenty-third chapter of Matthew contains an epitome of this warfare on his part, than which there is not a more withering philippic on record in all literature. Such denunciation necessarily provoked the most intense hatred on the part of such Pharisees as were too deeply imbued with the prevailing spirit of the party to be reached by the truth. By this very fact, however, they made it more evident to the people that they deserved all the denunciation which he hurled against them. On the other hand, the Sadducees were so well pleased with his successful assaults upon their hereditary and too powerful enemies, that they forgave, in some degree, his known opposition to their favorite doctrine, and felt for him some friendly sympathy.

With the apostles the relations of these parties were as naturally reversed. Instead of assaulting, in detail, the doctrinal tenets of any party, they confined their labors, at first, to testimony concerning the resurrection and glorification of Jesus. This confirmed the chief distinctive doctrine of the Pharisees, who believed in a resurrection, and it left their other tenets, for the time being, unnoticed. But the whole force of this preaching was leveled against Sadduceean infidelity in reference to the resurrection, and it therefore aroused this party to an activity never exhibited before. They rushed in and arrested Peter and John, "being indignant that they taught the people, and preached, through Jesus, the *resurrection from the dead*." They were seconded in this violent movement by the priests who were at the time officiating in the temple, and who were either identified with the Sadducees, or were enraged because the apostles, in the very midst of the temple, were drawing away the people from waiting upon their services. The "captain of the temple," with his guard, was doubtless subject to the orders of the chief of the officiating priests, and executed the arrest.

4. The audience who had been listening to Peter must have been thrown into intense excitement by the arrest, and the disciples among them, doubtless, expected to see re-enacted, in the persons of Peter and John, the murderous scenes which had terminated the life of their master. Notwithstanding this excitement, however, the words of Peter were not without a decided effect upon the hitherto unbelieving portion of his hearers; for Luke says: (4) "*But many of those who were hearing the word believed, and the number of the men became about five thousand.*" Whether this number includes the three thousand who were added on Pentecost or not, has been a matter of some dispute, but it is generally agreed by critics that it does. If those who believed on the present occasion were alone intended, the writer would have said the number ἦν, *was*, instead of ἐγενήθη, *became*, about five thousand.

5, 6. The prisoners having been arrested late in the afternoon, all further proceedings were adjourned till the next day, and Peter and John had the quiet of a night in prison for reflection and mutual encouragement ere they were brought to trial. (5) "*And it came to pass, on the morrow, that their rulers and elders and scribes,* (6) *and Annas the high priest, and Caiaphas, and John and Alexander, and as many* *as were of the kindred of the high priest, were gathered together in Jerusalem."* This assembly was the great Jewish Sanhedrim, and the parties here named are the different officials who constituted that tribunal. Who John and Alexander were is not now known. Annas and Caiaphas are historical characters, conspicuous in the history of the trial of Jesus, and also prominent on the pages of Josephus. Between the latter and Luke there is an apparent discrepancy, in reference to their official position at this time, Luke calling Annas the high priest, and Josephus attributing that dignity to Caiaphas. According to Josephus, Valerius Gratus, the immediate predecessor of Pontius Pilate, had removed Annas from the high priesthood, and after having appointed and removed three others, one of them, Eleazar, the son of Annas, finally left Caiaphas in office, when he was superseded by Pilate.* The Apostle John informs us that Caiaphas was son-in-law to Annas.† According to the law of Moses the high priest held office during life; hence, in deposing Annas, the Roman governor violated the Jewish Law, and the act was religiously null and void. Annas was still high priest by right, and for this reason is so styled here by Luke. The Jews, also, recognized his right, by taking Jesus before him for trial, though he, not daring to claim the office, sent them to Caiaphas. In his former narrative, Luke also mentions them both as being high priests at the same time. ‡ This is best explained by the fact that one was rightfully entitled to the office, and the other was exercising it by illegal appointment.

The "kindred of the high priest" embraced not only the chief members of his immediate family, but also some of the deposed high priests, who were all, in great probability, connected with the one high priestly family, and thereby entitled to seats in the Sanhedrim.

7. When the court was assembled, the prisoners were introduced, and the cripple who had been healed had the boldness to appear by their side. (7) *"And placing them in the midst, they asked, By what power, or by what name, have you done this?"*

This was not the first time that Peter and John had been together in the presence of this august assembly. As they gazed around for a moment, and recognized the faces of their judges, they could not fail to remember that terrible morning when their master stood there in bonds, and they themselves, full of fearful misgivings, stood in a distant part of the hall, and looked on. The fall, and the bitter tears of Peter, on that occasion, were now a warning and a strength to them both, and their very position brought to mind some solemn words of Jesus which had never acquired a present value till now. "Beware of men: for they will deliver you up to the councils, and they will scourge you in their synagogues, and you shall be brought before governors and kings for my sake, for a testimony to them and the Gentiles. But when they deliver you up, be not anxious how or what you shall speak; for it shall be given you in that same hour what you shall say. For it is not you that speak, but the spirit of your father that speaks in you." || Cheered by this promise, they now stand up before their accusers and judges with a boldness unaccountable to the latter.

Jos. Ant. B. xviii, chap. 2.   † John xviii : 13–24   ‡ Luke iii : 2. || Matt. x : 17–20.

ACTS IV: 8-13.

The prisoners had been arrested without a formal charge being preferred against them, and the court was now dependent upon what might be extorted from them, for the ground of their accusation. The question propounded to them is remarkable for its vagueness. By what *power*, or, in what *name*, have you done *this?* Done *what?* might have been the answer. Done this preaching? or this miracle? or *what?* The question *specified* nothing. There was no one particular thing done by Peter, on which they dared fix attention; but they frame an indefinite question, in attempting to answer which they evidently hoped he would say something on which they might condemn him.

8–10. They could not, however, have asked a question which suited Peter any better. It left him at liberty to select any thing he had done as the subject of reply, and, therefore, he chose to select that deed, which, of all that had been done, they were most unwilling to hear mentioned. He frames his answer, too, with a more direct reference to the other terms of their question, than they either desired or anticipated. (8) "*Then Peter, filled with the Holy Spirit, said to them: Rulers of the people, and elders of Israel,* (9) *If we are examined this day concerning the good deed done to the impotent man, by what means he has been saved,* (10) *be it known to you all, and to all the people of Israel, that by the name of Jesus Christ of Nazareth, whom you crucified, whom God raised from the dead, by him doth this man stand before you sound.*" This statement needed no proof, for the Sanhedrim could not deny, with the man standing before them, that the miracle had been wrought, nor could they, with plausibility, attribute the deed to any other power or name than that assumed by Peter. To deny that it was a divine power would have been absurd in the estimation of all the people; but to admit that the power was divine, and yet reject the explanation given by those through whom it was exercised, would have been still more absurd.

11, 12. Realizing the advantage which he had now gained, Peter pushes his adversaries into still closer quarters, by adding: (11) "*This is the stone which was despised by you builders, which has become the head of the corner.* (12) *Neither is there salvation in any other; for there is no other name under heaven, given among men, by which we must be saved.*" In this passage, he places his proud judges in the ridiculous attitude of searching about vainly for a stone to fit the corner of the foundation, while persistently rejecting the real corner-stone, without which the building can not be reared. And, leaving the figurative language of David, he more plainly declares, that there is no salvation for man except in the name of the very Jesus whom they had crucified. This proposition is universal, and shows that the redemption effected by Jesus will include every human being who shall finally be saved.

13, 14. Instead of answering evasively and timidly, as was expected of men in their social position, when arraigned in such a presence, the apostles had unhesitatingly avowed the chief deed of yesterday's proceedings, with the name in which it had been done, stating all in the terms most obnoxious to their hearers. (13) "*Now, seeing the freedom of speech of Peter and John, and perceiving that they were illiterate and private men*, they were astonished, and recognized them, that they had been with Jesus. (14) *But beholding the man who was healed standing with them, they could say nothing against it.*" There was total silence for awhile, when Peter ceased speaking. Not a man in the Sanhedrim could open his mouth in reply to Peter's brief speech. He had avowed every obnoxious sentiment on account of which they had been instigated to arrest him, yet not one of them dares to contradict his words, or to rebuke him for giving them utterance. The silence was painful and embarrassing.

15, 16. Finally, the silence was broken by a proposition that the prisoners be withdrawn. (15) *"And having commanded them to go aside out of the Sanhedrim, they conferred among themselves,* (16) *saying, What shall we do to these men? For that, indeed, a noted miracle has been wrought by them, is manifest to all who dwell in Jerusalem, and we can not deny it."* This admission, in their secret deliberations, shows the utter heartlessness and hypocrisy of their proceedings, and it is astonishing that they could any longer give each other countenance in such a course.

17. The real motive which controlled them, and under the influence of which they kept each other in countenance, was an unconquerable desire to maintain their old influence with the people. This is manifested in the conclusion to which they came. (17) *"But, that it may be spread no further among the people, let us strictly threaten them, that they speak, henceforth, to no man in this name."* The man who made this proposition no doubt thought that he had most satisfactorily solved a difficult problem, and the majority were too well pleased to find some means of escape from their present awkward predicament, to look very shrewdly into the probable success of the measure proposed. It was a safe course, if not a very bold one, and as there was no obstacle in the way but conscience, they could find no difficulty in pursuing it.

18. The resolution was no sooner formed than acted upon. (18) *"And they called them, and commanded them not to speak at all, nor teach in the name of Jesus."* How Luke learned the particulars of the secret consultation which resulted in this injunction, we are not informed, though it is not difficult to imagine. Gamaliel, Saul's teacher, and perhaps Saul himself, was present as a member of the Sanhedrim; and a great company of the priests themselves afterward became obedient to the faith.* These and other conversions from the ranks of the enemy opened up channels for such information in abundance.

19, 20. The apostles, if at all anxious concerning their personal safety, might have received this stern command in silence, and retired respectfully from the assembly. (19) *"But, Peter and John answered and said to them, Whether it is right, in the sight of God, to hearken to you rather than to God, do you judge.* (20) *For we can not but speak the things which we have seen and heard."* This was an open defiance of their power, with a direct appeal to their own consciences for a vindication of it. The apostles were not willing that their silence should be construed into even a momentary acquiescence in such a

* Chap. vi: 7, *below.*

command, and they spoke in such a manner as to be distinctly understood.

21, 22. It was a sore trial to the haughty spirits of the Sanhedrim to brook such defiance; but a desire to conciliate the people, mingled, no doubt, with a secret fear of the consequences of putting to death men who had exercised such power, restrained their wrath. (21) "*And when they had further threatened them, they let them go, not finding how they might punish them, because of the people; for all glorified God for that which was done.* (22) *For the man on whom this miracle of healing was wrought was more than forty years of age.*"

23-30. The apostles had now humbled the pride of their adversaries, and went away from the assembly in triumph. But they were uninflated by their present prosperity, as they had been undaunted by their recent danger. They had now attained that lofty degree of faith and hope which enables men to maintain a steady calmness amid all the vicissitudes of life. The course they immediately pursued is worthy of remembrance, and of all imitation. (23) "*And being let go, they went to their own company, and reported what the high priests and the elders had said to them.* (24) *And when they heard it, they lifted up their voice to God with one accord, and said: Sovereign Lord, thou God who hast made the heavens, and the earth, and the sea, and all that is in them;* (25) *who through the mouth of thy servant David hast said, Why did the Gentiles rage, and the people imagine vain things?* (26) *The kings of the earth stood up, and the rulers were gathered together against the Lord and against his anointed.* (27) *For, of a truth, against thy holy son Jesus whom thou hast anointed, both Herod, and Pontius Pilate, with the Gentiles and the people of Israel, were gathered together,* (28) *to do what thy hand and thy counsel determined before to be done.* (29) *And now, Lord, behold their threatenings; and grant to thy servants, that with all boldness they may speak thy word,* (30) *by stretching out thy hand to heal, and that signs and wonders may be done through the name of thy holy son Jesus.*" This prayer was uttered by one of the brethren, and the expression, "they lifted up their voice with one accord," indicates the perfect unity of sentiment with which they followed the words of the leader.

In all the prayers of the apostles, we observe strict appropriateness, in the ascription to God with which they open, and a remarkable simplicity in presenting the exact petition, and no more, which the occasion demands. On a former occasion, they had set before him two men, that he might choose one for the apostolic office, and they addressed him as the "heart-knower;" now they desire his protecting power, and they style him the "Sovereign God who made heaven and earth, and the sea, and all that is in them." They remind him that, according to his own words by David, kings and rulers, in the persons of Herod and Pilate, had risen up against his anointed, while the people and the Gentiles were imagining vain things; and they pray him to "behold their threatening," and grant to his servants boldness to speak the word in defiance of all opposition.

In these days of passion and war, in which it is common for prayers to be filled with earnest entreaties for victory over our enemies, and sometimes with terrible maledictions against those who are waging war against our supposed rights, it is quite refreshing to observe the tone of this apostolic prayer. These men were not in danger of losing some mere political power or privilege, but the dearest and most indisputable right they had on earth was denied them, and they were threatened with death if they did not relinquish it: yet, in their prayers, they manifest no vindictive nor resentful spirit; but, in reference to their enemies, they simply pray, Lord, behold their threatenings. Their gentle spirits never could have conceived that unblushing impiety which now so often brings men upon their knees for the very purpose of pouring out in the ears of God those violent and destructive passions which he has forbidden us to allow a place even within our hearts. By such prayers men seek to make God a partisan in every angry contention among men, as though he were nothing more than themselves. Much needs to be said upon this unhappy theme, but it can not be said here.

In praying for boldness the apostles give an intimation of the manner in which they expected it to be imparted to them. It was not by some direct and internal spiritual impact, but by external manifestations of his continued presence and favor: "*by stretching out thy hand to heal, and that signs and wonders may be wrought through the name of Jesus.*"

31. The prayer for boldness was answered at once, and in the way they had requested. (31) "*And when they had prayed, the place in which they were assembled together was shaken, and they were all filled with the Holy Spirit, and spoke the word of God with boldness.*" The shaking of the house, attended by a conscious renewal of the miraculous power of the Holy Spirit, gave them the boldness for which they prayed, because it assured them that God was still with them.

32–35. From this brief account of the first conflict of the young congregation, Luke again turns, to view more minutely the internal condition of the Church. Their religious life was now more fully developed, than at the period glanced at in the close of the second chapter, and his description is more in detail. (32) "*Now the multitude of those who believed were of one heart and one soul; neither did one of them say that aught of the things which he possessed was his own, but they had all things common. (33) And with great power the apostles gave testimony concerning the resurrection of the Lord Jesus, and great favor was upon them all. (34) Neither was there any among them who lacked; for as many as were possessors of lands, or houses, sold them, and brought the prices of the things that were sold, (35) and laid them at the feet of the apostles; and it was distributed to each, as any one had need.*"

Considering the immense numbers of this congregation, and that they were so suddenly drawn together from every class of society, it is certainly remarkable, and well worthy of a place in this record, that they were "*of one heart and of one mind.*" But the most signal proof of the power of the gospel among them was the almost entire subsidence of selfishness. Among the heathen nations of antiquity, systematic provision for the wants of the poor was unknown; and even among the Jews, whose law was watchful for the welfare of the poor in many respects, those who became insolvent were sold into

ACTS IV: 36. 67

temporary bondage to pay their debts. It was, therefore, a new thing under the sun, to see a large community selling houses and lands to supply the wants of the poor. It could but give additional weight to all that was said by the apostles, and for this reason Luke breaks the thread of his statements concerning it, to throw in the remark, that "With great power the apostles gave testimony concerning the resurrection of the Lord Jesus, and great favor was among them all." This remark does not mean that the testimony of the apostles was more distinct or positive, or that it was sustained by more signal miracles than before; for neither of these is possible. But it means that their testimony had more power with the people; and this is attributed to the harmony observed within the Church, together with their unheard-of benevolence, which combined to give them "great favor" with the people.

The fact that distribution was made to each as he had need, shows that it was only the needy who received any thing, and that there was no equalization of property. The sale of property and the consecration of the proceeds was voluntary with each individual, and not an established law of the Church. This is evident from the question of Peter to Ananias, below: "While it remained, was it not your own? And after it was sold, was it not in your own control?"*

36. After stating that many brethren who had property sold it, and gave up the proceeds, Luke now gives an individual instance of this liberality, introduced, no doubt, on account of the subsequent celebrity of the individual. (36) "*Now Joses, who was surnamed Barnabas by the apostles, (which is, when translated, son of exhortation,) a Levite, a Cyprian by birth, having land, sold it, and brought the money, and laid it at the feet of the apostles.*" This surname was given to Joses on account of his excellence in hortatory addresses, and not on account of the *consolation* which he afforded by his liberality. The original term παρακλήσις, rendered *consolation* in the common version, is a verbal noun used to express both the *act* of the verb παρακαλειν and the *effect* produced by it. We have no one word in English to represent it in these two senses; but *exhortation* expresses the act, and *consolation* the effect. We have, therefore, *exhortation* eight times in the common version, when the παρακλήσις is connected with the agent,† but always *consolation* when the reference is to the recipient. As Barnabas is contemplated as the agent, in this case, it should be *exhortation*, not *consolation*. This criticism is confirmed by the history of Barnabas. When the Church in Jerusalem heard that a congregation was planted in Antioch, they sent Barnabas thither, who "*exhorted* them all, that with purpose of heart they should cleave to the Lord."‡ This *exhorting* being the object for which he was sent, his selection for the mission indicates his superiority in that kind of talent. Perhaps it was chiefly on account of this talent, in which Paul was deficient, that Barnabas became the traveling companion of this apostle. It is a talent much more rare than mere logical power, and has always been highly prized by the Churches.

---

* See also vi: 1.
† Acts xiii: 15; Rom. xii: 8; 1 Cor. xiv: 3; 1 Thess. ii: 3; 1 Tim. iv: 13; Heb. xii: 5; xiii. 22; 2 Cor. viii: 17. ‡ Acts xi: 23.

It is quite probable that the land sold by Barnabas constituted his whole estate. Having no family dependent on him, he consecrated his life to unrequited missionary labor.*

V: 1, 2. In close connection with this unprecedented liberality of the brethren, we are now introduced to a remarkable case of corruption, of which it was the occasion. The praise always lavished on disinterested benevolence sometimes prompts illiberal men to make a pretense of liberality. But the mere desire of praise is incapable of subduing selfishness, so as to make a truly liberal heart; for it is itself a species of selfishness. In contrast with the course of Barnabas, we are told: (1) "*But a certain man named Ananias, with Sapphira his wife, sold a possession,* (2) *and kept back part of the price, his wife being also privy to it, and brought a certain part and laid it at the feet of the apostles.*" This language implies, what is distinctly avowed by the wife below, that this part was represented as the whole price of the possession.

3, 4. "*But Peter said, Ananias, why has Satan filled thy heart, to lie to the Holy Spirit, and to keep back part of the price of the land?* (4) *While it remained, was it not your own? And after it was sold, was it not in your own control? Why hast thou put this thing in thy heart? Thou hast lied not to men, but to God.*" Here Peter brings together the influence of Satan, and the free agency of the tempted, just as he had, in former discourses, the free agency of men, and the purposes of God.† He demands of Ananias, "Why has *Satan filled thy heart* to lie to the Holy Spirit," and, in the same breath, "Why hast *thou* put this thing in thy heart?" The existence and agency of the tempter are distinctly recognized, yet it is not Satan, but Ananias who is rebuked; and he is rebuked for doing the very thing that Satan had done, showing that he is as guilty as though Satan had no existence. Indeed, he is rebuked *for* what Satan had done. The justice of this is manifest from the fact that Satan had no power to fill his heart with evil, without his co-operation. That he had rendered this co-operation, threw the responsibility upon himself.

Peter's knowledge of the deception was the result not of human information, but of the insight imparted to him by the Holy Spirit. This is necessary to the significance of the entire incident, as well as to the purport of Peter's own words.

5. The exposure of Ananias was very surprising, but neither the audience, nor perhaps Peter, was prepared by it for the event which immediately followed. (5) "*And Ananias, hearing these words, fell down and expired. And great fear came upon all who heard these things.*" There is no evidence that Peter had any will of his own in this matter; but it was an act of divine power exerted independent of the apostolic agency. The responsibility, therefore, attached not to Peter as an officer of the Church, but to God as the moral governor of the world. The propriety of the deed may be appreciated best by supposing that Ananias had succeeded in his undertaking. His success would not only have turned the most praiseworthy feature of the new Church into a source of corruption and hypocrisy, but it would have brought discredit upon the inspiration of the apostles, by show

* 1 Cor. ix: 6. † See Com. iii: 17–18.

ing that the Spirit within them could be deceived. Thus the whole fabric of apostolic authority, which was based upon their inspiration, would have fallen, and precipitated the entire cause into hopeless ruin. The attempt, therefore, presented a crisis of vital importance, and demanded some such vindication of their inspiration as could neither be mistaken nor forgotten. The immediate effect of the event was just the effect desired: "great fear came upon all who heard these things."

6 The scene was too awful for lamentation, or for needless funeral services. As when Nadab and Abihu fell dead at the door of the tabernacle with strange fire in their censers,* there was no weeping nor delay. All were stricken with horror, as they saw the curse of God fall upon the wretch. (6) "*And the young men arose, wound him up, and carried him out, and buried him.*"

7. Sapphira was not present. (7) "*And it was about the space of three hours after, when his wife, not knowing what was done, came in.*" How she remained so long ignorant of the fate of her husband, we are not informed, though it is a most extraordinary circumstance. He had died suddenly, in a manner which had excited everybody; had been buried; and three hours had passed; yet his wife, who must have been in the vicinity, has no intimation of it, but comes into the very assembly where it had occurred, without a word reaching her ear upon the subject. There is no way to account for this, but by the supposition that there was a concerted determination on the part of the whole multitude to conceal the facts from her. This was a most unnatural determination, and one difficult of execution, except on the further supposition that Peter commanded the multitude to restrain their natural impulses, and let her know nothing until he himself was ready to reveal it to her. This course was necessary in order to effectually expose her.

8–10. She came in prepared to act out fully the part which she had agreed upon with her husband. (8) "*Then Peter answered her, Tell me whether you sold the land for so much? She said, Yes; for so much.* (9) *Then Peter said to her, Why is it that you have agreed together to put to proof the Spirit of the Lord? Behold, the feet of them who have buried thy husband are at the door, and they shall carry thee out.* (10) *Then she immediately fell at his feet and expired: and the young men coming in found her dead, and carried her out, and buried her by her husband.*" In her case, Peter knew what was about to take place, and declared it; but there is no indication that he exerted his own will or miraculous power to cause her death. We regard her death, like that of Ananias, as a miracle wrought independent of the power lodged in the apostles.

In the question "Why have you agreed together to put to proof the Spirit of the Lord?" Peter expresses the result of their agreement, though it may not have been what *they* had in view. They did put the Spirit to proof, by testing his powers. If he had failed under the test, the consequences, as we have suggested above, would have been disastrous. But now that the test applied has triumphantly vindi-

* Lev. x: 1–7.

cated the fullness of apostolic inspiration, it was not likely that such another attempt could be made.

11. The failure of the plot proved as propitious to the cause of truth as its success would have been disastrous. (11) *"And great fear came upon all the Church, and upon all who had heard these things."* This fear was excited, not only by the sudden and awful fate of the guilty pair, but also by the fearful nature of that spirit-searching knowledge imparted to the apostles. The disciples were now filled with more just conceptions than before of the nature of inspiration, and the unbelieving masses who heard of the event were awed into respect and reverence.

12, 13. Increased activity of the apostles followed, and their office was still further magnified. (12) *"And through the hands of the apostles many signs and wonders were done among the people. And they were all, with one accord, in Solomon's Portico, (13) and of the rest no man dare join himself to them, but all the people magnified them."* It was the apostles alone who were in Solomon's Portico, as is evident from the fact that the term apostles, in the first clause of the 12th verse, furnishes the only antecedent to the pronoun *they*, in the statement "they were all, with one accord," etc. This being so, "the rest," who dared not join themselves to them, must include the other disciples, as well as the unbelieving multitude. It need not be concluded, from this, that the disciples stood off at the same fearful distance with unbelievers; but that they were so filled with awe by the exhibition connected with the fate of Ananias and Sapphira, that they dared not approach the apostles with the familiarity which had marked their former intercourse with them. Such a feeling was at first experienced by the apostles themselves in the presence of Jesus, and was well expressed by Peter, when he and his companions made the first miraculous draught of fishes: falling down at the knees of Jesus, he exclaimed, "Depart from me; for I am a sinful man, O Lord."* That such a feeling was also experienced by the whole Church, at this time, has just been stated by the historian, in verse 11, where he says, "Great fear came upon all the Church."

14. The statement just made, that "of the rest no man dared to join himself to them," can not mean that persons dared not join the Church, for the reverse is now stated. (14) *"And believers were the more added to the Lord, multitudes both of men and women."* The increased awe in the presence of the apostles, with which the people were inspired, made them listen with increased respect to their testimony concerning Jesus, and brought them in greater numbers to obedience.

15, 16. The connection of Luke's next statement, introduced by the adverb *so that*, is somewhat obscure: but I presume he intends to state a result of all the facts just mentioned. Signs and wonders were done by the apostles; the people magnified them, and believers were the more added to the Lord. (15) *"So that they brought forth the sick into the streets, and laid them on beds and couches, that at least the shadow of Peter passing by might overshadow some of them.* (16) *There*

* Luke v: 8.

came also a multitude out of the cities round about to Jerusalem, bringing the sick and those vexed by unclean spirits, who were all healed."

17–18. The excitement which now prevailed throughout Jerusalem and the neighboring villages, and found utterance in the most enthusiastic praise of the apostles, was too much for the equanimity of the dignitaries who had so strictly forbidden them to preach or teach in the name of Jesus. (17) *" Then the high priest rose up, and all who were with him, being the sect of the Sadducees, and were filled with zeal,* (18) *and laid their hands on the apostles, and put them in the public prison."* Here we have the same Sadducees at work who had arrested and threatened Peter and John. They were "filled with zeal;" but it was a zeal inspired less by love for their own cause, than by hatred for that which was triumphing over it. The advocates of error will generally appear quite easy, and, sometimes, even generous, when their cause is merely standing still; but their zeal is always kindled when the truth begins to make inroads upon them. The zeal of these Sadducees was fanned to its fiercest heat by recent events, and they determined to execute the threats with which they had recently dismissed two of the apostles, making all the twelve their present victims.

19–21. When they were all seized and cast into prison together, the apostles could but expect that they would now feel the entire weight of the wrath which was treasured up against them. (19) *"But an angel of the Lord opened the prison doors in the night, and led them forth, and said,* (20) *Go stand in the temple, and speak to the people all the words of this life.* (21) *And having heard this they entered into the temple early in the morning, and taught. But the high priest came, and those who were with him, and called together the Sanhedrim, and all the eldership of the children of Israel, and sent into the prison to have them brought."* The apostles were already in the temple, teaching the early worshipers as if nothing unusual had occurred, when the Sanhedrim met and sent to the prison for them.

22, 23. After some delay, the officers returned into the presence of the Sanhedrim without their prisoners. (22) *"But when the officers arrived, and did not find them in the prison, they returned and announced,* (23) *saying, The prison we found closed with all safety, and the guards standing before the doors; but when we opened them, we found no one within."* This appalling circumstance would have been sufficient, with less determined men, to stay all hostile proceedings, and even to disperse the court who had assembled for the trial of the apostles.

24–26. The startling announcement was not without serious effect even upon the stubborn Sadducees. They were staggered by it, and knew not at first what to do or think. (24) *" Now when the high priest, and the captain of the temple, and the chief priests heard these words, they were perplexed concerning them, what this might come to.* (25) *But some one came and announced to them, Behold, the men whom you put in prison are standing in the temple and teaching the people."* This announcement relieved the perplexity of the Sanhedrim, by enabling them to proceed with business, and relieving them from the unpleasant necessity of dispersing without a good excuse. They now dispatch a more honorable guard after the apostles than they had, at first; for the captain of the temple himself takes command. (26) "*Then the captain went with the officers, and brought them without violence, for they feared the people, lest they should be stoned.*" The clause, "lest they should be stoned," is so arranged as to furnish a reason for both the preceding statements, that they "*feared* the people," and that they "brought them without *violence.*" The enthusiasm of the people had been much increased, no doubt, by the angelic deliverance, which was by this time well known about the temple.

27, 28. We have now a very lively and graphic description of the arraignment and trial of the apostles. (27) "*And having brought them, they placed them in the Sanhedrim, and the high priest asked them,* (28) *saying, Did we not strictly command you not to speak in this name? And behold, you have filled Jerusalem with your teaching, and intend to bring this man's blood upon us.*" These words contain two specific charges against the apostles, disobedience to the Sanhedrim, and an effort to bring upon them the blood of Jesus.

29–32. To these charges the apostles candidly and fearlessly respond. (29) "*Then Peter and the other apostles answered and said, We ought to obey God rather than men.*" This answers the first charge. They plead guilty, but justify themselves by the authority of God. Peter and John had left the Sanhedrim before, with the words, "Whether it is right in the sight of God to hearken to men more than to God, do you judge." Now, as if that question was decided, they declare, "We *ought* to obey God rather than men." They then answer the second charge by a restatement of the facts: (30) "*The God of our fathers has raised up Jesus, whom ye slew, having hung him on a tree.* (31) *This man has God exalted to his own right hand, a Prince and a Savior, to grant repentance to Israel, and remission of sins.* (32) *And we are his witnesses of these things, and so is the Holy Spirit whom God has given to those who obey him.*" This was repeating, with terrible emphasis, the very thing which was charged against them as a crime.

In the declaration that Jesus had been exalted a Prince and a Savior, "to *grant* repentance to Israel and remission of sins," it is implied that repentance, as well as remission of sins, is in some sense *granted* to men. But to *grant* repentance can not mean to bestow it upon men without an exercise of their own will; for repentance is enjoined upon men as a duty to be performed by them. How, then, can that which is a duty to be performed, be said to be *granted* to us? We will readily perceive the answer to this question, by remembering that repentance is produced by sorrow for sin, and that it belongs to God to furnish men with the facts which will awaken this sorrow. Without revelation, men would never be made to feel that sorrow for sin which works repentance; but in the revelation of Jesus Christ we are furnished with the chief of these motives, and because of this, he is said to *grant* repentance.

33. The Sanhedrim had been astonished at the boldness of Peter and John on their former trial, but had contented themselves with severe threatenings. Now, both their commands and their threats having been despised, and the bold innovators daring to defy them once more, they lost, for a moment, all the restraint which had been

imposed by fear of the multitude. (33) "*Now when they heard this, they were exasperated, and determined to slay them.*"

34–39. At this crisis the madness of the Sadducees was suddenly checked by the prudent counsel of one of the opposite party. The Pharisees were less exasperated, because their leading dogma was sustained by the apostles, and they saw that any imprudent proceedings were likely to involve the whole Sanhedrim in trouble, without regard to party; therefore Gamaliel interposes his advice. (34) "*But a certain Pharisee in the Sanhedrim, named Gamaliel, a teacher of the law, honored by all the people, arose and commanded to put the apostles out for a little while.*" This removal of the prisoners, like that of Peter and John before, was designed to prevent them from taking encouragement from any admissions which might be made during the pending discussion. They were, accordingly, withdrawn. (35) "*And he said to them, Men of Israel, take heed to yourselves what you are about to do respecting these men:* (36) *For before these days, Theudas arose, declaring himself to be somebody; to whom a number of men, about four hundred, attached themselves; who was slain, and all, as many as obeyed him, were scattered and brought to nothing.* (37) *After this man, Judas the Galilean rose up, in the days of the enrollment, and drew away many people after him. He also perished, and all, as many as obeyed him, were dispersed.* (38) *And now I say to you, refrain from these men, and let them alone; for if this purpose or this work is from men, it will be destroyed;* (39) *but if it is from God, you are not able to destroy it; lest you even be found to fight against God.*"

A question has been raised as to whether Luke is not guilty of an anachronism in this report of Gamaliel's speech, by making him refer to a Theudas, who is mentioned by Josephus, and who flourished many years later, under the reign of Claudius Cæsar. Such a reference could not possibly be made by Gamaliel; and if it was made by Luke, he is not only guilty of the anachronism, but, what is far worse, of giving a false report of Gamaliel's speech. Rather than admit a hypothesis involving such consequences in reference to a historian of unimpeached veracity, we must suppose that some impostor by the name of Theudas did flourish at the time here alluded to by Gamaliel. Judas the Galilean is also mentioned by Josephus, whose account of him agrees with this given by Gamaliel. The enrollment is most likely the same referred to in Luke ii: 1.

Upon the fate of these two impostors, Gamaliel bases his advice to the Sanhedrim in reference to the apostles. The moral merits of this advice may be differently estimated, according to the point of view from which we contemplate it. If we regard it as a general rule of procedure in reference to religious movements, it must be regarded as mere time-serving policy. Instead of waiting to see whether such a movement is going to prove successful or not, before we take ground in reference to it, the lover of truth will promptly investigate and decide its merits without regard to public opinion. But if we regard Gamaliel as only giving a reason why men should not *persecute* a cause which they are not prepared to accept, it was certainly most judicious advice. When we have decided against a cause, we should render a reason for our decision, and then leave it to the developments of Providence, well assured that whatever is not from God will come to nothing without any violent agency on our part. We should also be afraid to resist with violence or passion any thing bearing a semblance to truth, lest we fight against God, and be ourselves overthrown.

The last clause in Gamaliel's speech, "Lest you be found even to fight against God," indicates a suspicion, on his part, that such a result was by no means impossible. In view of the many miracles which had been wrought by the apostles, and their miraculous deliverance from prison the very night before, it is strange that something more than a suspicion to this effect did not possess the mind of Gamaliel, and of all the Sanhedrim. It was, doubtless, owing to serious misgivings on this point, that the embittered Sadducees yielded so readily to advice from the opposite party.

40. There was no opposition to Gamaliel's advice. (40) *"And they obeyed him; and having called the apostles, and scourged them, they commanded them not to speak in the name of Jesus, and let them go."* Scourging was so common in the Roman empire, even of men untried and uncondemned, and was so common a fate of Christians at the time Luke was writing, that he mentions it here rather as a matter of course. It is the first time, however, that it was experienced by the apostles, and was, probably, harder to endure than it ever was afterward.

41, 42. However painful the scourging was, it did not cause any resentful manifestations on the part of the sufferers, but they bore it cheerfully. (41) *"Then they departed from the presence of the Sanhedrim, rejoicing that they were thought worthy to be dishonored for his name.* (42) *And every day, in the temple, and from house to house, they ceased not to teach and to preach Jesus Christ."* The Sanhedrim had now tried both threats and scourging upon the apostles without checking their activity, and as there was nothing further for them to try but death, which they were not yet prepared to inflict, they relinquished for awhile their efforts. In this first contest, therefore, the apostles were completely victorious, and compelled their adversaries to abandon the field.

The apostles taught and preached not only publicly in the temple, but "from house to house." In this they give an example to the ministry of all ages, which is well worthy of imitation. Private instruction and admonition bring the teacher and the taught into closer contact, and secure an individuality of effect not attainable in a public assembly. It can not, therefore, be well dispensed with; but he who employs it most diligently will, other things being equal, employ his energies most successfully.

VI: 1. From the preceding account of the struggle between the apostles and the Sadducees, Luke now turns to consider, briefly, the internal condition of the Church during the same period. Though the mass of the disciples had attained many of the excellencies of Christian character, they were still but men, and liable to the partialities and prejudices of men. This became manifest in a manner which at first threatened serious consequences. (1) *"Now, in those days, the disciples having multiplied, there arose a murmuring of the*

ACTS VI: 2-4.

Hellenist against the Hebrews, because their widows were neglected in the daily ministration." The disciples in Jerusalem now numbered largely over five thousand. In so large a multitude, it was almost impossible to look after the wants of all with equal care, and some unintentional oversight must unavoidably occur. The "daily ministration" is undoubtedly that distribution from the funds contributed by the brethren, which was made "to every one according as he had need." That it was made daily, confirms our former conclusion, that there was no general equalization of property, but only a provision for the needy. The Hellenists were Jews of foreign birth and Greek education, and were so called because of their conformity to the manners of the *Hellenes*, as the Greeks were called. Many of them were, perhaps, not permanent residents in Jerusalem, but had remained there after Pentecost on account of their interest in the new religion. They were the more likely to be neglected, because less familiarly known to the apostles and their assistants.

2–4. This unforeseen circumstance suggested to the apostles the propriety of instituting a new office in the Church. Though the Holy Spirit was given to guide them into all the truth, its additional instruction was given only as circumstances required. They were not theorists, with a constitution and by-laws drawn up in advance, to which, under all circumstances, the Church must conform; but they allowed the condition of the congregation, from time to time, to dictate the provisions which should be made, and therefore the provisions which were made were precisely such as were needed. Hitherto the Church had been without an officer of any kind, except the apostles; for the supposition advanced by some writers, that the young men, οἱ νεώτεροι, who buried Ananias and Sapphira, were regularly-appointed officers, is without foundation, except in the analogy of later and unscriptural organizations. Seeing, then, that the Church in Jerusalem existed for a time under the control of the apostles alone, it follows that a Church may now exist under the written teaching alone of the same apostles. But seeing, further, that when circumstances required it, other officials were appointed, it follows that all Churches among whom similar wants arise should provide themselves in the same way. All Churches, however, will inevitably find need for such officers as the New Testament authorizes; hence they should procure them without unnecessary delay.

When the murmuring came to the ears of the apostles they acted promptly. (2) *" Then the twelve called the multitude of the disciples to them and said, It is not well that we should leave the word of God and serve tables.* (3) *Therefore, brethren, look out among you seven men of good repute, full of the Holy Spirit and wisdom, whom we may appoint over this business.* (4) *But we ourselves will continue in prayer and the ministry of the word."* The alternative with the apostles was to "leave," in some degree, "the word of God," and serve the tables satisfactorily, or turn this business over to other hands, and "continue in prayer and the ministry of the word" as uninterruptedly as before. They showed their superior regard for the latter ministry by choosing the latter course.

It seemed good to the Holy Spirit and the apostles that the whole "multitude of the disciples" should take part in the selection of these officers. No ingenuity of argument can evade the conclusion that this gives the authority of apostolic precedent for the popular election of officers of the Church. The multitude were limited, however, by apostolic authority, to the choice of men of a certain description. They must be men of "good repute;" not merely good men, but men whose goodness was accredited among the brethren.

They must also be men who were "full of the Holy Spirit." Whether this means that they must be possessed of miraculous powers, or merely that they must exhibit abundantly the fruits of the Spirit, it is difficult to determine. The circumstances, that up to this time no miracles had been wrought, so far as we know, by any but the apostles, and that, immediately after the appointment of the seven, Stephen appears "doing great wonders and miracles among the people," seem to indicate that they were merely full of the Holy Spirit in the ordinary way, but received miraculous powers when the hands of the apostles were laid upon them. On the other hand, the expression, "full of the Holy Spirit," generally means possessed of the miraculous powers of the Spirit. Whatever may be the decision of this question, it is certain that when a disciple was "full of the Spirit" in either sense, the religious sentiments were in lively exercise, and this is all that can be required in a candidate for the same office at the present day.

The office which the apostles are about to institute and fill is easily identified with that of the deacon as described in the third chapter of First Timothy. The seven are not styled διάκονοι, *deacons*, but they were selected to attend to the daily διακονία, (verse 1) and their service is expressed by the verb διακονέω, (verse 2) the same which expresses the duty of the deacons in 1 Tim. iii: 10–13. The chief duty for which they were appointed, was "*to serve tables*," διακονεῖν τραπέζαις; yet this duty need not prevent them from discharging any other functions for which they were qualified, and for which they could find time. God exacts the employment of every talent that is committed to us, and has appointed no work to be done which is too holy for the humblest disciple. We therefore find one of the seven deacons soon after in the front rank of the defenders of the faith; while another, after the dispersion of the Church, preaches in Samaria, and immerses both the Samaritans and the Ethiopian nobleman. Those who deny to deacons, at the present day, the same privileges, impose a restriction which is in direct conflict with the word of God. As to the title *evangelist*, afterward applied to Philip, see the "Commentary on Acts," xxi: 8.

5, 6. The proposition of the apostles so wisely provided for an obvious want, that there could be no hesitation about prompt compliance with it. (5) "*And the saying pleased the whole multitude; and they chose Stephen, a man full of faith and of the Holy Spirit, and Philip, and Prochorus, and Nicanor, and Timon, and Parmenas, and Nicolas, a proselyte of Antioch,* (6) *whom they placed before the apostles. And having prayed, they laid their hands on them.*" It is a remarkable proof of the generosity of the Church at large, that all these are Greek names, indicating that they were selected from the very party whence the murmuring had proceeded. It was as if the Hebrews had said to the Hellenists, We have no selfish ends to accomplish, nor any jealousy toward you who complain, therefore we give the whole business into your hands, and will fearlessly trust our poor widows to your care. So generous a trust could not be betrayed, except by the basest of men. All that is now known of five of these men is the fact of their appointment to this office. Their names are not again mentioned in the New Testament. It need not be presumed, from this, that they were subsequently inactive or unfaithful, but simply that Luke selected, for his brief narrative, a chain of events in which others were the actors. Of Nicolas, it is said that he was "a proselyte of Antioch," which means that he was a Gentile who had been proselyted to Judaism before he was converted to Christ. Thus we see that, even at this early period, the apostles had no objection to the reception of Gentiles, provided they had been circumcised.

Stephen is specially described as "a man full of faith and of the Holy Spirit," not because the others were destitute of these excellencies; for one of the qualifications necessary to a selection was that they should be men "full of the Holy Spirit." But if the seven were distinguished above others in this respect, Stephen may have been distinguished in the same way among the seven.

The object of the imposition of hands, on this occasion, has been a subject of some dispute; some contending that it was merely to impart miraculous gifts to the seven, and others, that it was the ceremony of their induction into office. Miraculous gifts were often conferred by the apostles in this way, and there is much probability, to say the least, that they were now conferred upon the seven; but the context forbids us to suppose that this was the only object of the ceremony. The apostles had commanded the disciples to do one thing, and they themselves proposed to do another. The multitude were to "*look out*" the men, "whom," say the apostles, "we may *appoint* over this business." The part performed by the apostles was their *appointment* to office. But all the apostles did was to pray and lay on their hands; hence, this was the ceremony of their appointment. It stands upon record as a precedent, and should be complied with in similar cases. The fact that men can not now confer a miraculous gift by laying on hands, does not relieve them from the obligation to impose hands as a ceremony of appointment to office. The question as to who should perform this ceremony should give no trouble. The parties who directed in the organization of the Church were the officials on this occasion, and so, according to the precedent, should it always be. Whoever plants a Church, or sets one in order, should lay hands on its officers. When there are peculiar circumstances not anticipated by the precedent, they should be provided for according to the wisdom of those concerned, being careful not to violate the precedent. The example of the apostles is binding in this, as in all cases not peculiar to the apostolic office, or to the condition of the early Churches.

7. The appointment of the seven over the business of daily ministration to the poor was intended to supply an existing deficiency in the organization of the Church. The more efficient organization gave greater efficiency to the labors of all. (7) "*And the word of God increased, and the number of disciples in Jerusalem was greatly*

multiplied, and a great multitude of the priests became obedient to the faith." This is the first intimation of the accession of any of the priests to the new faith It was the most signal triumph yet achieved by the gospel, for the priests of the old religion were more interested in maintaining it than were any other class among the Jews. The peculiar relation which the priesthood sustain to any system of religion must always render them the chief conservators of obsolete forms, and the most formidable opponents to the introduction of new truth. When the *priests* of an opposing system begin to give way, it is ready to fall. No fact yet recorded by Luke shows so strikingly the effect of the gospel upon the popular mind in Jerusalem.

The expression used concerning these priests, that they became "obedient to the faith," is worthy of notice as implying that there is something in the faith to be *obeyed*. This obedience is not rendered in the act of believing; for that is to *exercise* the faith, not to *obey* it. But faith in Jesus as the Messiah requires obedience to him as Lord; hence obedience rendered to him is styled obedience to the faith. It begins with immersion, and continues with the duties of a religious life. Paul declares that the grand object of the favor and apostleship conferred upon him was "for obedience to the faith among all nations."* Without it, faith itself is of no avail, for all who "*obey* not the gospel," whatever may be their faith, will be "destroyed from the presence of the Lord and the glory of his power."†

There is another expression in this verse worthy of notice, because of its singular contrast with modern phraseology in such connections. It is said "The word of God increased," and the specifications are, that the number of disciples was greatly multiplied, and that a great multitude of the priests became obedient. At the present day such incidents are often introduced by remarks of this kind: "There was a precious season of grace;" "The Lord was present in his saving power;" "A gracious outpouring of the Holy Spirit," etc. So great a departure from Scripture phraseology clearly indicates a departure from scriptural ideas. When men are engrossed with the conception that conversion is an abstract work of the Holy Spirit in the soul, they are likely to express themselves in this unauthorized manner. But Luke, who had no such conception, saw in the increase of the disciples an increase of the word of God; by which he means not an increase in the quantity of revelation, but in its effects. The more favorable circumstances which now existed within the Church, by the cessation of recent murmuring, and the introduction of a better organization, gave greater weight to the word that was preached, and greater success was the consequence.

8. We are now introduced to a very thrilling account of the labors and death of Stephen. His career, previous to the final conflict, is thus briefly sketched: (8) "*Now Stephen, full of faith and of power, did great wonders and signs among the people.*" The power by which he wrought these miracles is connected with the fact that he was "full of faith." This accords with the fact already observed, (iii: 16,) that the degree of miraculous power exerted by those who possessed spiritual gifts depended upon the degree of their faith.

* Rom. i: 5.   † 2 Thess. i: 7, 8, 9.

ACTS VI: 9, 10.

9, 10. The activity of Stephen, though probably not greater than that of the apostles during the same period, naturally attracted to him more especial attention, because he was a new actor in the scene, and one who had hitherto occupied a subordinate position. The opponents of the gospel were aroused into renewed activity. The first persecution occurred upon the surprising success of Peter and John in Solomon's Portico; the second, upon the triumphs which followed the death of Ananias and Sapphira; and the third now springs up upon the appearance of new advocates of the faith. (9) *"Then there arose certain persons from the synagogue called the synagogue of the Freedmen and Cyrenians, and those from Cilicia and Asia, disputing with Stephen; (10) and they were not able to withstand the wisdom and the spirit by which he spoke."*

The policy of the opposition is now changed. Having been deterred, by fear of the people, and by division of sentiment in their own ranks, from resorting to extreme violence, and finding that threats and scourging were unavailing, they now resort to discussion, expecting, by superior learning, to *confound* men who could not be *forced* into silence. The parties who entered the lists of debate were all foreign-born Jews. The Freedmen were Jews who had been set free from Roman slavery; the Cyrenians and Alexandrians were from the north of Africa; the Asians and Cilicians from the peninsula of Asia, the last-named being from the native country of Saul of Tarsus.

The fact that Saul was a leader in the contest now begun* identifies the attacking party as Pharisees; for he was a Pharisee, the son of a Pharisee, and "brought up in this city, at the feet of Gamaliel."† The violent proceedings of the Sadducees having been checked, in part, by the counsel of Gamaliel—the great teacher of the Pharisees—the apostles had gone on in their ministry, not merely proclaiming the resurrection of Jesus, but prosecuting the second part of their commission, "teaching them to observe and do all whatsoever Christ had commanded." This somewhat relieved the Sadducees from the brunt of attack, and turned it upon the Pharisees, whose traditions were directly assailed by the maxims of true piety and morality. The consequence was, a rallying of this party to an activity not manifested before since the death of Christ. Having nearly all the learning and talent of their nation in their ranks, and especially the literary culture and wealth of the foreign Jews, they resorted with great confidence to disputation. The seven deacons, who were also foreigners, were naturally brought into more direct contact with these foreign-born disputants; and Stephen, who was the most gifted of the seven, soon found himself engaged, single-handed, in a conflict with them all.

This is the first time the disciples measured the strength of their cause in open discussion. Hitherto the young converts had enjoyed no opportunity to compare the arguments by which they had been convinced with those which learning and ingenuity might frame against them. But now they were to hear both sides of the great question presented, with the odds of number, learning, and social position all on the side of their opponents. It was an interesting crisis,

* See vii: 5, 8 below † xxii: 3; xxiii: 6.

and it needs no very vivid imagination to realize the palpitating anxiety with which the disciples resorted to the place of discussion. Their fondest hopes were realized; for it soon became evident that Stephen had all the facts and the statements of Scripture in his favor, so that "they were not able to resist the wisdom and the spirit by which he spoke." By the "spirit by which he spoke," I suppose Luke refers to the Holy Spirit, who supplied him with whatever knowledge and wisdom he may have lacked.

In entering freely into this discussion, Stephen acted in accordance with the example of his master, and that of all the apostles. Their example makes it the duty of all disciples to whom God has given the necessary wisdom, to defend in discussion, against all opposition, the truth as it is in Jesus. Whoever does so, in the fear of God, and with a devout zeal for the salvation of men, will find his enemies unable to resist him.

11-14. When the advocates of error are defeated in discussion, they always resort to slander, or to violence. They tried both against Stephen. The Pharisees having the management of the case, we find their subsequent proceedings governed by the same policy which they pursued in the case of Jesus. (11) "*Then they suborned men, who said, We have heard him speaking blasphemous words against Moses and God.*" This was the indictment upon which the further proceedings were based, and it was circulated boisterously among all classes. (12) "*And they stirred up the people, and the elders, and the scribes, and came upon him, and seized him, and led him into the Sanhedrim; (13) and set up false witnesses, who said, This man ceases not to speak blasphemous words against this holy place and the law: (14) For we have heard him saying, that this Jesus of Nazareth will destroy this place, and change the customs which Moses delivered to us.*"

This is the first time that "the people" are represented as taking part against the disciples. During the first two persecutions the "fear of the people" had restrained the violence of the persecutors, which renders their present opposition the more remarkable. But the Sadducees, who had conducted those persecutions, had but little popular influence, and had contented themselves with merely asserting the authority of the Sanhedrim, without the aid of any ingenious policy. The Pharisees were more influential and more cunning. They put in circulation a slanderous report, which was cunningly directed against a single individual, and which their great popular influence enabled them to circulate with effect; and by this means they aroused a strong popular feeling in their own favor.

The general charge against Stephen was speaking blasphemy "against Moses and God," otherwise expressed, "against this holy place, and the law." The change of phraseology arises from the fact that the temple and law were the visible representatives of Moses and of God. The specifications under this charge were these: "We have heard him saying that this Jesus will *destroy this place, and change the customs* which Moses delivered to us." It is quite likely that Stephen was guilty of the specifications; but they fell very far short of the crime of blasphemy against Moses and against God. In thus teaching, he was really honoring Moses, by insisting upon the very termination which Moses himself had assigned to his own law, while he honored God by receiving him whom God had sent.

15. As Stephen stood before the Sanhedrim, thus falsely and hypocritically accused, and fully aware of a determination to condemn him without regard to evidence or justice, he could but remember the similar accusation of Jesus, of Peter and John, then of all the apostles; and his heart must have swelled at the thought of being identified with them in suffering. The baseness of his persecutors—who, under pretense of zeal for Moses and the law, were violating the one and dishonoring the other, by seeking the lives of the only men who believed his words—must have filled him with indignation, while love for the truth which he was defending, and for the Redeemer for whom he was suffering, was kindled afresh, and the power of a glorious hope inspired him with the most invincible courage. Emotions so intense and so lofty spread a glow upon his countenance which attracted the attention of the whole audience. (15) *"And all who sat in the Sanhedrim, looking earnestly upon him, saw his face as if it were the face of an angel."* There is no need to suppose any thing supernatural in his appearance, such as a halo of light enveloping his countenance; for a countenance naturally fine and expressive, when lit up by emotions so intense and heavenly as those which must then have swelled the breast of Stephen, would be sufficient to suggest such a comparison. If there were any brethren present, with what tearful delight they must then have gazed upon the hero of faith! And if any of the members of the Sanhedrim were still capable of nobler sentiments, how intense must have been their agitation! The trial proceeds:

VII: 1. *"Then said the high priest, Are these things so?"* Stephen responds in a long and powerful discourse.

There is great diversity of opinion among commentators, as to the logical bearing and connection of this discourse. We would naturally expect to find in it—if we regard it as properly a defense—a formal response to the charge which had been preferred. But it contains no direct answer to any of the specifications. He neither admits nor denies what was charged in reference to the destruction of the temple by Jesus and the changing of the customs delivered by Moses; though his silence may be regarded as an admission that the witnesses had spoken the truth on these points. Neither does he formally answer to the charge of blasphemy against Moses and against God, or against the holy temple and the law. The only thing in the discourse that has even an indirect bearing in this way, is his frequent reference to facts contained in the writings of Moses, which has been understood, by some commentators, as intended to indicate a degree of respect for Moses inconsistent with a disposition to speak blasphemy against him. But if such was his purpose, it is unaccountable that he should have pursued so indirect a course, instead of distinctly avowing the sentiments he intended to indicate. Again, this supposition can not account for the introduction of so many facts connected with the persecution of various individuals.

The best statement of the drift of the discourse, I think, is this: The charge against him was hypocritically preferred, and his judges had no intention to investigate it, but were using it merely as an excuse for his predetermined condemnation to death. They were now giving him somewhat the form of a trial, to keep up appearances before the people. Under such circumstances, Stephen knew that it would be useless to offer a formal defense; and, therefore, he does not undertake it. He sees, however, that his persecutors were identifying themselves, by their proceedings, with the unbelieving and persecuting portion of their forefathers, and he determines to make them stand forth to the people in this their true position. In prosecuting this purpose he selects his material from the writings of Moses, and shows that his accusers are with the persecuting party, while his Master and himself are side by side with Moses and others whom they had persecuted: Thus he hurls back upon them, and fastens on them, effectually, the charge which they had falsely preferred against him.

2–4. We will now take up the different sections of the discourse, treating each separately, and showing their connected bearing upon his main purpose. Before exhibiting the manner in which Moses was treated by the ancestors of his audience, he first shows that the mission on which Moses came was a subject of prophesy: thus indicating, at the outset, an analogy between it and that of Christ. To do this, he must begin with Abraham, to whom this prophesy was first given; but his reference to Abraham is only for the historical introduction of his main theme. (2) *"And he said: Men, brethren, and fathers, hearken. The God of glory appeared to our father Abraham, when he was in Mesopotamia, before he dwelt in Haran, (3) and said to him, Get thee out from thy country, and from thy kindred, and come into a land which I will show thee. (4) Then he came out of the land of the Chaldeans, and dwelt in Haran: and thence, after his father died, he removed into this land in which you now dwell."*

5–8. Having now introduced Abraham, and brought him into the land of Canaan, Stephen quotes the prophesy, connected with the fulfillment of which he is to find the chief points of his argument. (5) *"And he gave him no inheritance in it, not a footprint: and he promised to give it for a possession to him and to his seed after him, when as yet he had no child. (6) But God spoke thus: That his seed should sojourn in a strange land, and they should bring them into bondage, and afflict them four hundred years. (7) And the nation to whom they shall be in bondage I will judge, said God, and after these things they shall come forth, and serve me in this place. (8) And he gave him the covenant of circumcision; and so he begot Isaac, and circumcised him the eighth day; and Isaac, Jacob; and Jacob, the twelve patriarchs."*

The period of four hundred years is taken by Stephen from Genesis xv: 13, where God expresses himself, in round terms, of a period which was, more accurately, four hundred and thirty years, as we find in Exodus xii: 40, 41. This was not the period of their actual sojourn in Egypt; but, as we learn from Paul, (Galatians iii: 17,) and from the genealogical tables in Genesis and Exodus, it extended from the call of Abraham to the departure from Egypt.

9–16. The speaker next proceeds to recount the circumstances which brought the people down into Egypt, in order that the rejection of Joseph, and the final salvation of the whole family through him, might stand out before his hearers, and be made to bear upon his final conclusion. (9) "*And the patriarchs, moved with envy, sold Joseph into Egypt. And God was with him,* (10) *and delivered him out of all his afflictions, and gave him favor and wisdom in the sight of Pharaoh, king of Egypt, and he made him governor over Egypt and all his house.* (11) *Now, there came a famine on all the land of Egypt and Canaan, and great affliction; and our fathers found no sustenance.* (12) *But Jacob, having heard that there was grain in Egypt, sent out our fathers the first time.* (13) *And at the second time Joseph was made known to his brothers, and Joseph's kindred was made known to Pharaoh.* (14) *Then Joseph sent and called to him his father Jacob and all his kindred, seventy-five souls.* (15) *And Jacob went down into Egypt, and died, he and our fathers,* (16) *and were carried over into Sychem, and laid in the sepulcher which Jacob bought for a sum of money from the sons of Emmor, the father of Sychem.*"

There is a numerical discrepancy between Moses and Stephen, in reference to the number of Jacob's family when they went into Egypt. Stephen here makes them *seventy-five*, while Moses states them at seventy, including Joseph's family, and Jacob himself.* The Septuagint translation of Genesis agrees with Stephen. Various methods of reconciling these statements are proposed, of which the only satisfactory one is this. The number given by Moses includes all "who came out of his loins, besides Jacob's sons' wives."† The number given by Stephen must, then, include *five of their wives,* who were, probably, all that were then living. The translators of the Septuagint, having some historical evidence, now lost to us, that five of their wives went with them, saw fit to fill up the number in their translation, and Stephen followed their enumeration.

It was Jacob, and not Abraham, who purchased the sepulcher from the sons of Emmor, as is certain from the history given in Genesis xxxiii: 19, 20; yet it is attributed to Abraham here in the common version, and most of the Greek manuscripts. It is far more likely, however, that the manuscripts should err, in a case of this kind, than that the error should have been committed by Stephen or by Luke. I have, therefore, not hesitated to insert the name of *Jacob,* instead of Abraham, in the text. Dr. Bloomfield says, "The best critics are of the opinion that *Abraham* is spurious."

17–29. From this glance at the leading points in the history of Joseph, Stephen advances to the case of Moses, showing that his brethren rejected him in like manner, and were also finally delivered by him. (17) "*But when the time of the promise of which God had sworn to Abraham was drawing near, the people increased and were multiplied in Egypt,* (18) *until another king arose who knew not Joseph.* (19) *The same dealt craftily with our kindred, and afflicted our fathers, so that they cast out their young children, in order that they might not live.* (20) *In which time Moses was born, and was exceedingly beautiful. He was nourished in his father's house three months.* (21) *And when he was cast out, Pharaoh's daughter took him up, and nourished him for her own son.* (22) *And Moses was educated in all the learning of the Egyptians, and was powerful both in words and in deeds.* (23) *And when he was full forty years old, it came into his heart to look after his brethren, the children of Israel.* (24) *And seeing one of them suffer wrong,*

---

* See Gen. xlvi: 26, 27.   † Gen. xlvi: 26

he defended and avenged him who was oppressed, smiting the Egyptian. (25) Now he thought that his brethren would understand that God would, by his hand, give them salvation; but they did not understand. (26) The next day he appeared to them as they were fighting, and would have brought them to peace, saying, Men, you are brethren; why do you wrong one another? (27) But he who was wronging his neighbor thrust him away, saying, Who made you a ruler and a judge over us? (28) Do you wish to kill me as you killed that Egyptian yesterday? (29) Then Moses fled at this word, and became a sojourner in the land of Midian where he begot two sons."

In the rejection of Moses by his countrymen, when he was seeking to deliver them from bondage, according to the promise of God, Stephen has before the minds of the Sanhedrim another case bearing upon his final conclusion. It is true, that as yet they could not anticipate the use he intended to make of it, but the obscurity of his design awakened their curiosity, and rendered their mortification the more intense when at last it was suddenly developed. If they could have anticipated it, they would have stopped his mouth at the beginning.

30–37. There were other incidents in the life of Moses fully as much to his purpose as this; and to these he proceeds to advert. (30) *"And when forty years were completed, there appeared to him, in the wilderness of Mount Sinai, an angel of the Lord in a flame of fire in a bush. (31) When Moses saw it, he wondered at the sight, and as he drew near to observe it, the voice of the Lord came to him. (32) I am the God of your fathers, the God of Abraham, and the God of Isaac, and the God of Jacob. Then Moses trembled, and did not dare to observe it. (33) And the Lord said to him, Put off thy shoes from thy feet; for the place on which thou standest is holy ground. (34) I have surely seen the affliction of my people who are in Egypt, and have heard their groaning, and have come down to deliver them; and now, come, I will send thee into Egypt. (35) The same Moses whom they rejected, saying, Who made thee a ruler and a judge? the same did God send to be a ruler and a deliverer, by the hand of the angel who appeared to him at the bush. (36) He led them out, after doing wonders and signs in the land of Egypt, and in the Red Sea, and in the wilderness forty years. (37) This is the same Moses who said to the children of Israel, A prophet shall the Lord your God raise up to you from your brethren like me; him shall ye hear."* In this passage, the speaker has not only presented, in a most emphatic manner, the contrast between the rejection of Moses by his brethren, and his appointment by God to the very office of ruler and deliverer, which they refused him, but has also made a further advance toward his final purpose, by introducing the prophesy uttered by this same Moses concerning the Messiah. This prophesy was still more apposite, because it refuted the charge that he had spoken blasphemy against Moses, in saying that Christ would change the customs appointed by him. If Moses himself foretold the coming of a successor who should supersede him, he alone pays proper respect to Moses who submits to his successor.

38–40. To keep prominent the ill treatment received by Moses at the hands of the people, the speaker proceeds to note their conduct in the wilderness. (38) "*This is he that was in the congregation in the wilderness, with the angel who spoke to him at Mount Sinai, and with our fathers, who received the living oracles to give to us.* (39) *Whom our fathers were not willing to obey, but thrust him from them, and in their hearts turned back into Egypt,* (40) *saying to Aaron, Make us Gods who shall go before us; for this Moses, who led us out of the land of Egypt, we know not what is become of him.*" This instance of their rejection of Moses was much more flagrant than the first, seeing that it occurred immediately after the most splendid manifestations of God's presence with him; and that, in the very words which they addressed to Aaron, they acknowledged that it was he who had brought them out of Egypt. These circumstances also render more striking the analogy which Stephen is about to develop between him and Jesus; for he also had been rejected, notwithstanding the admission, by his enemies, that he had wrought miracles.

41–43. Stephen next shows that the same people who so often rejected the servants of God, likewise rejected God himself. (41) "*They made a calf in those days, and brought sacrifice to the idol, and rejoiced in the works of their own hands.* (42) *And God turned, and gave them up to serve the host of heaven, even as it is written in the book of the prophets, O house of Israel, have you offered to me slain beasts and sacrifices during forty years in the wilderness?* (43) *You have even taken up the tabernacle of Moloch, and the star of your god Remphan, figures which you made, to worship them; and I will carry you away beyond Babylon.*" With this brief glance at the subsequent fate of the people who had so often rejected their deliverers, covering a period of many centuries, and terminating with their captivity in Babylon, Stephen concludes his summary of facts; but, previous to the final application, which he saw would raise a storm in the Assembly, he has a few words in reference to the temple.

44–50. Instead of either admitting or denying the charge of blasphemy against the temple, he undertakes to show the true religious value of that building. This he does, by first alluding to the movable and perishable nature of the *tabernacle*, which preceded the temple, and then, by showing, from the prophets, that the presence of God is not limited to temples made with hands. (44) "*Our fathers had the tabernacle of witness in the wilderness, as he had appointed, saying to Moses that he should make it according to the pattern which he had seen;* (45) *which also, our fathers, having received, brought in with Joshua within the possession of the Gentiles, whom God drove out before the face of our fathers until the days of David,* (46) *who found favor before God, and desired to find a dwelling for the God of Jacob.* (47) *But Solomon built him a house.* (48) *Yet the Most High dwells not in temples made with hands,* as says the prophet, (49) *Heaven is my throne, and the earth my footstool. What house will you build for me? says the Lord; or what is my place of rest?* (50) *Did not my hand make all these things?*" By this statement, the speaker intrenches himself behind undisputed facts of their own history, and the sentiments of their own prophets, in reference to the temple, and is now ready to spring upon them the whole concealed power of the carefully-arranged facts from the life of Moses and of Joseph.

51-53. As Joseph, the divinely-selected savior of his brethren, had been sold by those brethren into slavery; and as Moses, divinely selected to deliver Israel from bondage, was at first rejected by them to become a sojourner in Midian, and was then sent back by the God of their fathers to be rejected by them again and again, notwithstanding the most indisputable manifestations of God's presence with him; and as all the prophets had met with a similar fortune, so, now, the final prophet, of whom Moses and all the prophets had spoken, had been rejected and slain by the sons of these persecuting fathers. The combined power of all these facts and analogies is now concentrated in the closing paragraph of the speech, and expressed in these terrific words: (51) *"Stiff-necked and uncircumcised in heart and ears, you are always resisting the Holy Spirit. As your fathers did, so do you. (52) Which of the prophets did not your fathers persecute? They murdered those who announced before concerning the coming of the Just One, of whom now you have been the betrayers and murderers; (53) who received the law through ranks of angels, and have not kept it."*

The pent-up fires which had burned within the breast of Stephen from the beginning of these unjust proceedings, and had given an angelic glow to his features at the beginning of his speech, had been carefully smothered and controlled during the progress of his argument; but now that the restraints of the argument were withdrawn, they had burst forth in these scorching and blazing words.

54-60. The exasperation of the Sanhedrim was the more intense, from the fact that the denunciation hurled upon them was not a sudden burst of passion, but the deliberate and sustained announcement of a just judgment. They had not been able to resist, in debate, the wisdom and the spirit by which he spoke, and now their efforts to convict him of crime had recoiled terribly upon their own heads. They had no course now left them, but the usual resort of unprincipled partisans when totally discomfited, and to this they rushed with fearful rapidity. (54) *"When they heard these things, they were exasperated, and gnashed their teeth upon him. (55) But he, being full of the Holy Spirit, looked steadfastly into heaven, and saw the glory of God, and Jesus standing at the right hand of God, (56) and said, Behold, I see the heavens opened, and the Son of Man standing at the right hand of God. (57) Then they cried out with a loud voice, and stopped their ears, and rushed upon him with one accord, (58) and cast him out of the city, and stoned him. And the witnesses laid off their garments at the feet of a young man called Saul. (59) And they stoned Stephen, calling on the Lord, and saying, Lord Jesus, receive my spirit. (60) And he kneeled down, and cried with a loud voice, Lord, lay not this sin to their charge. And when he had said this, he fell asleep. And Saul was consenting to his death."*

This was a strange way for a court to break up; the whole body of seventy grave rabbis, whose official duty it was to watch for the faithful and regular proceedings of law, leaving their seats, and rushing with the wild mob, amid hideous outcries and tumultuous rage, to the sudden execution of a prisoner absolutely untried and uncondemned. But the maddest pranks ever played upon this mad earth are witnessed when wicked men set themselves in uncompromising opposition to God and his holy truth. So uniformly has this been true in history, that, at the present day, when such opposition is to be sustained, whether on great or insignificant occasions, no well-informed man expects aught else than disregard of all the rules of justice and propriety. If the infuriated scenes which have been enacted under such circumstances, in the history of Christianity, could be dramatically represented, the performance might be appropriately styled, The Madman's Drama.

The vision witnessed by Stephen, while the Jews were gnashing their teeth upon him, need not be understood as a real opening of the heavens, so that the things within them could be seen by the human eye, but only a representation to his eyes, such as those granted to John in the Isle of Patmos. It was vouchsafed both for his own encouragement in the hour of death, and that the remembrance of the words in which he described it, and the hue of countenance with which he gazed upon it, might remain indelibly impressed upon the minds of those who were present. There was at least one in the audience upon whom, we have reason to believe, this impression was deep and lasting. The young man Saul never forgot it; but, long afterward, when bending under the weight of many years, he makes sad mention of the part he took in these dreadful proceedings.*

The death of Stephen was an event of most thrilling interest to the young Church, and well deserves the large space allotted to it by the historian. The disciples had embarked, with all their interests, both temporal and eternal, in the cause of one, who, though he proved himself mighty to deliver, while present with them, had now gone away beyond the reach of vision, and no longer held personal converse with them. They had struggled on faithfully thus far, and, amid many tears, some stripes, and much affliction, they had still found a deep satisfaction of soul in his service. It was demonstrated that their faith could sustain them in life, even amid very bitter trials; but it was not yet known how it would sustain them in the hour of death. No one of their number had yet tried the dread reality, and no man can now tell how much their spirits may have wavered in the prospect, and inclined backward toward the faith of their fathers, distrustful of the new arm of salvation. How great the strength, therefore, and how sweet the consolation imparted to every heart, when the first who died was so triumphant in the pangs of death! After witnessing the scene, they could go onward in their tear-dimmed course of suffering, without one fear or care for that within the grave, or beyond it. At the late day in which we live, which has been preceded by the happy death of millions of Christians, and which is often yet made deeply glad by their triumphs in the trying hour, we are not able to appreciate the eagerness with which the first disciples drank in the consolations of this glorious death. It was a fortuitous and most fitting preparation for the fiery ordeal through which the Church were immediately afterward called to pass.

We omit any notice of the part taken by Saul in this shocking tragedy till we come to comment on the ninth chapter, where his career becomes the leading theme of the historian.

* 1 Tim. i: 1-13.

VIII: 1–4. The enemies of the disciples had now tried and exhausted all the ordinary methods of opposing the truth. Under the leadership of the Sadducees they had tried, first threatening, then imprisonment, and then stripes. They were about to follow this with the death of the twelve, when the milder counsels of the yet unexasperated Pharisees had prevailed, and resort was had to discussion. But the cause which had prospered under the imprisonment and scourging of its chief advocates bounded forward with astonishing rapidity when the strength of its plea was brought before the people in open discussion. Its learned opponents were completely discomfited. Foiled in their efforts, the Pharisees were now ready to unite with the Sadducees in a common persecution. They selected Stephen as the first victim, because he had been their most formidable opponent in the discussion. They had determined to proceed in their bloody purpose with the forms of law; but, in a moment of frenzy, they had broken loose from all restraint, and dispatched their victim with the violence of a mob. Once embarked in this mad career, nothing less than the utter extermination of the Church could satisfy them. Hence the historian proceeds to inform us that, (1) "*On that day there arose a great persecution against the Church in Jerusalem, and they were all scattered abroad through the regions of Judea and Samaria, except the apostles.* (2) *Yet devout men carried Stephen to burial, and made great lamentation over him.* (3) *But Saul wasted the Church; entering into the houses, and dragging forth both men and women, he committed them to prison.* (4) *Nevertheless, they who were scattered abroad went everywhere preaching the word.*"

The grief of a community at the loss of a good man is more intense when he falls in the performance of some part characteristic of his life. But it is most intense when death, at such a moment, is precipitated by injustice and violence. It is not surprising, therefore, that the burial of Stephen should have been attended with "great lamentation." The perilous condition of the congregation—some of whom were being hourly cast into prison, and most of whom were contemplating flight—could but deepen their grief. The funeral services were soon followed by a general dispersion of the disciples. With much bitterness of heart, they left behind them their native city and their individual homes, to seek refuge among strangers. But the bitterness of their temporal loss must have been slight, to the truly devoted among them, compared with the disappointment of their brightening hopes concerning the speedy triumph of the gospel. How bitter, too, must have been the disappointment of the twelve, at suddenly finding themselves left alone in the great city, the congregation of many thousand disciples whom they had collected—all scattered and gone! While they thought of the brethren and sisters fleeing for life, and of the many already languishing in prison, they could but have regarded their own lives as in imminent danger. But, supposing that the time for which Jesus had limited their stay in Jerusalem had not yet expired, they courageously stood at their post, regardless of consequences.

The present distress and flight of the disciples had resulted, not from the mere fact that they believed in Jesus, but more especially from the zeal and persistency with which they pushed his claims upon the attention of others. Seeing that they had now lost every thing, by this course, a worldly prudence would have taught them to be, thenceforward, more quiet and unobtrusive in the propagation of their faith. Even the interests of the cause itself, which had been jeopardized by the boldness with which Stephen had attacked the prevailing iniquity, might have been urged in favor of a change of policy. But this timeserving expediency was reserved for the disgrace of a later age. It never took large possession of the heroic hearts of the early disciples. On the contrary, the scattered disciples "*went everywhere preaching the word.*" The result was the rapid spread of the gospel into the cities of Judea, and even into Samaria. Thus, the apparent ruin of the single Church in Jerusalem resulted in the springing up of many Churches throughout the province—proving, for the thousandth time in the world's history, how impotent is the hand of man when fighting against God. As the blows of the blacksmith's hammer upon the heated iron scatter the scintillations in every direction, so the effort of wicked Jews to crush the Church of Christ only scattered its light more widely abroad.

5. Among the many who now went everywhere preaching the word, the historian chooses to relate here the labors of only one. (5) "*Then Philip went down into the city of Samaria and preached Christ to them.*" This Philip was one of the seven, and his name stands in the list next to that of Stephen.* The reason why Luke selects his labors for this place in the history, is because he was the first to preach the gospel in Samaria. Jesus had commanded them to testify first in Jerusalem; then in Judea; then in Samaria; and then to the uttermost part of the earth. Luke follows them in the regular prosecution of this programme.

6-11. When Philip first entered the city of Samaria, the public mind was in a condition most unfavorable to the reception of the gospel. The practice of magical arts was quite common among the Jews and Samaritans of that age; and the masses of the people of all nations were very superstitious in reference to them. At the time now referred to, the people of Samaria were so completely under the influence of a magician, that one less bold than Philip would have had no hope of success in preaching the gospel to them. But he had confidence in the power of the gospel, and commenced his labors with a firm purpose. His success was far beyond what could have been anticipated. (6) "*And the multitudes, with one accord, attended to the things spoken by Philip, in hearing and seeing the miracles which he wrought. (7) For unclean spirits, crying with a loud voice, came out of many who had them, and many, paralyzed and lame, were healed. (8) And there was great joy in that city. (9) But a certain man named Simon was in that city before, practicing magic and astonishing the people of Samaria, saying that he himself was some great one: (10) to whom they all gave attention, from the least to the greatest, saying, This man is the great power of God. (11) And they gave attention to him because he had astonished them with magic arts for a long time.*"

We are here introduced to another case of conversion, with a very brief account of the means and influences by which it was effected.

---
* Acts vi: 5.

These demand careful consideration. It is in order that the perfect adaptation of the gospel means employed by Philip may the more strikingly appear, that Luke is particular to state the previous mental condition of the people. They had been so much astonished by the magic arts of Simon, that the prevailing conviction was, "This man is the great power of God." The dreamy genius of Neander has caught up some vague tradition of the fathers concerning a supposed theosophy involved in this expression; and, by a common sympathy in mysticism, rather than by the force of his reasoning, has transmitted it to many recent commentators. But the sober judgment, content with more natural conclusions, finds in it only the impression which such arts as Simon practiced usually make upon a superstitious multitude. The tricks of his legerdemain they supposed to be exhibitions of divine power. The first work for Philip to do was to prostrate the influence of Simon by undeceiving the people.

To accomplish this object, he has recourse to the power of the Holy Spirit. This power, addressed to the eye in the healing of lameness and paralysis, and the casting out of demons; and to the ear, in preaching Christ to them, soon arrested the attention of the multitude. There was a prompt and universal decision in the public mind in favor of the miracles wrought by Philip, and against the pretensions of Simon. What was the distinction between these miracles and Simon's astonishing tricks, which led to so prompt a decision, we are not able to say, because we know not what these tricks were. Suffice it to say, that this single incident should put to silence forever that species of skepticism which resolves all the miracles of Christ and the apostles into occult arts and optical illusions; for here are these arts, in their most delusive form, brought into direct conflict with apostolic miracles; and so palpable is the distinction, that it is at once discovered and acknowledged by the whole multitude.

12. The unmistakable reality of the miracles wrought by Philip convinced the people that he was attended by the *power* of God; and this was enough to make them acknowledge the *authority* of God in what he communicated to them. In order that men may believe the Gospel, it is only necessary that they believe it to be, in reality, the word of God. But the Holy Spirit convinced them that what they heard was the word of God, by attending it with a sensible demonstration of the power of God. That they believed was but the natural result of what they saw and heard. (12) *"But when they believed Philip preaching the things concerning the kingdom of God and the name of Jesus Christ, they were immersed, both men and women."* Being convinced that they heard the word of God, they believed it because it was the word; and, for the same reason, they yielded to its authority. Their obedience was not the result of any inherent power in the word, apart from its authorship; for if it were believed to be the word of man, it would have no authority, and no power. All the authority and power which are in it, therefore, result from the belief that God is its author. This belief was effected, in the present instance, by the Holy Spirit, through miraculous attestations; hence, the whole change wrought in the parties may be styled the work of the Holy Spirit. The simple facts of the kingdom over which Christ was reigning, thus

attested, were set forth before the people, and, upon belief of these, attended by a willingness to comply with their requirements, they were immersed without delay. This was but a faithful execution of the commission, which says, "He that believeth and is immersed shall be saved."

13. The most signal triumph achieved on this occasion was that over Simon himself. Luke gives it the prominence of a separate statement, in these words: (13) *"And Simon himself also believed, and when he was immersed he continued with Philip, and, beholding the signs and great miracles which were done, he was astonished."* The commentators nearly all agree that Simon's faith was not real, but feigned; and that the statement that he believed is made according to the appearance, and not according to the reality. They urge that subsequent developments prove the insincerity of his professions, and compel us to adopt this conclusion. It must be confessed, that at the time Philip might have been deceived by him; but this could not be said of Luke, who wrote subsequent to all the developments in the case. If his object was to describe the event as it appeared to Philip, he might retain, in the first instance, the mistake of Philip; but we would expect, on this supposition, a subsequent correction. No such correction, however, is given; neither is there any evidence that Luke intended to represent the case as it appeared to Philip. On the contrary, he speaks from his own stand-point, and had all the facts before him which we have before us. His statement, therefore, should control our judgment, and he says, not that Simon *feigned* belief, but that he *believed.* We conclude, then, that he did, in the true and proper sense of the word, *believe.*

Some commentators, disposed to admit the statement that Simon believed, still deny the sufficiency of his faith, and urge that it was deficient in its object.* But the historian makes no distinction between what Simon believed, and what was believed by the Samaritans. They "believed Philip preaching the things concerning the kingdom of God, and the name of Jesus Christ;" and Luke adds, without qualification, that "Simon himself also believed." He believed, then, what Philip preached; he believed the gospel. This conclusion is based upon statements too positive and unambiguous to be set aside because of any difficulty in reconciling them with facts subsequently developed.

14–17. Before recording the sequel of Simon's case, Luke introduces an incident, which, on account of its singularity in New Testament history, demands very careful consideration. (14) *"Now when the apostles, who were in Jerusalem, heard that Samaria had received the word of God, they sent to them Peter and John;* (15) *who, when they were come down, prayed for them, that they might receive the Holy Spirit.* (16) *For as yet he had fallen upon none of them, only they were immersed into the name of the Lord Jesus.* (17) *Then they laid hands on them, and they received the Holy Spirit."*

It would be useless to incumber these pages with the many unsatisfactory explanations of this procedure with which commentaries abound. We will be content with a simple effort to learn what it

* See Barnes, *in loco.*

teaches, by a careful consideration of the facts. We notice, then, *first*, That the Samaritans had believed the gospel, and been immersed. They were, then, according to the commission, and according to Peter's answer on Pentecost, pardoned, and in possession of that "gift of the Holy Spirit" which was promised on condition of repentance and immersion.* *Second*, After they had been in possession of this gift, for a period sufficient for the news to reach Jerusalem, the whole body of the apostles united in sending to them Peter and John. *Third*, Previous to the arrival of Peter and John, none of them had received the *miraculous* gift of the Spirit. *Fourth*, Upon the imposition of hands by the two apostles, accompanied with prayers, the Holy Spirit fell upon them, conferring miraculous gifts. From these facts we may draw several conclusions. 1st. Whatever other objects may have been contemplated in the mission of the two apostles, such as confirming the faith of the disciples, and assisting Philip in his labors, it is quite certain that the chief object was the impartation of the Holy Spirit. What they did when they arrived in Samaria was certainly the object for which they went. But the chief thing which they did was to confer the Holy Spirit; hence, this was the chief object of their visit. If, however, *Philip* could have conferred this gift, the mission, so far as the chief object of it is concerned, would have been *useless*. This affords strong evidence that the miraculous gift of the Spirit was bestowed by no human hands except those of the apostles. That such was the conclusion of Simon, who was an interested witness of this whole proceeding, is evident from the proposition he made to Peter, to purchase from him this power. If all who had the Spirit could impart it to others, he need only to have sought the gift himself, knowing that this would include the power to impart it. But his offer to buy this power, and that from an apostle, shows that the apostles alone possessed the power of imparting the Spirit. This conclusion is confirmed by the fact that in the only other instance of the kind recorded in Acts, that of the twelve disciples in Ephesus, the same gift was bestowed by the hands of an apostle.†

The case of Timothy is no exception, as has been supposed, to this conclusion; for, although Paul states that the gift which was in him was given him through prophesy and "the laying on of the hands of the eldership;"‡ yet he exhorts him, in the second epistle, "Stir up the gift of God, which is in thee, by the putting on of *my* hands."|| These two statements can be reconciled either by supposing that Paul refers to the gift of *office* in the former, and the gift of the *Spirit* in the latter; or, that the eldership united with Paul in laying on hands, while it was the apostolic part of the service which imparted the Spirit, the eldership participating, because at the same time he was ordained to the work of an evangelist.

2d. From the fact that these disciples enjoyed pardon and membership in the Church before receiving the miraculous gift, it is evident that this gift was not necessary to the enjoyment of either of these blessings. Yet, strange to say, the mystic power of an ultra spiritualism has thrown these plain facts into the utmost confusion in the minds of some great men. Witness the following from Neander, in reference to

* Acts ii: 38. † Acts xx: 6. ‡ 1 Tim iv: 14. || 2 Tim. i: 6.

the condition of the Samaritans previous to the visit of Peter and John. "They had not yet attained the consciousness of a vital communion with the Christ whom Philip preached, nor yet to the consciousness of a *personal divine life*. The *indwelling* of the Spirit was as yet something *foreign* to them, known only by the wonderful operations which they saw taking place around them."* This assertion is evidently in direct conflict with the commission, and with the promise of Peter, that those who would repent and be immersed should *receive the gift* of the Holy Spirit. Paul also teaches that the indwelling of the Spirit is characteristic of all who are Christ's;† and certainly all are Christ's who have been immersed into the name of Christ,‡ as had been these Samaritans.

3d. The statement that "as yet he had fallen on none of them, only they were immersed into the name of the Lord Jesus," thrown in paranthetically in explanation of the mission of Peter and John, necessarily implies that there was no such connection between immersion into Christ and the miraculous gift of the Spirit, as that the latter might be inferred from the former. This gift, then, was not common to the disciples, but was enjoyed only by those to whom it was specially imparted.

Seeing that this extraordinary gift of the Spirit was not necessary to the conversion and pardon of these parties, nor to the indwelling of the Spirit, it is proper to inquire for what purpose it was bestowed. We have already observed, in commenting on Acts i: 8, that the design of bestowing it upon the apostles was to endow them, intellectually, with power to establish the kingdom, and to furnish miraculous attestation of their mission. In general, miracles were designed to indicate the divine sanction of the procedure with which they were connected; but when the miracle assumed a mental form, it was designed to qualify the party for some mental labor. The young Church in Samaria had hitherto been guided by the infallible teaching of Philip, and, more recently, by that of Peter and John. But these brethren must, in executing their high commission, soon depart to other fields of labor. If, in doing so, they should leave the Church in the condition in which Peter and John found it, there would be no means left them of increasing their knowledge of the new institution, and none but their uncertain memories of retaining with accuracy what they had already learned. To supply this defect, chiefly, and, secondarily, to leave among them the means of convincing unbelievers, the gift of inspiration was bestowed—not upon all the disciples, for this is not necessarily implied in the text, but upon a sufficient number of chosen individuals. For further information upon the design of such gifts, I refer the reader to the twelfth and fourteenth chapters of First Corinthians. A complete discussion of the subject would belong to a commentary on that epistle, rather than to one on Acts. Suffice it here to add, that these gifts served as a temporary provision, until the facts, doctrine, commandments, and promises of the new covenant were committed to writing by inspired men, when the prophesies, tongues, and miraculous knowledge of individual teachers gave place to the written record.‖

* Planting and Training. † Rom. viii: 9. ‡ Gal. iii: 26–29. ‖ See 1 Cor. xiii: 8.

18, 19. In the above remarks upon the incident before us, we have assumed that the gift imparted was miraculous. This assumption is justified by the fact that it was a matter of observation by those who were not recipients of it, as is evident from the next statement of the text. (18) *"And when Simon saw, that through the laying on of the apostles' hands the Holy Spirit was given, he offered them money,* (19) *saying, Give me also this authority, that on whomsoever I lay hands he may receive the Holy Spirit."* The form of this proposition shows that the Holy Spirit did not come upon these persons directly from heaven, as upon the apostles on the day of Pentecost, but that it was imparted through imposition of hands. This marks the difference between the *immersion* in the Holy Spirit, to which the event on Pentecost belongs, and the *impartation* of the Holy Spirit, to which we refer the present case. The latter was effected through human agency; the former without it.

In order to account for the impious proposition of Simon, we must remember his former mode of life, and consider the mental habits which it must have cultivated. Having been accustomed to the performance of astonishing tricks as a means of making money, and to the increase of his stock in trade by purchasing the secret of every new trick which he met with among his brother magicians, he had acquired the habit of looking upon every thing of an astonishing character with reference to the *money* which might be in it. When, now he saw that by imposition of the apostles' hands the miraculous power of the Spirit was imparted, and remembered that there were many even among the disciples, who had not yet received the coveted gift he at once perceived that the power to impart it could be made a source of great profit. His overruling avarice, mingled with intense fondness for popular influence, prompted him to seek this power. The blinding influence of these passions prevented him from seeing the impropriety either of offering to buy it, or of intending to sell it; for certainly, if he had realized the light in which his proposition *should* be regarded, he would not have ventured to make it.

20–23. Nothing could be more abhorrent to the feelings of an apostle than such a proposition. It was well calculated to arouse the impulsive spirit of Peter, and his response is marked by his characteristic vehemence. (20) *"But Peter said to him, Your silver go with you to perdition, because you have thought to purchase the gift of God with money.* (21) *You have no part nor lot in this matter, for your heart is not right in the sight of God.* (22) *Repent, therefore, of this your wickedness, and pray God, if, perhaps, the purpose of your heart may be forgiven you.* (23) *For I perceive that you are in the gall of bitterness, and the bond of iniquity."* This description of Simon's spiritual condition shows clearly that he was not, at that time, in a state of mind acceptable to God. "The gall of bitterness" is a forcible expression of the wretchedness of his condition; and "the bond of iniquity," of the dominion which sin exercised over him. His heart was not right in the sight of God, and he was in the way to perdition. The declaration that he had "no part nor lot in this matter" depends, for its interpretation, upon the meaning of the expression, "this matter." Whether it refers to the gospel, or to the impartation of the Spirit, is

ACTS VIII: 24.

not altogether certain. In either case, the declaration is true; for it is certain that he had no part in the impartation of the Spirit; and equally certain that he was then under the condemnation of God.

Whether we are to suppose that Simon's destitute and miserable condition was the result of having forfeited the favor of God by falling into sin after his immersion, or that his confession and immersion had been insincere, so that he had never been pardoned, is not to be determined, as many suppose, by the grossness of his present conception concerning the Holy Spirit. The question resolves itself into this: whether the discovery that a man is under the control of some wicked passion soon after his immersion is proof that he had not been a proper subject for immersion. If conversion involves so complete a renovation, that old mental habits are entirely eradicated, never to exert their influence again, then Simon was not a genuine convert. But if, as both Scripture and experience teach, the turning of a sinner to God is simply the triumph of conscience and the better feelings over the passions, while the latter still exist in a latent state, ready to spring into activity on the approach of temptation, we must admit that Simon *may* have been a penitent believer at the time of his immersion. That he was a believer is asserted by Luke; but whether he was to such a degree penitent as to receive pardon when he was immersed, is not certainly determined by the text. For aught that is affirmed of him, he may either have been influenced by sinister motives in confessing his faith, or have been truly penitent at the time, and afterward, under spur of the temptation which the splendid gifts bestowed by Peter were the occasion of, have yielded to the sudden impulse of his ruling passion.

Whichever of these hypotheses we adopt, the case affords no objection to the immediate immersion of all who confess faith in Christ, and indicate a desire to obey him, no evidence of their insincerity being apparent. The inspired example of Philip is an authoritative guide for us, and if it appear that he occasionally immersed an unprepared subject, modern evangelists can not be censured for following his example, though they should occasionally meet with the same misfortune.

The supposition that Philip and Peter both, by the power of discerning spirits, knew from the beginning that Simon's heart was not right, but, for wise reasons, withheld the announcement until his wickedness was developed before the people, is entirely gratuitous. The gift of "discerning spirits," mentioned in 1 Cor. xii: 10, was the power of testing the claims of those who professed to be inspired. There is no evidence that it was ever used by the apostles or others to detect the concealed thoughts and emotions of the soul. The detection of Ananias and Sapphira is not a case in point, for it was effected not by discerning their thoughts, but by a direct revelation to Peter that the story which they told was a lie.

24. The conclusion of the conversation between Peter and Simon leaves us in doubt as to the final fate of the latter. Peter had exhorted him to repent, and pray to God for pardon. (24) "*Then Simon answered and said, Pray ye to the Lord for me, that none of these things which ye have spoken come upon me.*" This response indicates very

clearly that the scathing speech of Peter had a good effect. It doubtless awoke Simon to a clearer perception of his own character, filled him with more becoming awe of the Holy Spirit, and aroused some fear of the terrible consequences of his sin. As the curtain of history here falls upon him, he disappears in a more promising state of feeling, but without leaving us fully assured that he recovered from the dominion of his unholy passions. Many things are said of his subsequent career, in ancient and modern commentaries, but nothing that is sufficiently authenticated to deserve our serious attention.

25. In connection with the prime object of their visit to Samaria, Peter and John also furthered the efforts of Philip in preaching and teaching. This we learn from an incidental remark in connection with the statement of their departure for Jerusalem. (25) "*Now they, having testified and spoken the word of the Lord, returned into Jerusalem and preached the gospel in many villages of the Samaritans.*" This labor in the Samaritan villages was performed on their journey toward Jerusalem, which may have been somewhat circuitous, according to the situation of the villages which they desired to visit. Thus these primitive preachers of the gospel made all the stations of their journeys through the country successive points for disseminating the truth.

26. When the congregation in Samaria had been supplied *with spiritual gifts*, and sufficiently instructed to justify leaving them to their own resources for edification, Philip was called away to other fields of labor.

We are now introduced to another of those minutely detailed cases of conversion which are recorded for the purpose of instruction in reference to the means of turning men to God, and inducting them into the kingdom. The purpose of bringing him to a knowledge of salvation was formed in the divine mind, and specific means of accomplishing it put into operation, ere the man himself was aware of it. The narrative traces the steps by which this purpose of God was accomplished, and enables us to know, when God determines upon the conversion of an individual, how he proceeds to effect it.

The first step taken in the case was to send an angel from heaven. But where does the angel make his appearance? To the man for whose benefit he came? So it must be, if he is to hold any direct communication with him. But, strange to say, while the man was south of Jerusalem, traveling toward Gaza, the angel descends into Samaria, to the north of Jerusalem, and appears to Philip. (26) "*And an angel of the Lord spoke to Philip, saying, Arise and go toward the south, into the road which goes down from Jerusalem to Gaza. This is a desert.*" This is all that the angel has to say; and now his part of the work, which was simply to start the evangelist in the direction of the person to be converted, is accomplished. He retires from the scene.

The statement "this is a desert" is correctly supposed, by the best commentators, to be no part of the angel's speech to Philip, but to have been added by Luke to note the singularity of a preacher being thus peremptorily sent away from a populous country into a desert. The term desert is not here to be understood in its stricter sense of a barren waste, but in its more general acceptation, of a place thinly inhabited. Such an interpretation is required by the geography of the country, and by the fact that water was found for the immersion of the eunuch. The only road from Jerusalem to Gaza, which passed through a level district suitable for wheeled vehicles, was that by Bethlehem to Hebron, and thence across a plain to Gaza. According to Dr. Hackett, this is "the desert" of Luke i: 80, in which John the Immerser grew up. Dr. S. T. Barclay, who traversed this entire route in May, 1853, says that he traveled, after leaving "the immediate vicinity of Hebron, over one of the very best roads (with slight exceptions) and one of the most fertile countries that I ever beheld."*

27, 28. Philip promptly obeyed the command of the angel, and was soon in close proximity to the intended convert, though, as yet, he knew nothing of him. (27) *"He arose and went; and behold a man of Ethiopia, an eunuch of great authority under Candace, queen of the Ethiopians, who had charge of all her treasure, and had come to Jerusalem to worship, (28) was returning, and sitting in his chariot, was reading the Prophet Isaiah."*

29. Just as Philip entered the road to which he had been directed by the angel, and saw the chariot before him, the Holy Spirit began to work for the conversion of the treasurer. And where does he begin his work? In the heart of the sinner, by direct communication? No. Like the angel, he begins with the preacher. (29) *" Then the Spirit said to Philip, Go near, and join yourself to this chariot."* This was a miraculous communication from the Spirit, such as frequently directed the labors of inspired men. The object of it was the same as that of the angel's visit, to bring the preacher and the subject for conversion face to face.

30. The purpose of the angel's visit and the Spirit's miraculous communication was now accomplished. (30) *" Then Philip ran to him, and heard him reading the Prophet Isaiah, and said, Do you understand what you are reading?"* Considering the relative position of the parties, one an humble footman, and the other a chief officer of a powerful kingdom, sitting in his chariot, this question appears rather an abrupt and inappropriate introduction to the conversation. But it was, in reality, the most natural and appropriate question that Philip could ask. Hearing the man reading aloud, in what we call the fifty-third chapter of Isaiah, that touching description of the sufferings of Christ, he knew that it was unintelligible to him if he was not acquainted with the gospel; whereas, if he had learned the story of the cross, he could not fail to understand it. The question, "Do you understand what you are reading?" was, then, the very question to determine where he stood, and how to approach him.

31-35. The man's response was definite and satisfactory. (31) *"And he said, How can I, except some man should guide me? And he invited Philip to come up and sit with him. (32) Now the place of the Scripture which he was reading was this: He was led as a sheep to slaughter, and as a lamb silent before his shearer, so he opens not his mouth. (33) In his humiliation, his condemnation was extorted, and who shall fully describe his generation? For his life is violently taken from the earth. (34) And the eunuch answered Philip, and said, I pray you, of whom*

* City of the Great King, p. 576.

does the prophet speak this? Of himself, or of some other man? (35) *Then Philip opened his mouth, and beginning at the same Scripture, preached to him Jesus.*"

We have now before us all the influences and agencies employed in this man's conversion, and may restate them, as follows: He was reading a remarkable prophesy concerning Christ, and had paused upon it, with the inquiry, Of whom is this written? He could recollect nothing in the history of the prophet himself, or of any other man, to which it would apply. He was, therefore, unable to understand it; and if he had learned to pray as David did, the prompt impulse of his heart was, "Open thou mine eyes, that I may behold wondrous things out of thy law." In this frame of mind he was best prepared for the influences which God, who knows the secrets of all hearts, was preparing for him. If his eyes can be made to penetrate the darkness of that prophesy, and his heart to feel the power of the truth which lies there hid from his gaze, all will be well. But there is no human being present to teach him, nor does any friend of Jesus know even of his existence. What, then, will be done? God employs his Spirit to open the eyes and touch the hearts of men; will he not, then, immediately distill a heavenly influence upon the man's soul, to enlighten him and save him? He does not do it. And if not in this case, where no human agent is at hand, who shall say that he does in any other? The word of God is silent in reference to any such abstract influence, and he who assumes its existence gets behind the curtain of revelation.

But God also employs angels in ministering to those who shall be heirs of salvation. In the absence of human agency, will not some angel be dispatched to the aid of this waiting subject for salvation? An angel is truly sent; but his mission is, to start a *man* in the direction of the chariot. When the man gets within sight of the chariot, the Holy Spirit begins to work; but he works by first bringing the man to the side of the chariot, and next, through his lips, speaking to the man in the chariot. Thus we see, that, though an angel from heaven has appeared, and the Holy Spirit has operated miraculously for the conversion of the sinner, there is still an insuperable necessity for the co-operation of a *man*. Unless that *man* does his part of the work, all that has been done by both the angel and the Spirit will prove unavailing. Not the slightest influence from either of the heavenly messengers reaches the sinner's mind or heart, until the preacher begins to speak, and then it reaches him *through the words which are spoken.*

The further process is easily traced. As Philip opens up item after item of the prophesy, and shows its fulfillment in Jesus, the eyes of the eunuch begin to penetrate the Scripture, until, at last, he sees a flood of heavenly light where all was darkness before. His eyes are opened, and he sees the wondrous glory of a suffering Savior beaming from the inspired page which lies before him. This is effected, not by an abstract influence of the Spirit, enabling him to understand what was before obscure, but by the aid of a fellow-man providentially sent to him for the purpose.

The treasurer may have heard of Jesus, in Jerusalem; but, if so,

ACTS VIII: 36.

he heard of him through those with whom he had been up to worship, the bitter enemies of the cross; and knew him only as an impostor who had been deservedly crucified, though now worshiped by a few deluded Jews as their Messiah. But now, with a prophesy before him which he had tried in vain to find fulfilled in the history of any other man, but which finds its complement in the life and death of Jesus; and informed, by a man whose astonishing knowledge of the word of God is a guarantee of his honesty, that Jesus is risen from the dead, his honest heart interposes no wicked obstacles to his faith, and he believes. The demonstration strikes him with the greater force, because it is so unexpected. The Jews could not explain that prophesy, for they could not find its facts in the life of any of their great heroes; and though the reference to the Messiah was so palpable as to at once suggest itself to every reader, they would not apply it to him, because their conception of his earthly glory conflicted with the humiliation and suffering described by the prophet. Until now, this very difficulty had been puzzling the mind of the treasurer. But he now sees the prophesy fulfilled; and while the demonstration compels him to believe, the true conception of a bleeding Messiah touches his heart. All this is effected by the Holy Spirit *in* Philip, *through the words* which Philip spoke.

36. "*And as they went along the road, they came to a certain water. And the eunuch said, What hinders me to be immersed?*" The appearance of the water to which they had come suggested this question, but it could not have done so unless the eunuch had been taught something concerning immersion as a religious ordinance. But he had enjoyed no opportunity for instruction on this subject, except through the teaching of Philip. Had Philip, then, preached him a sermon on immersion? No. Luke says Philip "preached to him Jesus." How, then, had he, while hearing Jesus preached, obtained instruction in reference to immersion? There is only one answer to this question. It is, that to *preach Jesus*, after the apostolic method, involves full instruction upon the subject of immersion. The prejudice, therefore, which exists at the present day against frequent introduction of this subject in discourses addressed to sinners, is altogether unscriptural; and those only preach Jesus correctly who give to it the same prominence which belongs to it in apostolic discourses. It was a part of Peter's sermon on Pentecost, of Philip's preaching to the Samaritans, and of his present discourse to the Ethiopian; and we will yet see, in the course of this commentary, that it always occupied a place in the preaching of inspired men on such occasions. Indeed, it would be impossible to preach Jesus fully without it. For the beginning of the gospel, historically, according to Mark,* is the immersion of John, to which Jesus submitted, and near the conclusion of it is the commission given in the last words of Jesus on earth, commanding every believer to be immersed.† Thus he who preaches Jesus has immersion in the beginning and in the end of his sermon.

37. By the almost universal consent of recent critics, the whole of this verse is excluded from the original text, and should be from all versions. For the reasons on which this decision is based, we refer

* Mark 1: 1. † Mark xvi: 15, 16.

the reader to "Bloomfield's Commentary" on the passage, "Tregelle's History of the Printed Text," and other critical works.

This verse has been used chiefly for the purpose of determining the confession which was made originally by candidates for immersion. The fact that it is an interpolation must modify the argument on this subject, but does not invalidate it. The fact that such a confession as is here put into the mouth of the eunuch was uniformly required by the apostles, is evident from other passages of Scripture. It is quite certain that it was confessed by Timothy. Paul says to him: "Fight the good fight of faith; lay hold on eternal life, into which you were called, and did *confess the good confession* before many witnesses."* This confession was made at the beginning of his religious career; for it is connected with his call to eternal life. It is the same confession which is attributed to the eunuch; for Paul immediately adds: "I charge thee before God, who gives life to all things, and Jesus Christ, who bore testimony under Pontius Pilate, to *the good confession*," etc. Now, what is here called "the good confession" is certainly the confession that he was the Christ, made before the Sanhedrim, under Pontius Pilate. But this is identified, by the terms employed, with the confession which Timothy had made, which is also "the good confession." Timothy, then, made the confession that Jesus is the Christ, the same attributed to the eunuch. Moreover, this confession was so conspicuous, at the time of Paul's writing, that it was known as *the* confession, and so highly esteemed as to be styled *the good* confession.

That Timothy was not alone in making this confession is evident from the following statement of Paul: "The word is nigh thee, in thy mouth and in thy heart; that is, the word of faith which we preach, That if thou wilt confess with thy mouth the Lord Jesus, and believe in thy heart that God has raised him from the dead, thou shalt be saved."† From this it appears that one item in "the word of faith" which the apostles preached, was *the confession of the Lord Jesus with the mouth.* Paul assumes that this word was in the mouths and hearts of the brethren in Rome, whom he had never seen, and with whose conversion he had nothing, personally, to do. This assumption can be justified only on the ground that it belonged to "the word of faith" everywhere preached. He argued, from the universal practice of the apostles, to a particular conclusion in reference to their converts in Rome. We have, therefore, both his premises and his conclusion, to sustain us in deciding that this confession was universal in the primitive Church, as a part of the apostolic ritual.

We here have use for the interpolated verse now under consideration. The fact that it is interpolated does not prove that the eunuch did not make the confession. On the contrary, when rightly considered, it establishes the presumption that the passage, as it now reads, is a faithful account of the event. The interpolation is easily accounted for. The text read: "The eunuch said, See, here is water; what hinders me to be immersed? And he commanded the chariot to stand still, and they went down both into the water." Now, the object of the interpolator was to fill up what appeared to be a historic blank,

---

* 1 Tim. vi: 13. The terms ὁμολόγιω, and ὁμολογία, should be uniformly rendered con- *fess* and con*fession*. † Rom. x: 8, 9.

so that Philip should not appear to have led the man into the water too abruptly. In doing so, he, of course, inserted what he supposed to be the apostolic custom; and the fact that he inserted this confession shows that he believed that the apostles required candidates for immersion to make the confession. Furthermore, the interpolator would naturally be guided by the prevailing custom of his own day, so that his amendment might be received by his cotemporaries. In whatever age, therefore, the interpolation was made, it indicates both the custom of that age and the opinion then prevalent as to the apostolic custom. Whether these considerations have any force or not, depends upon the proximity of the age in question to the apostolic period. But this interpolation was known to Irenæus, A. D. 170,* and this proves that the confession which the Scriptures show to have been universal in the days of the apostles was perpetuated into the latter part of the second century.

Both the custom of confessing Christ, and the formula employed, originated in the most natural way, and without any positive precept. Jesus appeared in Galilee and Judea, proclaiming himself the Christ and the Son of God. As men became convinced of his claims, they would say, "*I* believe that he *is* the Christ." Others would say, "*I* believe that he is a prophet, but I *deny* that he is the Christ." Thus the confession or denial of this proposition was the first mark of distinction between believers and unbelievers. The Pharisees, therefore, "agreed that if any man did *confess that he was the Christ*, he should be put out of the synagogue." † The confession was, then, all that was necessary to identify one as a disciple of Jesus. Hence, with special reference to this state of things, Jesus said, "He that *confesses* me before men, him will I confess before my Father in heaven; but he that *denies* me before men, him will I *deny* before my Father in heaven." After the commission was given, enjoining the immersion of all believers, the confession was still perpetuated, and immersion naturally took position immediately after it.

A confession thus necessarily originating from the grand issue that Jesus presented to the world, and involving the earliest distinction between his friends and his foes, could not fail to have an important position in the formation of those friends into a great organization. The Church of Christ, like every other useful organization, is created and sustained by the obligations of some truth. This truth may be properly styled the foundation of the organization, because it is that from which it springs, and without which it could not exist. The truth declared in the confession, that Jesus is the Christ, the Son of God, is, beyond controversy, the foundation of the Church of Christ, and is so declared by Jesus himself.‡ Without it no Church of Christ could possibly exist. It had to exist as a truth, and be demonstrated to men as such, before the Church could begin to be. The truth itself, however, and the confession of it, are two things entirely distinct. The former is the foundation; the latter a means of building on it. There is no way to build an organization of men and women on a truth, except by a mutual confession of it, and an agreement to live together according to its obligations. When individuals, believing that Jesus

* Hackett, *in loco*. † John ix: 22. ‡ Matt. xvi: 16-18.

is the Christ, mutually confess it, and agree to unite in the observance of its obligations, the *immediate* and *necessary* result is a Church. In this way the confession became an organic element in the ecclesiastical constitution.

Inasmuch as some have conceived that Jesus in person is the foundation of the Church, it may be well to observe here that there is no way in which an organization can be built on a person, except by believing something in reference to him. It is not the fact that there is such a *person* as Jesus, but that that person is the *Christ* which gave existence to the Church.

Inasmuch as members of the Church are built upon the true foundation, in part, by a mutual confession of its truth, the confession, formally made, is both an acknowledgment of the obligations which the truth imposes, and a pledge to all the duties of a member in the Church. It is true, that the confession, like immersion, and eating bread and wine, may occur amid the careless scenes of a wicked life, without any religious import. But this is only to say that the specific acts which God calls upon us to perform in religious ordinances may be performed by wicked men without religious intent. And this, again, is only to say, that, in adapting his institutions to us, instead of inventing new and unheard-of performances, he has lifted up certain actions and words already familiar, into association with religious truth and obligation. This arrangement is a proof of his wisdom; for by it the mind is averted from the mere physical act, which might otherwise have usurped too much consideration, and is compelled to associate the value of the deed with the thoughts which surround it. Such is pre-eminently the case with the confession, which, though a very simple declaration of faith, in reference to the most familiar fact in the scheme of redemption, is a formal assumption of all the obligations of a Christian life.

The kingdom of Christ is not limited to earth, but was designed to bind together, in one harmonious whole, God, angels, and men. God himself was the first to present himself for this great union. Over the bank of the Jordan he made the same confession which is required of us, and thereby not only bore testimony to the fact that Jesus was his Son, but, also, voluntarily placed himself before the universe in the attitude which the incipient mediatorship required him to occupy. By this formal confession he pledged himself to accept the mediation of Christ, just as we, by the same confession, pledge ourselves to accept the blessings which that mediation procures for us. If God had never confessed Jesus, in this or some equivalent manner, we would have no direct assurance from him that he was in Christ reconciling the world to himself.

Like men on earth, the angels in heaven passed into the privileges of the kingdom of God, by making this same confession. When Jesus ascended up on high, the Father said to him, "Sit on my right hand, till I make thine enemies thy footstool."* Then he "sat down at the right hand of the throne of God,"† and God said, "Let all the angels of God worship him."‡ Then were fulfilled the words of Paul, "God hath highly exalted him, and given him a name that is above every name, that at the name of Jesus every knee should bow, of things in

* Heb. i: 13. † Heb. xii: 2. ‡ Heb. i: 6.

heaven, and things on earth, and things under the earth, and that every tongue should *confess that Jesus is Lord*, to the glory of God the Father." The angels all confessed the good confession, receiving Jesus as their Lord, and rendering thus their first act of worship to the Son of Mary. The one identical confession, therefore, has brought together, in one harmonious whole, God, angels, and men; the latter being pledged by it to eternal worship, and the former pledged forever to accept their grateful homage through Christ.

That this confession was the only one required of candidates for immersion by the apostles, is universally admitted by those who are competent to judge. It is likewise admitted that they regarded it as a sufficient confession. This fact alone should teach men to be satisfied with it now. He, indeed, who is guided by the Bible alone, can not require of men any other confession than such as he finds authorized by Bible precedents. Neither is it possible that he who implicitly follows the apostolic precedent can be misled, unless the apostles, the Holy Spirit, the New Testament, can mislead him. Fidelity to the word of God, therefore, binds us to this confession alone, and, in clinging to it, we have every assurance which inspiration can give that we are right.

Departure from apostolic precedent is never justifiable, except when the precedent itself was the result of circumstances peculiar to the apostolic age. The primitive practice of washing the feet of brethren who came into the house from the highway, was an accidental, and not a necessary result of the law of hospitality. Growing out of the peculiar habit of wearing sandals, it ceased to be a matter of duty as soon as the circumstances which gave rise to it disappeared. If a similar change of circumstances has taken place in reference to the confession, rendering it insufficient for our times, then we are no longer bound by the precedent. That such is the case is affirmed by many of our cotemporaries, and we must extend these remarks sufficiently to consider the reasons offered in support of this opinion.

It is often argued that, in the days of the apostles, the moment men became convinced that Jesus was the Christ they were ready to submit to his service; but now, every Church is surrounded with men and women who are convinced of this fact, but still persist in wickedness; hence some more effectual test should now be applied. This argument is based upon a false assumption in reference to results of primitive preaching; for we read of many rulers of synagogues who believed in Jesus, but would not confess him for fear of the Pharisees;[*] of Joseph of Arimathea, who, though a disciple, kept it secret;[†] of Felix, who trembled under the preaching of Paul, but said, Go thy way for the present; and of Agrippa, who was *almost*, though not altogether, persuaded to be a Christian. If these men in high stations were deterred by fear, or by worldly lusts, from making the confession, how much more the common people, who had much more to fear! Witness the parents of the blind man who had been healed by Jesus, who gave evasive answers in the synagogue for this very reason.[‡] There is no evidence that men were more prompt to yield to their convictions then than they are now.

Sometimes it is argued, quite inconsistently with the above, that the

---

[*] John xii: 42.   [†] John xix: 38.   [‡] John ix: 22.

danger of being known as a Christian in those days rendered the simple confession a sufficient test of a man's devotion; but now, when Christianity is popular, it is entirely insufficient. It must be granted, that sometimes it was dangerous to property and life to become a Christian, yet it was true then, as it is now, that many insincere persons found their way into the Churches. Jude complains that "ungodly men, turning the favor of God into lasciviousness, and denying the only Lord God, and our Lord Jesus Christ," had "crept in unawares."* Paul echoes the same sentiment in reference to "false brethren, unawares brought in, who came in privily to spy out our liberty which we have in Christ Jesus, that they might bring us into bondage."† There were those "who went out from us because they were not of us," and there was Demas, who forsook Paul in the hour of danger, "having loved this present world." And what more shall I say? For the time would fail me to tell of Simon the sorcerer, of Alexander the coppersmith, of Phygellus and Hermogenes, of Hymeneus and Alexander whom Paul delivered over to Satan that they might learn not to blaspheme, and of many others who proved insincere in their confession, or false to its obligations. Surely, if a test of sincerity which could let into the fold such wolves as these was sufficient for the inspired apostles, we may be content with the same, unless we affect a wisdom and a zeal superior to theirs.

But the most popular argument against the present sufficiency of the good confession is this: that the immense multiplicity of doctrinal errors now prevalent requires a severer test of soundness in the faith than was used by the apostles before these errors had an existence. Unfortunately, however, its historic assumption is as baseless as that of the two we have just considered. For not only were the Churches surrounded with most pernicious errors in doctrine, but were sickened by the poison of those errors within their own bosoms. Pharisees in Jerusalem crept in to spy out the liberty of the new covenant, and bring the brethren back into bondage to the law;‡ and there were Sadducees in the Church in Corinth who denied the resurrection.‖ There were philosophers, such as "Hymeneus and Philetus, who concerning the faith have erred, saying that the resurrection is already past, and overthrow the faith of some,"§ and there were transcendentalists, who denied that "Jesus Christ had come in the flesh,"¶ having speculated his bodily existence into the essence of moonshine, or something equally unreal. James had to warn some against being deceived into worship of the heavenly bodies, by assuring them that "every good gift comes down from the *Father* of lights," and not from the lights themselves; while Paul fights many a hard battle against brethren who were disposed to openly countenance fornication, incest, and the sacrificial banquets of heathen worship. Under the pressure of all this influx of falsehood and iniquity, why did not these inspired men see their mistake, and, discarding the simple confession, draw up a masterly catechism, which would shut out every error, and guard the purity of the Church? How sad the reflection, that men so ingenious in other respects, were so stupid in this! And how fortunate for

* Jude iv. † Gal. ii: 4. ‡ Gal. ii: 4.
‖ 1 Cor. xv: 12. § 2 Tim. ii: 17, 17. ¶ 1 John iv: 1-3.

ACTS VIII: 38, 39.

us, that the wiser heads of Rome, Geneva, Augsburg, and Westminster have supplied this deficiency in the work of the apostles!

We have thus far argued upon the broadest assumption in reference to the inefficiency of the good confession in guarding the purity of the Church. We might retort upon the advocates of creeds and catechisms, by showing that these devices can not be, and have not been, any more efficient; but we prefer to show the real exclusiveness of the good confession. It is certainly exclusive enough to keep out the pagan, the Jew, the Mohammedan, the atheist, and the infidel; for none of these can honestly make the confession. It will exclude the Unitarian and the Universalist; for while they are willing to confess that Jesus is the Christ, in the next breath they deny him, by contradicting some of his most emphatic declarations. It will also exclude the wicked and impenitent; for it is offered only to penitent believers. If this is not considered sufficient, we may advance still further, and say that it will exclude the Roman Catholic, who persists in having other intercessors in heaven besides the high priest of our *confession.*"* It will exclude the devotee of the mourning bench, who waits for an operation of the Spirit before he comes to Christ. It will exclude the pedobaptist, who is satisfied with his sprinkling; for it requires an immediate immersion. None of these characters can scripturally make the good confession without some specific change in views or in character. Lest the tune of the objector should now be changed, and he should cry, "Your confession is too exclusive," we add, that it receives all whom the apostles would receive, and excludes all whom they would exclude.

. 38, 39. When Philip ascertained that the eunuch believed in the Lord Jesus, and desired to obey him, there was no delay, but his desire to be immersed was immediately gratified. (38) *"And he commanded the chariot to stand still, and they went down into the water, both Philip and the eunuch, and he immersed him.* (39) *And when they were come up out of the water, the Spirit of the Lord caught away Philip; and the eunuch saw him no more, for he went on his way rejoicing."*

This is one of the passages which the conflict of contending parties has rendered familiar to every reader of the New Testament. The questions in controversy are: *First,* Whether Philip and the eunuch went *into* the water, or only *to it; Second,* Whether the facts in the case afford any evidence that the eunuch was immersed.

The determination of the first question depends upon the exact force of the antithetical expressions, κατέβησαν εἰς τὸ ὕδωρ, and ἀνέβησαν ἐκ τοῦ ὕδατος. If the latter means, "they went *up out* of the water," then the former necessarily means, "they went down *into* the water;" and *vice versâ.* There are two methods of inquiry, therefore, by which to determine whether they went into the water: *First,* The direct method, which depends upon the meaning of the words supposed to declare this fact; *Second,* The indirect method, which determines whether they went *into* the water, by determining whether they went *out* of it.

In dealing with this question, Dr. Moses Stuart, one of the most learned and candid of the disputants on the pedobaptist side, does great injustice to his own reputation. He says: "That εἰς, with the verb

* Heb. iii: 1.

106   ACTS VIII: 38, 39.

καταβαίνω, often means going down *to* a place, is quite certain; *e. g.* 'Jesus went down *to* Capernaum;' 'Jacob went down *to* Egypt;' 'They went down *to* Attalia;' 'They went down *to* Troas;' 'He went down *to* Antioch;' 'Going down *to* Cæsarea.'"* How strange it is that the learned author did not perceive that in every one of these examples the meaning is necessarily *into!* If he had paused to ask himself whether Jesus went *into* Capernaum, and Jacob *into* Egypt, and so of the others, or merely went to the boundary line of those places, he would have spared his reputation by erasing this paragraph. He would also have saved himself the utterance of another unfortunate sentence on the same page: "I find but one passage in the New Testament where it seems to mean *into* when used with καταβαίνω. This is in Romans x: 7, Who shall go down, εἰς ἄβυσσον, *into the abyss?"* Besides the examples mentioned above, he must have searched with very little industry not to have discovered the following: "Let him that is on the housetop not *go down into,* καταβατω εἰς, the house."† "Now that he ascended, what is it but that he also first *descended into,* κατέβη εἰς, the lower parts of the earth?"‡ "This man *went down into,* κατέβη εἰς, his house, justified rather than the other."‖ "A certain man was *going down,* καταβαίνει, from Jerusalem *into,* εἰς, Jericho."§ "The road that *goes down,* καταβαίνουσαν, from Jerusalem *into,* εἰς, Gaza."¶

These are all the instances in the New Testament in which these two words occur together; and the reader can but see, that in every single instance the controverted expression means *to go down into*. By our first method of inquiry, therefore, it is settled that Philip and the eunuch *went down into the water.*

It is not logically necessary to pursue this discussion any further; but, lest it might be imagined that the conclusion we have already reached should be modified by the force of the other member of the antithesis, we must give some attention to the meaning of ἀνέβησαν ἐκ τοῦ ὕδατος. And here I must take exceptions to another sweeping declaration of Dr. Stuart's. He says: "Ἀναβαίνω is never employed in the sense of *emerging from a liquid substance.* The preposition ἐκ, here, would agree with this idea—although it, by no means, of necessity implies it; but ἀναβαίνω forbids us to thus construe it." Why is this apparently broad assertion so cautiously limited to the single case of "emerging from a *liquid* substance?" Is it possible that Dr. Stuart knew that the expression meant to *go up out of,* but, thinking that it did not occur in any other passage in connection with a liquid, framed his proposition to suit such an *accident?* It is humiliating in the extreme to see so great a mind descend to such special pleading on so grave a subject. If ἀναβαίνειν ἐκ means *to go up out of,* nothing but the most determined obduracy can preclude the admission that it means the same when referring to liquids as to other substances. Now, it is a fact, and it must have been known to Dr. Stuart, if he examined into the ground of his own statements, that, in every single occurrence of these two words in connection, in the New Testament, they mean *to go up out of.*** Moreover, in one of these occurrences they are "employed

---
* Stuart on Baptism, Nashville, 1856, p. 95.   † Mark xiii: 15.   ‡ Eph. iv: 9.
‖ Luke xviii: 14.   § Luke x: 30.   ¶ Acts viii: 26.
** See John xi: 55; Luke ii: 4; Rev. viii: 4; ix: 2; xi: 7; xiii: 1; xiii: 11; xvii: 8.

in the sense of emerging from a *liquid* substance." In Revelations xiii: 1, John says: "I stood upon the sand of the sea, and saw a beast, ἐκ της θαλάσσης ἀναβαίνον, *rising up out of the sea.*" Notwithstanding this broad assertion of Dr. Stuart's, therefore, the expression in question does, without a single exception, invariably mean *to go up out of.* Philip and the eunuch, then, *went up out of the water*; hence, they must first have *gone down into* it. By both methods of inquiry, the conclusion is established.

The most astonishing display of partisan blindness on this passage is yet to be noticed. It is an argument employed by Moses Stuart, in which he is followed by Dr. Alexander. He says: "If κατέβησαν εἰς το ὕδωρ is meant to designate the action of *plunging, or being immersed into the water*, as a part of the rite of baptism, then was Philip baptized as well as the eunuch: for the sacred writer says they both went into the water. Here, then, must have been a rebaptism of Philip; and, what is at least singular, he must have baptized *himself* as well as the eunuch." This argument proceeds upon the assumption that immersionists regard the act of going down into water as the act of immersion, than which there could not be a grosser perversion of their meaning. When a strong mind descends to arguments so weak and childish as this, we have the clearest evidence that the cause in which it is employed is felt to be weak and untenable.

We must now address ourselves to the inquiry, whether this passage affords any evidence in favor of immersion. This much-controverted question may be discussed either as a philological question, or as a question of fact. In the former method, the controversy turns upon the meaning of the Greek word βαπτίζω. In the latter, upon the *action* performed by the apostles, when they *baptized* men. Questions of fact are much more tangible than those in philology, especially when the philological inquiry runs into a foreign language. We prefer, therefore, to discuss this question as a simple matter of fact; and this method is the more appropriate in this work, which treats of *acts* performed by apostles. It can be most easily determined what act was performed when men were baptized, without any discussion as to the meaning of the word βαπτίζω.

If the passage before us contains any evidence that the eunuch was immersed, outside of the meaning of the word, it must be circumstantial evidence, and not direct testimony. In ordinary jurisprudence, the former is often more conclusive than the latter; for living witnesses may be bribed, or voluntarily bear false testimony; but facts, however grossly they may be misinterpreted, can never give real utterance to falsehood. Circumstantial evidence is that derived from facts which transpired in such connection with the main fact assumed as to indicate its existence or character. There are two conditions necessary to its conclusiveness: *First,* That the facts which constitute the circumstances be fully authenticated; *Second,* That they shall be such as can not be accounted for without the admission of the main fact at issue. The first condition is always satisfied in scriptural inquiries, because the facts are asserted by infallible witnesses. Every thing depends, therefore, upon compliance with the second condition. This compliance may be so various in degree, as to admit of every possible degree of conclusiveness, from the slightest presumption up to absolute certainty. When the circumstances are as easily accounted for without the fact assumed as with it, they afford no evidence at all. When they can be better accounted for with the fact than without it, the evidence is probable. When they can not possibly be accounted for without the fact, and are fully accounted for by the fact, the evidence is irresistible.

When the facts constituting the circumstances are actions performed by men, this introduces an additional element into the argument. In this case, if the agent is a rational man, he must be supposed to act for a reason, and his actions, as circumstances, may be regarded with reference to the reasons for which they were performed. We further observe, that the question, What act was performed by the apostles under the name of baptism? has not reference to an indefinite number of actions, but is confined, by the nature of the controversy, to two. It was either immersion or affusion; the latter term embracing both the specific acts of sprinkling and pouring. This is admitted by all parties; for, although some contend that either act will serve the purpose of a valid baptism, no one, at the present day, contends that the *apostles* practiced *both*. Those who contend for affusion deny that the apostles or John the harbinger practiced immersion; while those who contend for immersion deny that they practiced affusion. It is as if A and B were brought into court for trial in reference to the murder of C. It is admitted by both the parties, and known to the counsel, the jurors, the judge, the sheriff, and the spectators, that the murder was committed by one of these two parties. Now, whatever evidence might be presented to exculpate A, would have precisely the same tendency to the conviction of B. And if the demonstration of A's innocence were complete, the jury would render a verdict against B, though not a witness had testified directly to his guilt. Just so in the present case. Whatever evidence can be found against the affusion of the eunuch and others, is good to the same extent in favor of their immersion, and *vice versâ*.

The circumstances by which this question is to be decided are divided into two distinct classes, which we may style, respectively, circumstances of fact, and circumstances of allusion. We will consider them in the order in which they are here named.

There are some circumstances of fact which afford no evidence upon this question whatever. For instance, three thousand persons were baptized in Jerusalem on the day of Pentecost, in one afternoon. Now, if it were impossible for the agents employed to immerse so many in so short a time, or if sufficient water for the purpose could not have been found in Jerusalem, the two circumstances of place and time would furnish evidence against immersion. But as the facts on which this evidence would depend did not exist,* no such evidence is here found. All the circumstances involved in the transaction can be accounted for by the supposition of either affusion or immersion; hence they furnish no evidence in favor of either as against the other. In like manner, the command of Ananias to Saul, to *"Arise and be baptized,"* though it supplies the fact that previous to being baptized

* See Com. ii: 41.

ACTS VIII: 38, 39.

he must *arise* from his prostrate or recumbent position, furnishes no evidence bearing upon our question, because it is consistent with either immersion or affusion. If it were proved that C was murdered with a club, this in itself would be no evidence against A, or in favor of B, seeing that either of them could have used a club.

But there are other circumstances of fact which afford unmistakable evidence upon this question. The agent about to perform the act in dispute selected for the purpose a *river*, as the Jordan,* or a place where there was "*much water*," as in "Ænon near to Salim."† When the parties about to perform the act were in an ordinary dwelling, they went out of doors for the purpose, though it were the hour of midnight, as in the case of the Philippian jailer.‡ When they came to the water selected, both the administrator and the subject went down *into* it, as in the case of the eunuch, and the baptism was performed while they were *in* it. These are all unquestionable facts, for they are declared in unambiguous terms by infallible witnesses. They are also actions performed by rational men, and, therefore, each of them must have been performed for some reason. Moreover, the reason for each was furnished by the nature of the main act, for the purpose of accomplishing which each of these subordinate actions was performed. But the supposition of *affusion* furnishes no conceivable reason for any one of these actions. It can not, therefore, be the main act in question.

Again: If the main act could have been as well and as conveniently performed without these subordinate actions as with them, then all these agents acted without a reason. But certainly affusion, even of the multitudes baptized by John, could have been performed as conveniently to himself and the people, at some well or fountain centrally located, as at the Jordan, or in Ænon. Paul could have sprinkled the jailer as conveniently in the house at midnight, as out of doors; and Philip could have sprinkled or poured water on the eunuch as well at the brink of the water, as by going down into it. Each of these subordinate actions, therefore, was an irrational one, if affusion was the main act performed.

But, still further, there are good and valid reasons *against* such a line of action as we are considering, such as have sufficed, in every age and country, and among all ranks of society, to cause those who perform affusion to pursue a course the reverse of this in every particular. To save time and labor, and to avoid personal discomfort, instead of going to rivers and places of much water, they administer the rite at home or at church. Instead of going out of doors at night, if they happen to be out of doors, they prefer to go into the house. And, instead of going down *into* the water, they dip into it merely the tips of their fingers, or, avoiding all contact with the water themselves, they pour it from a vessel upon the subject. To suppose, in the face of all these reasons, which are controlling with rational men, that the apostles performed the various actions which we know they did, for the purpose of affusion, is to suppose them to act not only *irrationally*, but *contrary* to all the reasons which govern rational men. But they were rational men; therefore, he who reasons thus concerning them is convicted, beyond question, of drawing an irrational conclusion.

* Mark i: 5.   † John iii: 23.   ‡ Com. xvi: 33.

So far as the circumstances of fact are concerned, we might logically rest the case here; for, having sustained the negative proposition that affusion was not the act in question, we have no alternative but to conclude that it was immersion. But the same circumstantial evidence which brings us to so solid a conclusion by this indirect method, serves the purpose equally well when applied to the direct proof of immersion. The supposition of immersion furnishes the desired reason for each one of the subordinate actions we have been considering. It accounts for the selection of a river or a place of much water; for leaving the house at midnight, and for going down *into* the water. It is the only supposition which *can* account for them; and, therefore, their existence demands the existence of immersion. We must either deny these facts, which would be infidelity; deny that the apostles acted rationally, which would be the hight of folly and impiety; or admit that immersion, and not affusion, was the apostolic practice.

The circumstances of allusion are equally conclusive with those already considered. Their force may be stated thus: When parties who are certainly acquainted with the facts in dispute let drop incidental remarks indicative of the nature of the facts, such remarks afford evidence, by indicating the knowledge possessed by the speaker. If, in the case of trial for murder above supposed, it were known that D was cognizant of all the facts, any incidental statetement of his, inconsistent with the supposition that he knew A to be the murderer, would afford circumstantial evidence in favor of A, and against B. Now, Jesus and the apostles were cognizant of all the facts in reference to baptism, and they have made certain allusions to it, which, so far as the nature of the act is concerned, are incidental, but which indicate what they knew the act to be. If, upon a collation of these allusions, we find them inconsistent with the knowledge, on their part, that baptism was affusion, but just such as imply the knowledge that it was immersion, the evidence from this source will be conclusive.

Of the many allusions at hand, we will select, for our present purpose, only a few, the bearing of which appears least liable to dispute. First, in the words of our Savior, "Except a man be *born of water* and the Spirit, he can not enter into the kingdom of God." That the expression, "born of water," is an allusion to baptism, is admitted by all standard commentators and critics known to the writer, and is disputed by none but those who are incapable of being candid upon this subject. The term is used metaphorically, and, therefore, indicates some connection with water, which is analogous to a birth. But there is no conceivable analogy between a birth and an application of water by affusion; hence it is impossible that Jesus could have known the act alluded to to be affusion. The expression forces the mind to something like a birth, which can be found only in the act of drawing the body out of water, which takes place in immersion. This, alone, could have suggested the metaphor to the mind of Jesus, and to this our minds intuitively run when we hear the words pronounced. It is intuitively certain, therefore, that Jesus alluded to immersion, and not to sprinkling.

The next allusion to which we invite attention is that in which

Jesus calls the unspeakable sufferings which were to terminate his life, "The *baptism* with which I am to be *baptized*."* Here the term baptism is used metaphorically for his sufferings, which could not be unless there is, in literal baptism, something analogous to the overwhelming agonies of Gethsemane and Calvary. The soul revolts at the supposition that a mere sprinkling, or pouring of water on the face, could have supplied this analogy, and intuitively demands something like the sweep of water over the sinking body, which is witnessed in immersion. Immersion supplies the analogy, and it must be the meaning of the term baptism, if there is any meaning in the Savior's mournful words.

One allusion from the Apostle Paul, and one from Peter, will suffice for our present purpose. Paul exhorts the brethren to draw near to God, "having our hearts sprinkled from an evil conscience, and our *bodies washed* with pure water."† Here is an allusion to the sprinkled blood of Christ, as cleansing the heart from an evil conscience, and to baptism as a *washing of the body*. But this language is inconsistent with the idea of sprinkling or pouring a little water on the face, which could, by no propriety of speech, be styled a *washing of the body*. Nothing but immersion will meet the demands of the expression, for the words describe what takes in immersion, and in no other ordinance of the New Testament. Peter's allusion is quite similar to this. He says: "Baptism doth also now save us, not the putting away of the filth of the flesh, but the seeking of a good conscience toward God." Now Peter could not have supplied the words, "Not the putting away of the filth of the flesh," unless there was something in baptism which might possibly be mistaken for this. But it would be impossible for any one to so mistake sprinkling, while immersion might be readily mistaken for a cleansing of the flesh. Peter, then, knew that immersion, and not affusion, was baptism, and so indicates by this language.

We now have before us, from Jesus and Paul and Peter, who certainly knew what baptism was, unmistakable allusions to it, which could not have been made if they knew it to be affusion, and which force us to the conclusion that they knew it to be immersion. It is difficult to conceive how circumstantial evidence could be more conclusive.

We might add to our list of circumstances of allusion the statement of Paul in Romans vi: 4, and Colossians ii: 12, that in baptism we are buried and raised again. But I regard this as *direct testimony* to what is done in baptism, and not a mere allusion to it. If any man were to try to frame a statement of what takes place in the act of immersion, he could not do so in more unambiguous terms than to say "We are buried and raised again." If he were to say "We are *immersed*," it would not be so specific a description of the act, nor so little liable to dispute as to its real meaning.

The last clause of the passage under consideration demands some notice ere we introduce another section of the text. It is said that "when they came up out of the water, the Spirit of the Lord caught Philip away; and the eunuch saw him no more, for he went on his way rejoicing." No doubt the influence of the Spirit by which Philip

* Matt. xx: 22. † Heb. x: 22.

was caught away was the same as that which had at first joined him to the chariot. It was that monition of the Spirit by which the movements of inspired men were frequently directed. We will notice frequent instances of the kind in the course of this work.

When Philip was caught away to other labors, the eunuch "went on his way rejoicing." So universally does joy pervade the hearts of those whose sins are forgiven, that many sectaries of modern times have mistaken it for the *evidence* of pardon. The fallacy which they commit is to assume, without authority, that a real pardon from God is the only cause which can induce this feeling. Now, we know that joy must spring up in the heart, under the belief that pardon has been dispensed, however mistaken that belief may be. The convict awaiting execution would be just as happy if deceived by a counterfeit pardon, as if it were genuine. So with the penitent sinner. When his soul has been racked, for hours and days together, by the torture of an awakened conscience, it is likely, by the reaction of its own powers, or through exhaustion of the nervous system, to become calm. Now, if he has been taught that the supervening of this calm is an indication of pardon, immediately upon the consciousness of its presence there will spring up that joy which he alone feels who believes his sins are pardoned. Such individuals, however, generally have serious doubts, at times, whether they did not mistake the natural for the supernatural, and they seldom obtain more than a *hope* that their sins were forgiven. The rejoicing of the eunuch was based upon far different and more solid ground. Taught by Philip, according to the commission, and according to the preaching of Peter, who had been Philip's own teacher, that the penitent believer was to be immersed for the remission of sins; realizing, in his own consciousness, that he was a penitent believer; and having been immersed, his conviction that his sins were pardoned was as solid as his confidence in the word of God and in his own consciousness. In neither of these could he well be mistaken, and, therefore, his joy was not alloyed by any harassing doubts.

We now part company with this noble man, whose ready faith and prompt obedience give evidence of such a character that we would love to travel with him further; but here the curtain of authentic history drops upon him, and we see him no longer. Happily, the echoes that come back to us, as he passes on, are notes of joy, and we may hope to meet him at the point where all our journeys meet, and rejoice with him forever.

40. The historian brings the present section of his narrative to a close by a brief notice of the subsequent labors of Philip. (40) *"But Philip was found at Azotus; and, passing along, he preached the gospel in all the cities till he came to Cæsarea."* The town of Azotus, the Ashdod of the Old Testament, was westward of the route the eunuch was pursuing, on the shore of the Mediterranean. Philip's further tour extended northward, along the sea-shore, to Cæsarea. We are not yet prepared to bid him a final adieu; but will meet him again, after the shifting scenes of many years, to say farewell amid many tears.*

* See Acts xxi: 8.

ACTS IX: 1, 2.

IX: 1, 2. There is a sudden transition in our narrative at this point, and it assumes more the character of a biography. The writers of sacred history, in both Testaments, devote the greater part of their space to biographical sketches. The greater familiarity of the masses of the people with such portions of the Bible fully attests the wisdom of this course. This familiarity is the result of a deeper impression made upon the heart, and, consequently, upon the memory We accept it, therefore, thankfully, that Luke, in his sketch of apostolic labors, was directed to record, somewhat connectedly, the labors of Paul, rather than detached sketches from the lives of all the apostles. What is lost to our curiosity in reference to the other apostles is far overbalanced by the more thrilling effect of a continuous personal narrative. This effect is all the more thrilling, from the selection of him, who, among all the apostles, was "in labors most abundant."

Saul has already been introduced to the reader in the account of Stephen's martyrdom. By the aid of his own subsequent statements concerning himself, we are able to trace his history to a still earlier period. The early education and ancestral remembrances of a man have much to do in forming his character and shaping his career. Those of Saul were calculated to thrust him into the very scenes in which he first figures in history. He was born in the city of Tarsus, in Cilicia, not far from the period at which Jesus was born in Bethlehem. He was of pure Jewish extraction, of the tribe of Benjamin, and descended from pious ancestry. This insured his careful instruction in Jewish history, and such portions of the law of Moses as he could understand in childhood. His parents were Pharisees, and, therefore, his understanding of the Scriptures was modified by the peculiar interpretations and traditions of that sect, while his prejudices were all enlisted in its favor.*

Besides this religious instruction, he was taught the trade of tent-making. The goat's hair which was used in this manufacture was produced in Cilicia in such abundance, and of so fine a quality, that the manufactured article acquired the name *Cilicium*, from the name of the province. The wisdom of his parents in teaching him this trade as a means of providing against the unfortunate contingencies of life, will be fully exemplified in the course of this narrative.

The child was being educated, under the eye of an overruling Providence, for a future unthought of by either himself or his parents. His residence in a city where the Greek language prevailed was not the least important circumstance bearing upon this education. Like the children of foreigners in our own country, though the ancestral tongue was the language of the fireside, on the streets and in all places of public resort he was compelled to employ the language of the adopted country. In this way he acquired that familiarity with the Greek, which enabled him, in after-life, to employ it with facility both in writing and speaking.

It was only his earliest childhood that was thus devoted to parental instruction, and to the acquirement of the Greek language and a trade; for he was "brought up" in the city of Jerusalem, at the feet of Gamaliel.† Under the instruction of this learned Pharisee, whose prudence

---

* See Phil. iii : 4, 5 ; 2 Tim. i : 3. † Acts xxii : 3.

and whose calm indifference to the cause of Christ we have had occasion to notice, in commenting on the second trial of the apostles,* his Pharisaic prejudices must have been intensified, while his knowledge of the law was enlarged, and his zeal for it inflamed.

A youth of Paul's intellectual capacity would be expected to make rapid advances with the opportunities which he now enjoyed, and so, he tells us, he did. "I made progress in the Jew's religion above many my equals in age in my own nation, being more exceedingly zealous for the traditions of my fathers."† This pre-eminence among his school-fellows was accompanied by the strictest propriety of religious deportment; so that he could appeal, after the lapse of many years, to those who knew him in his youth, though now his enemies, to testify that, "according to the strictest sect of our religion, I lived a Pharisee."‡ He could even declare that he was, "touching the righteousness that is in the law, blameless."‖ Such was his character, and his reputation, when he finished his course of instruction in the school of Gamaliel.

If the usual supposition concerning Saul's age is correct, it is not probable that he was in Jerusalem at the time of the crucifixion, or for several years previous. If he had been, it would be unaccountable that in all his epistles he makes no allusion to a personal knowledge of Jesus. The supposition that he was at that time still confined in the school of Gamaliel is not only inconsistent with his supposed age, which could not have been less than thirty at the time he is introduced to us, but it is insufficient to account for his ignorance of events over which the very children of Jerusalem rejoiced.§ The supposition that he left the school and returned to Tarsus previous to the immersion preached by John, and reappeared in Jerusalem after the ascension of Jesus, is most agreeable to all the known facts in the case. By an absence of a few years he had not forfeited his former reputation, but appears now as a leader in the movements against the Church. We have already, in commenting on Acts vi: 9, ventured the assumption, that among the Cilicians there mentioned as opponents of Stephen, Saul bore a leading part as a disputant. Such a position his superior learning and piety would naturally assign him, and his prominence at the stoning of Stephen affords evidence in favor of this assumption. The law required that the witnesses upon whose testimony an idolater was condemned to death should throw the first stones, in the execution of the sentence.¶ In accordance with this law, the witnesses against Stephen, preparatory to their cruel work, laid off their cumbrous outer-garments at the feet of Saul, who "was consenting to his death."** After the death of Stephen, he still maintained the position of a leader, and continued to commit men and women to prison, until the Church was entirely dispersed. Many of those committed to prison met with the fate of Stephen. This fact is not stated by Luke, but is confessed by Paul in his speech before Agrippa.†† Many others were beaten in the synagogues, and compelled to blaspheme the name of Jesus as the condition of release from their tortures.‡‡

* Acts v: 34–39.   † Gal. 1: 14.   ‡ Acts xxvi: 5.   ‖ Phil. iii: 6.   § Matt. xxi: 15.
¶ Deut. xvii: 7.   ** Acts vii: 58; xxii: 20.   †† xxvi: 10.   ‡‡ xxii: 19; xxvi: 11.

ACTS IX: 1-3. 115

After the congregation in Jerusalem had been dispersed, Saul doubtless thought that the sect was effectually crushed. But soon the news came floating back from every quarter, that the scattered disciples were building up congregations in every direction. One less determined than Saul might have despaired of final success in destroying a cause which had thus far been promoted by every attack made upon it, and which even sprung up with increasing strength from apparent destruction. But his was a nature which gathered new resolution as obstacles multiplied before him; and thus he appears in the present text, which, after so long delay, we must now have before us. (1) "*But Saul, yet breathing out threatening and slaughter against the disciples of the Lord, went to the high priest,* (2) *and requested from him letters to the synagogues in Damascus, that, if he found any of that way, whether men or women, he might bring them bound to Jerusalem.*"

Why he selected Damascus as the scene of his first enterprise, rather than some of the cities of Judea, is acknowledged by Olshausen as "difficult to determine." But when we remember the sensitiveness of patriots, in reference to the reputation of their country and its institutions in foreign lands, the difficulty disappears. The ancestral religion of the Jew was his pride and boast in every land. It was bitter enough to the proud Pharisee that it should be brought into disrepute among a portion of the population at home; but when the hated authors of this reproach began to spread it abroad in surrounding kingdoms, it was beyond endurance. When the news reached Jerusalem that this dishonoring heresy had begun to spread in the ancient and celebrated city of Damascus, where thousands of Jews then lived, and had obtained a religious influence over a large portion of the population, the exasperation of the Pharisees knew no bounds, and Saul, with characteristic ardor, started in pursuit of the fugitives. He had reason, of course, to believe, that, upon requisition of the high priest, the authorities of Damascus, which was then embraced within the dominions of the Arabian king Aretas, would deliver up the disciples as fugitives from justice. That he was correct in this is sufficiently demonstrated by the zeal with which the governor afterward lent the aid of his guards to the orthodox Jews, for the purpose of seizing Saul himself.*

3. The storm of passion with which Saul started from Jerusalem would naturally subside, in some degree, in the course of the five or six days necessary to perform on foot the journey of one hundred and forty miles, leaving him in a calmer mood, and better prepared for the scenes which transpired near the close of the journey. (3) "*And as he journeyed, he came near to Damascus, and suddenly there flashed around him a light from heaven.*" This occurred at noon, when the sun was shining with full meridian strength upon the sandy plain which he was traversing,† yet the light from heaven was "above the brightness of the sun."‡

We are now fairly introduced to the history of Saul's conversion,

---
* Comp. ix: 23–24, with 2 Cor. xi: 32.
† For a description of the natural scenery, see Life and Epistles of Paul, vol. i, page 86. Throughout the remainder of this volume I will draw freely from the rich resources of this valuable and exhaustive work. ‡ Acts xxvi: 13.

and must note carefully the entire process, both with reference to the specific changes effected, and the influences which produced them. In order that we may have the case fully before us, we will draw upon the parallel passages in the twenty-second and twenty-sixth chapters for such additional facts as they furnish.

4. *"And he fell upon the earth, and heard a voice saying to him, Saul, Saul, why do you persecute me?"* He not only heard this voice, but, gazing, while his eyes could endure it, into the midst of the glory, he saw distinctly the being who spoke to him.* The question he heard, by the simple force of the word *persecute*, carried his mind forward to his bloody purpose in Damascus, and back to his bloody deeds in Jerusalem. Nor was this the only involuntary motion of his mind upon the instant; for here we must locate the additional words, "It is hard for thee to kick against the goads."† This language reveals to us that Saul's conscience had not been altogether at rest during his persecutions, but that, like an unruly ox, he had been kicking against a goad, which urged him to a different course. Although he had acted ignorantly, and in unbelief, yet it was with so many misgivings, that he ever afterward regarded himself as the *chief of sinners*, having been the chief of persecutors.‡ His conscience must have been instantaneously aroused by this reference to its past goadings.

5, 6. Though his conscience was now aroused, and he knew full well that the vision before him was from heaven, he can not comprehend it until he knows who it is that speaks to him and asserts him self the object of his persecutions. (5) *"And he said, Who art thou, Lord? And the Lord said, I am Jesus, whom you persecute."* It is impossible for us, who have been familiar with the glory of our risen Savior from our infancy, to fully appreciate the feelings which must have flashed, like lightning, into the soul of Saul, upon hearing these words. Up to this moment he had supposed Jesus an impostor, cursed of God and man; and his followers blasphemers worthy of death; but now, this despised being is suddenly revealed to him in a blaze of divine glory. The evidence of his eyes and ears can not be doubted. There he stands, with the light of heaven and the glory of God around him, and he says, "I AM JESUS!" "Now is Jesus risen from the dead, and become the first fruits of them that slept." Stephen was a blessed martyr, and I have shed innocent blood. My soul is guilty. "O wretched man that I am, who shall deliver me from the body of this death?" I have gloried in my shame. All that I have gained is lost. It is filth and refuse. I will throw myself upon his mercy. (6) *"And he, trembling and astonished, said, Lord, what wilt thou have me to do?"* The die is cast. The proud spirit yields, and the whole mighty current of that soul is turned back in its channel, to flow forever, deeply and strongly, in the opposite direction.

The glorious power of the one great gospel proposition was never more forcibly illustrated than on this occasion. A moment ago, Saul was sternly, and with fearful calmness, pressing to the destruction of the cause of Jesus, but now he is a trembling suppliant at his feet. What has produced this change? It is not the fact that he has seen a light, and heard a voice. For when he fell to the ground in alarm,

* 1 Cor. xv: 8. † Acts xxvi: 14. ‡ 1 Tim. i: 13-15.

his unbelief and ignorance still remained, and he still had to ask the question, "Who art thou?" Thus far, he is no more convinced that Jesus is the Christ than he was before; but he is convinced that the vision is divine, and this prepares him to believe what he may further hear. When that heavenly being, whose word he can not doubt, says, "I am Jesus," one new conviction, that must, from its very nature, reverse all the purposes of his life, takes possession of his soul. To stifle its effects he is not able; to resist its impulse is contrary to the honesty of his nature; and he has no time, if he would, to steel his heart against it. The change flashes over him in an instant, and he lies there a *penitent believer*. The word of the Lord, miraculously attested, gives him faith. The conviction that Jesus, whom he had persecuted in the person of his disciples, is really the Lord of glory, brings him to repentance. He mourns over his sins, and yields his will. These facts reveal the glorious simplicity of gospel salvation; and while we contemplate them, the sickly talk about "irresistible grace," which floats, like the green scum on a stagnant pool, over the pages of many commentaries, in reference to this conversion, is swept away, while the sights and sounds which haunt the memory of many a superstitious convert are driven back to dwell with the ghosts and hobgoblins of a night of ignorance now nearly gone.

To the question, What wilt thou have me to do? the Lord gave an answer which naturally divides itself into two parts. One part is given by Luke, in the verse before us, and by Paul, in his speech to the Jerusalem mob; the other, in the speech before Agrippa. The latter contains his commission as an apostle, and is expressed in these words: "I have *appeared* to thee for this *purpose*, to appoint thee a minister and a witness of the things which thou hast seen, and of those in which I will appear to thee, delivering thee from the people and the Gentiles, to whom I now send thee, to open their eyes, that they may turn from darkness to light, and from the authority of Satan to God, that they may receive remission of sins, and inheritance among the sanctified, by faith in me."* In this sentence, which we will notice more at length in its proper connection, Jesus states the object of his *personal appearance* to Saul, and gives him his commission as an apostle. The former was necessary to the latter; for an apostle must be a witness of the resurrection,† and this he could not be without having seen him alive since his crucifixion.‡ Having now seen him, not only alive, but glorified, his evidence was afterward classed with that of the original apostles and witnesses.|| If he had been converted without having seen the Lord, he would not have been an apostle, unless the Lord had afterward appeared to him to make him one. Instead of this, the Lord chose to appear to him in connection with his conversion. While this appearance was necessary to his apostleship, we may not assume that it was necessary to his conversion, unless we take the strange position that it was impossible for him to be convinced in any other way.

Before Saul could enter upon the office of an apostle, it was necessary that he should become a citizen of the kingdom of which he was to be a chief officer. The other portion of the Savior's reply has

---

* Acts xxvi: 16–18. † See Com. i: 22. ‡ 1 Cor. ix: 1. || 1 Cor. xv: 8.

reference to his duty in this particular. It is stated by Luke in these words, constituting the last clause of verse 6, of which we have already quoted a part: "*Arise, and go into the city, and it shall be told thee what thou must do.*" Saul's own statement of it is more minute: "Arise, and go into Damascus, and there it shall be told thee concerning all the things which are appointed for thee to do." The things which he was to do as an apostle had just been told him, and concerning these there had been no previous *appointment*. The things which had been *appointed* for him to do concerned him in common with all other penitent sinners. These having been already appointed by the Lord himself, and their execution committed to the hands of faithful men, the Lord shows respect to his own transfer of authority, by sending the suppliant to Damascus to learn them.

During his personal ministry, Jesus sometimes spoke pardon, at once, to penitent sinners.* But, since his resurrection from the dead, and the appointment, by formal enactment, of the terms of pardon, there is no instance of this kind. Moreover, his refusal to tell Saul his appointed duty, or to pardon him on the spot, establishes the presumption that he will not do so in any case. If there ever was an occasion on which we would expect the glorified Savior to speak pardon, in person, to a sinner, it is here, when he is in actual conversation with the penitent, and the request is formally preferred. But he refuses to do so. Those, therefore, who imagine themselves to have received a direct communication of pardon from Christ, either orally, or by an abstract spiritual agency, are deluded. They claim for themselves what was not accorded to Saul, and what is inconsistent with the order established in the kingdom of Christ. The reply to all inquirers, if Christ should now speak, would be, as it was then, Go to Damascus, and it shall be told you; Go to the apostles and evangelists of the New Covenant, and the answer will now be given you by Peter, Philip, Ananias, in the same words, and by the same authority, that 't was then.

7. While the conversation was passing between Saul and Jesus, the conduct of his companions is thus described by Luke. (7) "*Now, the men who were journeying with him stood speechless, hearing the voice, but seeing no man.*" Paul gives a different account of their demeanor, by saying that they *all fell to the ground;*† but the two accounts harmonize very naturally. The first effect of such an apparition would naturally be to prostrate them all; but his companions, not being held in this position by any direct address to them, would naturally arise after the first shock was over, and, fleeing to a safe distance, there stand gazing, in mute terror, upon the glory which enveloped their leader. This supposition is confirmed by the fact that Paul represents the falling to the earth as occurring *before* the voice was heard, while their standing speechless is connected by Luke with the *close* of the conversation.

This supposition helps to account for a well-known verbal discrepancy between these two accounts. Luke says they *heard* the voice; Paul says "they *heard not* the voice of him that spoke to me." The discrepancy arises from the ambiguous use of the verb *hear*. There is

* Matt. ix: 16; Luke vii: 37-50.　　　　† Acts xxvi: 14.

nothing more common, among all nations, than for one who is listening to a speaker, but, either from his own confusion or the indistinctness of the speaker's articulation, can only catch an occasional word, to exclaim, "I don't *hear* you;" although the sound of the voice reaches him continually. It is in this sense of the word *hear*, that the companions of Saul, in the confusion of their effort to escape from the scene, failed to *hear* the voice. They heard the sound, but did not understand the words.

8, 9. When the vision disappeared, Saul promptly obeyed the commandment given him. (8) *"And Saul was raised from the earth, but when his eyes were opened he saw no one, and they led him by the hand and brought him into Damascus.* (9) *And he was there three days without seeing, and did neither eat nor drink."* The physical effect of the intense light into which he had gazed upon his eyesight was not more painful than the moral effect of the whole scene upon his conscience. The former made him blind; the latter filled him with remorse. To this feeling alone can we attribute his total abstinence from food and drink. The awful crime of fighting murderously against God and Christ was pressing upon his soul, and as yet he knew not what to do that he might obtain pardon. His Jewish education, if not his natural instinct, prompted him to *pray*, and this he was doing with all fervor;* but the hands he lifted up were stained with blood—the blood of martyrs; and how could he hope to be heard? No penitent ever had greater cause for sorrow, or wept more bitterly than he.

10–12. While this scene of anguish was transpiring in the presence of the astonished Jews who surrounded Saul, the Lord was not unmindful of the promise he had made him. As he had sent him to Damascus to learn what to do, he provides for him a teacher. (10) *"Now there was a certain disciple in Damascus, named Ananias. And the Lord said to him in a vision, Ananias! And he said, Behold, I am here, Lord.* (11) *And the Lord said to him, Arise, and go upon the street called Straight, and inquire in the house of Judas, for one named Saul of Tarsus. For behold, he is praying,* (12) *and has seen in a vision a man named Ananias coming in and putting his hand upon him that he might receive his sight."* It will be observed, that, in these directions, the Lord does not tell Ananias what to tell Saul to *do*. This omission only proves that Ananias already knew perfectly what such a person *should* be told to do, and corresponds with the fact that the things in which he was to be instructed were "the things *appointed* for him to do."

It is well to pause for a moment here, and inquire what progress has been made toward the conversion of Saul, and by what means the progress made has been effected. That he is now a believer, it is impossible for any man who has followed the narrative intelligibly to doubt. That he is also a penitent is equally certain. But the Holy Spirit—by whose direct agency alone, it is taught by many, a man can be brought to faith and repentance—has not yet been imparted to him, nor does he receive it till after the appearance of Ananias.† Such an agency of the Spirit, then, is not necessary to faith and repentance. Moreover, as we have already observed, the only influence yet brought to bear upon him was that of the words of Jesus, proved to be of divine

* Verse xi.   † Verse xvii.

authority by the miraculous vision. He was convinced, then, by the same means that the eunuch and the three thousand on Pentecost had been, by the word of the Lord miraculously attested. His case differs from both of those, in that the Lord himself was his preacher, instead of an inspired man; and from that of the eunuch, in that the miraculous attestation was a physical display in his case, and the fulfillment of prophesy in the eunuch's. The *nature* of the influences was the same in them all.

Saul is now a believer, and a penitent believer; but he is not yet justified. The theory, therefore, drawn from his own words in the epistle to the Romans, that a man is justified by faith only, the moment he believes, is proved false by Paul's own experience. He says, "Being justified by faith, we have peace with God."* But he had faith for three days before he was justified, or obtained peace with God. Interpreting his words, then, by his experience, we conclude that men are justified, not by. faith only, nor the moment they believe, but when they are led by faith, as he was, to *do* what is *appointed* for penitent believers to do.

There is another fact in the case worthy of notice just here. There is some such necessity for the co-operation of a fellow-man, in order to one's conversion, that, although the Lord himself has appeared to Saul, and conversed with him, he can not find peace of mind, though he weeps and groans and prays for three days and nights, until *Ananias* comes to him. In this particular, also, his case is like that of the eunuch, whose conversion could not be effected, though an angel had been sent from heaven, and the Spirit had operated miraculously, until the *man Philip* took his seat in the chariot. The necessity, in his case, differs from that of the eunuch, in that he needed not the man to preach Jesus to him; for this had already been done by Jesus himself. But there was *something* to be done before he obtained pardon, which a *man* must do; and the sequel will show what that something is. In the mean time, let it be observed, that all these pretended conversions of the present day, which are completely effected while the subject is in his bed at night, or alone in the grove, or praying in some solitary place, lack this something of being scriptural conversions. No man was so converted in the days of the apostles.

13–16. Ananias had already heard of Saul, doubtless through fugitive brethren from Jerusalem, and such was the horror which his name inspired, that he was reluctant to approach him, even when commanded by the Lord to do so. (13) "*Then Ananias answered, Lord, I have heard from many concerning this man, how much evil he has done to thy saints who are in Jerusalem,* (14) *and here he has authority from the high priests to bind all who call on thy name.* (15) *But the Lord said to him, Go; for he is to me a chosen vessel, to bear my name before the Gentiles, and kings, and the children of Israel.* (16) *For I will show to him how great things he must suffer on account of my name.*" Here we have a statement that the Lord had made a special choice of Saul for a certain work, and a prediction that he would suffer in the execution of it. The latter demonstrates the foreknowledge of God concerning human conduct, and the former shows that he

* Rom. v: 1.

ACTS IX: 17-19.   121

makes choice beforehand of suitable individuals to execute his purposes.

17-19. The assurance given by the Lord was sufficient to remove his fears. (17) *"And Ananias went away and entered into the house, and laid hands upon him, and said, Brother Saul, the Lord, even Jesus who appeared to you in the road in which you came, has sent me that you may receive sight, and be filled with the Holy Spirit.* (18) *And immediately there fell from his eyes something like scales, and he received sight forthwith, and arose and was immersed;* (19) *and taking food, he was strengthened."* In laying hands on Saul to restore his eyesight, Ananias imitated the example of Jesus, who wrought similar miracles, at one time by touching the eyes of the blind,* and at another by putting clay on them and directing that it be washed away.†

It is quite common to assume that Ananias also conferred the Holy Spirit upon him, by imposition of hands. But this is neither stated nor implied in the text; nor is there any evidence that any besides the apostles ever exercised the power of imparting the Spirit. The fact that this power is not known to have been exercised by any other than the apostles, establishes a strong presumption that it was not exercised by Ananias. This presumption, in the entire absence of proof to the contrary, would alone be conclusive. We do not forget that Ananias says, "Jesus has sent me that you may be filled with the Holy Spirit." This shows that his reception of the Spirit in some way depended upon the presence of Ananias, but does not imply that he received it by imposition of hands. All the other apostles received it direct from heaven, without human agency.‡ They also received it after they had been immersed; for the fact that Jesus preached the immersion of John, and caused the twelve to administer it under his eye, is proof that they themselves had submitted to it. Moreover, in every other case in the New Testament, with the single exception of Cornelius, the gift of miraculous power followed immersion. These facts furnish a firm basis for the conclusion that Saul's inspiration was awaiting his immersion; and that it depended upon the visit of Ananias, because he was sent to immerse him that he might receive pardon and be filled with the Holy Spirit. To conclude otherwise would be to make his case an exception to that of all the other apostles in reference to *manner* of receiving the Spirit, and to nearly all other disciples, including the apostles, in reference to the *time* of receiving it.

The manner in which Ananias proceeded when he reached the house of Judas presents a most remarkable contrast with the course of most Protestant preachers of the present day. Leaving out of view the miraculous restoration of Saul's eyesight, Ananias was simply sent to a man in a certain house, who had been a persecutor, but was now praying. He has no special directions as to the instruction he shall give the man, but is left to his own previous knowledge of what is proper in such cases. He comes into the house, and finds him prostrate upon the floor, almost exhausted from want of food and drink, which his wretchedness makes him refuse; and he is still praying in great agony. No man of this generation can hesitate as to the course

* Matt. ix: 29.   † John ix: 6.   ‡ Acts ii: 1-4.

one of our modern preachers would pursue in such a case. He would at once urge him to pray on, and quote to him many passages of Scripture in reference to the answer of prayer. He would tell him to believe in the Lord Jesus, and that the moment he would cast his soul entirely upon him he would be relieved. He would pray with him. Long and fervently would he call upon God to have mercy on the waiting sinner, and send down the Holy Ghost to speak peace to his troubled soul. If these efforts did not bring relief, other brethren and sisters would be called in, and their prayers united with those of the preacher. Pathetic hymns would alternate with zealous prayers and warm exhortations, until both the mourner and his comforters were exhausted, the latter every moment expecting to hear from their wretched victim a shout of joy, as the touch of God would roll away the burden from his soul. If all these efforts failed, the man would go mourning over his still unpardoned sins, perhaps for the remainder of his life. Fortunate would it be for him, if the terrible conclusion that all religion is but hypocrisy, or that he himself is an inevitable reprobate, did not take possession of his soul. This picture is not overdrawn; for my readers can testify that far deeper colors could be spread over it, by copying accurately from many thousands of cases which have occurred in popular "revivals."

Such is the baleful influence of this gross departure from the word of God, that men who are under its influence are constantly denouncing as *heretics* those who venture to follow the example of Ananias. He finds the man to whom he is sent, praying to the Lord Jesus; but, instead of commanding him to pray on, and praying with him, he says to him, "Why do you tarry? Arise, and be immersed, and wash away your sins, calling on the name of the Lord." * There are many Churches at the present day, professing to derive their creeds from the Bible, whose clergy dare not follow this example, upon pain of excommunication. Engaged in a public debate, a few years since, with a Doctor of Divinity of a numerous and powerful party, I determined to apply to him a test which had been employed before by some of my brethren, and charged that he dare not, as he valued his ministerial position, and even his membership in the Church, give to mourners seeking salvation the answers given by inspired men, in the very words which they employed. He interrupted me, by asking if I intended to insinuate that he would not preach what he believed to be the truth. I replied, that I had no disposition to question his honesty, but that I was stating a startling fact, which ought to be made to ring in the ears of the people. I then told the audience I would put my statement to a test at once, and turning to the Doctor, I said: "Sir, if you had a number of mourners before you, as Peter had on Pentecost, pierced to the heart with a sense of guilt, and exclaiming, What shall we do? would you *dare* to say to them, '*Repent* and be *baptized*, every one of you, in the name of Jesus Christ, *for the remission of sins*, and you shall receive the gift of the Holy Spirit?' Or, if you were called into a private house, like Ananias, to see a man fasting and weeping and praying, would you *dare* to say to him, 'Why do you tarry? Arise, and be baptized, and wash away your sins, calling on

* Acts xxii : 16.

the name of the Lord?' I pause for a reply." I stood waiting, and the immense audience held their breath, until the silence became painful; but the Doctor hung his head and answered *not one word.*

It is high time that the people were won back from such delusions, and made to feel the necessity of following the word of God. Ananias was guided by the apostolic commission. Seeing there were three conditions of pardon, faith, repentance, and immersion, and that Saul had already complied with the first two, he does not tantalize him by telling him to believe or urging him to repent, but commands him to do the one thing which he had not yet done, "Arise, and be immersed." He instantly obeyed; and then, for the first time since he saw the vision by the way, he was sufficiently composed to take food and drink. "Taking food, he was strengthened." Like the eunuch, it was *after* he came up out of the water that he rejoiced.

His composure and peace of mind, after being immersed, was the proper result of intelligent obedience in that institution. If he had not already learned its design, by what he knew of apostolic preaching, the words of Ananias conveyed it without ambiguity. To a sinner mourning over his guilt, seeking pardon, and knowing that the Lord alone could forgive sins, the command to be immersed and wash away his sins could convey but one idea, that, upon the washing of water over the body in immersion, the Lord would remove his sins by forgiving them. That such was the idea intended in the metaphorical expression, "wash away," would need no argument, if it had not suited the theories of modern sectaries to call it in question. It is a common assumption that Saul's sins had been *really* forgiven before his immersion, and Ananias required him only to *formally* wash them away. But this is a mere combination of words to hide the absence of an idea. How can a man *formally* do a thing which has already been *really* done, unless it be by going through a *form* which is empty and deceptive? If Saul's sins were already washed away, then he *did not* wash them away in immersion, and the language of Ananias was deceptive. But it is an indisputable fact, that at the time Ananias gave him this command he was still unhappy, and, therefore, unforgiven. Immediately after he was immersed, he was happy; and the change took place in the mean time, which connects it with his immersion. In precise accordance, therefore, with the commission, with Peter's answer on Pentecost, and with the eunuch's experience, his sins were forgiven when he was immersed.

These individual cases of conversion are of great value to one studying the plan of salvation, because they present more in detail the entire process than can be done in describing the conversion of a multitude. We now have before us two such, and will have a third in the tenth chapter, when we will find it profitable to institute a close comparison between them.*

19-22. No sooner had Saul obeyed the gospel and obtained pardon, than he began to devote all his energies to building up what he had sought to destroy. (19) "*Then Saul was some days with the disciples in Damascus,* (20) *and immediately he preached Christ in the synagogues, that this is the Son of God.* (21) *And all who heard him were aston-*

---

* See Com. x: 47, 48.

ished, and said, Is not this he who destroyed those in Jerusalem who called upon this name, and came hither for this purpose, that he might take them bound to the high priests? (22) *But Saul increased the more in strength, and confounded the Jews who dwelt in Damascus, proving that this is the Christ."* The one great gospel proposition, that Jesus is the Christ and the Son of God, the belief of which had wrought in him all the wondrous change on the road to Damascus, is now his constant theme. The synagogues being for a time open to him, and the curiosity of the people intensely excited, in reference to his change of conduct, it is probable that he had more ready access to the unbelieving Jews in Damascus than had been enjoyed by those who preceded him. Whatever opponents he encountered, were "confounded" by the proofs he presented.

In addition to proofs employed by the other apostles and teachers, Saul stood up in the synagogues as a new and independent witness of the resurrection and glorification of Jesus. He had seen him alive, and arrayed in divine glory. He had conversed with him face to face. If any man doubted the truth of his statements in reference to the vision, his traveling companions, who saw the same light, and heard the same voice, could testify with him. If any man, still incredulous, ventured the supposition that all of them were deceived by an optical illusion, or by some human trickster, the actual blindness which remained after the vision had passed away, and was witnessed by both believers and unbelievers, proved, indisputably, that it was a reality. No illusion or deception could have produced this effect. If it were suspected that Saul and his companions had made up the story, in order to deceive, the suspicion was silenced by the fact that the blindness was real, and could not be feigned. Whether, therefore, they regarded him as honest or dishonest, such was the combination of facts that they could not find an excuse for doubting his testimony. No wonder that he "*confounded* the Jews who dwelt in Damascus."

Such was the force of Saul's testimony, as it was addressed to his cotemporaries in Damascus. To others, not eye-witnesses of his career, and to men of subsequent generations, it stands thus: If the vision which he claimed to have witnessed was a reality, then Jesus is the Christ, and his religion is divine. But if it was not a reality, then Saul was deceived, or was himself a deceiver. His blindness precludes the supposition that he could have been deceived. Was he, then, a deceiver? His whole subsequent career declares that he was not. All the motives, in reference to both time and eternity, which can prompt men to deception, were arrayed against the course he was pursuing. His reputation among men, his hopes of wealth and power, his love of friendship, and his personal safety, all demanded that he should adhere to his former religious position. In making the change, he sacrificed them all, and, if he was practicing deception, he exposed himself, also, to whatever punishment he might suppose the wicked to incur in eternity. It is possible to believe that a man might, through miscalculation as to the immediate results, *begin* to practice a deception which would involve such consequences; but it is entirely incredible that he should continue to do so after his mistake was discovered, and persist in it through a long life of unparalleled sufferings. It is in credible, therefore, that Saul was a deceiver. And, as he was neither deceived himself, nor a deceiver of others, his vision must have been a reality, and Jesus *is* the Christ.

There is no way to evade the force of this argument, except by denying Luke's account of Saul's career, after his supposed conversion. But this would be to deny to Luke even the ordinary credibility attached to ancient history; for the argument depends not upon miracles, but upon the ordinary events of Saul's life, which are in themselves most credible. Supposing this much to be granted, as a basis for the argument, (and it is granted by all who are acquainted with history,) the proof of the Messiahship of Jesus from the conversion of Saul is perfectly conclusive.

23–25. Saul now begins to see enacted in Damascus scenes similar to those in which he had played a part in Jerusalem; but his own position is reversed. He begins to experience, in his turn, the ill-treatment which he had heaped upon others. (23) *"Now, when many days were fulfilled, the Jews determined to kill him; (24) but their plot was known to Saul; and they watched the gates, day and night, that they might kill him. (25) Then the disciples took him by night, and let him down through the wall in a basket."* The Jews were not alone in this plot. Dwelling as strangers in a foreign city, they would hardly have ventured upon so murderous an undertaking without the connivance of the authorities. Paul himself informs us that the governor of the city lent them his active co-operation. He says: "In Damascus, the governor under Aretas, the king, kept watch over the city with a garrison, desiring to apprehend me."* From the same passage in Second Corinthians, we learn that it was through a *window* in the wall that he was let down. Even to the present day there are houses in Damascus built against the wall, with the upper stories projecting beyond the top of the wall, and containing windows which would anwer admirably for such a mode of escape. The observations of modern travelers are constantly bringing to light topographical facts which accord most happily with the inspired narrative. Another such is the fact that there is yet a street in Damascus running in a straight line from the eastern gate for about a mile, to the palace of the Pasha, which can be no other than "the street called Straight," on which Judas lived, and where Ananias found Saul.†

It was three years from the time of his conversion that Saul made this escape from Damascus. The whole of this period had not been spent in that city, but he had made a preaching tour into Arabia, and returned to Damascus. This we learn from his own pen: "I conferred not with flesh and blood, neither went I up to Jerusalem to them who were apostles before me; but I went into Arabia, and returned again into Damascus. Then, after three years, I went up to Jerusalem to see Peter."‡ It is quite probable that some excitement attendant upon his preaching in other parts of the dominions of King Aretas had some influence in securing the ready co-operation of the Arabian governor with the Jews, in trying to take his life.

26, 27. The mortification of Saul at being compelled to thus escape from Damascus was remembered for many years, to be mentioned

---
*2 Cor. xi: 32, 33.   † Kitto's Encyclopedia, Art. Damascus.   ‡ Gal. i: 16–18.

when he would "glory in the things which concerned his infirmities."* He had not yet seen any of those who were apostles before him since he left them in Jerusalem to go on his murderous mission to Damascus. He turns his steps in that direction, resolved to go up and see Peter.† We will not attempt to depict the probable emotions of the now devout apostle, as the walls of Jerusalem and the towering hight of the temple came once more into view. As he approached the gate of the city, he passed by the spot where Stephen was stoned, and where he himself had stood, "consenting to his death." He was about to meet again, on the streets, and in the synagogues, his old allies whom he had deserted, and the disciples whom he had persecuted. The tumult of emotions which the scenes about him must have excited, we leave to the imagination of the reader, and the pages of more voluminous writers.‡ We know the reception which awaited him both from friends and foes. (26) *"And when he arrived in Jerusalem he attempted to join himself to the disciples, but they were all afraid of him, not believing that he was a disciple.* (27) *But Barnabas took him and brought him to the apostles, and related to them how he had seen the Lord in the way, and that he had spoken to him, and how he had spoken boldly in Damascus in the name of Jesus."* This ignorance of the brethren in reference to the events of the past three years in Damascus is somewhat surprising; but it only proves that they had no rapid means of communication with the brethren in that city. It is not probable that Barnabas had any means of information not enjoyed by the other brethren. Doubtless he obtained his information from Saul's own lips, either because he was prompted to do so by the generous impulses of his own heart, or because Saul, having some knowledge of his generosity, sought him out as the one most likely to give him a candid hearing. In either case, it would not be difficult for him to credit the unvarnished story, told, as it must have been, with an earnestness and pathos which no impostor could assume. When Barnabas was once convinced, it was easy for him to convince the apostles; and the warm sympathy which he manifested for Saul was the beginning of a friendship between them which was fruitful in blessings to the Church and to the world.

28, 29. Though the brethren, even at the solicitation of Barnabas, may have received him with some misgivings, the course he pursued soon won their confidence. (28) *"And he was with them coming in and going out in Jerusalem,* (29) *and spoke boldly in the name of the Lord Jesus, and disputed against the Hellenists; but they undertook to kill him."* During his three years' absence from Jerusalem, the persecution of which he had been the leader had so far abated that the Hellenists were once more willing to debate the points at issue. But they found in their new opponent one equally invincible with Stephen, and, in the madness of defeat, resolved that Stephen's fate should be his.

30. In this emergency, the brethren found opportunity to make amends for the suspicion with which they had at first regarded him. (30) *"And when the brethren knew this, they took him down to Cæsarea, and sent him forth to Tarsus."* We learn, from Paul's own account of this movement, that it was not controlled by his own judgment, nor

---

* 2 Cor. xi: 30–33. † Gal. i: 18. ‡ See Life and Ep., vol. 1, p. 101.

entirely by that of the brethren. While praying in the temple, he fell into a trance, in which the Lord appeared to him, and said, "Make haste, and get quickly out of Jerusalem; for they will not receive your testimony concerning me." Saul had, himself, come to a very different conclusion. Notwithstanding the murderous disposition of his opponents, he still believed that his labors among them would prove successful. He argued upon the supposition that his former position as a persecutor, like them, would now give peculiar weight, with them, to his testimony and arguments; and he ventured to urge this consideration upon the attention of the Lord: "Lord, they know that I am imprisoned and beat in every synagogue those who believe on thee; and when the blood of Stephen thy witness was shed, I was myself standing by and consenting to his death, and keeping the raiment of those who slew him." But he had erred in overlooking the peculiar odium attached to the character of one who could be styled a *deserter*, inclining men to listen more favorably to an habitual opponent than to him. The Lord did not argue the case with him, but peremptorily commanded him, "Depart; for I will send you far hence to the Gentiles."* The fears of the brethren were confirmed by this decision of the Lord, and they promptly sent him to a place of safety.

After reaching Cæsarea, a short voyage on the Mediterranean and up the Cydnus brought him to Tarsus, the home of his childhood, and perhaps of his earlier manhood. He returns to his aged parents and the friends of his childhood, a fugitive from two great cities, and a deserter from that strictest sect in which he had been educated; but he comes to bring them glad tidings of great joy. He disappears, at this point, from the pages of Luke; but he does not retire into inactivity. His own pen fills up the blank that is left here by the historian. He says that he went "into the regions of *Syria* and *Cilicia*, and was unknown by face to the Churches in Judea who were in Christ; but they 'heard only that he who once persecuted us is now preaching the faith which he once destroyed. And they glorified God in me."† Not long after this we find mention of *brethren* in Syria and Cilicia, which renders it probable that his labors there were attended with his usual success. We have reason also to believe that he encountered, during this interval, a portion of the sufferings enumerated in the eleventh chapter of Second Corinthians; such as the five times that he received from the Jews forty stripes save one, the three shipwrecks, and the night and day that he spent in the deep. We can not refer them to a later period; for, from this interval to the time of writing that epistle, we have a continuous history of his life, in which they do not occur.

We now part company with Saul for a time, and while he is performing labors, and enduring afflictions, the full detail of which we will never learn till we meet him in eternity, we turn with our inspired guide, to contemplate some instructive scenes in the labors of the Apostle Peter.

31. Preparatory to this transition in the narrative, the historian glances rapidly over the territory to which we are about to be introduced, stating the condition of things immediately after Saul's depart-

* Acts xxii: 17-21. † Gal. i: 21-24.

ure for Tarsus. (31) "*Then the Churches had peace throughout all Judea, and Galilee, and Samaria; and being edified, and walking in the fear of the Lord, and the consolation of the Holy Spirit, they were multiplied.*" Thus times of peace and quiet were seen to be propitious to a cause which had sprung up amid strife and opposition, showing that it was not the obstinacy of human passion, but the legitimate working of unchangeable truth, which had brought it into being. According to the philosophy which Gamaliel had urged in the Sanhedrim,* its claim to a divine origin was now vindicated.

32–35. We have just seen Saul sent "far hence to the Gentiles;" but as yet we have had no account of the admission of uncircumcised Gentiles into the Church; it is time that this account should be before us, and Luke proceeds to give it. He approaches the subject by relating the circumstances which led Peter, who was the chosen instrument for opening the gates of the kingdom to the Gentiles, into the city of Joppa, where the messengers of Cornelius found him. We parted company with this apostle on his return with John from the visit to Samaria. We meet him again, engaged in active labor through the rural districts of his native country. (32) "*Now it came to pass that Peter, passing through all quarters, came down also to the saints who dwelt at Lydda. (33) And he found there a certain man named Æneas, who had kept his bed eight years, and was paralyzed. (34) And Peter said to him, Æneas, Jesus the Christ heals you. Arise, and make your bed. And he arose immediately. (35) And all who dwelt at Lydda and Saron saw him and turned to the Lord.*" The long continuance of painful disease makes the afflicted individual well known to a large circle of neighbors, and fixes their attention upon the disease itself as one difficult to cure. Hence, the effect upon this community of the cure of Æneas, like that of the lame man at the Beautiful gate of the temple, was decisive and almost universal. It was a demonstration of divine power in Jesus the Christ, whom Peter had declared the agent of the cure, which the honest people of Lydda and Saron could not gainsay, and therefore they had no honest alternative but to yield to his claims.

36–43. From the midst of these happy and peaceful triumphs of the truth, Peter was suddenly called away to Joppa. The circumstances which led to this event are thus related by Luke: (36) "*Now, in Joppa, there was a certain disciple named Tabitha, which, translated, is Dorcas.† This woman was full of good works and alms which she did. (37) And it came to pass, in those days, that she took sick and died. They washed her, and laid her in an upper room. (38) And Lydda being near to Joppa, the disciples, hearing that Peter was in that place, sent two men to him, entreating him not to delay to come to them. (39) Then Peter arose and went with them. When he arrived, they led him up into the upper room, and all the widows stood by him, weeping, and showing the tunics and mantles which Dorcas made while she was with them. (40) But Peter put them all out, and kneeled down and prayed: and, turning to the body, he said, Tabitha, arise. She opened her eyes; and, seeing Peter, she sat up. (41) Giving her his hand, he caused her to stand up;*

* Acts v: 34–39. † Which, again translated into English, is a *gazel.*

and, having called the saints and widows, he presented her alive. (42) *It became known throughout all Joppa, and many believed in the Lord.*"

Nothing could be more graphic and simple than this narration, or more touching than the incident itself. Amid the array of solemn and stately events which are moving before us, it is dropped in, like a flower in the forest. It opens a vista through the larger events of history, and lets in light upon the social sorrows of the early saints, awakening a closer sympathy between our hearts and theirs. We here see enacted among them scenes with which we are familiar, when one who has been noted for good works sickens and dies: the same anxiety felt by all; the same desire for the presence of him who had been their religious counselor; the same company of weeping sisters, and brethren standing by in mournful silence. As each good deed of the departed is recounted by some sobbing voice, and the garments "which she made while she was with us," to clothe the poor, are held up to view, how the eyes gush! how the heart swells! These are sacred hours. The labors of a whole life of piety are pouring their rich influence, unresisted, into softened hearts. How blessed are the dead who die in the Lord! They rest from their labors, but their works do follow them, still working while they are at rest. When Peter came into that company of weeping disciples, he seems to stand once more beside his master, as once he and all who were with him wept with Mary and Martha over the tomb of Lazarus. But he remembers that his compassionate master is now in heaven. With deep solemnity, he motions the mourners all aside. He is left alone with the dead, and the company without have hushed their sobs into silent suspense. He kneels down and prays. How the heart turns to God beside the bed of death! How fervent our prayers are then! The prayer of faith is heard. The eyes of the dead are opened, and the faith and hope which glowed in them ere they were closed are in them now. She sees the loved apostle, and rises to a sitting posture. He takes her by the hand, raises her to her feet, and calls in her friends. Who can describe the scene, when brothers and sisters in the flesh and in the Lord, wild with conflicting emotions, rushed in to greet the loved one recovered from the dead! And if that is indescribable, what shall we say or think of that scene when all the sainted dead shall rise in glory, and greet each other on the shores of life? May Christ our Savior help us to that day! We have no Peter now, to wake up our sleeping sisters, and give them back to us; but we do not regret it, for we remember that Dorcas had to die again, and we would not wish to weep again, as we have wept, over the dying bed, and the fresh sods of the silent grave. We would rather let them sleep on in the arms of Jesus, till both we and they shall rise to die no more.

43. Peter was engaged, at this time, in general evangelizing among the Jews, adapting his stay at a given point, and his change of place, to the exigencies of the cause. The restoration of Dorcas, doubtless, opened a wide field for usefulness in the surrounding community, (43) "*and he tarried many days in Joppa, with one Simon, a tanner.*" Here the historian leaves him for awhile, and introduces us to the circumstances which removed him from this to another field of labor.

X: 1–2. The scene changes from Joppa to Cæsarea, about thirty miles northward along the Mediterranean shore; and we are introduced to another case for conversion, a Gentile and a soldier (1) *"There was a certain man in Cæsarea named Cornelius, a centurion of the cohort called Italian, (2) a devout man, and one who feared God with all his house, who gave much alms to the people, and prayed to God continually."* We desire to examine, with great care, the process of this man's conversion, and begin by noticing the present religious elements of his character. He is a "devout man"—a man of deep religious feelings. He is not a devout pagan, but he "fears God," the true God. He must, then, be somewhat acquainted with the Jewish religion. He is not identified with the Jews, being uncircumcised. He is not a timid or unfaithful worshiper of God, but has taught all his family the same worship. He gives much alms to the people, and is a praying man.

At first glance, it might appear strange that such a man should *need* conversion. There are many men, at the present day, in whose favor not so much can be said, who flatter themselves that their prospects for eternity are good. They are honest in their business, honorable in their intercourse with men, good husbands and fathers, generous to their neighbors, and benevolent to the poor; what have they to fear at the hands of a just and merciful God? They forget that their obligations to God are infinitely higher than those to men, even to the dearest friends on earth; and that, therefore, it is the most inexcusable of all sins to persistently refuse him the worship which is his due. This offense takes the hue of the blackest ingratitude, when we remember the blood which has been shed to touch our hearts, and to open up to us the way of pardon and eternal life. Of this crime every man is guilty who does not worship the living God, and submit to the ordinances of Jesus Christ. But Cornelius was a praying man, a devout worshiper of God, besides possessing every other virtue claimed by self-righteous sinners; yet it was necessary for even him to hear "words by which he *might be saved*."* Until a man can claim for himself something more than is here said of him, he may not flatter himself with the hope of salvation.

Under the former dispensation, the piety and fidelity of Cornelius would have given him an honorable place among the holy men of God; but this alone could not suffice him now. Jesus the Christ had stepped in between God and man, and opened, through the rent vail of his flesh, the only access to God. All heaven had confessed his authority, and the holy disciples on earth had come to the Father by him. But Cornelius was still calling upon God, without the name of Christ, and seeking to approach him by the old, not by the new and living way. He was in the same condition with any pious but unbelieving Jew of that or of our own age. It was necessary to his salvation that he should believe in Jesus and obey him. This would secure to him the pardon of his sins, which he had not and could not secure by worshiping according to the law.

3-6. This defect in his religious character was not a fault; it was only a misfortune. He was doing the best he knew how; and, if we may infer what he prayed for, from what he obtained in answer to his

* Acts xi: 14.

prayers, he was praying for additional knowledge, and perhaps for an interest in the salvation offered through Christ. Such a prayer, offered by such a man, is always acceptable to God. On a certain day he had fasted till in the afternoon, and at three o'clock was praying within his house,* when (3) "*He saw distinctly in a vision, about the ninth hour of the day, an angel of God coming in to him and saying to him, Cornelius.* (4) *He looked intently upon him, and was full of fear, and said, What is it, Lord? He said to him, Thy prayers and thine alms have come up for a memorial before God.* (5) *And now, send men to Joppa, and call for one Simon who is surnamed Peter.* (6) *He is lodging with a certain Simon, a tanner, whose house is by the sea-shore. He will tell you what you ought to do.*"

Here is an unconverted man praying, and his prayer is answered. But the circumstances of the man, the nature of the prayer, and the answer given, are all essentially different from those of unconverted men who are taught to pray by the Protestant sects of the present day. The man was not instructed in a knowledge of the Redeemer, and the way of salvation, and of his own interest in the same, but neglecting his duty, as is the case with the modern sinner. Neither was he praying for pardon, while postponing obedience to the gospel, as in these cases; but his prayer was for a *knowledge* of his duty, and he had no one by to instruct him. The answer to his prayer was given, not, as is now so often pretended, by sending forth the Spirit into his heart to speak his sins forgiven, but by sending an angel to tell him where he can find a *man* who will guide him in the way of salvation.

In the case of the eunuch, an angel appeared to the preacher and sent him to the inquirer. In this case, the angel appears to the inquirer, and tells him to send for the preacher. In both cases, the only work of the angel was to bring the two men together, face to face. Thus, again, we see an insuperable necessity, in case of a scriptural conversion, for the presence and co-operation of a human agent, showing that the divine influences, whatever, and however numerous they may be, reach the heart *through* the word of truth. The prayer of Cornelius was answered, like that of Saul, by referring him to inspired authorities within the Church. This shows how vain, at the present day, must be every prayer for direct answers from heaven, in reference to the pardon of sins. If a verbal answer to such prayers could be obtained, we are bound to conclude, from these precedents, that it would still be, "Go to Damascus and it shall be told you," or "Send men to Joppa for Simon whose surname is Peter, and he will tell you what you ought to do." Peter and Ananias are before us now, with the same instruction which they gave then, and it is useless for us to offer for what we have in hand, prayers which Saul and Cornelius offered for what had not yet been granted. The directions given by the two teachers, in these cases, and by other inspired men, is all that God granted to sinners then, and it is certainly all that we have a right to ask for now.

The necessity for the spoken word in order to the conversion of men is not only exhibited in these missions of angels, but it also ex-

* Verse 30.

plains the occurrence, in the two cases of Cornelius and the eunuch, of an agency not discernible in other cases. If no heavenly messenger had been sent to Philip, he could not have known that there was an Ethiopian on the road to Gaza, reading his Bible, and ready to hear the gospel. And if no angel had appeared to Cornelius, he could not have known that he had any interest in the blood of Jesus, or any right to send for Peter. No human being could have informed him, because all others, including Peter, were as ignorant of it as himself. An interposition from heaven is necessary; but when it occurs, it provides only for just such demands of the case as could not be supplied without it. The multitude on Pentecost needed no such angelic aid, for the preacher was before them, and each party was conscious of the right to speak, on the one hand, and the right to obey, on the other. So with us. When we wish any information, or the enjoyment of any religious privilege, we have the apostles before us, face to face. Their words are in our hands, and may be in our minds and hearts. We have no need for heavenly apparitions or illuminations; and if we expect them, we will be disappointed, or deluded. If a man in ignorance prays for a knowledge of salvation, this incident in the case of Cornelius, instead of encouraging him to pray on, actually answers his prayer, by telling him to send for some man who understands the gospel, and will guide him as Peter did Cornelius.

Before proceeding further in this case of conversion, we wish the reader to observe that enough has occurred already to secure Cornelius's recognition as a genuine convert, by the prevailing Protestant parties of this day. Let any man come before the Church with such an experience as his, saying, "I have been for many years a devout man, worshiping God as well as I knew how, giving alms to the poor, praying continually, and teaching all my family the fear of God. Yesterday afternoon, at three o'clock, I was praying, according to my custom, when suddenly a holy angel stood before me, and said, Thy prayers and thine alms have come up for a memorial before God." Who would doubt that he was "powerfully converted," or dare to insinuate that there was any thing else necessary in the case? He would receive the right-hand of fellowship at once. Yet, so different was the apostolic procedure, that the man was now only prepared to *hear words* by which he *might* be saved. How long will religious men allow their inventions and traditions to nullify the word of God?

7–8. (7) "*And when the angel who spoke to Cornelius went away, he called two of his household servants, and a devout soldier of those who attended him,* (8) *and having fully related all these things to them, he sent them to Joppa.*" The two servants are included in the household, who with him feared God, and the soldier selected had also learned the same great lesson. None but men of such character would be suitable messengers in a case like this.

9–16. The scene of the narrative now changes again, from Cæsarea back to Joppa, and to the house of the tanner, where we left the Apostle Peter. Leaving the messengers of Cornelius on the way, Luke anticipates their arrival, and relates how Peter was prepared for the favorable reception of their message. (9) "*Now, on the next day, while they were on their journey, and were drawing near to the city, Peter went*

ACTS X: 10–16.

up upon the house to pray, about the sixth hour. (10) *He was very hungry, and desired to eat; but while they were preparing, he fell into a trance,* (11) *and saw heaven opened, and saw a certain vessel descending, like a great white sheet tied by the four corners, and let down to the earth;* (12) *in which were all kinds of four-footed animals and wild beasts and reptiles of the earth, and birds of the air.* (13) *And there came a voice to him, Rise, Peter; kill and eat.* (14) *But Peter said, Not so, Lord; for I have never eaten any thing common or unclean.* (15) *And the voice spoke to him again the second time, What God has cleansed, do not you call common.* (16) *This was done three times, and the vessel was taken up again into heaven."*

In order to fully appreciate the necessity for this vision, we must remember the prejudice of the Jews against uncircumcised Gentiles. Previous to the Babylonish captivity, they had too great an inclination to intimacy with their idolatrous neighbors; but that terrible affliction cured them of idolatry, and when they returned to their own land, they put away, at the instigation of Nehemiah, all the idolatrous wives among them.* This was the beginning of a reaction toward the opposite extreme, and such a state of feeling was finally induced, that, in the traditions of the elders, it was regarded as a sin even to go into the house of one who was uncircumcised. The disciples of Jesus had been educated from their childhood to an intense degree of this prejudice, and there were facts in the history of Jesus calculated to foster rather than to eradicate it. They had heard him say, "I am not sent save to the lost sheep of the house of Israel."† They had seen him work no miracle for a Gentile except under the protest, "It is not proper to take the children's food and cast it to dogs."‡ And when he had sent them out on their first mission, he had commanded them, "Go not into the way of the Gentiles, and enter not into a city of the Samaritans; but go rather to the lost sheep of the house of Israel."|| It is true, that in their final commission he had commanded them to disciple and immerse all nations; but they very naturally interpreted this in the light of past experience, and concluded that all nations were to be gradually absorbed into the Jewish commonwealth by circumcision, and afterward brought into the Church. They had not hesitated, therefore, to immerse proselytes, and even to give them office in the Church,§ though they still regarded it as a sin to enter the house of a Gentile who was uncircumcised.¶

This fact in the mental state of the apostles shows that they were not guided by the Holy Spirit into all truth at once, but their knowledge was extended according to the demands of the occasion. It was a prejudice, however, belonging to them as Jews, which had prevented them, thus far, from perceiving the particular truth here involved; and this involves the conclusion that prejudices previously imbibed were capable of impeding the inspiring influence, so that special measures were required for their eradication.

The time had now arrived when this prejudice must be uprooted from the heart of Peter. If it were a part of the work of the indwelling

---

* Neh. xiii : 23–31. † Matt. xv : 24. ‡ Matt. xv : 26.
|| Matt. x : 5 6. § See Com. vi : 5. ¶ Acts xi : 3.

Spirit to act immediately upon the heart, then there need be nothing more done with Peter than for the Spirit thus to act. But there is not the slightest intimation of any such action. On the contrary, influences of an entirely different nature are brought to bear upon him, and to them the effect is plainly attributed. A series of significant objects are presented to his eye, certain words are addressed to his ear, and a combination of facts are brought to bear upon his understanding. Falling into a trance, while hungrily awaiting his noonday meal, he sees, descending from heaven, and then spread out before him, a great sheet full of animals, both clean and unclean. This vision conveys no meaning, until he hears the words, "Arise, Peter; kill and eat." He now understands it as indicating that he shall eat unclean animals. But this is so shocking to his sense of propriety that he exclaims, in perplexity, even to the invisible God who had spoken to him, "Not so, Lord; for I have never eaten any thing common or unclean." But he is commanded, "What I have cleansed, do not you call common." The vessel is brought near to him, and the same words repeated three times. Then the vision closes, and he recovers from the trance.

17–20. Restored now to his natural state of mind, Peter remains upon the house-top, reflecting upon the vision, and wondering if there was not some meaning in it besides that in reference to unclean animals. The question was soon solved. (17) *"Now when Peter was doubting in himself what this vision which he had seen could mean, behold, the men who were sent from Cornelius, having inquired out the house of Simon, were standing at the gate:* (18) *and calling, they inquired if Simon surnamed Peter was lodging there.* (19) *But Peter was still thinking of the vision, and the Spirit said to him, Behold, three men are seeking you.* (20) *Arise, therefore, and go down and go with them, doubting nothing, for I have sent them."* In the skillful arrangements of divine wisdom, all the separate influences which are to remove Peter's prejudices are adjusting themselves for combined and harmonious action. Those men have been on their journey two days, but God had measured their steps to the house of Simon, and timed the appearance of the vision to the motion of their feet, so that when they reach the gate he is still on the house-top, absorbed in reflection; but ere they are admitted to the house, the Spirit has sent him down to meet them, and to go with them.

21–22. He knows nothing, as yet, of the nature of their mission, neither does he yet understand any better than before the meaning of the vision. (21) *"Then Peter went down to the men, and said, Behold, I am he whom you are seeking. What is the cause for which you are come?* (22) *And they said, Cornelius, a centurion, a just man, and one who fears God, and of good report among all the nation of the Jews, was warned from God by a holy angel to send for you into his house, and to hear words from you."* Upon hearing these words, the whole truth at once flashed upon the mind of Peter, and the agencies which for two days had been preparing to uproot his prejudice, sprang upon it with their combined force. No less than an angel from God has sent these men to call me into the house of a Gentile, to preach the gospel to him. My vision of clean and unclean beasts is explained. God has cleansed the Gentiles, and I am no longer to call them unclean. The Spirit has commanded me to go with these men, without doubting. The authority of God, of an angel, of the Holy Spirit, all impel me. I can resist no longer. His prejudice is gone, and doubtless he feels a new thrill of joy as his heart tremulously enlarges to take the whole world within the embrace of his philanthropy.

23. As the Spirit had directed, he does not hesitate as to the line of duty, but at once announces to the messengers that the journey shall begin to-morrow. (23) "*Then, calling them in, he lodged them; and on the next day Peter went out with them, and certain brethren from Joppa went with him.*" It was a wise precaution that he took other brethren with him, so that the whole of this new movement might be properly attested by competent and disinterested witnesses.

24. During the four days which had elapsed, Cornelius had made no secret of the vision he had witnessed, but had communicated it to such friends as were likely to take the same interest in it with himself. Having presumed, with all confidence, that Peter would come, and knowing the time that the journey would require, all was in readiness for his arrival. (24) "*On the next day they entered into Cæsarea. Cornelius was waiting for them, having called together his kinsmen and intimate friends.*" These friends and relatives, it must be remembered, and not the mere *family* of Cornelius, were the chief part of the audience about to be addressed by Peter.

25–27. (25) "*Now as Peter was coming in, Cornelius met him, and fell down at his feet and worshiped.* (26) *But Peter raised him up, and said, Stand up. I myself also am a man.* (27) *And conversing with him, he came in and found many who had come together.*" It is not in keeping with the character of Cornelius to suppose that he rendered to Peter such worship as is due to God. But prostration was the common attitude of approach to a superior, as it yet is in eastern countries, and Cornelius was but complying with this custom. To Peter, however, it appeared as if he intended something more, and hence the rebuke.

28, 29. Upon entering the house of this Gentile, side by side with him, and into the presence of others who were likewise uncircumcised, Peter deemed it proper to inform them of his reason for thus departing from a well-known Jewish custom. (28) "*And he said to them, You know that it is unlawful for a Jew to attach himself to, or to come into the house of one of another nation. Yet God has showed me that I should not call any man common or unclean.* (29) *Therefore, I came without objecting when I was sent for. I ask, then, for what purpose you sent for me?*" This speech shows clearly that Peter had interpreted the vision of unclean beasts as referring to *men* as well as to animal food.

30–33. (30) "*Then Cornelius said, Four days ago I was fasting until this hour, and at the ninth hour I was praying in my house, and behold, a man stood before me in bright apparel,* (31) *and said, Cornelius, your prayer is heard, and your alms are had in remembrance before God.* (32) *Send, therefore, to Joppa, and call for Simon who is surnamed Peter.*

He is lodging in the house of Simon, a tanner, by the sea-shore. When he comes he will speak to you. (33) *Immediately, therefore, I sent for you, and you have done well that you have come. Now, then, we are all present here before God to hear all things which are by God commanded you."* In this last remark Cornelius speaks for his friends who were assembled, as well as for himself. As was becoming the occasion, he had gathered in, to hear the expected messenger, only those who were willing to hear him as a messenger of God. In the statement that they were all present before God to hear what he had commanded, there was an implied pledge to obey what they might hear, and there is no doubt, from the sequel, that such was their purpose.

34, 35. The scene before Peter enlarges his conceptions of the purpose of God; for he now sees that his mission is designed not for the benefit of Cornelius alone, but for a large number of his Gentile friends; and if for all these, then, there is to be no further national limitation to the gospel. He gives utterance to this conception. (34) *" Then Peter opened his mouth and said, In truth I perceive that God is not a respecter of persons; (35) but, in every nation, he that fears him and works righteousness is acceptable to him."* This expansive thought was sufficient to burst asunder all the exclusive bonds of the Mosaic institution, and should be sufficient now to explode the equally injurious theory of an arbitrary predestination of certain men and angels to their eternal destiny.* It is a positive declaration that God respects not *persons* but *character*. To *fear* him, and to *work righteousness*, and not any other distinction between persons, is the ground of acceptability with him.

36–38. Cornelius has now related to Peter such an experience, as, we have seen above, would secure him recognition as a genuine convert to Christ among Protestant sects; but Peter was so far from regarding it in this light, that he proceeds to preach to them as he would to other sinners. We will consider his speech by the sections into which it naturally divides itself. (36) *" You know the word which God sent to the children of Israel, preaching peace through Jesus Christ, (he is Lord of all,) (37) the word which was published throughout all Judea, beginning from Galilee after the immersion which John preached, (38) concerning Jesus of Nazareth, how that God anointed him with the Holy Spirit and with power; who went about doing good and healing all who were oppressed by the devil, because God was with him."* From this it appears that Cornelius and his friends were familiar with the personal history of Jesus, and even with the message of peace which God had caused him to preach to the children of Israel. The information which they lacked, therefore, was only that which referred to their own interest in that message.

39. Not content with assuming that these facts were familiar to them, he gives them a surer foundation for their convictions, by presenting the testimony upon which he relies to prove the facts. (39) *"And we are witnesses of all things which he did both in the land of the Jews and in Jerusalem, whom they slew, hanging him upon a tree."* In view of the fact that Cornelius had been "warned from God by a holy

---

* See Westminster Conf., ch. iii: sec. 5.

angel," to send for Peter and hear what he had to say, no confirmation of this his testimony was needed. They were prepared to receive every thing he might say to them as a message from God.

40, 41. The crowning fact of the gospel comes next in the statement. (40) "*Him God raised up the third day, and showed him openly,* (41) *not to all the people, but to witnesses chosen by God beforehand, even to us, who did eat and drink with him after he arose from the dead.*" Here Peter states, by way of commending to his hearers the evidence of the resurrection, a fact which has been so differently construed by infidels, as to be made a ground of objection to it; that is, that the witnesses were chosen for the occasion. Whether Peter or the infidels are right in judgment, depends entirely upon the grounds of the choice. If they were chosen because of a dishonest desire to prove the fact, or because of the ease with which they might be deceived into the belief of a fact which had no real existence, then it may be rightly regarded as a suspicious circumstance. But the reverse is true in both particulars. Such was the situation of the witnesses, that there was great danger both to property and person, in giving their testimony, and therefore every motive to dishonesty prompted them to keep silent rather than to testify. They were also the least likely of all the men of Israel to be deceived, because of their long familiarity with the person of him who was to be identified. Peter, then, was right; for the fact that *such* witnesses were chosen beforehand is proof that no deception was intended; while the fact that they "did eat and drink with him after he arose from the dead," rendered it impossible for them to be deceived.

42, 43. Having now followed the career of Jesus from the beginning to his resurrection and exhibition of himself alive to the witnesses, Peter proceeds in regular order to the next historical fact, the giving of the apostolic commission. (42) "*And he commanded us to preach to the people, and to testify that it is he who is ordained by God the judge of the living and the dead.* (43) *To him all the prophets testify that every one who believes in him shall, through his name, receive remission of sins.*"

The declaration that every one who believes in him shall receive remission of sins has been construed as proof that remission of sins is dependent on faith only. But the fact that Peter is here stating what Jesus commanded the apostles to preach should prevent such a construction of his words; for, in the commission to which he refers, immersion is connected with faith, as a condition of pardon. His words must be construed consistently with this fact. There is no difficulty in doing this, for it is a common apostolic usage to employ faith as an equivalent for all the conditions of pardon. To deny that immersion is for remission of sins, because, in a condensed statement like this, it is not specifically mentioned, is not less subversive of the truth than to deny that repentance is a condition because *it* is not mentioned. It is not sufficient to reply to this, that repentance was always *implied* in genuine faith; for it certainly was not more uniformly attendant upon faith than was immersion. It would be as difficult to find, in apostolic times, a penitent believer who was not *immersed*, without unnecessary delay, as a genuine believer who was not *penitent.* All believers who repented were invariably immersed. Of course, we exclude from this remark all cases which occurred previous to the date of the commission.

If any one, dissatisfied with this explanation, is disposed to insist that Peter's declaration, that *every one* who believes in Jesus shall receive remission of sins, must include those—if any there be—who believe, but are not immersed, we have but to show the absurdity of the assumption by referring to a parallel case in which there can be no dispute. The Apostle John says: "*Whosoever* shall confess that Jesus is the Son of God, God dwells in him, and he in God."* He who would conclude, from this remark, that the only condition of communion with God is to *confess* that Jesus is his Son, subverts the truth no more than he who makes the assumption in question; for the universality of the declaration is the same in both, and there is no limitation expressed in either.

There is no one fact more distinctly stated in Acts than that believers should repent and be immersed for the remission of sins:† hence, there can scarcely be a grosser perversion of the word of God than to construe other statements of the Scripture so as to deny the truth of this. A condition of pardon once stated can never be set aside by any less than express divine authority.

It should be observed, further, that the statement in question is not absolutely that "every one who believes in him shall receive remission of sins;" but that he shall receive it "*through his name.*" The expression, "through his name," was not thrown in here at random; for the inspired apostles never spoke at random. It has a well-defined meaning, and was intended to qualify the sentence of which it forms a part. What we receive *through* his name certainly can not reach us until we attain some connection *with* his name. But we are *immersed into* his name with that of the Father and the Holy Spirit; hence it is at the time of this immersion, that the believer receives remission of sins *through* his name.

44–46. We are next informed of a fact which is new to this narrative, and was very surprising both to Peter and his companions. (44) "*While Peter was yet speaking these words, the Holy Spirit fell upon all those who were hearing the word,* (45) *and the believers of the circumcision who came with Peter were astonished, because on the Gentiles was poured out the gift of the Holy Spirit.* (46) *For they heard them speaking in tongues, and magnifying God.*" The matter of astonishment to the Jewish brethren was not merely that these men received the Spirit; for if Peter had gone on to finish his discourse, promising them the gift of the Holy Spirit as he did on Pentecost,‡ and had then immersed them, these brethren would have understood, as a matter of course, that they received the Holy Spirit. And if, after this, he had laid hands on them, as he did on the Samaritans, even miraculous manifestations of the Spirit could have created no surprise. The circumstances which caused the astonishment were: *First,* That the Holy Spirit was "poured out" upon them directly from God, as it had never been before on any but the apostles; *Second,* That this unusual gift was bestowed upon *Gentiles.*

* 1 John iv: 15. † See Acts ii: 38. ‡ Acts ii: 38.

ACTS X: 44-46.

In attempting to classify the manifestations of the Holy Spirit known in this history, we are compelled to distinguish the case before us from the gift of the Spirit enjoyed by all disciples in common, by the fact that these parties "spoke in tongues;" and from the gift of the Spirit bestowed on the Samaritans, by the fact that it was bestowed without prayer or imposition of hands. We have no event with which to classify it except that which occurred on Pentecost. That these two events constitute a class by themselves is further evident from the fact that these parties alone are said to be "*immersed* in the Holy Spirit."* These two are the only instances of immersion in the Holy Spirit on record, and they are distinguished from other gifts of tongues, in that they alone were bestowed without human agency.

There is only one passage of Scripture in even apparent conflict with this conclusion, which, from the interpretation frequently given to it, demands some notice in this connection. It is the statement of Paul: "By one Spirit we were all immersed into one body, whether Jews or Greeks, whether bond or free, and have all been made to drink of one Spirit."† If the apostle intends by this to assert that all the disciples "were immersed in the Holy Spirit," then this immersion was not peculiar to the apostles and the house of Cornelius. The question turns upon the reference of the word *immerse;* whether it is to immersion in water or immersion in the Spirit. It is settled by the fact that the immersion here spoken of is that which introduces "into the one body." We know by the commission that immersion in water brought its proper subjects "into the name of the Father, and of the Son, and of the Holy Spirit." But when, and by whatever means, men were brought into the relation expressed in these words, it is indisputable that they were brought into the one body. It was immersion in water, therefore, by which "all were immersed into one body." Moreover, the immersion in the Holy Spirit did not have this effect; for the apostles were in the one body *before* they were immersed in the Spirit, and Cornelius was immersed in the Spirit *before* he was immersed into the name of the Father, Son, and Holy Spirit. This makes it certain that the passage in question is not in conflict with our conclusion. As to Paul's assertion that the immersion into one body was "*by* one Spirit," the words "by one Spirit" are a declaration that the immersion had taken place under the *direction* of the one Spirit who was the author of all the gifts mentioned in the connection in which the passage occurs.‡

The immersion of Cornelius and his friends in the Holy Spirit previous to their immersion in water has been urged as proof that remission of sins takes place before immersion. But it can furnish no such proof unless it be first proved that the Holy Spirit could not be imparted to a man who was yet unpardoned. If Cornelius had been a man of gross wickedness, there would seem to be some incongruity in such an impartation; but, in view of his real character, and the fact that God had previously sent an angel to express his approbation of his conduct, there appears no incongruity in this circumstance.

This incident in the conversion of Cornelius can not, in any way, be held as a precedent for us; from the fact that it was a miraculous

* Compare i: 5 with xi: 16. † 1 Cor. xii: 13. ‡ See 1 Cor. xii: 3-13.

gift, and therefore peculiar to the age of miracles. It may as well be regarded as necessary to see the Lord as Saul did, in order to a genuine conversion, as to be immersed in the Spirit as Cornelius was. It is, therefore, a very gross deception to urge upon the people that they should receive the Spirit, after the precedent of Cornelius, before they are immersed.

47, 48. The true explanation of this unusual circumstance is given in the following words, together with Peter's own explanation of it in the eleventh chapter: *" *Then Peter answered*, (47) *Can any man forbid water, that these should not be immersed, who have received the Holy Spirit as well as we?* (48) *And he commanded them to be immersed in the name of the Lord. Then they requested him to remain some days.*" The use that Peter made of it expresses the design of its occurrence. That use was to remove all possible objection to the immersion of the parties. In any other case which had occurred, or which occurred after this, no such objection could have existed. The very fact, therefore, which led to this unusual occurrence, was an exceptional circumstance, which furnishes the strongest proof that this case is not a precedent for imitation in this particular.

Before he was interrupted, Peter had already proceeded so far with his discourse as to reach the subject of faith, and of remission of sins, and immersion must have been the next word upon his lips, if he had proceeded after the model of his sermon on Pentecost. The interruption, therefore, did not break the thread of his discourse, but enabled him to proceed with greater confidence to the very conclusion which he had intended. He first appeals to the brethren, to know if any objection yet lingered in their minds, and finding none, he commanded them to be immersed *in the name of the Lord.*

Let us now recall the fact that Cornelius had been directed to send for Peter to hear "words by which he and all his family might be saved."† Peter has come, and delivered his message. He has told him of Christ, in whom the man now believes. He has commanded him to be immersed, and it has been done. This is the whole story of the conversion. When it was accomplished, the painful anxiety which he must have experienced during the last four days was removed, and his present happiness is indicated by the cordiality with which he invites Peter to remain with him some days.

We now have three individual cases of conversion before us, each detailed with great minuteness. In some particulars they are precisely alike; in others, they are quite different. But they are all three genuine cases of conversion; and, therefore, the points in which they differ are not essential to conversion, but are accidental circumstances arising from the peculiarities of the individual case. Now, in order that we may learn what is essential to conversion, and what among all the cases on record, are accidental circumstances, we must be guided by the following rule. Whatever is common to all cases is necessary to a scriptural conversion; but whatever we find in one case which certainly did not occur in all others, is a peculiarity of the individual cases in which it occurs. The points in which all the recorded cases agree are the points in which all subsequent conversions must agree

* Acts xi: 15. † Acts xi: 14.

with them. The points in which they differ are points in which subsequent conversions may differ from them. In order to determine that certain features are not essential, it is only necessary to find cases in which they do not occur. In order to determine that any one is essential, we must find it in all cases, or find it prescribed in some general law expressly designed to govern all cases.

While the three cases already before us are fresh in the memory, and before points of difference become multiplied by additional cases, so as to confuse the understanding, we propose to institute a comparison between them, in the light of the rule just prescribed. Leaving out of view the difference in character, occupation, and social position, of the eunuch, Saul, and Cornelius, which show only that the gospel is adapted to all men without regard to previous character or position, we will only notice those differences which might form the ground of erroneous conclusions. *First*, then, in the cases of the eunuch and Cornelius, there was the visible appearance of an angel; and many converts of modern times have related, as part of their experience in conversion, similar apparitions. But there certainly was not in Saul's case the appearance of an angel; therefore, such an appearance is not necessary to conversion. *Second*, The Lord himself appeared to Saul and conversed with him; but he certainly did not to either the eunuch or Cornelius. It is not necessary, then, to see the Lord. *Third*, Saul mourned and prayed for three days after he believed, and before he was immersed; but Cornelius and the eunuch did not; therefore, protracted sorrow and prayer are not necessary to conversion. *Fourth*, Cornelius was immersed in the Spirit, but Saul and the eunuch were not; therefore, immersion in the Spirit is not essential, but a circumstance arising from the peculiarity of a single case.

The points in which these cases agree are chiefly these: they all heard the gospel preached, with miraculous evidence to sustain it; they all believed what they heard; they were all commanded to be immersed; they all were immersed; and after immersion they were all happy. If, then, we do not hereafter encounter recorded cases from which some of these items are certainly absent, we must conclude that at least all of these are necessary to scriptural conversion. When other cases are before us, we will institute further and more complete comparisons.

We would be glad to know more of the history of Cornelius, so as to determine how far, even in times of peace, the profession of arms is compatible with the faithful service of the Prince of Peace. He is the only soldier of whose conversion we have an account in the New Testament, and of his subsequent career we know nothing. Whether, amid the scenes of blood and desolation not many years after most wickedly visited upon Judea by the army in which he was an officer, he resigned his office, or made shipwreck of the faith, we can not know till the great day. Let it be noted, however, that his is an instance of a soldier becoming a Christian, not of a Christian becoming a soldier. It furnishes a precedent for the former, but not for the latter. Whether Peter instructed him to resign his position in the army or not, is to be determined not by the *silence* of the historian in reference to it, but by first determining whether military service is compatible with the moral teachings of the New Testament. If Jesus and the apostles had been, for more than thirty years previous to the publication of Acts, teaching that Christians should not take the sword, it was not at all necessary for Luke to say that Peter so instructed Cornelius.

XI: 1–3. The novel scene which had transpired in Cæsarea was soon reported abroad over the country. (1) "*Now the apostles and brethren throughout Judea heard that the Gentiles had received the word of God.* (2) *And when Peter went up to Jerusalem, they of the circumcision disputed with him,* (3) *saying, You went into the house of men uncircumcised, and did eat with them.*" The prejudice from which Peter had been delivered was still preying upon the hearts of his Jewish brethren, including the other apostles. The same change is now to be wrought in them which had already been effected in him. But there is no repetition, in their case, of the vision and voices which had occurred in his. On the contrary, there is nothing brought to bear upon them but what is contained in the *words* of Peter.

4–17. (4) "*But Peter related the matter to them in order from the beginning, saying,* (5) *I was in the city of Joppa, praying, and saw, in a trance, a vision, a certain vessel like a great sheet descending, let down from heaven by the four corners, and it came to me.* (6) *Having looked intently into it, I perceived and saw four-footed animals, and wild beasts, and reptiles of the earth, and birds of the air.* (7) *And I heard a voice, saying to me, Arise, Peter; kill and eat.* (8) *But I said, Not so, Lord; for nothing common or unclean has at any time entered into my mouth.* (9) *But the voice from heaven again answered me, What God has cleansed, do not you make common.* (10) *This was done three times, and all was drawn up into heaven again.* (11) *And behold, three men immediately came to the house in which I was, sent to me from Cæsarea,* (12) *and the Spirit told me to go with them, doubting nothing. But these six brethren also went with me, and we entered into the man's house.* (13) *Then he told us that he had seen an angel in his house, standing and saying to him, Send to Joppa, and call for Simon who is surnamed Peter,* (14) *who will speak words to you by which you and all your house will be saved.* (15) *And while I was beginning to speak, the Holy Spirit fell upon them as upon us in the beginning.* (16) *Then I remembered the word of the Lord, that he said, John immersed in water, but you shall be immersed in the Holy Spirit.* (17) *Since, then, God gave to them the same gift as to us who already believed on the Lord Jesus Christ, who was I, that I should be able to withstand God?*" The events here rehearsed by Peter had removed his own prejudice, and now, *through the words* which he addressed to the brethren, the same vision of unclean animals, with the command to kill and eat; the same command of the Spirit to go with the Gentile messengers; the authority of the angel who had ordered him to be sent for; and, finally, the same immersion of those Gentiles in the Holy Spirit, are all pressing upon their minds and hearts, with precisely the same import that they did upon his.

18. The effect of these influences was the same upon them that it had been upon Peter. (18) "*When they heard these things they held their peace, and glorified God, saying, Then has God to the Gentiles also*

granted repentance in order to life." So greatly are their hearts enlarged, that they now glorify God for the very things on account of which they had just been censuring Peter.

We have, in this incident, an exhibition of the actual method by which the minds of Christians were enlightened, and their hearts enlarged. We see that Peter was first enlightened by a combination of facts, visions, and words, so as to *understand* the will of God in the matter, and that *through* this enlightened understanding he was made to *feel* the weight of divine authority. Although the Spirit of God dwelt in him continually, and imparted ideas to his understanding directly, yet, when his *heart* was to be relieved from an injurious prejudice, the end was accomplished by means of ideas communicated to his understanding. Thus the case stands with Peter, who occupies the position of an original recipient of truth.

With the brethren in Jerusalem, who occupied the exact position toward this particular subject which we do to all revealed truth, there is this difference, that *all* the influence, both upon the understanding and the emotional nature, exerted in their case, reached them *through* Peter's words. Still, the influence was not inherent in the *words*, but in the *facts* of which the words were the medium of communication. Moreover, the facts had such an influence only because they indicated the will of God. It was then, at last, the moral power of God, embodied in the facts reported by Peter, but brought to bear through the *words* of Peter, which so changed their hearts. They had only to believe what Peter reported, in order to feel this power. If they had retained their prejudice after this, they would have felt that they were resisting God.

In precisely this way the converting and sanctifying influence of the Holy Spirit reaches the hearts of men now. We do not have direct communications with heavenly beings, as Peter had, but, like the brethren in Jerusalem, we hear from his lips, and the lips and pens of other original recipients, the same truth which affected their minds and hearts, and we find ours affected by it in the same way. When we resist, we are resisting not Peter and Paul, but the Holy Spirit, by whom they spoke and wrote. The fact that the Holy Spirit dwells in us is no proof that his action upon our moral sentiments is direct or immediate; for he dwelt in Peter, and in the apostles who arraigned Peter; yet his action upon even their hearts was *mediate*, through ideas communicated. He who asserts for us a species of spiritual influence which was not exerted even upon the apostles and other inspired men, is, to say the least, a daring speculator.

19. The scene of the narrative is now about to change to another Roman province, and to the city of Antioch. Preparatory to this transition, the historian glances back over a period of several years, to the dispersion of the Jerusalem Church. He had made that event his point of departure in rehearsing the labors of Philip and the early history of Saul, and now, with a degree of system in his arrangement which should not be overlooked, he starts again at the same point to sweep over another part of the wide field before him. (19) *" Now they who were scattered abroad from the persecution which arose about Stephen, traveled as far as Phenicia, and Cyprus, and Antioch,*

speaking the word to none but Jews." From this we learn that w .ile Philip was preaching in Samaria, and Saul in Damascus and Arabia, others of the brethren were spreading the truth into Phenicia, the island of Cyprus, and Antioch in Syria. Thus the knowledge of salvation was sounded out from Jerusalem simultaneously into all the surrounding provinces.

20–21. Among the brethren engaged in these labors, Luke chooses to follow in the narrative only those who founded the Church in Antioch. (20) "*And some of them were men of Cyprus and Cyrene, who, having come into Antioch, spoke to the Hellenists, preaching the Lord Jesus.* (21) *The hand of the Lord was with them, and a great number believed and turned to the Lord.*" These men were not immediately from Cyprus and Cyrene, but were a part of those dispersed from Jerusalem. The expression, "Some of them," referring to the preceding sentence, thus designates them. The Hellenists were doubtless numerous in Antioch, from the fact of its being the chief commercial city of Western Asia; and these brethren, being also Hellenists, were best suited for reaching their ears.

22–24. Jerusalem was still the chief center of religious influence, being the chief residence of the apostles. They kept a watchful eye upon the movements of brethren in all directions, supplying help and counsel according to the demand of circumstances. They were anxious to hear of every new success, and the brethren were equally glad to report it. (22) "*Then tidings of these things came to the ears of the Church in Jerusalem, and they sent forth Barnabas to go as far as Antioch.* (23) *When he arrived and saw the favor of God, he rejoiced, and exhorted them all with purpose of heart to cling to the Lord.* (24) *For he was a good man, and full of the Holy Spirit and faith; and a great multitude were added to the Lord.*" It is not often that Luke bestows a direct encomium upon the characters of whom he writes, as he does here upon Barnabas. But it was proper, in this case, that the selection of Barnabas for this mission, in preference to other brethren, should be accounted for by stating the noble qualities which led to the choice. He was certainly a most proper man to send to a congregation of young disciples, to exhort them to cling to the Lord.

25. While Barnabas was engaged in these faithful labors in Antioch, he seems to have longed for the co-operation of a kindred spirit. He had not forgotten the converted persecutor, whom he had kindly taken by the hand when all the apostles were suspicious of him, and introduced to the confidence of the brethren. An act of kindness often makes as deep an impression on the heart of the benefactor as on that of the recipient. The heart of Barnabas had followed Saul when the brethren sent him away to Tarsus, and now that he needs a fellow-laborer, his heart directs him where to seek. (25) "*Then Barnabas departed to Tarsus to seek Saul; (26) and having found him he brought him to Antioch.*" The attachment being mutual, he found no difficulty in securing the object of his mission.

26. The united efforts of two such men as Barnabas and Saul, in a community where the gospel was already favorably heard, could not fail of good results. (26) "*And it came to pass, that during a whole year they were associated together in the Church, and taught a great multitude;*

and the disciples were called Christians first in Antioch." There has been much dispute as to whether this new name was given by Barnabas and Saul under divine authority, or by the Gentiles of Antioch, or by the disciples themselves. It would serve no practical purpose to decide between the latter two suppositions, for, with whichever party it originated, it was subsequently accepted by the disciples in general.

As to the supposition that the name was given by direct revelation through Barnabas and Saul, a thorough discussion of its merits would require more verbal criticism than is suited to the design of this work, and, at the same time, be less decisive in reference to the authority of the name in question, than the course of investigation which we prefer to institute. We retain, therefore, the common version of the passage, which is sustained by the great mass of critics of all ages and all parties, while we seek a more certain basis on which to rest the divine authority of the new name than verbal criticism can establish.

If the New Testament furnishes any names for the people of God, its authority in reference to their use is not less imperative than in reference to any other use of language. We can have no more right, in this case, to substitute other names for them, or to add others to them, than to do the same in reference to the names of the apostles, of the Holy Spirit, or of Christ.

Religious names are significant. They not only distinguish the bodies to which they belong, as do modern names of individuals, but they distinguish them by a condensed description of their peculiarities. All the peculiarities of a religious denomination are expressed by the denominational name in its current import. Hence, to call a Baptist by the name Methodist would be worse than to call Smith by the name of Jones; for, besides miscalling him, it would be misrepresenting his religious principles. It is true, that, in thus miscalling the Baptist, you have not changed him into a Methodist, for he remains the same by whatever name you call him. Still, you have miscalled him and done him injustice. Truth and justice, therefore, require us to use religious names with reference to their significance.

If denominational names are significant, those originally applied to the body of Christ are not less so. They distinguish the people of God by designating some of their peculiarities. These peculiarities were found either in the relations which they sustained, or in the character which they exhibited to the world. The first relation which attracted the attention of the world, as they followed Jesus from place to place, was that of teacher and pupils. This suggested the name *disciples*, or *learners*, by which they were first designated, and which is the most common designation in the gospel narratives. From the fact that there were disciples of John, with whom they might be confounded, they were, at first, styled "disciples of Jesus." But when John had decreased, and Jesus had increased, the limiting words were dispensed with, and the term *disciple* was *appropriated*, so that, standing alone, it always meant a disciple of Jesus. In the four gospels the limiting words are commonly employed; but in Acts, where Luke is giving some of their history as a great people spreading through the earth, after once calling them "disciples of the Lord," at the time

Saul starts after them to Damascus, he drops the limiting words, and thence throughout the whole narrative he calls them simply the "disciples."

When the disciples assumed a new relation to their teacher, it necessarily brought them into a new relation to one another. From the nature of the moral lessons which they were learning, and which they were required to put into immediate practice, this relation became very intimate and very affectionate. It gave rise to their designation as "*the brethren.*" They were so styled first by Jesus, saying to them: "Be not called Rabbi; for one is your teacher, and all you are *brethren.*"* This term, however, as a distinctive appellation of the whole body, is used only once in the gospel narratives, where John says of the report that he would not die: "This saying went abroad among *the brethren.*"† In Acts it frequently occurs in this sense; but still more frequently in the Epistles. The latter being addressed to the brethren, and treating of their mutual obligations, this term most naturally takes precedence in them, and the term disciple, which is used in speaking *of* a brother rather than *to* him, is as naturally omitted. This accounts for the fact that the latter term is not once found in the Epistles.

This increasing currency of the term *brethren* in the later apostolic age is intimately associated with the introduction of another name which came into use in the same period. Jesus frequently called the disciples his own brethren, and taught them, in praying, to say "*Our Father, who art in heaven;*" but the title, "children of God," which grew out of the relation thus indicated, was not applied to them during this early period. It is not so applied in any of the gospels but John's, and in this only in two instances, where it is evident that he is using the phraseology of the time in which he writes rather than of the period of which he writes.‡ This appellation, as a current and cotemporaneous title, is found only in the Epistles, being brought into use after the disciples had obtained more exalted conceptions of the blessed privileges and high honors which God had conferred upon them. It extorted an admiring comment from John, in his old age: "Behold, what manner of love the Father has bestowed upon us, that we should be called the *sons of God!*"∥

By this time the disciples exhibited to the world a well-defined character. It was such as identified them with those who, in the Old Testament, were called *saints*, and this suggested the use of this term as one of their appellations. The persecutions which they were enduring still further identified them with the holy "prophets who were before them." This name occurs first on the lips of Ananias when he objected to approaching Saul of Tarsus. He says to the Lord, "I have heard by many of this man, how much evil he has done to thy *saints* in Jerusalem." In the Epistles this name is used more frequently than any other.

All of the names we have now considered are well adapted to their specific purposes; but all of them presuppose some knowledge of the people whom they are intended to distinguish. An entire stranger would not at first know who was meant by *the disciples,* or *the brethren;*

* Matt. xxiii: 8.   † John xxi: 23.   ‡ John i: 12; xi: 52.   ∥ 1 John iii: 1.

but would ask, Disciples of whom? brethren of whom? Nor would he know who were the *children of God*, or the *saints*, until you had informed him to what certain characters these terms apply. There was need, therefore, of a name less ambiguous to those who had the least information on the subject—one better adapted to the great world. This, like all the others, originated from circumstances which demanded it for immediate use. When a Church was established in Antioch, it became an object of inquiry to, strangers, brought thither by the pursuits of commerce, from all parts of the world. They were strangers to the cause of Christ in reference to all but the wonderful career of its founder. The whole world had heard something of Christ, as the remarkable personage who was put to death under Pontius Pilate, though many had heard nothing of the early history of his Church. From this fact, when strangers came to Antioch, and heard the new party who were attracting so much attention there, called *Christians*, they at once recognized them as followers of that *Christ* of whom they had already heard. This explains the fact stated in the text, that "the disciples were called *Christians first* in Antioch." The fact that Luke here adopts it, and that both Paul and Peter afterward recognized it, gives it all the validity of inspired usage, and, therefore, all the weight of divine authority. That it is a New Testament name is undisputed, and this renders its divine authority indisputable.

This name, whether given by divine or by human authority, was not designed as an exclusive appellation, seeing that the others were continued in use after its introduction. It merely took its proper place among the other names, to answer its own special purpose.

To sum up the facts now adduced, the New Testament usage in reference to names is this: When the followers of Jesus were contemplated with reference to their relation to him as their great teacher, they were called *disciples*. When the mind of the speaker was fixed more particularly on their relation to one another, they were styled *brethren*. When their relation to God was in the foreground, they were called *children of God*. When they were designated with special reference to character, they were called *saints*. But when they were spoken of with the most general reference to their great leader, they were called *Christians*. A practical observance of the exact force of each of these names would soon conform our speech to the primitive model, and would check a tendency to exalt any one name above another, by giving to each its proper place.

The names now enumerated are all that are furnished by the New Testament. We have assumed above that it would be subversive of divine authority for disciples to adopt any other names. The truth of this assumption is demonstrated by the rebuke which Paul administers to the Corinthians for this very sin. He says to them: "It has been declared to me, my brethren, by them who are of the household of Chloe, that there are contentions among you. Now this I say, that each of you says, I am of Paul, and I of Apollos, and I of Cephas, and I of Christ. Is Christ divided? Was Paul crucified for you? Or were you immersed into the name of Paul?"* Now, if it was sinful for these brethren to assume the names of men, how can it be

* 1 Cor. 1: 11-13.

innocent in us to do the very same thing? This question demands the most solemn and trembling consideration of this generation.

It is no extenuation of this fault to urge that the divisions which now exist are of a different character from those in Corinth; for the difference is entirely in their favor. They had not gone so far as to divide the Church into separate organizations, but had merely formed parties within it, like the parties of the present day, which sometimes exist within a single denomination. The sin of to-day is, therefore, much greater than theirs.

It is equally vain to excuse our sin, by urging that the party names now worn are necessary, in order to distinguish the parties from one another. If the existence of the parties themselves were authorized by the Scriptures, this excuse would be valid; for we could not censure ourselves for the unavoidable results of that which is itself right. But the existence of party divisions constitutes the *chief* crime in the case, and *leads* to the sin of party names, as stealing leads to lying. The thief must inevitably lie, or acknowledge his theft; so the partisan must either cling to his party name, or give up his party. The name, in the mean time, is a necessary evil, but, being self-imposed, it is none the less evil from being necessary.

Not to multiply words upon this point, it is sufficiently evident, from the above considerations, that parties and party names among Christians should be obliterated. If we say that it is *impossible* to obliterate them, we are simply saying that it is impossible to bring Christians back to the New Testament model—for, in the New Testament period, there were no such divisions, and therefore a restoration of that state of the Church would be the destruction of parties and party names. If this is impossible, it can only be from one cause, and that is, that men professing to take the word of God as their guide are so hypocritical in this profession, that they will, at all hazard, persevere in despising its authority in reference to a prominent item of duty. How shameful it is, that men will uphold parties and party names, which they know perfectly that a strict conformity to the New Testament would utterly destroy! There is only one means of escape from this crying sin. Those who love God must break loose at once, as individuals, from the bondage of party, and take a position where they may be upholders of no party, and wearers of no party name. All who act thus will find themselves planted together on the plain letter of the Scriptures, as their only rule of faith and practice.

In addition to the observations already submitted on this topic, we remark that every significant name which a man wears imposes some obligation upon him, and appeals to him incessantly, though silently, to discharge this obligation faithfully. Does a man in a foreign country declare himself an *American*, he realizes that there is a peculiar demeanor required by the fact, and feels constantly called upon to act worthy of the name he wears. Even a man's patronymic, which means no more than that he belongs to a certain family, is forever warning him not to disgrace the name of his father. So it must be with all religious names.

Is a man called a *disciple of Jesus?* He remembers that it is the part of a disciple to learn what his teacher imparts, and to imitate his example. Whenever he is reminded that this is his name, he feels the necessity of studying the teachings of Jesus, and walking in his footsteps. Whenever he finds himself neglecting these duties, his very name rebukes him. This thought was not overlooked by the great Teacher himself. He says to those Jews who believed on him, "If you continue in my *word*, you are truly my *disciples*, and you shall *know* the *truth*, and the truth shall make you free."* Again he says, "It is enough for the *disciple* to be as his *teacher;*" and "whosoever does not *bear his cross* and come *after* me, can not be my *disciple.*"† Thus he gives emphasis to that exhortation which the name itself is constantly sounding in the ear of conscience.

But the disciple is also one of the *brethren*—a brother to the Lord Jesus, who is the oldest brother of a large family. This name is full of affection and sympathy. I can not meet a man and call him *brother*, without some thought of the fraternal sympathy which should exist between us. If, when my heart is poisoned by unkind feelings toward a disciple, he meets me and calls me *brother*, I feel reproached by the word, and am choked in the attempt to pronounce it in return. It will never let me forget the law of love. Its influence is recognized by Peter, who says, "Seeing you have purified your souls in obeying the truth through the Spirit unto unfeigned love of the *brethren*, see that you love one another with a pure heart fervently."‡

There is another obligation involved in this name, arising from the fact that the brothers in one family stand on an equal footing in reference to authority, no one having supremacy over the others, but all subject to the father. Jesus makes use of this fact as the ground of a serious injunction. "Be not called Rabbi; for one is your teacher, and all you are *brethren;* and call no man on earth your *Father*, for One who is in heaven is your Father; neither be called *Leaders*, for one is your Leader, the Christ."|| The fact that we are *brethren* is thus made to bear directly against that thirsting for titles of distinction, and for rank and authority in the Church of Christ, which is invariably the offspring of an unholy ambition. The modern *Leaders* of sects—the ghostly *Fathers* of mystic Babylon, and the swelling titles by which *Doctors of Divinity*, and the *Reverend* and *Right Reverend* Bishops and Archbishops of the present age are distinguished, exhibit the most flagrant contempt for this solemn commandment of the Lord. A man who understands the meaning of the fact that he is one among many *brethren*, is guarded, by the humility of this title, from participation in a sin like this.

If such are the obligations implied in the names *disciple* and *brethren*, what shall we say of that more exalted title, *children of God?* It originates from a supposed likeness between them and their Father. We are commanded to love our enemies, to bless them who curse us, to do good to them who hate us, and to pray for them who persecute us, *that we may be* children of our Father who is in heaven.§ Thus the very highest moral obligations imposed in the word of God must ever press upon the soul of him who wears this title, inciting him to become a partaker of the divine nature.

* John viii: 31, 32. † Matt. xi: 24; Luke xiv: 27. ‡ 1 Peter i: 22.
|| Matt. xxiii: 8, 10. § Matt. v: 44, 45.

When, in addition to these appellations, you call a man a *saint*, you thrust him as a companion into the midst of all the holy men of old, and make him struggle to be like them. So palpable is the force of this name, that the mass of professed Christians have long since ceased to wear it. When men apostatized from what its meaning indicates, it hung so heavily upon the conscience, that it became like a coal of fire on their heads, and they found relief in throwing it off from themselves and appropriating it to a few of the worthy dead. If we would ever come back from the long apostasy of ages, we must learn to wear the name saint, and walk worthy of the company with which it identifies us. The term *saint* means *a holy one*, and Peter exhorts, "As he who called you is holy, so be ye holy in all manner of behavior; because it is written, Be ye holy for I am holy."*

The name *Christian* embodies within itself, in a more generic form, all the obligations specifically expressed by the other names. Being derived from the name of him who is "head over all things for the Church," whose name is above every name, it is a title of peculiar honor and glory. It calls upon the man who wears it to act a part in consonance with the historic memories which cluster around it, and encourages him with the reflection that he wears a high dignity even when despised and spit upon by the powers of earth. So thought Peter, when this name was most despised. He says, "If any suffer as a *Christian*, let him not be ashamed, but let him glorify God on this account." " If you are reproached for the name of Christ, happy are you; for the spirit of glory and of God rests upon you."†

When the servant of Christ remembers that all these names belong to him; that, because he is supposed to be learning of Christ, he is called a *disciple;* because he is one of the happy and loving family of equals, they call him *brother;* because the Father of that family, whose character he strives to imitate, is God himself, he is called a *child of God;* that, because he is presumed to be holy, he is called a *saint;* and that, for all these reasons, he wears the name of him who by his mediation and intercession enables him to be all that he is, how powerful the incentive to every virtue, constantly yet silently pressing upon his conscience, and how stern the rebuke to every vice!

When we turn from this deep and holy philosophy of scriptural names, to consider the import of mere partisan badges, how heartless they all appear! The constant and only influence of party names is to intensify mere partisan feelings. The man who wears the name Methodist feels called upon by the fact to simply act like a Methodist; and when that name is appealed to among those who honor it, it is only to exhort one another to diligence in that which is peculiarly expected of a mere Methodist. So with all other party names. There is nothing in any of them to excite the longings of a sin-sick soul, and hence they are never appealed to when sinners are exhorted to repent. On the contrary, the most zealous partisans are often heard to assure sinners, "Our object is not to make *Presbyterians* of you, or *Methodists*, or *Baptists;* but we want you to become *Christians.*" How strange it is that men will pertinaciously cling to names which they are thus ashamed of in the presence of penitent sinners, when there are others

* 1 Peter i: 15, 16.   † 1 Peter iv: 14-16.

ACTS XI: 27-30; XII: 1, 2.

at hand given by God himself, full of honor to the wearer. and of attraction to all who seek salvation!

27-30. We have dwelt long upon the new name given in Antioch; we must now consider other interesting events which occurred there about the close of the year in which Barnabas and Saul labored there together. (27) "*In those days prophets came down from Jerusalem to Antioch, (28) and one of them, named Agabus, arose and signified through the Spirit that there would be a great famine throughout the whole world, which also occurred in the days of Claudius. (29) Then the disciples, every one according as he was prospered, determined to send relief to the brethren who dwelt in Judea; (30) which also they did, sending it to the elders by the hand of Barnabas and Saul.*"

This is the first account we have of the gift of prophesy among the disciples, but Agabus and his companions appear to have been already known as prophets, doubtless from previous exercises of this gift. The brethren, therefore, did not hesitate to give full credit to the prediction, and knowing that such a famine must cause peculiar distress among the extremely poor in Judea, they were prompt to supply their wants even before the period of distress arrived. Their benevolence is not less remarkable than that of the Church in Jerusalem at the beginning. The poor for whom that Church provided were in their midst, and suffering from present want; but the disciples in Antioch anticipate a state of distress yet in the future, on the part of brethren to whom they are personally unknown, and provide for it in advance. No more striking evidence could be given, at once, of their benevolence, and their confidence in the predictions of their own prophets.

This benevolent supply was sent to the *Elders*, by whom, we are to understand, it was distributed to the final recipients. This is the first time that elders, as a distinct class, are mentioned in connection with the congregations of disciples. They are mentioned, however, as a class of officials then well known, and, consequently, we must infer that they had been appointed in the Churches at a still earlier period.

XII: 1, 2. The historian does not follow Barnabas and Saul in their tour through the districts in Judea, but, leaving them for awhile, introduces a very interesting episode concerning events that were then transpiring in Jerusalem. (1) "*Now, about that time, Herod the king stretched forth his hand to afflict certain persons of the Church, (2) and killed James the brother of John with the sword.*" The persecutions which we have hitherto noticed were conducted by religious partisans in Jerusalem, without any active assistance on the part of the civil authorities. We are now introduced to one in which the reigning prince is the leader, while the old enemies of the truth are working behind the curtain, if it all.

This Herod was a grandson of that Herod by whom the infants of Bethlehem were slaughtered, and a nephew of "Herod the Tetrarch," by whom John the Immerser was beheaded. He grew up in Rome, where he wasted what fortune he had inherited in princely extravagance; but while doing so he acquired an intimacy with Caius Cæsar, afterward the famous Caligula of history. When the latter ascended the throne, at the death of Tiberius, he elevated his friend Agrippa, as this Herod was most usually called, to a kingdom, which was subsequently enlarged by Claudius until it embraced all the territory ruled by his grandfather Herod the Great. He was now in the zenith of his power, and living in the utmost magnificence.* Why he undertook this persecution it is difficult to tell, unless he was instigated to it by the old enemies of the Church. This appears most probable from Luke's statement below, that he seized Peter because he saw that the death of James pleased the Jews.†

A number of brethren suffered in this persecution, though James the brother of John is the only one who is said to have suffered death. He is designated as the "brother of John" to distinguish him from the other James, who is the author of the epistle bearing this name. He was the first of the apostles to suffer death, and his brother John was the last. In the death of both were fulfilled the words of Jesus, uttered on a memorable occasion, when they asked him for a seat, one at his right hand and the other at his left. He asked them if they were able to undergo the immersion which he would undergo. They said, "We are able." He replied, "You shall, indeed, drink of my cup, and be immersed in the immersion in which I am immersed; but to sit on my right hand and on my left is not mine to give, but to them for whom it is prepared by my Father." As the sword of the executioner was made bare, and the neck of James laid upon the block, he could but remember these words. He understood, too, far better than when he first made the request, what it is to sit at the right hand of Jesus.

Why James was selected for this murderous example, in preference to any other of the apostles, we are not informed; but we have already seen that the brunt of persecution uniformly fell upon those most prominent in the scenes which were the immediate occasion of it. This consideration gives some ground for the conclusion that, though Peter and John had hitherto acted the most prominent part in Jerusalem, at this time James stood in the foreground in the conflict with unbelieving Jews.

3, 4. When a man engages in a wicked enterprise, his conscience makes him timid while left to himself; but the applause of the multitude enables him to drown the voice of conscience, and rush on madly to the end. Agrippa may have hesitated when he found his hands stained with the blood of an apostle; but when the people applauded he hesitated no longer. (3) *"And seeing that it was pleasing to the Jews, he proceeded to seize Peter also. But it was in the days of unleavened bread. (4) And having apprehended him, he put him in prison, delivering him to four quarternions of soldiers to guard him, intending, after the Passover, to bring him out to the people."* A public execution during the feast of unleavened bread would have been exceedingly incongruous with the religious solemnities of the occasion: hence this delay.

The four quarternions of soldiers who guarded Peter consisted of sixteen men, each quarternion consisting of four. It was enough to keep four men on guard during each of the four watches of the

---

* For a detailed and very interesting history of this prince, see Josephus's Ant., Books 18 and 19.　　　　† Acts xii : 3.

night. They, together with the strength of the prison-doors, were deemed sufficient for the utmost security.

5. We have noticed that when Peter and John were dismissed from the Sanhedrim, with a threat of violence if they dared any more to speak or teach in the name of Jesus, they came to their own company, and all united in prayer to God for courage.* Now that James has been murdered, and Peter is in prison awaiting the same fate, we find the brethren once more unitedly appealing to God. (5) "*Peter, therefore, was kept in prison, but fervent prayer was made by the Church to God for him.*" When we reflect that the circumstances affecting the disciples were calculated in the highest degree to exasperate them against the murderers of their brethren, and stimulate them to active measures for the defense of their own lives, it is exceedingly to their credit that they were engaged in fervent prayer. If they had been taught the modern doctrine that Christians may rightly resist, with violence, the assaults of tyrannical rulers, and, whatever the weakness on their own part, may confidently appeal to the God of battles in vindication of their rights, their feelings and their conduct, under these circumstances, must have been far different from what they were. If ever there was an occasion on which the boasted first law of nature, the right of self-defense, would justify violent resistance to oppression, it existed here. But, instead of the passion and turmoil of armed preparation, we hear from the midnight assemblies of the disciples the voice of fervent prayer. Where prayer is, acceptable prayer, there is no passion, no thirst for revenge, or purpose of violence. These men were disciples of the Prince of Peace.

6. Time wore away in painful suspense until the Passover was gone by. (6) "*And when Herod was about to bring him forth, in that night Peter was sleeping between two soldiers, bound with two chains, and the guards before the door were guarding the prison.*" He was securely kept, according to the most ingenious method of the Roman army. Besides the prison-doors, and the guards without, his arms were pinioned by two chains, each to the arm of a soldier on the right and left, so that he could not move without disturbing one or both. If Herod was actuated, in adopting these precautions, by a desire to prevent a rescue, he ought to have known that Peter's brethren never fought with carnal weapons, even to save the life of a brother. Or if he feared a miraculous escape of his prisoner, and intended that the guards should kill him upon the first movement of that kind, he ought to have remembered that all the twelve had once walked out of a prison in that city without hinderance either from the iron doors or the armed soldiers. But wicked men are prone to forget the warnings of the past, and continue to repeat, in endless succession, the blunders of their predecessors.

7-11. Though Peter undoubtedly expected to die the next day, he seems to have slept as soundly as the soldiers to whom he was chained. All was dark and still within the prison until a late hour of the night, when the scene suddenly changed. (7) "*And behold, an angel of the Lord stood by, and a light shone in the prison; and striking Peter on the side, he raised him up, saying, Rise up quickly. His chains fell from*

---
* Acts iv : 24.

his hands. (8) *And the angel said to him, Gird yourself, and bind on your sandals. He did so. And he said to him, Cast your mantle about you and follow me.* (9) *And he followed him, going out, and did not know that what was done by the angel was real, but thought he was seeing a vision.* (10) *But having passed through the first and second guard, they came to the iron gate which leads into the city, which opened to them of its own accord; and going out, they went forward one street, and immediately the angel departed from him.* (11) *Then Peter, coming to himself, said, Now I know in reality that the Lord has sent his angel, and delivered me from the hand of Herod, and from all the expectation of the Jewish people.*" It is not at all strange that Peter thought, at first, that he was dreaming; for the deliverance was entirely unexpected, and was effected in the most wonderful manner, and amid the bewilderment usual upon being suddenly aroused from deep sleep. When he found himself alone in the street, and had collected his senses, he knew that it was a reality, and felt like one waking from a singular dream.

12. When the angel departed, he stood in the street for awhile, reflecting upon the incident, and considering what he should do. In the house of Mary the sister of Barnabas,* a number of disciples were at that very hour engaged in prayer in his behalf. He knew nothing of this, but, guided either by the proximity of the house, or the well-known character of its inmates, he turned in that direction. (12) "*When he understood the matter, he went to the house of Mary the mother of John, whose surname was Mark, where many were gathered together praying.*"

13–16. Although the condition of Peter was the burden of the prayers of these disciples, they were by no means expecting his deliverance, and were most likely praying that he might be enabled to endure with fortitude a death which they regarded as inevitable. (13) "*And when he knocked at the door of the gate, a servant girl named Rhoda came to hear who it was.* (14) *And recognizing the voice of Peter, she opened not the gate for gladness, but ran in and told that Peter was standing before the gate.* (15) *But they said to her, You are mad. But she positively affirmed that it was really so. Then they said, It is his angel.* (16) *But Peter continued knocking, and when they had opened the door and saw him, they were astonished.*"

When we remember that these disciples were so familiar with miracles, it is rather surprising that the deliverance of Peter should have caused so much astonishment. It shows that they were still disposed, like ourselves, to estimate the probabilities of even what God may do, by the difficulties of the execution. This is really judging of God by the standard of human ability. While we are compelled to approach the unknown through the known, we will, perhaps, never rise above this weakness. Still, it should not, even in the most difficult cases, check the fervency of our prayers. They undervalued the power or the willingness of God to grant their desires, in the day of miracles, as we undervalue his power to work without miracles; yet their prayers were none the less fervent or persistent.

When Rhoda insisted that it was Peter at the gate, and the disciples said, It is his angel, they undoubtedly had allusion to the popular

* Compare verse 12 with Col. iv: 10.

superstition of their day, that a man's guardian angel sometimes assumed his form. Before this, the twelve had twice imagined that they saw a disembodied spirit; once when they saw Jesus walking on the water, and once when he miraculously entered a closed room where they were sitting.* These facts show how strong a hold the popular superstitions had upon their minds. But while the conception that angels sometimes assumed the forms of those whom they guarded, and that disembodied spirits were sometimes visible, was superstitious, we must not forget that beneath this superstition there was a solemn reality. Jesus says, "Take heed that you despise not one of these little ones; for I say unto you that in heaven *their angels* do always behold the face of my Father who is in heaven."† Paul asks, "Are they not all ministering spirits, sent forth to minister for those who shall inherit salvation?"‡ And David, under the old economy, says, in his own poetic style, "The angel of the Lord encampeth round about them who fear him."|| In view of these statements, we can not doubt that the ministration of angels in behalf of the saints is still a reality.

17. Apprehensive of a pursuit, Peter did not remain long with the brethren in the house of Mary. (17) "*But, beckoning to them with his hand to be silent, he related to them how the Lord had led him out of the prison, and said, Tell these things to James and the brethren. And going out, he went into another place.*" Whether this other place was a place of concealment in the city, or an entirely new field of labor, is not known.

The prominence given to the name of the surviving James, in this speech of Peter, shows that he already occupied a prominent position among the brethren. We will, hereafter, see that he continued to occupy this position.

18, 19. The escape of Peter had been altogether unobserved by the soldiers who guarded him. The two who were chained to him in the prison slept on till day, and those guarding the outside changed their watches at the regular hours without suspecting any thing wrong within. (18) "*Now when it was day, there was no small stir among the soldiers, what was become of Peter.* (19) *And when Herod had sought for him and found him not, he examined the guards and commanded that they should be put to death. And he went down from Judea to Cæsarea, and abode there.*" The military law of the Romans required that guards who allowed the escape of a prisoner, and rendered no satisfactory account of it, should be put to death. But it is impossible to believe that on this occasion Herod was governed by an honest sense of military duty. He must have known that the escape of Peter was miraculous, and the execution of the guards was an act of insane fury. A conscience stained by the blood of an apostle and of sixteen faithful soldiers could not find rest in the place where the deeds were done; and doubtless this had much to do with the removal of his residence to Cæsarea.

20–23. The historian pursues the history of this murderous prince a little further. (20) "*Now Herod was enraged against the Tyrians and Sidonians. But they came to him with one accord, and having made Blastus the king's chamberlain their friend, desired peace, because their*

* Matt. xiv: 26; Luke xxiv: 37.   † Matt. xviii: 10.   ‡ Heb. i: 14. | Ps. xxxiv: 7.

country was nourished by that of the king. (21) *And upon a set day Herod, arrayed in royal apparel, sat upon his throne, and made an oration to them.* (22) *And the people cried out, The voice of a God, and not of a man.* (23) *And immediately an angel of the Lord smote him, because he gave not God the glory, and being eaten by worms, he expired."* Josephus says of the "royal apparel" in which he was arrayed, that it was woven wholly of silver threads, the glittering of which, in the morning sun, suggested the idolatrous exclamation of the multitude. He also relates that Herod was seized with pains in the bowels, so violent that he had to be carried into the palace, and lingered five days in excruciating torments from the worms also mentioned by Luke. This historian mentions some circumstances of a superstitious character in connection with this terrible event, but his account agrees substantially with that of Luke. Thus was the righteous judgment of God, which is chiefly reserved for the future state, displayed even in this world, for the terror of wicked men and the encouragement of the righteous.

24. It was impossible that this providential and sudden death of Herod, occurring so soon after the murders which he had committed in Jerusalem, should not seriously affect the public mind. We are not surprised, therefore, that Luke adds: (24) *"But the word of the Lord grew and multiplied."* Once more the efforts of men to crush the cause of Christ resulted in the extension of its triumphs.

25. This narrative concerning the death of James, the imprisonment of Peter, and the miserable death of Herod, is thrown in between the arrival of Paul and Barnabas on their mission to the poor saints, and their return to Antioch. It is most probable that they were in Jerusalem at the feast during which Peter lay in prison. (25) *"Now Barnabas and Saul returned from Jerusalem, when they had fulfilled their ministry, and took with them John who was surnamed Mark."* This is the first appearance in public life of the evangelist Mark, whose education in the house of Mary his mother, and whose subsequent familiarity, first with Barnabas and Saul, and afterward with Peter, very happily fitted him for the gospel narrative which we have from his pen. We will have more to say of him hereafter.*

XIII. We have already seen that Barnabas and Saul had labored one whole year together in the city of Antioch, and we now learn that at the close of this period there were other inspired teachers associated with them. (1) *"Now there were in the Church in Antioch certain prophets and teachers, Barnabas and Simeon called Niger, and Lucius the Cyrenian, and Manaen, foster-brother of Herod the tetrarch, and Saul."* It will be observed that, in this catalogue of names, that of Barnabas stands first, and that of Saul last. As it was customary at that period to arrange names in the order of their notability at the time contemplated, we may infer that Barnabas still occupied a position of pre-eminence, while Saul was as yet comparatively undistinguished among the inspired teachers. Nothing more is known of Simeon, Lucius, and Manaen than is here stated; but this is enough to show that the future instruction of the congregation might be safely committed to their hands.

* See Acts xiii: 13; and xv: 37-39.

2, 3. (2) "*As they were ministering to the Lord and fasting, the Holy Spirit said, Separate for me Barnabas and Saul to the work to which I have called them.* (3) *And when they had fasted and prayed and laid hands on them, they sent them away.*" This command of the Holy Spirit is not the *call* of Barnabas and Saul to their peculiar work, but refers to a call which had been previously given. It shows that Barnabas as well as Saul had received a special call to labor among the Gentiles. They had, hitherto, most probably, been associated together mainly through geniality of spirit. This geniality may also have furnished the main reason why they were directed by the Holy Spirit to continue their labors together.

The design of the ceremony of fasting, prayer, and imposition of hands observed on this occasion, is variously understood. There are only two interpretations of it which are worthy of notice. *First*, it is assumed that the design was to confer on Barnabas and Saul the power of working miracles. The only proof offered in support of this assumption is the fact that neither of them is said to have wrought miracles previous to this time, while they both exhibited miraculous powers shortly after. But this is to argue from the *silence* of the Scriptures, and is, necessarily, inconclusive. They may have worked miracles before this time, notwithstanding this silence. In the case of Saul, indeed, there is almost positive proof that he did so. The Lord had given him a special commission as an apostle when he first appeared to him on the way to Damascus,* and Ananias was sent to him that he "might receive his sight, and be *filled* with the *Holy Spirit.*"† Immediately after his immersion he began to discharge his apostolic office, and had been thus engaged three years previous to his first return to Jerusalem.‡ Another whole year had been spent in the same work in Antioch,‖ besides the interval of his residence in Tarsus.§ But an essential mark of the apostolic office was the power to work miracles. This Paul himself assumes, in his Second Epistle to the Corinthians, among whom his apostleship had been denied. As conclusive proof of his apostleship, he says: "Truly the *signs* of an apostle were wrought among you, in all patience, in *signs* and *wonders* and *mighty deeds.*"¶ If these signs are the proof of apostleship, then he must have been able to exhibit them from the time that he began to be an apostle; and this was more than four years previous to the imposition of hands by the prophets and teachers in Antioch. This fact, coupled with the statement of Ananias, that he was sent to him that he might be filled with the Holy Spirit, indicates clearly that his miraculous endowments dated from his immersion. The first supposition, then, in reference to the design of the ceremony we are considering, proves to be not only unfounded, but inconsistent with the facts of the case.

The *second*, and doubtless the true interpretation, is this: That the imposition of hands, accompanied by fasting and prayer, was, in this case, as in that of the seven deacons, merely their formal separation to the special work to which they had been called. This, indeed, is sufficiently evident from the context. What they did was doubtless

* Acts xxvi: 16–18. † Acts ix: 17. ‡ Gal. i: 15–18.
Acts xi: 26. § Acts ix: 3; xi: 25. ¶ 2 Cor. xii: 12.

what they had been told to do by the Holy Spirit. But the Holy Spirit simply said to them, "*Separate* me Barnabas and Saul *to the work to which I have called them.*" The fasting, prayer, and imposition of hands was, then, merely their *separation* to this work. It was a ceremony deemed by infinite wisdom suitable to such a purpose; and, therefore, whenever a congregation has a similar purpose to accomplish, they have, in this case, the judgment and will of God, which should be their guide.

The solemn simplicity of this apostolic ceremony stands in striking contrast with the pompous mummery which often characterizes "ordination services" in modern Churches. No less striking is the contrast between the humility of Saul and the ambitious spirit of many modern clergymen who are extremely exacting in reference to the punctilios of ecclesiastical rank. Though an apostle by special commission, he was "ordained" by his humble fellow-laborers in Antioch. This fact shows that the idea of superior rank and authority had not then begun the work of ruin which it has since accomplished, in filling the minds of preachers with that same lust of office and power which characterizes the intrigues of political partisans.

4, 5. We now follow Barnabas and Saul to their new field of labor. Their departure from Antioch is thus announced by Luke: (4) "*So they, being sent forth by the Holy Spirit, went down to Seleucia, and thence sailed into Cyprus.* (5) *And when they were in Salamis, they preached the word of God in the synagogues. And they had John as an assistant.*" Seleucia was the seaport nearest to Antioch, distant some fifteen or eighteen miles, and near the mouth of the river Orontes, on the bank of which Antioch is situated. Embarking upon some trading vessel, they sailed to the port of Salamis, which is at the eastern end of the island of Cyprus.

In choosing this island as the first point in the wide world to which they directed their steps, they were, doubtless, guided not by the natural partiality which Barnabas may have felt for it as his native land,[*] but by that fixed principle in the apostolic labors which taught them to cultivate first those fields which promised the most abundant harvest.[†] The fact that this was the native island of Barnabas gave him hope of a more ready access to many old associates. Besides, the gospel had already been proclaimed here with some success among the Jews,[‡] and in the city of Salamis, as we learn from the text just quoted, there was more than one Jewish synagogue.

What duties were performed by John, in his capacity as "an assistant," can not be specifically determined with certainty. The term *assistant* would indicate that he performed, under their direction, a part in the same labor in which they were themselves engaged. The fact, however, that Saul was not in the habit of immersing his own converts, but imposed this duty on his assistants,[||] renders it highly probable that this was at least one of the duties performed by John.

6, 7. Luke is entirely silent in reference to the effect of the apostolic preaching in Salamis, leaving us to suppose that it was not great. After stating that they preached in the synagogues of the Jews, he

[*] Acts iv: 36.   [†] See Com i: 8.   [‡] Acts xi: 19, 20.
[||] Compare xviii: 8 with 1 Cor. i: 14–17.

ACTS XIII: 6-12.

follows them in their further progress through the island. (6) *"And having passed through the whole island as far as Paphos, they found a certain magician, a false prophet, a Jew whose name was Bar-jesus, (7) who was with Sergius Paulus the proconsul, a prudent man, who called for Barnabas and Saul, and desired to hear the word of God."* Every reader of ancient history has observed that statesmen and generals were in the habit of consulting oracles and auguries, and that they generally kept about them some one supposed to have the power of interpreting the signs of approaching good or evil. In this particular period, the educated Romans had become skeptical in reference to their heathen oracles, but Jewish pretenders still had access to their confidence on the credit of the ancient Jewish prophets. With a knowledge of the true God superior to that of even the greatest philosophers among the Greeks, because derived from the Jewish Scriptures, this Bar-jesus very naturally gained the confidence of even the prudent Sergius Paulus. When, however, two other Jews appeared in Paphos, claiming to bring *additional* revelations from the God of Israel, the same prudence which had prompted the proconsul to reject the heathen oracles in favor of the Jewish pretender, now prompted him to send for Barnabas and Saul, that he might hear the word of God from them. Such a mind as his could not fail to hear with profit.

8–12. While listening to the gospel, there were some indications that he was inclined to believe it. (6) *"But the magician Elymas, for so is his name translated, withstood them, seeking to turn aside the proconsul from the faith. (9) Then Saul, who is also Paul, filled with the Holy Spirit, fixed his eyes on him, (10) and said, O full of all subtilty and all mischief, son of the devil, enemy of all righteousness, will you not cease to pervert the right ways of the Lord? (11) And now, behold, the hand of the Lord is upon you, and you shall be blind, not seeing the sun for a season. And immediately there fell upon him a mist, and darkness, and he went about seeking persons to lead him by the hand. (12) Then the proconsul, seeing what was done, believed, being astonished at the Lord's teaching."*

This is the only miracle wrought by an apostle to the injury of any one's person. It is to be accounted for, not by supposed resentment on the part of Saul, nor by a desire to make a special example of Bar-jesus. But the case was such that some display of power over the person of the false prophet was the readiest way to convince the proconsul. When Moses went into Egypt he found it necessary to impose many personal inflictions upon the priests, in order to destroy Pharaoh's confidence in them. The present case was similar to that. The conflict in the mind of Sergius Paulus was between the claim of Bar-jesus to prophetic powers, and that of the apostles. The best way to settle this question was to denounce him in his true character as a son of the devil and an enemy of all righteousness, and then prove the justice of the denunciation, by exerting miraculous control over his person. As he groped about, calling upon one and another of the frightened bystanders to lead him by the hand, the falsity and iniquity of his pretensions stood confessed, and the divine mission of the apostles was demonstrated. The proconsul was fully convinced, and astonished at teaching which was attended by such power.

This triumph over Bar-jesus, and the consequent conversion of Sergius Paulus, forms an epoch in the life of the Apostle Paul. Hitherto he has occupied a subordinate position, and his name has come last in the list of himself and his fellow-laborers. But hereafter he is to occupy the foreground of almost every scene in which he acts. Heretofore, Luke has written "Barnabas and Saul;" hereafter he writes, "Paul and Barnabas." He had been, up to this time, known by no other name than Saul, being so called not only by Luke, but by Jesus and Ananias.* Luke, though writing long after this name had gone into disuse, remembering the custom which thus far prevailed, thus far retains it in his narrative. But, from this time forward he uses the name *Paul* exclusively; and that this was the universal custom, we infer from the fact that he is so called by all others who mention his name; by the Lord Jesus;† by the mob in Jerusalem;‡ by the centurion under Lysias;|| by his own nephew;§ by Lysias the chiliarch;¶ by Festus,** and by Peter.††

There are only two suppositions worthy of notice, by which to account for this change of name. *First*, that he had both the Hebrew name Saul, and the Latin name Paul, before this time, and perhaps from his infancy; but the conversion of the proconsul Paulus led to the exclusive use of his Latin name thereafter. This supposition, however, can not account for the entire absence of the name Paul previous to this event. Moreover, while it is true that many Jews of that day had both a Hebrew and a Latin or Greek name, there is no evidence that such had been the case with Saul.

The other supposition is, that he received this new name by common consent, in commemoration of the conversion of Paulus. This conversion was a signal triumph; it was accomplished by his instrumentality alone, and was the beginning of the pre-eminence which he afterward maintained over Barnabas and all subsequent fellow-laborers. So bold and startling an incident, though it might have been regarded as common-place in his subsequent career, attracted attention now, because it was the first of the kind in his history, and because it secured a conversion of which even Barnabas, under the circumstances, might have despaired. Surprised by the event, and observing the extreme similarity between his name and that of his distinguished convert, which differed only in a single letter, and sounded very much alike, his friends very naturally conceived the idea of changing his name, as they did. It was in perfect harmony with a prevalent custom of the times. Its universal reception soon followed as a matter of course.

It argues no vanity in Paul that he adopted this name; for he could scarcely avoid the adoption into his own use of a name by which he had become universally known. There is nothing in the event, therefore, to encourage men in pompously sounding abroad their own achievements, but much to encourage us in honoring a brother whose boldness and success are worthy of praise.

13. Without pausing to give more detailed accounts of the success of the gospel in Cyprus, our historian now hurries us away with the

---

* Acts ix: 4–17. † Acts xxiii: 11. ‡ Acts xxiii: 14. | Acts xxiii: 18.
§ Acts xxiii: 20. ¶ Acts xxiii: 24. ** Acts xxvi: 24. †† 2 Peter iii: 15.

ACTS XIII: 13-16.

two apostles upon the further prosecution of their tour. (13) "*Now those about Paul set sail from Paphos, and went to Perga of Pamphylia. But John, departing from them, returned to Jerusalem.*" So completely has Paul now become the central figure on the pages of Luke, that here, instead of following his former phraseology, and saying that "Barnabas and Saul" set sail from Paphos, the whole company are described as "those about Paul."

Why they chose the regions north of Pamphylia, in Asia Minor, as their next field of labor, we are not informed. Luke is equally silent in reference to the reason why John Mark, at this particular juncture, departed from them, and returned to Jerusalem. He informs us, however, at a later period, that Paul censured him for so doing.* It is very plausibly suggested by Mr. Howson, that he was influenced by fear of the dangers which lay in their way, the mountains before them being commonly infested with robbers.† He remarks that "No population, through the midst of which he ever traveled, abounded more in those ' perils of robbers ' of which he himself speaks, than the wild and lawless clans of the Pisidian highlanders."

14, 15. Luke does not linger to recount the dangers through which the two travelers may have passed in crossing the mountains, but describes their progress in these few words: (14) "*But they, having departed from Perga, arrived in Antioch of Pisidia, and entering into the synagogue on the Sabbath-day, they sat down.* (15) *And after the reading of the law and the prophets, the rulers of the synagogue sent to them, and said, Brethren, if you have any word of exhortation for the people, say on.*" This is a very life-like description of the order of worship in a Jewish synagogue, and of the readiness with which the apostles gained access to the ears of their Jewish kinsmen upon their first advent in a new field of labor. The direct invitation given them to address the people was doubtless prompted by some vague knowledge of their characters as public speakers, furnished, perhaps, by themselves.

16. To this invitation Paul responded, by immediately arising and addressing the audience. It need not be supposed, in order to account for the leadership which he now assumes, that he had laid formal claim to superiority over Barnabas; for when two men, of generous spirit, are co-operating together under trying circumstances, he who possesses the greater courage and promptness will eventually assume the foremost position, even without a special agreement to that effect. Such was the constant danger and embarrassment of the two missionaries, that the question was, who is willing to go forward, rather than, who has the right to be heard first. Paul's manner, in arising to open the gospel message among these strangers, was bold and commanding. It is thus described by Luke: (16) "*Then Paul stood up, and beckoning with his hand, said, Men of Israel, and ye who fear God, give audience.*" This gesture, described as beckoning with the hand, was characteristic of Paul's manner, as we shall have occasion to observe frequently hereafter, and was well calculated to arrest the attention of an audience. It is the manner of one who knows what he is about to say, and feels confident of its importance.

---
* Acts xv: 38.   † Life and Epistles, vol. i, pp. 162-3.

Besides the Jewish audience present, Paul addressed a number of Gentiles,* such as were in the habit of attending Jewish worship in almost every Gentile city, and many of whom, like Cornelius, had learned to worship the true God. He distinguishes the two classes, by addressing the former as "Men of Israel," and the latter, as "Ye who fear God."

17-24. After thus arresting the attention of his hearers, he approaches his main theme, by a rapid glance at some of the most cherished events in Jewish history. (17) "*The God of this people Israel chose our fathers, and exalted the people when they dwelt as strangers in the land of Egypt, and with a high hand led them out of it;* (18) *and about the time of forty years nourished them in the wilderness.* (19) *And having destroyed seven nations in the land of Canaan, he gave their land to them as an inheritance.* (20) *After these things, he gave them judges about four hundred and fifty years, until the prophet Samuel.* (21) *Then they desired a king, and God gave them Saul, the son of Kish, a man of the tribe of Benjamin, forty years.* (22) *And having removed him, he raised up to them David for a king, to whom he also gave testimony and said, I have found David, the son of Jesse, a man according to my own heart, who will do all my will.* (23) *From this man's offspring God has, according to his promise, raised up to Israel a Savior, Jesus;* (24) *John having preached, before his coming, the immersion of repentance to all the people of Israel.*"

This glance at the history of Israel, from their departure out of Egypt to the reign of David, is a very circuitous method of approaching the announcement of Jesus as a Savior; but, instead of being a defect in the speech, it is one of its chief excellencies. Every speech must be judged with reference to the special character of the audience addressed. The Jews had a glorious history, of which they were justly proud; and any happily expressed allusions to its leading facts always awakened in their hearts the most lively emotions. These incidents furnished the inspiration of their songs, the themes of their orators, the foundation of their national pride, and their comfort in persecution. Whoever, of their own people, appeared most deeply touched by these memories, had the readiest access to their sympathies, and he who would treat them with indifference or contempt, incurred their utmost hatred. Before such an audience, if Paul had abruptly introduced the name and the new doctrine of Jesus, he might have appeared an apostate from the Jewish faith, seeking to supplant it by something entirely new, and would therefore have kindled the resentment of his Jewish hearers at once. But, beginning with a happy reference to the history of the chosen tribes, and the reign of their most glorious king, and catching up the promise made to David, on which their own most cherished hopes were based, he leads them, by almost imperceptible steps, to the favorable consideration of the fulfillment of that promise in the appearance of Jesus as a Savior to Israel. The reference to John, whom all the Jews now accredited as a prophet, served the same purpose, while it designated more specifically the period in which Jesus had first appeared as a Savior.

* See verse 42, below.

ACTS XIII: 25-29.

The commentators have all noticed the striking similarity between this introduction of Paul's speech and that of Stephen before the Sanhedrim, of which Paul was probably a hearer. But the attentive reader of our comments upon the two speeches will observe that the similarity is merely in the facts referred to, not in the purpose for which the reference is made; Paul's object being merely to favorably introduce his main theme, while Stephen was gathering up a bundle of misdeeds in the history of the fathers, with which to lash the backs of sons who were so wickedly imitating their resistance to the Holy Spirit.

25. Having alluded to John's preparatory ministry, he next introduces the direct testimony which he bore to the Messiahship of Jesus. (25) "*Now, as John was fulfilling his course, he said, Whom think ye that I am? I am not he, but behold, there is coming after me one whose sandal I am not worthy to loose from his feet.*" This was a habitual saying of John, well known to all who heard his preaching, or had heard of it, and it brought to bear the whole weight of his testimony in favor of Jesus.

26. Those who have been accustomed to watch the sympathy between a speaker and his audience can readily perceive, in the change of Paul's manner just here, evidence that he discovered some favorable emotions at work in his audience. He interrupts the thread of his argument, by warmly remarking: (21) "*Brethren, children of the stock of Abraham, and those among you who fear God, to you is the word of this salvation sent.*" But his impetuosity was not so great as to make him forget, altogether, the deep-seated prejudices to be overcome in his audience, or to waive the convincing and persuasive proofs he had yet to present. He proceeds, therefore, with renewed deliberation, to a fuller statement of the argument.

27-29. After claiming that the Messiahship of Jesus was so well authenticated, it was necessary to give some explanation of the singular fact, that the Jews, who knew him well, had put him to death as an impostor. This he does in a way that not only removes all objection, but furnishes additional evidence in his favor. (27) "*For they who dwell in Jerusalem, and their rulers, not knowing him and the voices of the prophets which are read every Sabbath-day, fulfilled them in condemning him.* (28) *And though they found not the least cause of death in him, they requested Pilate that he should be put to death.* (29) *And when they had completed all that was written of him, they took him down from the tree and laid him in a sepulcher.*" Thus, his rejection and death at the hands of the Jews, which might have appeared to Paul's hearers an argument against his claims, are made to tell mightily in his favor, by the fact that this was but the fulfillment of what the prophets had written concerning the Messiah.

In this brief statement of the death and burial of Jesus, Paul makes no distinction between those who put him to death and those who "took him down from the tree, and laid him in the sepulcher." But this omission is entirely justifiable; for, although his friends, Joseph and Nicodemus, performed the last two acts, they did it by the express *permission* of Pilate, and it may be regarded as, in a proper sense, the act of his enemies.

30–33. The speaker proceeds to the climax of his argument; a proof of the Messiahship still more conclusive, if possible, than the testimony of John, or the fulfillment of prophesy. (30) *"But God raised him from the dead; (31) and he was seen many days by those who came up with him from Galilee to Jerusalem, who are his witnesses to the people. (32) And we declare to you glad tidings concerning the promise made to the fathers, (33) that God has fulfilled it to us, their children, by raising up Jesus; as it is also written in the second Psalm, Thou art my son; to-day have I begotten thee."* The fact of the resurrection of Jesus, so well attested by competent witnesses, is introduced, not only as the final proof of his Messiahship, but as happy tidings to these Jews, being no less than the fulfillment of the promise to the fathers, and the realization of their most cherished hopes.

The difficulty of applying the words of David, "Thou art my son; to-day I have begotten thee," to the resurrection of Jesus, has led many commentators to suppose that both it and the expression, "raising up Jesus," refer to his incarnation. But these words of David, in every other instance of their occurrence in the New Testament, are applied to his resurrection, and not to his natural birth. In Hebrews v: 5, Paul says: "Christ glorified not himself to be made a priest, but he who said to him, Thou art my son; to-day have I begotten thee." Now, as Christ was not a priest until after he had died as a *victim*, and was prepared to enter heaven with his own blood, it is clear that these words are applied to his resurrection, at the time of which he entered upon his priestly office. So, likewise, in Hebrews i: 5, the question, "To which of the angels said he at any time, Thou art my son; to-day have I begotten thee?" is adduced as evidence of his superiority to angels, and can not, therefore, refer to the period when he was "made a little lower than the angels."* That the term rendered *begotten* may be properly referred to the resurrection is evident from the fact that he is called the "first begotten from the dead,"† and the "first born from the dead,"‡ in which two expressions the Greek words are the same. He was the "only begotten son of God,"|| by his birth of the Virgin Mary; but he became the "first born from the dead," or the "first born of the whole creation,"§ when he was declared to be the Son of God with power by the resurrection from the dead.¶ In applying the quotation from the second Psalm, therefore, to the resurrection, and endeavoring to cheer the Jews in Antioch, with the thought that a long-cherished and familiar promise was thereby fulfilled, Paul was giving his real understanding of the passage quoted, and it is one as much more cheering than that which many commentators have gathered from it, as the exaltation of Christ from the grave to his throne in the heavens was a more glorious birth than that which brought him into this sinful world.

34–37. That we have given the true explanation of the clause last quoted is confirmed by the course of the argument in that which follows, in which the speaker continues to quote from David, to prove that, according to his prophesies, the Messiah should rise from the dead. (34) *"Now that he did raise him from the dead, no more to*

---

* Heb. ii: 9.   † Rev. i: 5.   ‡ Col. i: 18.
|| John i: 14, 18.   § Col. i: 15.   ¶ Rom. i: 4.

return to corruption, he spoke thus: I will give to you the sure mercies of David. (35) *Wherefore he also says in another psalm, Thou wilt not suffer thy Holy One to see corruption.* (36) *For David, after he had served his own generation by the will of God, fell asleep, and was added to his fathers, and saw corruption;* (37) *but he whom God raised up did not see corruption.*"

The words quoted from the fifty-fifth chapter of Isaiah, "I will give you the sure mercies of David," have given no little trouble to both translators and interpreters. No translator can feel well satisfied with rendering τὰ ὅσια Δαυὶδ τὰ πιστά, *the sure mercies of David;* yet the literal translators have generally adopted this as the best that can be done. I think the words mean *the holy things made sure to David.* The purpose of the quotation is to prove that God would raise the Messiah from the dead no more to return to corruption. He assumes, therefore, that the words quoted refer to the Messiah, and that his hearers would not dispute the reference. Whatever, therefore, might otherwise be our own understanding of the words, we must take this as their true reference. The promise is addressed not to the Messiah, but to the Jews; for the pronoun *you* (ὑμῖν) is in the plural number. It is a promise, then, to give to the Jews the holy things faithfully promised to David, among which was the promise already referred to, "Thou wilt not suffer thy Holy One to see corruption." It furnished, therefore, the required proof that the Messiah would rise, and not see corruption.

The only objection which his hearers would be likely to raise against the argument is, that in the words, "Thou wilt not suffer thy Holy One to see corruption," David spoke of himself. But this objection is anticipated by the remark that David had fallen asleep and seen corruption, whereas he, Jesus, whom God raised up, as was proved by the witnesses who saw him alive, did not see corruption; hence to him the words must refer. According, therefore, to the only possible application of David's words, and to the admitted reference of the words quoted from Isaiah, they were bound to admit that Jesus was the Messiah.

38, 39. Having now established, by brief, but unanswerable arguments, the Messiahship of Jesus, Paul proceeds to offer the audience the benefit of his mediation. (38) "*Be it known to you, therefore, brethren, that through this man is preached to you the remission of sins;* (39) *and in him every one who believes is justified from all from which you could not be justified in the law of Moses.*" The expression ἐν τούτῳ, *in him,* not *by him* as rendered in the common version, indicates that the parties to be justified must be *in* Christ, that is, in subjection to his authority; as the expression ἐν τῷ νόμῳ, *in the law,* applies to those who were under the law, and not to uncircumcised Gentiles who were not under it. The benefits of the Jewish law extended only to those who were born in, or properly initiated into the body of people to whom the law was given; and just so, the remission of sins is preached only to those who shall be *in* Christ by being properly initiated into his body.

By the antithesis here instituted between the law and the gospel, Paul assumes that there was no remission of sins enjoyed by those under the law. For he asserts that there were some things "from which they could not be justified in the law of Moses;" and in the expression "justified from *all* from which you could not be justified in the law," the true supplement after *all* is *sins*, taken from the preceding clause. He announces that remission of sins is preached through Jesus, and from *these* he assumes that under the law there was no justification. This point, indeed, would need no argument, even if the context did not settle it; for certainly, if there was any thing from which one under the law could not be justified, it was *sin;* and, on the other hand, in Christ we are justified from nothing but sin. The assumption is not, that justification can not be procured by *works of law*, for this is equally true under Christ; but that those under the law of Moses did not obtain remission of sins at all.

Paul argues this assumption at length, in the ninth and tenth chapters of Hebrews. The only provisions in the law at all connected with remission of sins were its sacrifices; and he asserts of them, "It is not possible that the blood of bulls and of goats should take away sins."* It can not be rightly assumed that he contemplates these sacrifices as considered apart from their typical meaning; for he makes no such distinction. He takes them just as he finds them, with all that belongs to them when offered in good faith, and makes the assertion that it is not possible for them to take away sins. In the preceding verses of the same chapter he presents a specific argument based upon this broad assertion: "The law, having a shadow of good things to come, and not the very image of those things, can *never*, by those sacrifices which they offer year by year continually, *make the comers thereunto perfect.*" He proves this proposition, and shows the particular in which they were still imperfect, by adding, "For then would they not have ceased to be offered? Because the worshipers, once cleansed, would have no more *conscience* of sins."† If a man had once obtained remission of particular sins, he would, of course, as is here argued, no longer offer sacrifices for those sins, seeing that his conscience would no longer annoy him in reference to them. But it is a fact, he argues further, that "In those sacrifices there is a remembrance of sins made every year."‡ The sins of the year, for which offerings had been made daily, were remembered again on the annual day of atonement, and new sacrifices offered for them, declaring to the worshiper that they were still remembered against him. As this continued, annually, throughout the life of the pious Jew, it left him in the same condition at the day of his death, and he was gathered to his fathers with his sins still unforgiven.

The same truth is taught in the very terms of the new covenant. In stating the points of dissimilarity between it and the old covenant made at Mount Sinai, the Lord says, "I will be merciful to their unrighteousness, and their sins and their iniquities will I *remember no more;*" implying that under the old covenant this blessing was not enjoyed.§

We can not dismiss this topic without paying some attention to the question which forces itself upon us, What did the saints, under the old covenant, enjoy in reference to forgiveness, and what is the mean-

* Heb. x: 4. † Heb. x: 1, 2. ‡ Heb. x: 3. § Heb. viii: 8-12.

ing of the promise so often attached to sin offerings, "The priest shall make an atonement for him concerning his sin, and it shall be *forgiven* him?"* If we had nothing but this promise to guide us, we could but conclude that the party was, at the time, really forgiven; but with Paul's comments upon it before us, we are compelled to avoid this conclusion, and seek some other explanation of the words. There can not be less than a *promise* of pardon in the words quoted; and as it can not be a promise fulfilled at the time, it must be a promise reserved to some future period for fulfillment.

That the promise of pardon made to Jews and patriarch was reserved for fulfillment to the death of Christ, Paul affirms in these words: "On this account he is the mediator of the new covenant, that by means of death for the redemption of the transgressions that were under the *first* covenant, they who were called, (that is, the ancient elect,) "might *receive* the *promise* of eternal *inheritance*."† Here the reception of the "promise of eternal inheritance," by those who were under the first covenant, is made to depend upon the redemption of their transgressions. This redemption was not effected till the death of Christ; therefore, till his death their transgressions remained unforgiven. Though they had the *promise* of pardon, and rejoiced in the full assurance that it would yet be granted, they were compelled to regard it as a blessing of the future and not of the present. Their enjoyment, as compared with that of the saints under the new covenant, was as that of one who has from God a promise of pardon, compared with him who has it already in possession. Their happiness, like ours, depended upon their faith in God's word.

40, 41. This passage in Paul's speech was most unwelcome to his Jewish hearers. It was an express disparagement of the law of Moses such as always fell harshly upon Jewish ears. We consequently see in the next and last paragraph of the speech an indication of a change in the aspect of the audience. It is only an audience in whom a most unfavorable change is discernible, that so watchful a speaker could address in these words: (40) "*Beware, then, lest that which is said in the prophets come upon you;* (41) *Behold, ye despisers, and wonder and perish; for I do a work in your days, a work which you will not believe though one should fully declare it to you.*" No doubt some evidence of their incredulity was visible in their countenances, if it was not exhibited by audible murmurings. The force of the quotation was to show, that if they did reject the gospel, they would only be identifying themselves with a class of whom this conduct had been predicted.

The surprise expressed by the prophet, that they would not believe though one should declare it to them, does not assume that they should believe facts so astounding upon the mere assertion of an individual; but the object of surprise is, that they would not believe though one should declare it *fully* to them, that is, with all the incontestible evidences of its reality. Undoubtedly the *work* referred to by the apostle, in his application of the prophet's language, is the work of raising up a savior to Israel in the person of Jesus.

42, 43. When Paul's speech was concluded, the synagogue was

---

* Lev. chapters iv and v, *passim*, and xvi: 30-34.   † Heb. ix: 15.

dismissed and the apostle had an opportunity to learn what particular effects had been produced. The people, candid and outspoken, left him in no doubt on the subject. (42) *"Now as they were going out, they entreated that these words should be spoken to them the next Sabbath, (43) and, the synagogue being dismissed, many of the Jews and devout proselytes followed Paul and Barnabas, who, talking to them, persuaded them to continue in the favor of God."* Thus, notwithstanding the majority of the Jews in the audience gave such evidence of incredulity as to extort the warning with which Paul closed his speech, some of them were ready to believe; while the Gentile proselytes, less affected by Jewish prejudices, and, therefore, better prepared to do justice to the speaker, were most deeply interested. The picture which Luke gives of their following Paul and Barnabas in a crowd away from the synagogue, and keeping up an earnest conversation, is a striking exhibition of the simple habits of the people, as well as of the interest which they felt in the new and thrilling theme of the discourse.

44. So deep an interest kindled in the synagogue, and taking hold of Gentile minds, could not fail to spread widely through the city during the following week, and its progress was doubtless furthered by the most active private exertions of Paul and Barnabas. The result was seen in the next assemblage at the synagogue. (44) *"On the next Sabbath almost the whole city were gathered together to hear the word of God."*

45. So large an assemblage of the people, to hear a doctrine which appeared disparaging to the law of Moses, and which had, on this account, already offended the mass of the Jews, could but arouse their utmost indignation. They acted according to their uniform policy under such circumstances. (45) *"But the Jews, when they saw the multitudes were filled with zeal, and contradicted the things spoken by Paul, contradicting and blaspheming."* This was one of the instances in which Paul could say, "I bear them witness that they have a *zeal* of God, but not according to knowledge."* It was useless to reason with them further, or to attempt to conciliate them.

46, 47. When men take a stand like this, nothing will satisfy them but an abandonment of the truth; and hence that conciliatory bearing which should mark our address to them up to this point, may, with propriety, be dismissed, and we may proceed without regard to their feelings. So the apostles acted. (46) *" Then Paul and Barnabas, speaking boldly, said, It was necessary that the word of God should first be spoken to you; but since you put it from you, and judge yourselves unworthy of everlasting life, behold we turn to the Gentiles. (47) For thus has the Lord commanded us, I have placed thee as a light of the Gentiles, that thou mayest be for salvation to the extremity of the earth."*† The remark that it was necessary that the word of God should first be spoken to them, before turning to the Gentiles, shows that the apostles understood that the gospel was not only to begin in Jerusalem, but that, in every distinct community, it was to *begin with the Jews.* Hence the frequent occurrence, in Paul's style, of the expression, "To the Jew first, and also to the Gentile."‡ The

* Rom. x: 2.   † Is. xlix: 6.   ‡ Rom. ii: 9, 10.

ACTS XIII: 48.

reason of this distinction has been discussed in the commentary on Acts i: 8.

48. In the next paragraph we have a statement, the meaning of which has excited no little controversy. (48) "*On hearing this the Gentiles rejoiced, and glorified the word of the Lord, and as many as were determined for eternal life believed.*" The controversy turns upon the meaning of the clause ὅσοι ἦσαν τεταγμένοι εἰς ζωὴν αἰώνιον, rendered, in the common version "as many as were *ordained* to eternal life." The Calvinistic writers unite in referring it to the eternal election and foreordination taught in their creeds. They contend, therefore, for the rendering "were ordained," or "were appointed." If their interpretation were admitted, it would involve the passage in some difficulties which none of them seem to have noticed. If it be true that "as *many* as were *foreordained* to eternal life believed," then there were none of the foreordained left in that community who did not believe. Hence, all those who did not then believe, whether adults or infants, were among the reprobate, who were predestinated to everlasting punishment. Now it is certainly most singular that so complete a separation of the two parties should take place throughout a whole community at one time; and still more singular that Luke should so far depart from the custom of inspired writers as to state the fact. Again, the same statement implies that all who believed on that occasion were of the elect. For, if the parties who believed were those who had been foreordained to eternal life, then none of the non-elect could have been among the number. Here is another anomalous incident: that on this occasion all who believed were of the number who would finally be saved, and that Luke should be informed of the fact and make it known to his readers. Certainly we should not adopt an interpretation involving conclusions so anomalous, unless we are compelled to do so by the obvious force of the words employed.

It is worthy of note that the efforts of Calvinistic writers to prove that this is the meaning of these words consist chiefly in strong assertions to that effect, and in attempts to answer the feebler class of the objections urged against it. Thus Dr. Hackett asserts: "This is the only translation which the philology of the passage allows." But he makes no effort to prove that the New Testament usage of the principal word involved allows this translation. The word rendered *ordained* in this passage is τασσω—a term which is not employed in a single instance in the New Testament in the sense of *foreordained.* Where that idea is to be expressed, other words are uniformly employed.

The word in question is a generic term, having no single word in English to fully represent it. Its generic sense is best represented by our phrase, *set in order*. In its various specific applications, however, we have single terms which accurately represent it. Thus, when Jesus ἐτάξατο *set in order* a certain mountain in Galilee as a place to meet his disciples,* or the Jews in Rome ταξάμενοι *set in order* a day to meet Paul,† we best express the idea by *appointed*.‡ But when

---
* Matt. xxviii: 16. † Acts xxviii: 23.
‡ It expresses the same idea in Luke vii: 8; Acts xxii: 10.

Paul says of civil rulers that "the existing authorities τεταγμέναι εἰσὶν *were set in order* by God,"* he does not intend to affirm that God had *appointed* those rulers, but merely asserts his general providence in their existence and arrangement. The idea is best expressed in English by using the phrase *set in order*, or by saying they were *arranged* by God. When he asserts of the household of Stephanas, in Corinth, that ἔταξαν ἑαυτοὺς they *set themselves in order* for ministering to the saints,† we would say they *devoted* themselves to ministering to the saints. But when the brethren in Antioch had been puzzled by the disputation between Paul and Barnabas and "certain men who came down from Judea," in reference to circumcision, and they finally ἔταξαν, *set in order*, to send some of both parties to the apostles and elders in Jerusalem for a decision, the common version very correctly renders it, "they *determined* that Paul and Barnabas and certain others of them should go."‡

In reference to the propriety of this last rendering, Dr. Hackett asserts that this term "*was not used to denote an act of the mind;*"|| but the awkward translation of this passage to which the assertion forces him is evidence conclusive against it. He renders it, "They *appointed* that Paul and Barnabas and certain others of them should go up to Jerusalem."§ This is an ungrammatical use of the word appointed. When a mission has been determined upon, we *appoint* the individuals who shall be sent, but we do not *appoint* that *they shall go*. Evidently, the state of the case was this: the brethren were at first *undetermined* what to do in reference to the question in dispute, but finally *determined* to send to Jerusalem for an authoritative decision of it. When a man is undetermined in reference to a pressing question, his mind is in *confusion;* but when he determines upon his course, it is no longer *confusion*, but is *set in order*. The term in question, therefore, meaning primarily to *set in order*, is most happily adapted to the expression of such a state of mind. Our English word *dispose* has a similar usage. It means *to arrange in a certain order*, and applies primarily to external objects; but when one's *mind* is found arranged in accordance with a certain line of conduct, we say he is *disposed* to pursue it.

We scarcely need observe, after the above remarks, that the specific meaning attached to the generic term in question, in any particular passage, is to be determined by the context. In the passage we are now considering, the context has no allusion to any thing like an *appointment* of one part, and a *rejection* of the other; but the writer draws a line of distinction between the *conduct* of certain Gentiles and that of the *Jews* addressed by Paul in the closing paragraph of his speech. To render the contrast between the two more conspicuous, he throws his words into antithesis with those of Paul. Paul had said to the Jews, "You put the *word* of God *from* you;" Luke says of the Gentiles, "They *glorified* the *word* of the Lord." Paul said, "You *judge* yourselves *unworthy* of everlasting life;" Luke says, many of the Gentiles "*were determined* for everlasting life." It is an act of the mind to which Paul objects on the part of the Jews, and it is as clearly an act of mind in the Gentiles which Luke puts in contrast with it. At some previous time in their history, these Gentiles, like

* Rom. xiii: 2.   † 1 Cor. xvi: 15.   ‡ Acts xv: 2. | Com. *in loco*.   § Com. xv: 2.

all others, had been undetermined in reference to everlasting life, either because they were not convinced that there was such a state, or because they hesitated to seek for it. But now their minds were *set in order* upon the subject, by being *determined* to labor for the eternal life which Paul preached. It now remains, in order to full elucidation of the passage, that we account for the connection indicated between their being determined for everlasting life, and their believing. The former stands as a cause which led to the latter. Let it be noted that everlasting life is not contemplated as the *object* of their belief, for, if it was, they would have had to *believe* in it, before they could *determine* for it; so that the order of the two mental acts would be reversed. But, in common with the Jews, who had been their religious instructors, they already believed in a future state, and what they now learned to believe by Paul's preaching was the gospel of Christ. Those of them who had, either through previous religious instruction, or through the influence of Paul's preaching, heartily determined for eternal life, were in a better frame of mind to appreciate the evidence in favor of that Christ through whom alone it could be obtained, than the others who were so undetermined upon the subject that they appeared to judge themselves unworthy of such a destiny. Such was the difference between the two classes in the audience, and Luke's object is to declare the result of this difference in the fact that the one class *believed*, and the other thrust the word of God from them. To say that the difference had been wrought in them exclusively by divine agency would be to rob them of responsibility. Or to say that the favorably-disposed party had become so exclusively by their own self-determining energy would be to deny the influence of divine truth. Neither of these positions can be true; but, while it was an act of their own minds to determine for eternal life, it was God who had induced them to do so; at the same time, the other party determined against eternal life, in despite of the same divine influence exerted upon them.

49–52. The animosity of the Jews, excited by the success of the apostles, finally resulted in their expulsion from the city. The account is given in brief terms: (49) "*And the word of the Lord was published throughout the whole region.* (50) *But the Jews stirred up the devout and honorable women, and the chief men of the city, and raised a persecution against Paul and Barnabas, and expelled them from their borders.* (51) *And they, shaking off the dust of their feet against them, went into Iconium.* (52) *But the disciples were full of joy and the Holy Spirit.*" The means by which this persecution was brought about serves to illustrate the relation which the Jews who were settled in Gentile cities sustained to the surrounding society. They had no political power in their own hands, and dared not lay violent hands upon the apostles. But certain "honorable women," wives of the "chief men of the city," had come under their influence by attending the synagogue worship, and through them they gained access to their unbelieving husbands so as to induce them to expel Paul and Barnabas. It is a suggestive fact, that the women who were made instruments of a transaction so discreditable are styled "*devout* women." It shows that *devotion* in the worship of God, like zeal when not according to knowledge, may be made to do the devil's own work. The more devout one's feelings, while his mind is corrupted by false conceptions of duty, the greater mischief he is likely to do; so far is it from being true, that to make the heart right is to make the whole man right. No man is safe without a proper *understanding* of his duty, derived from the word of God.

Paul and Barnabas were not without indignation when they were thus ignominiously expelled from the city; but the only exhibition which they made of it was that which the Savior had directed; "they shook off the dust of their feet against them."* This was not a mere idle or childish mark of resentment, as it would be in an uninspired teacher; but was designed as "a testimony against them," a solemn warning of the righteous judgment of God, whom they had rejected in rejecting his chosen messengers.†

We would imagine that the young disciples, from whom their religious teachers were thus violently driven away, would have been overwhelmed with grief and fear. But we are told, as quoted above, that they were "filled with joy and with the Holy Spirit." The full assurance given by the gospel of that everlasting life which they had "determined for," and the belief that the Spirit of God dwelt in their mortal bodies, supplied them with a joy which was no longer dependent on human agency, and of which human power could not deprive them.

XIV: 1, 2. In Iconium the two missionaries met with better success than in Antioch, but they encountered similar opposition, and from the same source. (1) "*Now it came to pass in Iconium, that they went together into the synagogue of the Jews, and so spoke that a great multitude, both of the Jews and the Greeks, believed.* (2) *But the unbelieving Jews stirred up and disaffected the minds of the Gentiles against the brethren.*" The multitude of Jews and Gentiles who believed must have been "great," not in comparison to the whole population, but to the number who were usually convinced under such circumstances, and especially to the number who had just been convinced in Antioch. For we see that the unbelieving Jews were still an influential body, and the remark that they "disaffected the minds of the Gentiles" indicates that the mass of the Gentiles were still unbelievers.

It should not escape the notice of the reader, that the conviction of these people is attributed distinctly to the force of what the apostles *spoke*. They "*so spoke* that a great multitude believed." This is one among many incidental remarks of Luke, which indicate that he had no conception of the modern doctrine that faith is produced by an abstract operation of the Holy Spirit, and which confirm by historic facts the doctrine of Paul, that faith comes by hearing the word of God.‡

3–7. This divided and excited state of the public mind continued during the whole time that Paul and Barnabas remained in the city. (3) "*They continued there a long time, speaking boldly respecting the Lord, who bore testimony to the word of his favor, and granted signs and wonders to be done through their hands.* (4) *Yet the multitude of the city was divided: some were with the Jews, and others with the apos-*

* Mark vi: 11.   † Luke x: 16.   ‡ Rom. x: 17.

tles. (5) *But when an onset was made by both Gentiles and Jews, with their rulers, to abuse and stone them,* (6) *they, being aware of it, fled down to the cities of Lycaonia, Lystra, and Derbe, and the surrounding country;* (7) *and there they preached the gospel."* In the rapid sketch which Luke is giving us of this rather hurried missionary tour, he makes no definite note of time, to indicate how long the two missionaries remained at any particular place. The above remark, that they continued in Iconium "a long time," is the only note of the kind in the tour, and it is very indefinite. It only indicates that their stay here was long in comparison with that at most other places during this tour.

Though their preaching here was not as successful as might have been expected from the length of time employed, it received abundant attestations of the Lord's approval. The proof of this fact adduced by Luke is quite different from that often adduced for a similar purpose by modern writers. Now, the proof that a man's ministry is "owned and accepted" by the Lord, is found in the "abundant outpourings of the Spirit" which attend it; and this, in other words, means the number of "powerful conversions" with which it is rewarded. But the Lord's method of bearing testimony to the word of his favor, according to Luke, was by "granting signs and wonders to be done" by the hands of the preachers; while not a word is said, either by him or any other inspired writer, of such a spiritual attestation as is now so confidently referred to. This shows that our modern revivalists have confounded the attestations of the word by signs and miracles, which was common, in apostolic times, with the exciting scenes which now occur in their revivals. This mistake not only confounds things essentially different, but assumes that the apostles were accustomed to scenes of which they never dreamed. Moreover, it erects a false and very injurious standard by which to judge whether a man's ministry is acceptable to God. If the preacher who is most successful in gaining converts is the one whose ministry is most acceptable to God, then there is not the same value in earnest piety, a blameless life, and watchful oversight of the flock which the apostolic epistles would lead us to believe; since it sometimes occurs that men who obtain the fame of great "revivalists," are quite deficient in these essential characteristics of an acceptable minister of the Word.

The onset made by the multitude, like the similar proceeding in Antioch, was instigated by the unbelieving Jews, though effected chiefly by the Gentiles and the rulers of the city. The escape of the missionaries must have been narrow, and was probably owing to the kindness of some stranger, whom Paul and Barnabas may have remembered with gratitude, but whose name will not be known to the great world till the day of eternity.

8–12. The district of Lycaonia, into which the apostles had fled, was an interior district of Asia Minor, lying north of the Taurus Mountains, but of very indefinite boundaries. The exact situation of the two towns, Lystra and Derbe, is not now known. With the character of the people, however, which is the important consideration in a narrative like this, we are made sufficiently acquainted by the narrative itself. It was one of those retired districts, remote from the great marts of trade and the routes of travel, where the people retained their primitive habits, spoke their primitive dialect, and knew little of either the civilization of the Greeks, or the religion of the Jews. This rude state of society will account for some of the peculiarities of the following narrative.

Finding no Jewish synagogues, to afford them an assembly of devout hearers, the missionaries took advantage of such other opportunities as offered, to get the ears of the people. Having succeeded in collecting a crowd in Lystra, they met with the following incident: (8) *"A certain man in Lystra was sitting, impotent in his feet, a cripple from his birth, who had never walked.* (9) *The same was listening to Paul speaking, who, looking intently upon him, and seeing that he had faith to be healed,* (10) *said with a loud voice, Stand upright on your feet;** *and he leaped and walked about.* (11) *The multitude, seeing what Paul did, lifted up their voice in the speech of Lycaonia, and said, The gods have come down to us in the likeness of men.* (12) *And they called Barnabas Jupiter, and Paul, because he was the chief speaker, Mercury."*

Although Paul had been speaking to them of the true God, and of his Son Jesus Christ, until the cripple, at least, believed; yet, when the miracle was wrought before them, all their heathenish ideas rushed back upon their minds, and they at once supposed that they stood in the presence of gods. Such was the natural conclusion of men who had been educated from childhood to believe the strange inventions of heathen mythology. It was an honest mistake, committed through ignorance.

Their conclusion as to which of the gods had appeared, was as natural and as instantaneous as their conviction that they *were* gods. They had a temple, or a statue, or perhaps both, in front of their city, as we learn below, to the honor of Jupiter; hence any god who might appear to them would be naturally taken for him. But when two gods appeared together, the one who acts as chief speaker could be no other than Mercury, the god of Eloquence, and the constant attendant of Jupiter in his terrestrial visits. The remark of Luke that Paul was called Mercury "because he was the chief speaker," shows that he was familiar with Greek mythology.

13. The people felt the warmest gratitude for the visit of their supposed gods, and gave expression to their feeling in the most approved method. (13) *"Then the priest of the Jupiter that was before the city brought bulls and garlands to the gates, and, with the people, wished to offer sacrifices to them."* The garlands of flowers were designed, according to a well-known custom of the ancients, to deck the forms of the bulls about to be offered. It is not altogether certain whether the "gates" referred to are those of a private court within which Paul and Barnabas may have retired when first greeted as gods, or the gates of the city, of which there may have been two or more in the same part of the wall, and near which the apostles may have remained with a part of the crowd. The latter I regard as the most probable supposition.† The sacrifices were to be offered to the supposed gods in person, and not to the image which stood before the city.

---

* On the faith to be healed. See Com. Acts iii: 16.
† The criticism of Mr. Howson, vol. 1, p. 193, *note* upon πυλωνις as meaning *only* the

14–18. Nothing could have been more unexpected or more painful to the humble missionaries, than a demonstration of this kind. The purpose of the priest and the crowd with him was, doubtless, communicated to them before the rites were commenced. (14) *"Which when the apostles Barnabas and Paul heard, they rent their clothes, and ran into the crowd, crying aloud,* (15) *and saying, Men, why do you do these things? We are men of like passions with yourselves, preaching the gospel to you, that you should turn from these vanities to the living God, who made the heavens and the earth, and the sea, and all things that are in them;* (16) *who in generations past suffered all the Gentiles to go on in their own ways;* (17) *although he did not leave himself without testimony, doing good, and giving you rains from heaven, and fruitful seasons, filling your hearts with food and gladness.* (18) *And by saying these things they with difficulty restrained the people from offering sacrifice to them."*

The habit of rending one's clothes under the influence of sudden passion, which Paul and Barnabas had inherited from their ancestors, and fell into on this occasion, appears very singular to the taste of western nations. The earliest historical traces of it are found in the family of Jacob,* and the example of Job;† and the latest in the instance before us, which is the only one recorded of the apostles. How so childish and destructive a custom could have originated, it is difficult to imagine; but when once introduced, it is easy to see how it might be transmitted by imitation, until the use of more costly garments would put a stop to it with the economical, or the restraints of a more enlightened piety would mollify the passions of the religious. It was, certainly, very inconsistent with the calm self-possession inculcated by Christ and the apostles; but we can excuse Barnabas and Saul on this occasion, in consideration of their early habits, which often spring unexpectedly upon men in a moment of sudden excitement.

In describing their effort to restrain the idolatry of the multitude, Luke once more reverses their names, saying Barnabas and Saul, as he did before the conversion of Sergius Paulus. This is because Barnabas was called *Jupiter*, and was the chief figure in this scene. The care with which Luke thus changes the order of their names, according as one or the other is most prominent, confirms what we have already said of the pre-eminence of Barnabas previous to the commencement of this missionary tour.‡

Though Barnabas, on this occasion, received the chief honor at the hands of the people, yet Paul continued to play the part of Mercury which the people had assigned him; for the speech to the idolaters bears unmistakable marks of his paternity. Mr. Howson notices the coincidence between the exhortation to the Lystrians, that they "should turn from these vanities to the living God," and his remark to the Thessalonians, that they had "turned from idols to serve the living and true God;" between the remark that "in generations past God suffered the Gentiles to go on in their own ways," and his state-

gates of a private court, is refuted by its frequent use in Revelations for the gates of a city, xxi: 12, 13, 21–25.
* Gen. xxxvii: 29–34. † Job i: 20. ‡ See Com. xiii: 9.

ment to the Athenians, that "the times of this ignorance God had overlooked;" and finally, between the argument by which he proves that God had not left himself without testimony among the heathen, and that in Romans, where he says, (to quote the common version,) "The invisible things of him, from the creation of the world, are clearly seen, being understood by the things that are made, even his eternal power and Godhead, so that they are without excuse." To which I would add, that the coincidence in *thought* between this speech, so far as reported, and that made in Athens to another company of idolaters is so striking, that the latter might be regarded as the same speech, only modified to suit the circumstances of the audience and the peculiarities of the occasion.

The speech and manner of the apostles finally brought the people back to their senses. It was a sad disappointment to know that their wonderful visitors were only men like themselves, and this conviction left them in great bewilderment as to the nature of the superhuman power which Paul had exerted.

19. This state of suspense was most favorable to the acceptance of Paul's own explanation of his miraculous power, and consequently to their belief of the gospel; and we can not doubt that some of the disciples, whom we afterward find there, owed their conviction, in part, to this circumstance. But with those who did not promptly embrace the faith, the same suspense made room for explanations unfavorable to conviction, and such explanations were soon given. (19) *"But Jews from Antioch and Iconium came thither, and having persuaded the multitude, and stoned Paul, they dragged him out of the city, supposing that he was dead."* The readiness with which a people who had so recently offered divine honors to Paul were persuaded to stone him to death, though at the first glance surprising, is but a natural result of all the circumstances. That portion of them who had been prominent in the idolatrous proceedings felt mortified at the discovery of their mistake, and were naturally inclined to excuse their own folly by throwing censure upon the innocent objects of it. The Jews stimulated this feeling by urging that Paul was an impostor, and that all the honorable women and chief men of Antioch and Iconium had united in driving him away from those cities. This enabled them to charge him with willful deception, and as their feelings were already keyed up to their utmost tension they were easily swayed to the opposite extreme, and at a nod from the Jews they were ready to dash him to pieces. That Paul, rather than Barnabas, was the victim of their wrath, resulted from the fact that both here and in the cities from which the Jews had come, he was the chief speaker. The same circumstance which had given him the inferior place in their idolatry, gave him, finally, the superior place in their hatred.

20. Although Paul's physical constitution was feeble, he had, as is often the case with such constitutions, great tenacity of life. The mob left him, thinking he was dead. (20) *"But while the disciples were standing around him, he rose up, and entered into the city, and the next day he went out with Barnabas into Derbe."*

21, 22. Having been compelled to fly from Antioch to Iconium, and from Iconium to Lystra, wading into deeper dangers at every step,

ACTS XIV: 21-23.   177

who can tell the feelings with which the wounded missionary enters the gate of another heathen city, bearing visible marks of the indignity he had suffered, to excite the contempt of the people? We know, from the expression given to his feelings on some other occasions, that now they must have been gloomy indeed. But he who brings light out of darkness caused a refreshing light to shine upon the darkening pathway of his faithful servant, by granting him here a peaceful and abundant harvest of souls. (21) "*And when they had preached the gospel in that city, and made many disciples, they returned to Lystra, Iconium and Antioch,* (22) *confirming the souls of the disciples, exhorting them to continue in the faith, and that through many tribulations we must enter into the kingdom of God.*" Luke passes hurriedly over these scenes; but the uninspired imagination loves to linger among them, to sympathize with the suffering apostles in their afflictions and comforts, and also with the congregations in the four cities, as the two brethren, who had come among them like visitors from a better world, were bidding them farewell, and leaving them to make their own way through many temptations into the everlasting kingdom of God.

23. They were left as "sheep in the midst of wolves;" but they were committed to the care of the great Shepherd of the sheep, and were supplied with under-shepherds to keep them in the fold. (23) "*And having appointed for them elders in every Church, and prayed with fasting, they commended them to the Lord, in whom they believed.*" Here we have the same prayer and fasting, connected with the appointment of elders, which we have already noticed upon the appointment of the seven deacons in Jerusalem, and upon the sending forth of Paul and Barnabas from Antioch. The laying on of hands, which was a part of the ceremony on those occasions, is not here mentioned; but as we have already seen that it was a part of the ceremony of appointment to office,* and as the apostles are said to have *appointed* these elders, we may safely infer that it was not omitted.

As the office exercised by these elders, and the number of them in each congregation, have been made subjects of controversy, we will devote some space to grouping a few facts which bear upon these points. The passage before us contains the earliest mention of the *appointment* of elders, yet these were by no means the first elders appointed. For Paul and Barnabas, when sent to Jerusalem with a contribution for the poor saints, delivered it to "the elders."† This shows that there were already elders in the Churches in Judea. Paul and Barnabas, on their present tour, appointed elders in *every* Church; Titus was left in Crete that he might set in order the things that were omitted, and appoint elders in *every* city;‡ and James takes it for granted that every Church has elders, by directing, in his *general* epistle, that the sick should call for the *elders of the Church*, to pray for them and anoint them with oil, with a view to their recovery.∥ In view of these facts, it can not be doubted that the office of elder was universal in the apostolic Churches.

That the term *elder* is used as an official title, and not merely to indicate the older members of the Church, is sufficiently evident from the fact that men became elders by *appointment*, whereas an appoint-

* Com. vi: 6; xiii: 3.   † Acts xi: 30.   ‡ Titus i: 5.   ∥ James v: 14.

ment can not make one an *old man.* The fact that these officers were called *elders* indicates that they were generally selected from the elderly class; still, it does not necessarily imply that, to be an elder officially, a man must be an elder in years. Terms which are appropriated as official titles do not always retain their original meanings. Whether advanced age is necessary to the elder's office is to be determined, not by the official title, but by the qualifications prescribed. But, inasmuch as no such qualification is anywhere prescribed, we conclude that any brother who possesses the qualifications which *are* prescribed, may be made an elder, though he be not an old man.

The term *bishop* in our common version, rendered in some English versions *overseer,* is but another title for this same officer. This is evident, *first,* from the fact that the same brethren of the congregation in Ephesus, who came down to Miletus to meet Paul, are styled by Luke "*elders* of the Church," and by Paul, *bishops.** *Second,* in the epistle to Titus, Paul uses the two terms interchangeably. He tells Titus that he left him in Crete to ordain *elders* in every city, prescribes some of the qualifications for the office, and assigns as a reason for them, "for a *bishop* must be blameless," etc. If Washington, in his Farewell Address, had advised the American people to always elect as *President* a man of known integrity, and had given as a reason for it that the *chief magistrate* of a great people should be of blameless reputation, it would be as reasonable to deny that the terms *president* and *chief magistrate* are used interchangeably, as that the terms *elder* and *bishop* are in this passage.

That there was a *plurality* of elders in each congregation could hardly be disputed by an unbiased reader of the New Testament. Two facts, alone, would seem sufficient to settle this question: *first,* the fact that Titus was to ordain *elders,* not *an elder,* in every city;† *second,* that they were *elders,* and not *an elder* from the Church in Ephesus, who came to meet Paul at Miletus.‡ The objection sometimes urged, that there may have been several Churches in each of these cities, and that the plurality of elders was made up of the single elders from the individual Churches, is based upon a conjecture utterly without historic foundation. But if the argument from these passages were waived, the issue is conclusively settled by the statement of our text, that Paul and Barnabas "appointed *elders* in every Church." A *plurality* of elders, therefore, and not a *single one,* were appointed for each Church.

A full exhibition of the duties of the elder's office, and of the moral and intellectual qualifications requisite to an appointment thereto, belongs to a commentary on the First Epistle to Timothy, rather than on Acts of Apostles. We will not, therefore, consider them here, further than to observe that the duties were such as can not be safely dispensed with in any congregation; while the qualifications were such as were then, and are now, but seldom combined in a single individual. Indeed, it can not be supposed that Paul found in the young congregations of Lystra, Iconium, Antioch, and every other planted during this tour, men who could *fill up* the measure of the qualifications

* Acts xx: 17, 28.   † Titus 1: 5.   ‡ Acts xx: 17.

which he prescribes for this office.* But he appointed elders in every Church, hence he must have selected those who came nearest the standard. It is not an admissible objection to this argument, that inspiration may have supplied the defects of certain brethren in each congregation, so as to fully qualify them; for moral excellencies, which are the principal of these qualifications, are not supplied by inspiration. The truth is, the qualifications for this office, like the characteristics prescribed for old men, aged women, young men and women, and widows, respectively, are to be regarded as a model for imitation, rather than a standard to which all elders must fully attain. It were as reasonable to keep persons of these respective ages out of the Church, until they fill up the characters prescribed for them, as to keep a Church without elders until it can furnish men perfect in the qualifications of the office. Common sense and Scripture authority both unite in demanding that we should rather follow Paul's example, and appoint elders in *every* Church from the best material which the Church affords.

The qualifications to be prescribed for one who would fill an office depend upon the duties of the office. Imperfection in the qualifications leads to proportionate inefficiency in the performance of the duties. Seeing, then, that but few men are found possessing, in a high degree, all the qualifications for the office of bishop, we should not be surprised that its duties have generally been more or less inefficiently performed. Much less should we, as so many have done, seek a remedy for this inefficiency, in an entire subversion of the Church organization instituted by the apostles. After all that can be said to the contrary, the apostolic plan has proved itself more efficient than any of those invented by men. Those congregations of the present day which are under the oversight of an efficient eldership, other things being equal, come nearer, in every good word and work, to the apostolic model of a Church of Christ, than any others in Christendom. And those which have a comparatively inefficient eldership will compare most favorably with those under an inefficient pastorship of any other kind. Finally, such inefficiency is not, after all, more frequently found in the eldership than in what is popularly styled the ministry. This must be so, from the fact that the qualifications for the office, public speaking alone excepted, are more frequently found combined in three or four men, than in *one*, whether *pastor*, or *class-leader*, or whatever may be his title. The folly, therefore, of abandoning the apostolic eldership in favor of any other organization, is demonstrated by history; while its wickedness must be apparent to every one who esteems apostolic precedents above human expedients. To seek an escape from the condemnation due for this wickedness, by asserting that the apostles left no model of Church organization, is only to add to the original crime by perverting the Scriptures to excuse it. So long as it stands recorded that Paul and Barnabas "appointed for them elders in every Church," and so long as the duties of these officers remain carefully prescribed in the apostolic epistles, so long will it be false to deny that the apostles left us a definite model of Church organization, and wicked in the sight of God to abandon it for any other.

* 1 Tim. iii: 1-7.

24–26. Leaving Antioch of Pisidia, the apostles returned as far as the sea-coast by the same route through which they had gone up into Pisidia. (24) *"And passing through Pisidia, they came into Pamphylia; (25) and having spoken the word in Perga, they went down to Attalia. (26) Thence they sailed to Antioch, whence they had been commended to the favor of God for the work which they had performed."* Perga, on the river Cestrus, a few miles above its mouth, was the point at which they had disembarked on their first arrival from Cyprus. They had made no delay there at first, but now we are told that they "spoke the word in Perga." Luke's silence in reference to the result of this effort is an indication that it was not very decided. It is probable that their design was simply to usefully employ an interval during which they were waiting for a vessel bound to Antioch. This conjecture is confirmed by the fact that they finally left Perga by land, and walked down to Attalia on the sea-coast, where they would be likely to meet with a vessel without so long delay. They were not disappointed; for "thence they sailed to Antioch."

27, 28. The apostles had now completed their missionary tour, and there could but be great anxiety in the congregation who had sent them forth, to know the result of their labors. It was the first mission ever sent to the heathen world. The missionaries were as eager to report the success with which their sufferings and toil had been crowned, as the congregation were to hear it. He who returns from a hard-fought field bearing good tidings, pants beneath the burden of his untold story. (27) *"And having arrived and assembled the Church together, they rehearsed all that God had done with them, and that he had opened a door of faith to the Gentiles. (28) And they continued there no little time with the disciples."* In the statement that God had "opened a door of faith to the Gentiles," there is an allusion both to the opening of that national inclosure which had hitherto confined the gospel almost exclusively to the Jews, and the introduction of the distant Gentiles through that door into the Church. Before this, faith had been to them inaccessible; for "how shall they believe on him of whom they have not heard?" But now that the preachers had been sent out to them, the door was open, and faith was accessible to all.

XV: 1. At this point in the narrative our historian makes a sudden transition from the conflicts of the disciples with the unbelieving world to one almost as serious among themselves. There never was a national antipathy more intense than that felt by the Jews to the whole Gentile world. It was the more intense, from the fact that it was imbedded in their deepest religious sentiments, and was cultivated in all their devotions. In the hearts of the disciples this feeling had, by this time, been so far overcome, that they had admitted the propriety of receiving uncircumcised Gentiles into the Church. But they found it more difficult to convince themselves that Gentiles were to be admitted into social and domestic intimacy. Hence, when Peter returned from the house of Cornelius to Jerusalem, the chief objection urged against him was, not that he had *immersed* Gentiles, but "Thou didst go *into the house* of men uncircumcised, and didst *eat* with them." This was the full extent to which the judaizing party in the Church were prepared, at that time, to push their objections. But when men take an unreasonable and obstinate stand against any cause, they frequently assume more extravagant ground as the cause they are opposing advances. While but a few Gentiles had come into the Church, the pharisaic party objected only to domestic association with them; but now that Paul and Barnabas had succeeded in opening a door of faith to the whole Gentile world, and it was likely that the Jews, who had hitherto constituted almost the whole body of the Church, were soon to become only a small element in its constituency, their fears were excited, and their demands became more exorbitant. Paul and Barnabas were still in Antioch. (1) *"And certain men came down from Judea, and taught the brethren, Unless you are circumcised according to the law of Moses, you can not be saved."* As we learn from a subsequent part of this chapter, they were not content with merely enjoining circumcision, but also exacted the observance of all the law of Moses, to which circumcision was only preliminary.* The success of this party would have perpetuated Judaism, and forever have neutralized those philanthropic principles of the gospel which the experience of the world and the wisdom of God alike had shown to be necessary to the moral renovation of the human race.

2. If Paul and Barnabas had ever been, since their conversion, blinded by these narrow views, their labors among the Gentiles would have wrought a change in their feelings, and prepared them to see the subject in a better light. They opposed the new propositions with all their powers; and though they did not succeed in silencing their opponents, they brought the discussion to a fortunate conclusion. (2) *"When therefore Paul and Barnabas had no small dissension and disputation with them, they determined that Paul and Barnabas, and certain others of them, should go up to Jerusalem to the apostles and elders about this question."*

If the brethren in Antioch had estimated at its proper value the authority of an inspired apostle, they would have yielded implicitly to Paul's decision without this mission to Jerusalem. But they were as yet too little accustomed to reflection upon the profound mystery of apostolic infallibility to properly accredit it; and their deep prejudices on the subject under discussion was a serious obstacle in the way of clear thought. It is probable that apostolic authority is more highly appreciated now than it was then; yet the prejudices of sect and party are so intense, that even now the *dictum* of a living apostle would prove insufficient, in millions of cases, to convince men of their errors. Like the disciples in Antioch, who had the testimony of Paul, men now are not easily satisfied with a single inspired statement upon a point in dispute, or with the statements of a single apostle, but demand an accumulation of even divine testimonies.

It is probable that Paul would have objected to making this appeal to the other apostles, on the ground of its apparent inconsistency with his own claims to inspired authority, had not the proposition been sustained by an express revelation of the divine will. In the second chapter of Galatians, where Mr. Howson very clearly proves that Paul has reference to this journey,† he says: "I went up by

* Acts xv: 24.   † Vol. i, p. 227, *et seq.*

revelation and communicated to them that gospel which I preach among the Gentiles." It was the divine purpose to settle the question, not for the Church in Antioch alone, but for all the world and for all time.

3. Their journey to Jerusalem, which was accomplished by land, lay through two sections of country which had already been evangelized to a considerable extent. (3) *"Being sent forward by the Church, they passed through Phenicia and Samaria, relating the conversion of the Gentiles: and they caused great joy to all the brethren."* The Churches in Samaria did not, of course, sympathize with the Jewish prejudices, and although in Phenicia there were doubtless many Jews, yet the Gentile element sufficiently predominated to enable the brethren there, like the Samaritans, to rejoice that the gospel was spreading into the heathen world.

4. After a pleasant journey among rejoicing Churches, they reached Jerusalem. (4) *"And when they arrived in Jerusalem, they were received by the Church, and by the apostles and elders, and they declared all that God had done with them."* They proceeded, in Jerusalem, as they had upon their return to Antioch, to give a history of their missionary tour. This was done in the presence of the Church, the apostles also being present.

5. The Judaizers did not hesitate to declare fully their own position. (5) *"But some of the sect of the Pharisees who believed, rose up, saying, It was necessary to circumcise them and to command them to keep the law of Moses."* This party are here identified as converts from the old sect of the Pharisees. We have had no account hitherto of any large accessions to the Church from this party; but this incidental remark shows that some of these obstinate opposers of the truth had yielded, and were now occupying positions of influence in the congregation. Paul now once more meets some of his old companions in the persecution of the disciples, not to harmonize with them, nor to dispute with them in the synagogues concerning the claims of Christ; but to contend, within the Church itself, against that same disposition to perpetuate the law which had made them formerly fight against the gospel. He had a bad opinion of some of them, which must have been well founded, or he would not have given the public utterance to it which he did at a subsequent period. He styles them, in the Epistle to the Galatians, "False brethren, unawares brought in, who came in privily to spy out our liberty which we have in Christ Jesus, that they might bring us into bondage."* Having witnessed a rapid increase of the congregations under the pressure of the persecutions and disputations to which they had formerly resorted, these wily enemies of the truth determined at length to corrupt and destroy, under the guise of friendship, a cause whose progress they could not impede by open enmity. They well knew, what some of the brethren had failed to discover, that the doctrine of Christ would be rendered powerless if it could only be hampered by bondage to the law. Even to this day the mass of religious teachers have failed to learn this lesson, though the experience of ages has demonstrated its truth. The essential issue between Paul and the Pharisees had reference to the

* Gal. ii: 4.

perpetuation of the law of Moses in the Church of Christ, and the same issue has been in debate, under various aspects, from that day to this. Paul defeated the attempt of these Judaizers to fasten *circumcision* on the Church; but subsequent Judaizers imposed *infant immersion*, and, finally, *infant sprinkling*, as a substitute. What the early Pharisees failed to accomplish in the face of apostolic opposition, the later Pharisees did accomplish under a thin disguise. The unsuccessful attempt of *those* Pharisees to "spy out the liberty which the disciples had in Christ Jesus, and bring them into bondage" under the law, has been successfully accomplished by *these*, in teaching men that the Church of Christ originated in Abraham's family, and that the Jewish tribes and the Christian congregations constitute but one identical Church. The Roman apostasy perpetuates the pompous ritual and daily sacrifice of the old temple; religious zealots slaughter Canaanites in the form of modern heretics; professed Christians go to war under the old battle-cry of "The sword of the Lord and of Gideon;" the Latter-day Saints emulate the Turks in the multiplication of wives; and for all these corruptions authority is found in the laws and customs of ancient Israel. The intelligent reader of the New Testament knows scarcely which of these errors is most repugnant to the truth; but must, like Paul, struggle with untiring energy and ceaseless vigilance to uproot them all from the minds of men.

6. After the Pharisees had stated their position, distinctly affirming that the Gentiles should be circumcised and keep the law, it seems that the assembly adjourned to meet again at another hour. The next meeting is then announced in these words: (6) "*Now the apostles and elders came together to consider this matter.*" Neither this nor the former meeting was composed exclusively of the apostles and elders, for we have seen, from verse fifth, that the messengers were received by the Church, and we learn, from the twenty-second verse below, that at this second meeting the whole Church were present. There had been, however, previous to either of these, a private interview between Paul and the chief men of the Church, for the purpose of coming to some distinct understanding of the subject before it was laid before the multitude. This we learn from Paul himself, who says: "I communicated to them that gospel which I preached among the Gentiles, but *privately* to them who were of reputation, lest by any means I should run, or had run in vain."* This language implies that his course was approved by these brethren of reputation, who were, doubtless, the apostles and other inspired men. Their approval of his course shows that the objections afterward urged were preferred by another class of men. The public discussion was not for the purpose of bringing about an agreement among *inspired* men, for they really did not differ after the facts were stated by Paul and Barnabas. But it was an effort, on the part of the apostles, to bring the other brethren to the same conclusion in which they themselves had already united.

7-11. Luke does not report all that was said, but only those speeches that were decisive, and that brought the controversy to a close. Merely alluding, therefore, to the first part of the discussion, he says:

* Gal. ii: 2.

(7) *"And when there had been much discussion, Peter arose and said to them, Brethren, you know that, a good while ago, God made choice among us that the Gentiles through my mouth should hear the word of the gospel and believe. (8) And God, who knows the heart, bore witness for them, giving to them the Holy Spirit even as he did to us. (9) He made no difference between us and them, purifying their hearts by faith. (10) Now, then, why do you put God to the proof, by putting a yoke upon the neck of the disciples which neither our fathers nor we were able to bear? (11) But we believe that we shall be saved through the favor of the Lord Jesus Christ, in the same manner as they."* The position of the Pharisees not only condemned the course of Paul and Barnabas, but also involved a censure of Peter, who was the first of all the apostles, as he here asserts, to preach the Word to Gentiles. When arraigned once before for his conduct in the case of Cornelius, he had vindicated his procedure by relating the miraculous evidences of God's will which had been his guide; and now, to accomplish the same end with these brethren, he adduces the most decisive of those miracles, the gift of the Holy Spirit to uncircumcised Gentiles. Having given to them the same gift as to the apostles on Pentecost, and having imposed upon them none of the purifying rites of the law, but simply purifying their *hearts by faith*, he assumes that God had made no difference between them and the Jewish brethren. Now, to attempt to impose the law upon them, in the face of these evidences of God's will to the contrary, would be putting God to the proof of his determination to maintain his own authority. It would, moreover, be imposing a yoke which the Jews themselves had never been able to bear successfully. This yoke is not circumcision, for there is no difficulty in submitting to that; but it was the law, under whose provisions no man could live without incurring its condemnation. His concluding statement, that "*We believe that we shall be saved through the favor of the Lord Jesus, in the same manner as they*," involves two important conclusions: *First*, That it is not through the merit of obedience to the law that we are to be saved, but through the favor of the Lord Jesus Christ. This favor is extended in the pardon of sins. *Second*, That the Gentiles are saved in the same manner as the Jews. By using the plural, *we* believe, instead of *I* believe, he doubtless intended to express not only the conviction of his own mind, but that of the party with whom he acted, including the other apostles. It was a decision of the inspired teachers against the Pharisees.

12. This brief statement of facts had so good an effect upon the multitude, that Barnabas and Paul determined to follow it by a rehearsal of similar facts in the history of their own labors among the Gentiles. (12) "*Then all the multitude kept silence, and listened to Barnabas and Paul relating what signs and wonders God had wrought among the Gentiles through them.*" Their remarks on this occasion were not a repetition of what they had said in the former meeting, when they had set forth "all that God had done with them," but were confined to the "signs and wonders" by which God had indicated his approbation of their ministry.* The reversal of the order in which Luke now habitually names these two brethren indicates that Barnabas, whose

* Compare Acts xiv: 3.

name is first, was the first speaker. This gave Paul the closing argument on those events.

13–21. So far as recent indications of God's will were concerned, the argument was now complete and unanswerable; but the Jewish mind was prone to an underestimate of passing events, while they looked back with superior reverence to the law and the prophets. The Apostle James, knowing that they would reject all possible cotemporaneous evidences, if they appeared to conflict with the written word, determined to close up this avenue of escape from the argument already presented, by sustaining it with the authority of the prophets. (13) *"And, after they were silent, James answered, saying, Brethren, hear me.* (14) *Simeon has related how God first visited the Gentiles, to take out of them a people for his name,* (15) *and to this agree the words of the prophets, as it is written,* (16) *After this I will return and will rebuild the tabernacle of David which has fallen down. I will rebuild its ruins, and set it upright,* (17) *that the residue of men may seek after the Lord, even all the Gentiles upon whom my name is called, says the Lord, who does all these things.** (18) *Known to God from eternity are all his works.* (19) *Therefore, my judgment is, not to trouble those of the Gentiles who turn to God;* (20) *but to write to them that they abstain from the pollutions of idols, and from fornication, and from things strangled, and from blood.* (21) *For Moses, for generations past, has in every city those who preach him, being read in the synagogues every Sabbath."* In this speech James shows that God, who knows from eternity what his own works would be, had foretold, through the prophet, the work which he was then performing through the labors of Peter, Barnabas, and Paul. He had said that he would rebuild the tabernacle of David, in order that the residue of men, who had not known the Lord before, "even all the Gentiles, upon whom his name is called," should seek after the Lord; and now, he had, through these apostles, selected from among the Gentiles "a people for his name." The prophesy clearly covered all the ground claimed for it, and made the argument complete.

There was room for no other conclusion than the one which James deduced, that they should impose on the Gentiles, so far as the class of restrictions under consideration were concerned, only those *necessary* things which were necessary independent of the Mosaic law. Idolatry, with all the pollutions connected with it, was known to be sinful before the law of Moses was given; and so was fornication. The eating of blood, and, by implication, of strangled animals, whose blood was still in them, was forbidden to the whole world in the family of Noah.† In the restrictions here proposed by James, therefore, there is not the slightest extension of the law of Moses, but a mere enforcement upon the Gentiles of rules of conduct which had ever been binding, and were to be perpetual. They are as binding to-day as they were then. To deny this would be to despise the combined authority of all the apostles, when enjoining upon the Gentile world, of which we form a part, restrictions which they pronounce *necessary*. One would be surprised that it was thought necessary to mention to Gentiles, who had *turned to the Lord,* the sinfulness of fornication, did we

* Amos ix : 11, quoted from the Septuagint. † Gen. ix : 4.

not know that among heathen nations of antiquity it was deemed innocent, and even sometimes virtuous.

The controversy now pending, in reference to the identity of the Jewish Church with the Church of Christ, renders it necessary that we should here pay some special attention to one remark made by James in this speech. He applies the prophesy concerning the rebuilding of the "tabernacle of David" to the reception of Gentiles into the Church, and it is hence argued that this prophesy contemplated a reconstruction and extension of the dilapidated Jewish Church, and not the construction of a new one. The whole argument turns upon the meaning of the expression "tabernacle of David." If the metaphorical word *tabernacle* here means the Jewish Church, the argument would have force. But the Mosaic institution never sustained such a relation to David that it could, with propriety, be styled the "*tabernacle of David*." If such had been the reference, the expression would undoubtedly have been, the *tabernacle of Moses*, which would have been unambiguous. But David was a king, and had a promise from God, that his "*throne* should be established forever;"* that there should not fail him a man on the throne of Israel.† This promise God confirmed with an oath, saying, "I have made a covenant with my chosen, I have sworn to David my servant, Thy seed will I establish forever, and build up thy throne to all generations."‡ According to the *apparent* meaning of this promise, it had long since failed; for it had been many generations since a descendant of David had occupied his throne. It was during this period, in which the royal house of David was in ruins, that Amos uttered the prophesy, "I will return, and build again the tabernacle of David which is fallen down; I will build again the ruins thereof, and set it upright." The term *tabernacle*, therefore, must be put for the family who dwell in the tabernacle, and the reconstruction of it the re-establishment of the royal dignity which the family had lost. Hence, when the birth of Jesus was announced to Mary, the angel said: "The Lord shall give to him the throne of his father David, and he shall reign over the house of Jacob forever, and of his kingdom there shall be no end." ‖ Thus, the promise, when properly understood, is seen to refer neither to a continuous line of Jewish kings, descended from David, nor to a reconstruction of the Jewish Church, but to the perpetual reign of Jesus, the "seed of David according to the flesh." § When, therefore, Jesus sat down upon his throne in heaven, the tabernacle of David was rebuilt, and now, by the labors of Peter, Barnabas, and Paul, the remainder of the prophesy of Amos was being fulfilled, by the extension of his kingdom among the Gentiles.

The closing paragraph of this speech appears, at first glance, to have no immediate connection with the preceding argument. But it was, doubtless, designed to anticipate an objection. The Pharisees might object, If you thus ignore the statutes of Moses, his writings will fall into contempt, or be neglected by the people. No danger of this, says the speaker, for Moses is preached in every city, and read in the synagogues every Sabbath, and has been for generations past.

* 2 Sam. vii: 16.   † 1 Kings ii: 4.   ‡ Ps. lxxxix: 3, 4.
‖ Luke i: 32, 33.   § Rom. i: 3.

ACTS XV: 22-31.

22-29. The speech of James brought the discussion to a close. The will of God upon the subject was now so clearly exhibited that the opposition was totally silenced, and it remained only to determine the best method of practically carrying out the proposition submitted by James. (22) " *Then it pleased the apostle and the elders, with the whole Church, to send chosen men from among themselves with Paul and Barnabas to Antioch; Judas surnamed Barsabas, and Silas, leading men among the brethren,* (23) *writing by their hand these words: The apostles, and elders, and brethren, to the brethren from the Gentiles, in Antioch, and Syria, and Cilicia, greeting:* (24) *Since we have heard that certain persons who went out from us have troubled you with words, subverting your souls, telling you to be circumcised and to keep the law, to whom we gave no such commandment,* (25) *it seemed good to us, being of one mind, to send chosen men to you with our beloved Barnabas and Paul,* (26) *men who have hazarded their lives for the name of our Lord Jesus Christ.* (27) *We have sent, therefore, Judas and Silas, who also will tell you the same things orally.* (28) *For it seemed good to the Holy Spirit and us, to lay upon you no greater burden than these necessary things,* (29) *that you abstain from meats offered to idols, and from blood, and from things strangled, and from fornication: from which, if you keep yourselves, you will do well. Farewell.*"

By the construction of the Greek, we learn that it was Paul and Barnabas, and not Judas and Silas, who are commended in this letter as "men who have hazarded their lives for the name of the Lord Jesus."

30, 31. The object of sending Judas and Silas with Paul and Barnabas was doubtless that they, having been entirely unconnected with the conversion of Gentiles, and above suspicion of undue partiality toward them, might use their personal influence with the Jewish brethren to induce them to accept the teaching of the epistle. Their journey, and the effect of the epistle, are thus stated: (30) "*So, then, being sent away, they went to Antioch, and having assembled the multitude, they gave them the epistle.* (31) *When they read it, they rejoiced for the consolation.*" The brethren residing in Antioch had not become partisans in the controversy, but had been distressed by the conflict between Paul and Barnabas and the Pharisees from Jerusalem, and desired only a satisfactory settlement of the question. The epistle, therefore, afforded them "consolation," and they cheerfully yielded to its requirements.

The triumph of Paul and Barnabas over their pharisaic opponents was most signal and complete. And it appeared all the more signal to the brethren in Antioch, from a fact not recorded by Luke. We learn, from Paul's own account of the visit to Jerusalem, that Titus, who was a Gentile, went with him, and that strenuous efforts were there made to have him circumcised; but Paul returned to Antioch, with Titus still uncircumcised, and with his whole course indorsed by the apostles, the elders, and the whole Church. This ought to have settled the controversy forever.

Before dismissing the subject of this appeal to the apostles and elders in Jerusalem, we must notice briefly the use that is made of it by the advocates of representative assemblies in the Church, for judicial and legislative purposes. Romanists, and the advocates of episcopacy generally, find in the assembly in Jerusalem the first "*general council*," and have styled it "The Council of Jerusalem." The Presbyterians find in it the first synod; and others still appeal to it in general terms, as authority for assemblies of brethren to decide questions of doctrine and discipline. In order that it may properly be used as a precedent for any of these assemblies, it must be made to appear analogous to them in its essential features. But its essential features are: *First*, That it was occasioned by an appeal from *one* congregation to certain parties in *one other* congregation, in reference to a disputed question which the first felt unable to decide. *Second*, That the parties to whom the appeal was made were inspired men, who could say of their decision, when made, "It seemed good to the *Holy Spirit and us;*" *i. e.*, to the *Holy* Spirit as the divine arbiter, and to us as obedient subjects of his authority. It was the inspiration, and, consequently, the infallibility of the party appealed to, that suggested and that justified the appeal. In both these peculiarities all the councils and synods of Catholic and Protestant history are essentially deficient, for, instead of being called together at the request of some congregation, to decide some question presented, they consist of representatives from a number of congregations, or districts of country, assembled for the purpose of discussing and deciding whatever questions may come up among them; and instead of being infallible, their decisions are nothing but the fallible opinions of uninspired men, in reference to which it would be the hight of profanity to say, "It seemed good to the Holy Spirit and us." Not till we have an assembly under the guidance of *inspired* men can we allow them to authoritatively decide religious questions after the precedent of this assembly in Jerusalem. All the duties, responsibilities, and privileges of disciples have already been authoritatively propounded by inspired men; and for men now to meet together for the authoritative decision of such questions, is to assume a prerogative that belongs exclusively to inspired apostles and prophets, and, at the same time, is to assume that there are deficiencies in their infallible teachings to be supplied by uninspired men.

In arguing thus upon the merits of all judicial and legislative assemblies among the Churches, we must not be understood as condemning the co-operation of different congregations, or of individuals from them, in performing duties which *are* imposed by divine authority. The essential difference between assemblies for these two purposes is, that in the latter we are simply uniting our energies to perform duties appointed by the word of God; while, in the former, we undertake to decide what truth and duty *are*—a work which none but inspired men can perform.

32–34. We have said above, that the purpose for which Judas and Silas were sent to Antioch was to enforce, by their personal influence, the authority of the epistle. We find this statement confirmed by the further account of their labors. (32) "*And Judas and Silas, being themselves also prophets, exhorted the brethren with many words, and confirmed them.* (33) *And when they had remained some time, they were dismissed in peace from the brethren to the apostles.* (34) *But it pleased Silas to remain there.*"

The manner in which Luke connects the fact that these brethren were prophets, with the statement that they *exhorted* the brethren and *confirmed* them, shows that the chief work of New Testament prophets was not to foretell the future, but to exhort and confirm the brethren. He says, "being also themselves *prophets*, they *exhorted* the brethren and confirmed them;" which form of expression makes the fact of being prophets account for their exhortations. They differed from the Old Testament prophets only in that the latter gave their chief attention to foretelling future events. Still, even the predictions of the old prophets were made to answer the purpose of exhortations to their cotemporaries; so that the difference between the two is very slight.

35. The city of Antioch still continued to be a profitable field for apostolic labor, and the scene of interesting events. (35) "*Paul and Barnabas also continued in Antioch, with many others, teaching and preaching the word of the Lord.*" It is during this period that the most judicious commentators locate the visit of Peter to Antioch, and the rebuke administered to him by Paul, as recorded in the second chapter of Galatians: "When Peter came to Antioch, I withstood him to the face, because he was to be blamed. For before the coming of certain persons from James, he did *eat* with the Gentiles; but when they came, he *withdrew* and *separated* himself, fearing them of the circumcision. And the other Jews dissembled likewise with him, so that even Barnabas was carried away with their dissimulation."*

It has been erroneously supposed that Peter, in this affair, acted in direct conflict with the epistle which he had just united in addressing to the Gentile brethren. The harshness of this supposition has led some writers to hastily conclude that his improper conduct must have occurred at a period antecedent to the issuing of that epistle. It is also urged in favor of an earlier date of the incident, that, if it had occurred subsequent to the publication of that epistle, Paul would naturally have appealed to it in the controversy with Peter, which he seems not to have done. Both of these suppositions spring from a mistake as to the exact fault of which Peter was guilty. He did not insist that the Gentiles should be circumcised, or that they should keep the law; which were the points discussed in the apostolic epistle. But, still admitting the right of the uncircumcised to membership and its privileges, his fault was in refusing to *eat* with them in their private circles, although he had himself been the first to do so in the family of Cornelius, and had done so, for a time, even since he came to Antioch. In opposing such conduct, it would not have answered Paul's purpose to appeal to the epistle from Jerusalem; for it merely asserted the freedom of the Gentiles from the yoke of the law, without prescribing the intercourse that should exist between the circumcised and uncircumcised brethren. The course of argument which he did pursue was the only one available. He convicted Peter of inconsistency, saying, "If you, being a Jew, live like a Gentile, and not like a Jew, why do you require the Gentiles to live like Jews?"† He had lived like a Gentile while eating with them; but now, by withdrawing from them, he was virtually saying to them, You must live like the Jews. This was inconsistent, and made it appear that either he was now a transgressor,

* Gal. ii: 11-13. † Gal. ii: 14.

while building up the Jewish prejudices, or had formerly been, while seeking to break them down. "For if I build again the things which I destroyed, I make myself a transgressor."*

But the proof of inconsistency in an opponent never settles a question of truth or duty. After you have proved your opponent inconsistent, you have still to prove that his present course differs from what truth requires, as well as from his former course. Moral inconsistency convicts a man as a transgressor, but whether a transgressor now, or formerly, is still an open question. Paul, therefore, proceeded to prove Peter's present conduct improper, by stating as an undisputed fact, "I, *through* the law, am *dead* to the law, that I might live to God;"† that is, by the limitation which the law prescribes to itself, it has ceased to bind me, and I have ceased to live under it. This fact was decisive, because all the distinction assumed to exist between the circumcised and the uncircumcised was based upon the supposition that the former, at least, were still under the law.

This is the last passage in Acts connected with the Apostle Peter. Before leaving it, we must notice one fact in connection with this unhappy incident in his life which far outweighs the dissimulation rebuked by Paul. It is the manner in which he received this rebuke. There is not the least evidence of any resentment on his part, either for the rebuke itself, or for the subsequent publication of it to the Churches in Galatia. Most men become offended when thus rebuked by their equals, and would regard it as an unpardonable offense to give unnecessary publicity to a fault of this kind. But Paul knew so well the goodness of Peter's heart, that he did not hesitate to speak of it to the world and to future generations. That he did not overestimate the meekness of Peter, is evident from the fact that the latter subsequently spoke most affectionately of Paul, with direct allusion to his epistles, and with a publicity equal to that which his own sin had received.‡ This excellence of Peter's character was known to other brethren besides Paul, as is evident from the freedom with which all the four evangelists speak of his denial of the Lord. They might have omitted this incident from their narratives, if they had been influenced by that pride and sensitiveness which prompt men to hide the faults of their leaders, or if they had thought that the publication of it would give serious offense to Peter. But they knew Peter, and, we must presume, they knew that he was willing for any fault of his, however discreditable, to be published to the world, if it would do any good. This is the spirit of self-sacrifice with which every servant of God should offer himself to the cause of Christ.

36–41. We have lingered long upon the interval spent by Paul and Barnabas in Antioch. We are now to follow the former upon his second missionary tour. (36) "*But after some days, Paul said to Barnabas, Let us return and visit our brethren in every city in which we have preached the word of the Lord, and see how they do.* (37) *And Barnabas determined to take with them John surnamed Mark.* (38) *But Paul thought proper not to take with them him who had departed from them in Pamphylia, and did not go with them to the work.* (39) *Then there was a contention, so that they separated one from the other: and*

* Gal. ii: 18. † Gal. ii: 19. ‡ 2 Peter iii: 15, 16.

Barnabas took Mark and sailed into Cyprus. (40) *But Paul chose Silas, and departed, having been commended to the favor of God by the brethren;* (41) *and went through Syria and Cilicia, confirming the Churches."*
This journey, it should be observed, was undertaken for the prime purpose of revisiting the Churches where these brethren had previously labored, and not, primarily, to preach to the heathen. This shows that the solicitude with which the apostles watched for the welfare of the congregations was not less ardent than their zeal in spreading a knowledge of the gospel.

The desire of Barnabas to take John with them was, doubtless, prompted, in part, by partiality, arising from the relationship which existed between them.* John, of course, desired to go, and Barnabas wished to give him an opportunity to atone for his former dereliction. Paul's reason for refusing to let him go was based upon a want of confidence in one who would, either through fear or love of ease, desert him in a trying hour.† Each considered the reason for his own preference a good one; and as neither was willing to yield for the sake of remaining with the other, they ought to have parted in perfect peace. But some unpleasant feeling was aroused by the controversy, which Luke expresses by the term παροξυσμὸς, of which *contention* is rather a tame rendering, though *paroxysm*, which we have derived from it, would express too high a degree of passion. This incident shows that the best of men may differ about matters of expediency, and that, in contending for their respective conclusions, they may be aroused to improper feelings. But the good man, under such circumstances, will always be distinguished by the readiness with which such feelings will be repressed, and by the absence of all subsequent malice. We know that Paul afterward felt very differently toward John; for, during his first imprisonment at Rome, he mentions him to Philemon as a fellow-laborer there present;‡ and to the Colossians as one who had been a comfort to him;|| and, during his second imprisonment, he writes to Timothy: "Take Mark and bring him with you; for he is profitable to me for the ministry."§ The slight heat engendered between Barnabas and Paul also subsided in a short time; for Paul afterward speaks of him in most friendly terms, in the First Epistle to the Corinthians.¶

By returning with Mark to his native island, Barnabas revisited a portion of the brethren to whom he and Paul had preached, while Paul visited another portion of them by a different route. Thus, notwithstanding their disagreement and separation, they did not allow the good cause to suffer, but accomplished separately the whole of the proposed work. The separation of Barnabas from Paul is our separation from Barnabas. His name is not mentioned again by Luke. But as we bid him a final farewell, the sails are spread which are to bear him over the sea, that he may make the islands glad with a knowledge of salvation. The further incidents of his life will yet be known to all who shall sit down with him in the everlasting kingdom.

We turn with Luke to follow the history of him who was in labors more abundant and in prisons more frequent than all the apostles,

---

* Col. iv: 10.　　† See Com. xiii: 13.　　‡ Phil. 24.
|| Col. iv: 11　　§ 2 Tim. iv: 11.　　¶ 1 Cor. ix: 6.

and to form a better acquaintance with his new companion. The statement that Paul and Silas were "commended to the favor of God by the brethren," does not imply, as many writers have supposed, that they refused thus to commend Barnabas and Mark, or that the brethren sided with Paul against Barnabas in their contention. It is sufficiently accounted for by the fact that the attention of the writer is fixed upon the detail of Paul's history rather than that of Barnabas. No doubt the prayers of the brethren followed them both to their distant and dangerous fields of labor.

By a northern route through Syria, and then a westerly course through Cilicia, Paul approached the extremity of his recent tour in the interior of Asia Minor. He was not altogether a stranger along the journey, for he had spent some time in Syria and Cilicia before his first visit to Antioch;* and it is most probable that he now revisited, in these districts, Churches which he had planted by his own labors.

XVI: 1, 2. Without giving the least detail of Paul's labors in Syria and Cilicia, Luke hurries us forward to his arrival in Derbe and Lystra, the scenes respectively of the most painful and the most consoling incidents which occurred on his former tour. His chief object in this seems to be to introduce us to a new character, destined to play an important part in the future history. (1) "*Then he came down into Derbe and Lystra, and behold, a certain disciple was there, named Timothy, son of a believing Jewess, but of a Greek father;* (2) *who was well attested by the brethren in Lystra and Iconium.*" Not only the mother but also the grandmother of this disciple was a believer; for Paul afterward writes to him: "I call to remembrance the unfeigned faith that is in thee, that *first* dwelt in thy grandmother Lois, and in thy mother Eunice, and I am persuaded also in thee."† From this it seems that both the mother and grandmother had preceded him into the kingdom; for it is clearly of their faith in Christ, and not of their Jewish faith, that Paul here speaks. With such an example before him, it is not surprising that the young disciple should be found well attested by all the brethren who knew him. The fact that he was thus attested not only at Derbe and Lystra, within the vicinity of his residence, but also in the more distant city of Iconium, renders it probable that he was already known as a public speaker.

On the occasion of Paul's former visit to Lystra, we learned that while he lay dead, as was supposed, after the stoning, "the disciples stood around him." Timothy was doubtless in the group; for he was Paul's own son in the faith,‡ and must have been immersed previous to the stoning, as Paul left the city immediately after. This scene occurred just at that period in Timothy's religious life, the period immediately subsequent to immersion, when the soul is peculiarly susceptible to the impress of a noble example. The recesses of the heart are then open to their deepest depths, and a word fitly spoken, a look full of religious sympathy, or a noble deed, makes an impression which can never be effaced. In such a frame of mind Timothy witnessed the stoning of Paul; ‖ wept over his prostrate form; followed him, as if

---

* Comp. Gal. i: 21, with Acts ix: 30, and xi: 25.   † 2 Tim. i: 5.
‡ 1 Tim. i: 2.   ‖ Comp. 2 Tim. iii: 10, 11.

raised from the dead, back into the city; and saw him depart with heroic determination to another field of conflict in defense of the glorious gospel. It is not wonderful that a nature so full of sympathy with that of the heroic apostle as to extort from the latter the declaration, "I have no one like-minded with me,"* should be inspired by his example, and made ready to share with him the toils and sufferings of his future career.

3. The discriminating and watchful eye of Paul soon discovered qualities which would render this youth a fitting companion and fellow-laborer, and it was by his request that Timothy was placed in the position which he afterward so honorably filled. (3) *"Paul wished him to go forth with him, and took him, and circumcised him on account of the Jews who were in those quarters; for they all knew that his father was a Greek."*

The circumcision of Timothy is quite a remarkable event in the history of Paul, and presents a serious inquiry as to the consistency of his teaching and of his practice, in reference to this Abrahamic rite. It demands of us, at this place, as full consideration as our limits will admit.

The real difficulty of the case is made apparent by putting into juxtaposition two of Paul's statements, and two of his deeds. He says to the Corinthians, "Circumcision is nothing, and uncircumcision is nothing;"† yet to the Galatians he writes: "Behold, I, Paul, say to you, that if you are circumcised, Christ shall profit you nothing."‡ When he was in Jerusalem upon the appeal of the Antioch Church, brethren urgently insisted that he should circumcise Titus, who was with him, but he sternly refused, and says: "I gave place to them by subjection, no, not for an hour."|| Yet we see him in the case before us, circumcising Timothy with his own hand, and this "on account of certain Jews who were in those quarters." In order to reconcile these apparently conflicting facts and statements, we must have all the leading facts concerning this rite before us.

We observe, first, that, in the language of Jesus, circumcision "is not of Moses, but of the fathers."§ The obligation which the Jews were under to observe it was not originated by the law of Moses, or the covenant of Mount Sinai; but existed independent of that covenant and the law, having originated four hundred and thirty years before the law.¶ The connection between the law and circumcision originated in the fact that the law was given to a part of the circumcised descendants of Abraham. We say a part of his descendants, because circumcision was enjoined upon his descendants through Ishmael, through the sons of Keturah, and through Esau, as well as upon the Jews. Since, then, the law did not originate the obligation to be circumcised, the abrogation of the law could not possibly annul that obligation. We shall be forced, therefore, to the conclusion, that it still continues since the law, unless we find it annulled by the apostles.

Again: its perpetuity is enjoined in the law of its institution. God said to Abraham: "He that is born in thy house, and he that is bought with thy money, must needs be circumcised, and my covenant shall be

---
* Phil ii: 20.   † 1 Cor. vii: 19.   ‡ Gal. v: 1.
|| Gal. ii: 3–5.   § John vii: 22.   ¶ Gal. iii: 17.

in your flesh for an *everlasting* covenant."* An everlasting covenant is one which continues as long as both parties to it continue to exist. The covenant concerning Canaan was everlasting, because it continued as long as the twelve tribes continued an organized people to live in it. The covenant of Aaron's priestly dignity was everlasting, because it continued in Aaron's family as long as such a priesthood had an existence. So the covenant of circumcision must be everlasting, because it is to continue as long as the flesh of Abraham is perpetuated. This will be till the end of time; hence circumcision has not ceased, and can not cease, till the end of the world. This conclusion can not be set aside, unless we find something in the nature of gospel institutions inconsistent with it, or some express release of circumcised Christians from its continued observance.

Is it, then, inconsistent with any gospel institution? Pedobaptists assume that it was a seal of righteousness, and a rite of initiation into the Church; and as baptism now occupies that position, it necessarily supplants circumcision. It is true, that Paul says: "Abraham received the sign of circumcision, a seal of the righteousness of the faith which he had while yet uncircumcised;" but what it was to Abraham it never was to any of his offspring, seeing that the child eight days old could not possibly have any righteousness of faith while yet uncircumcised, of which circumcision could be the seal. Again: it was not to the Jew an initiatory rite. For, *first*, the law of God prescribing to Abraham the terms of the covenant says: "The uncircumcised man-child whose flesh of his foreskin is not circumcised, shall be *cut off* from his people; he has broken my covenant."† Now, no man can be *cut off* from a people who is not previously of them. Regarding the Jewish commonwealth, therefore, as a Church, the infant of eight days was already *in* the Church by natural birth, and circumcision, instead of bringing him *into* it, was a condition of his *remaining in it*. In the *second place*, this conclusion from the terms of the covenant is made indisputable by a prominent fact in Jewish history. While the twelve tribes were in the wilderness forty years, none of the children born were circumcised. The six hundred thousand men over twenty years of age who left Egypt all died in the wilderness, and an equal number were born in the same period; for the whole number of men at the end of the journey was the same as at the beginning.‡ When they crossed the Jordan, therefore, there were six hundred thousand male Jews, some of them forty years of age, who had not been circumcised, yet they had been entering the Jewish Church during a period of forty years. After crossing the Jordan, Joshua commanded them to be circumcised, and it was done.|| This fact not only demonstrates that circumcision was not to the Jews an initiatory rite, but throws light upon its real design. The covenant of circumcision was ingrafted upon the promise to Abraham of an innumerable fleshly offspring, to keep them a distinct people, and to enable the world to identify them, thereby recognizing the fulfillment of the promise, and also the fulfillment of various prophesies concerning them. In accordance with this design, while they were in the wilderness, in no danger

* Gen. xvii: 9-14. † Gen. xvii: 14.
‡ Num. 1: 45, 46; Comp. xxvi: 51, 63-65. || Joshua v: 2-7.

of intermingling with other nations, the institution was neglected. But, as soon as they enter the populous land of Canaan, where there is danger of such intermingling, the separating mark is put upon them.

From these two considerations, we see that there is no inconsistency between circumcision and baptism, even if the latter is admitted to be a *seal of the righteousness of faith*, which language is nowhere applied to it in the Scriptures. Neither is there inconsistency between it and any thing in the gospel scheme; for Paul declares: "In Jesus Christ neither *circumcision* availeth any thing, nor *uncircumcision;* but faith which works by love."* Thence, he enjoins: "Is any man called, being circumcised, let him not be uncircumcised; is any called in uncircumcision, let him not be circumcised."† So far as faith in Christ, and acceptability with him are concerned, circumcision makes a man neither better nor worse, and is, of course, not inconsistent with the obedience of faith in any respect whatever.

We next inquire, Are there any apostolic precepts which release converted Jews from the original obligation to perpetuate this rite? Paul does say, "If you are circumcised, Christ shall profit you nothing;" and this, certainly, is a prohibition to the parties to whom it is addressed. If it was addressed to Jewish Christians, then it is certainly wrong for the institution to be perpetuated among them. But neither Paul nor any of the apostles so understood it. That Paul did not is proved by the fact that he circumcised Timothy; and that the other apostles did not, is proved conclusively by the conference which took place in Jerusalem upon Paul's last visit to that place. James says to him: "You see, brother, how many thousands of the Jews there are who believe, and they are all zealous of the law. And they are informed of you, that you teach all the Jews who are among the Gentiles to forsake Moses, saying that they *ought not to circumcise their children*, neither to walk after the customs. Do this, therefore, that we say to you. We have four men who have a vow on them. Take them, and purify yourself with them, and pay their expenses, in order that they may shave their heads, and all may know that the things of which they were informed concerning you are *nothing*, but that you yourself walk orderly, and keep the law."‡ This speech shows that James considered it slanderous to say that Paul taught the Jews not to circumcise their children; and Paul's ready consent to the proposition made to him shows that he agreed with James. Yet this occurred after he had written the epistle to the Galatians, in which he says, "If you are circumcised, Christ shall profit you nothing." There could not be clearer proof that this remark was not intended for Jewish Christians.

Even James, in the speech from which we have just quoted, makes a distinction, in reference to this rite, between the Jewish and the Gentile Christians. He says: "Concerning the Gentiles who believe, we have written, having decided that they *observe no such thing;* save, only, that they keep themselves from idols, and from blood, and from things strangled, and from fornication."‖ This remark refers to the decree issued by the apostles from Jerusalem, which Paul was carrying with him at the time that he circumcised Timothy.§ It should

---

* Gal. v: 6. † 1 Cor. vii: 18. ‡ Acts xxi: 20-24. ‖ Acts xxi: 25. § Acts xvi: 4.

be observed, that there never did arise among the disciples any difference of opinion as to the propriety of circumcising Jews. This was granted by all. But the controversy had exclusive reference to the Gentiles; and the fact that the Judaizers based their plea for circumcising Gentiles upon the continued validity of the rite among the Jews, is one of the strongest proofs that all the disciples considered it perpetual. If Paul, in disputing with them, could have said, that, by the introduction of the gospel, circumcision was abolished even among the Jews, he would have subverted, at once, the very foundation of their argument. But this fundamental assumption was admitted and acted upon by Paul himself, and no inspired man ever called it in question.

That it was the Gentiles alone who were forbidden to be circumcised, is further evident from the context of this prohibition in Galatians. This epistle was addressed to Gentiles, as is evident from the remark in the fourth chapter, "Howbeit, then, when you knew not God, you did service to them who by nature are no gods?" The circumcision of the Gentiles is not, however, considered apart from the purpose for which it was done. It is often the purpose alone which gives moral character to an action; and in this case it gave to this action its chief moral turpitude. The purpose for which the Judaizers desired the Gentiles to be circumcised was that they might be brought under the law as a means of justification. Hence Paul adds to the declaration we are considering: "I testify again to every man who submits to circumcision, that he is a debtor to do the whole law. You have ceased from Christ, whoever of you are being justified by the law, you have fallen away from favor."* This can not refer to Jews, for it would make Paul himself and all the Jewish Christians "debtors to do the whole law;" a conclusion in direct conflict with one of the main arguments of this epistle.† It must, then, refer to Gentiles who were considering the propriety of circumcision as a condition of justification by the law.

We can now account for Paul's stern refusal to circumcise Titus. He was a Gentile, and could not with propriety be circumcised unless he desired to unite himself nationally with the Jewish people. But if, with Paul's consent, he should do this, his example would be used as a precedent to justify all other Gentile disciples in doing the same; and thus, in a short time, circumcision would cease to be a distinguishing mark of the offspring of Abraham, and the original design of the rite would be subverted. Moreover, to have circumcised him under the demand that was made by the Pharisees, would have been a virtual admission that it was necessary to justification, which could not be admitted without abandoning the liberty of Christ for the bondage of the law.

The case of Timothy was quite different. He was a half-blood Jew, and therefore belonged, in part, to the family of Abraham. He could be circumcised, not on the ground of its being necessary as a part of a system of justification by law, but because he was an heir of the everlasting covenant with Abraham. This, however, was not the chief reason for which Paul circumcised him, for Luke says it was "on account of the Jews who dwelt in those quarters; for they all knew that

* Gal. v: 3, 4.   † Gal. iii: 23–25.

his father was a Greek." In this reason there are two considerations combined, the latter qualifying the former. The fact that his father was known to be a Greek is given to account for the fact that Paul yielded to the prejudices of the Jews. If his father and mother both had been Jews, Paul might have acted from the binding nature of the Abrahamic covenant. Or if both had been Greeks, he would have disregarded the clamor of the Jews, as he had done in the case of Titus. But the mixed parentage of Timothy made his case a peculiar one. The marriage of his mother to a Greek was contrary to the law of Moses.* Whether the offspring from such a marriage should be circumcised, or not, the law did not determine. The Jewish rabbis taught that the mother should not circumcise the child without the consent of the father,† which was to admit that his circumcision was not obligatory. Paul did not, then, feel bound by the Abrahamic covenant to circumcise him, but did so to conciliate the "Jews who dwelt in those quarters," who had, doubtless, already objected to the prominent position assigned to one in Timothy's anomalous condition. It was, as all the commentators agree, a matter of expediency; but not, as they also contend, because it was indifferent whether *any one* were circumcised or not, but because it was indifferent whether one like *Timothy* were circumcised or not. It was an expediency that applied only to the case of a half-blood Jew with a Greek father; and it would, therefore, be most unwarrantable to extend it to the case of full-blooded Jews.

The remark of Paul that "Circumcision is nothing, and uncircumcision is nothing, but keeping the commandments of God,"‡ is readily explained in the light of the above remarks, and of its own context. It is immediately preceded by these words: "Is any man called being circumcised, let him not become uncircumcised. Is any called in uncircumcision, let him not be circumcised." And it is immediately followed by these words: "Let every man abide in the calling wherein he is called." So far, then, is this text from making it indifferent whether a Christian become circumcised or not, that it positively forbids those who had been in uncircumcision before they were called, to be circumcised; while it equally forbids the other party to render themselves uncircumcised; which expression means to act as if they were uncircumcised by neglecting it in reference to their children. For to become uncircumcised literally is impossible. That circumcision is nothing, and uncircumcision nothing, means, therefore, simply that it is indifferent whether a man had been, before he was called, a Jew or a Gentile; but it is far from indicating that it is innocent in a Jew to neglect this rite, or in a Gentile to observe it.

If we have properly collated the apostolic teaching on this subject, the conclusion of the whole matter is this: that Christian Jews, Ishmaelites, or Edomites, are under the same obligation to circumcise their children that the twelve tribes were in Egypt, and that the descendants of Ishmael and Esau were during the period of the law of Moses. This being so, the pedobaptist conceit that baptism has taken the place of circumcision is shown to be absurd, by the fact that circumcision still occupies its own place. It is undeniable that during

* Ex. xxxiv: 16; Deut. vii: 3.   † See Bloomfield, *in loco*.   ‡ 1 Cor. xii: 18-20.

the whole apostolic period Jewish disciples observed both baptism and circumcision, and as both these could not occupy the same place at the same time, their proper places must be different. According to apostolic precedent, both should still continue among the Jews; neither one taking the place of the other, but one serving as a token of the fleshly covenant with Abraham, the other as an institution of the new covenant, and a condition, both to Jew and Gentile, of the remission of sins.

4, 5. After so long delay upon the circumcision of Timothy, we are prepared to start forward again with the apostles, cheered as they were by this valuable addition to their company. (4) *"And as they passed through the cities they delivered to them to observe the decrees which had been adjudged by the apostles and elders in Jerusalem. (5) And the Churches were confirmed in the faith, and were daily increasing in number."* These decrees were everywhere needed, in order to unite in harmonious fellowship the Jewish and Gentile converts. Presented by Paul, who had been sent to Jerusalem for them, and by Silas, who had been sent out with high commendation by the apostles, to bear them to the Gentiles, they came with their full force to the ears of the brethren, and produced the happiest effects. The peace and harmony which they produced helped to confirm the brethren in the faith, and the daily increase in number was the result of this happy condition of the Churches.

6–8. The neighboring cities of Derbe and Lystra, where Paul was joined by Timothy, constituted the limit of his former tour with Barnabas into this region of country. He makes them now the starting point for an advance still further into the interior, and to the western extremity of Asia Minor. (6) *"Now when they had gone through Phrygia and the district of Galatia, being forbidden by the Holy Spirit to speak the word in Asia, (7) they went to Mysia, and attempted to go on through Bythinia, and the Spirit did not permit them. (8) So passing by Mysia they went down to Troas."*

From this hurried sketch of the tour through Phrygia and Galatia, it might be inferred that nothing of special interest occurred during its progress. But we learn from Paul himself that it was far otherwise in Galatia. In his epistle to the Churches there, he lifts the vail of obscurity thrown over this part of his life, and brings to light one of the most touching incidents in his eventful career. More than one congregation sprang up under his personal labors there,* who owed their knowledge of salvation to an afflicting providence affecting himself. He writes to them: "You know that on account of infirmity of the flesh I preached the gospel to you at the first."† This statement does not mean merely that he was suffering in the flesh at the time; but the expression δι' ἀσθένιαν indicates that the infirmity was the *cause* which led to his preaching to them. The infirmity was evidently that "thorn in the flesh, the messenger of Satan to buffet him," which he had prayed in vain to the Lord to take from him.‡ For he says to them: "My temptation which was in my flesh you despised not, nor rejected, but received me as an angel of God, even as Christ Jesus."‖ It is probable that he had intended to pass through this region with-

* Gal. i: 6; iv: 19.   † Gal. iv: 13.   ‡ 2 Cor. xii: 7.   ‖ Gal. iv: 14.

stopping, but some unusual violence of the humiliating and irritating malady compelled him to forego the more distant journey, and make some stay where the Word was so gladly received by these brethren. Though Paul felt that strangers like these would be likely to despise him and reject him, on perceiving the malady with which he was afflicted, yet this people listened to his annunciation of eternal truth as if they heard an angel of God, or Jesus Christ himself. His distress of mind and weakness of body were calculated to give a mellower tone to his preaching, and to awaken a livelier sympathy in truly generous hearts, and such was the effect on them. He says: "I bear you witness, that if it had been possible, you would have plucked out your own eyes and have given them to me."* Thus, out of the most unpropitious hour in which this faithful apostle ever introduced the gospel to a strange community, the kind providence of God brought forth the sweetest fruits of all his labors; for there are no other Churches of whose fondness for him he speaks in terms so touching. This serves to illustrate the meaning of the Lord's answer, when Paul prayed that the thorn might depart from his flesh: "My favor is sufficient for you; for my strength is made perfect in weakness."† His weakest hour, wherein he expected to be despised and rejected, he found the strongest for the cause he was pleading, and the most soothing to his own troubled spirit. It was experience like this which enabled him, in later years, to exclaim, "Most gladly, therefore, will I rather glory in my infirmities, that the power of Christ may rest upon me. Therefore I take *pleasure* in infirmities, in reproaches, in necessities, in persecutions, in distresses for Christ's sake; for when I am weak, then am I strong."‡

Paul's own judgment seems to have been much at fault, during this period, in reference to the choice of a field of labor. Contrary to his purpose, he had been delayed in Galatia "on account of infirmity of flesh;" and then, intending to enter the province of Asia, of which Ephesus was the capital, he was "forbidden by the Holy Spirit to speak the Word there." Finally they attempted to go into Bythinia, "and the Holy Spirit did not permit them." Feeling his way around the forbidden territory, he finally went down to Troas, on the shore of the Ægean Sea.

9, 10. Here he learns the object which the Spirit had in view, while turning him aside from one after another of the fields which he himself had chosen. (9) "*Then a vision appeared to Paul in the night. There stood a man of Macedonia, entreating him, and saying, Come over into Macedonia and help us.* (10) *And when he saw the vision, we immediately sought to go forth into Macedonia, inferring that the Lord had called us to preach the gospel to them.*"

This overruling of Paul's purpose, coupled with the absence of it at other times, indicates something of the method by which the journeyings of inspired men were directed. While their own judgment led to a judicious choice, it was permitted to guide them; but when it failed, as was likely to be the case, through their ignorance of the comparative accessibility of different communities, or the circumstances of individuals, they were overruled by some controlling providence, like

* Gal. iv: 15.   † 2 Cor. xii: 9.   ‡ 2 Cor. 9, 10.

Paul in Galatia; directed by angels, like Philip in Samaria; or by the Spirit, like Peter in Joppa; restrained from some purpose, like Paul and Silas when attempting to enter Asia and Bythinia; or called away across the sea, as he was now, by a vision at night. We will yet see that, as in the cases of Philip and of Peter, the prayers of individuals ready to hear the gospel were connected with the divine interference by which Paul and Silas were now being directed.*

Preachers of the present day have no authoritative visions by night to guide them, and the supposition indulged by some, that they are at times prompted by the Spirit as Paul was, is nothing more than the conceit of an enthusiast, while it is nothing less than a claim to inspiration. But Paul was often guided merely by the indications of Providence, and so may it be with us. If we are attentive to these indications, we shall be under the guidance of that same All-seeing Eye which chose the steps of Paul. If the way of our choosing is entirely blocked up, at times, or some stern necessity turns us aside from a settled purpose, we may regard it as but the firmer pressure of that hand which leads us, for the most part, unseen and unfelt.

11, 12. An opportunity was offered without delay, for the apostolic company to make the contemplated voyage to Macedonia. (11) *"Therefore, setting sail from Troas, we ran by a straight course to Samothrace, and the next day to Neapolis;* (12) *and thence to Philippi, which is the first city of that part of Macedonia, and a colony. And we abode in that city some days."*

Samothrace is an island in the Archipelago, about midway between Troas and Neapolis. Neapolis was a seaport of Macedonia, and the landing place for Philippi. The remark that they sailed to Samothrace, and the *next day* to Neapolis, shows that they spent the night at Samothrace, which accords with the custom of ancient navigators, who generally cast anchor at night, during coasting voyages, unless the stars were out. This voyage occupied a part of two days.

Philippi was not the *chief* city of that part of Macedonia, as rendered in the common version, but the *first* city; by which is meant, either that it was the first which Paul visited, or the first in point of celebrity. I think the latter is the real idea; for it is obvious from the history that this was the *first* city Paul *visited*, and of this the reader need not be informed. But it was the first city of that region in point of celebrity, because it was the scene of the great battle in which Brutus and Cassius were defeated by Marc Antony. Thessalonica was then, and is yet, the *chief* city of Macedonia.

The observant reader will here notice a change in the style of the narrative, which indicates the presence of the writer among the companions of Paul. Hitherto he had spoken of them only in the third person; but when about to leave Troas, he uses the first person plural, saying, "*we* sought to go forth into Macedonia," and "*we* ran to Samothrace," etc. It is only by such a change in the pronoun employed, from the third to the first person, and from the first to the third, that we can detect the presence or absence of Luke. From this indication we conclude that he first joined the company in the interior of Asia Minor, just previous to entering the city of Troas. The company with

* See Com., below, verses 13, 14.

ACTS XVI: 13-15. 201

whom we are now traveling is composed of Paul and Silas, Timothy and Luke.

13-15. Upon entering this strange city, the first on the continent of Europe visited by an apostle, Paul and his companions must have looked around them with great anxiety for some opportunity to open their message to the people. The prospects were sufficiently forbidding. They knew not the face of a human being; and there was not even a Jewish synagogue into which they might enter with the hope of being invited to speak "a word of exhortation to the people."* By some means, however, they learned that on the bank of the river Gangas, which flowed by the city, some Jewish women were in the habit of congregating on the Sabbath-day, for prayer. Thither the apostles directed their steps, determined that here should be the beginning of their labors in Philippi. (13) *"And on the Sabbath-day we went out of the city by a river-side, where prayer was wont to be made, and sat down, and spoke to the women who had collected there. And a certain woman named Lydia, a seller of purple, of the city of Thyatira, who worshiped God, was listening; whose heart the Lord opened, so that she attended to the things spoken by Paul. (15) And when she was immersed, and her house, she entreated us, saying, If you have judged me to be faithful to the Lord, come into my house, and remain there. And she constrained us."*

With Bloomfield, I reject the criticism of most recent commentators, who render the second clause of verse 13, "*where was wont to be a place of prayer.*"† Besides the reasons suggested by this learned author, I would observe, *first*, that the term προσευχή is nowhere else in the New Testament used in the sense of a *place of prayer*, but always means *prayer*. Nothing but a contextual necessity, therefore, would justify a different rendering here. Again, the expression ἐνομίζετο εἶναι means *was accustomed to be*, and it is never said of a place, or building, that it is *accustomed* to be where it is.

We now see one reason for that singular prohibition which had been steadily turning Paul aside from the fields which he had preferred, until he reached the sea-shore; and of that vision which had called him into Europe. These women had been wont to repair to this riverbank for prayer. God had heard their prayers, as in the case of Cornelius, and he was bringing to them the preacher through whose words they might obtain faith in Christ, and learn the way of salvation. Long before either they or Paul knew anything of it, God was directing the steps of the latter, and timing the motion of the winds at sea, with reference to that weekly meeting on the river's bank, as he had once done the flight of an angel and the steps of Philip with reference to the eunuch's chariot. Now, as in those two cases, he has brought the parties face to face. He answers the prayers of the unconverted, not by an enlightening influence of the Spirit in their hearts, but by providentially bringing to them a preacher of the gospel who knows the way of salvation.

The statement that the Lord opened the heart of Lydia, that she attended to the things spoken by Paul, is generally assumed by the commentators as a certain proof that an immediate influence of the

---

* Acts xiii: 15. † Hackett, and authors referred to by him.

Spirit was exerted on her heart, in order that she should listen favorably to the truth. Their interpretation of the words is expressed in the most orthodox style by Bloomfield, thus: "The opening in question was effected by the grace of God, working by his Spirit with the concurrent good dispositions of Lydia." Dr. Hackett says her heart was "enlightened, impressed by his Spirit, and so prepared to receive the truth." Whether this is the true interpretation or not, may be determined by a careful examination of all the facts in the case.

First: The term *open* is evidently used metaphorically, but in a sense not at all obscure. To *open* the *mind* is to expand it to broader or more just conceptions of a subject. To *open* the *heart* is to awaken within it more generous impulses. What exact impulse is awakened, in a given case, is to be determined by the context.

Second: The impulse awakened in Lydia's heart was not such a disposition that she *listened* favorably to what Paul said, but, "that she *attended* to *things*" which he spoke. The facts, in the order in which they are stated, are as follows: 1st. "We spoke to the women." 2d. Lydia "was listening." 3d. God opened her heart. 4th. She *attended* to the things spoken. The fourth fact is declared to be the result of the third. It was *after* she "was listening" that God opened her heart, and *after* her heart was opened, and *because* of this opening, that she *attended* to what she had heard. What the exact result was, then, is to be determined by the meaning of the word "*attended.*" The term *attend* sometimes means to *concentrate the mind* upon a subject, and sometimes to *practically observe* what we are taught. The Greek term προσεχω, here employed, has a similar usage. It is used in the former sense, in Acts viii: 6, where it is said the people "*attended* to the things spoken by Philip, in *hearing* and *seeing* the miracles which he wrought." It is used in the latter sense in 1 Tim. iv: 13, where Paul says, "Till I come, *attend* to reading, to exhortation, to teaching;" and in Heb. vii: 13, where to *attend* to the altar means to do the service at the altar. That the latter is the meaning in the case before us is clearly proved by the fact that she had already *listened* to what Paul spoke, or given mental attention to it, before God opened her heart so that she *attended* to the things she had heard. Now, in hearing the gospel, she learned that there were certain things which she was required *to attend* to, which were, to believe, to repent, and to be immersed. To *attend* to the things she heard, then, was to do these things. That immersion was included in the things which Luke refers to by this term is evident from the manner in which he introduces that circumstance. He says, "And *when* she was immersed," etc., as if her immersion was already implied in the preceding remark. If such was not his meaning, he would not have used the adverb *when*, but would simply have stated, as an additional fact, that she was immersed.

Having the facts of the case now before us, we inquire whether it is necessary to admit an immediate influence of the Spirit, in order to account for the opening of her heart. We must bear in mind, while prosecuting this inquiry, that the opening in question was such a change in her heart as to induce her to believe the gospel, to repent of her sins, and to be immersed, thereby devoting her life to the service of Christ. Her heart had been contracted by the narrowness of Jewish prejudices, which were obstacles, in some degree, to the reception of the gospel; but she was a "worshiper of God," which inclined her to do whatever she might learn to be the will of God. In seeking to account for the change effected, we must also bear in mind the well-settled philosophical principle, that when an effect can be accounted for by causes which are known to be present, it is illogical to assume a cause which is not known to be present. Now, in Lydia's case, it is not asserted that an immediate action of the Spirit took place in her heart; neither can it be known that such a cause was present, unless this is the only cause which could produce the effect. But it is known that all the power which can be exerted through the words of an inspired apostle preaching the gospel of Jesus Christ, was present. And it can not be denied, that when the gospel, thus presented, is listened to by one who is already a sincere worshiper of God, as Lydia was, the heart may be so expanded by it from the narrowness of Jewish prejudice as to admit of faith, repentance, and obedience. The assumption, therefore, that her heart was opened by an abstract influence of the Spirit, is entirely gratuitous and illogical, while the real cause is patent upon the face of the narrative in the preaching done by Paul.

If it be objected to this conclusion, that it is said *God* opened her heart, and not Paul, we answer, that God by his Spirit was the real agent of all that was effected through the words of Paul. For it was the Spirit in Paul who spoke to Lydia, and it was the fact that the Holy Spirit was in him which compelled her to believe what he might say, and gave his words all their power. Hence, so far is this statement of the text from being inconsistent with our conclusion, that the opening of her heart through Paul's words is the clearest proof that it was effected by the Holy Spirit as the prime agent.

If, in conclusion of this inquiry, we compare Lydia's case with that of the eunuch, or of Cornelius, who were in similar states of mind previous to conversion, and needed a similar opening of the heart, we find that it was effected in the same way, through the power of miraculously attested truth, and that the only difference is in the phraseology in which Luke chooses to describe it. If, from these facts, we attempt a general conclusion, it is, that when any narrowness of heart, produced by improper education, or otherwise, stands in the way of salvation, the Lord removes it, and opens the heart, by the expanding and ennobling influence of his truth. This is true of the saint as well as the sinner, as is well illustrated by the case of Peter and the other apostles in connection with the family of Cornelius.*

The statement that Lydia's household were immersed with her has been taken by nearly all pedobaptist writers as presumptive evidence in favor of infant baptism. Olshausen, however, while affirming that "the propriety of infant baptism is undoubted," has the candor to admit that "It is highly improbable that the phrase *her household* should be understood as including infant children." He also affirms that "There is altogether wanting any conclusive proof-passage for the baptism of children in the age of the apostles, nor can the necessity of it be deduced from the nature of baptism."† Dr. Alexander also remarks that "The real strength of the argument lies not in any

* See Com. x: 9-16, *et seq.*, and xi: 18. † Com. *in loco*.

one case, but in the repeated mention of whole households as baptized." But Dr. Barnes states the argument in the more popular style, thus: "The case is one that affords a strong presumptive proof that this was an instance of *household* or infant baptism. For, (1) *Her* believing is particularly mentioned. (2) It is not intimated that *they* believed. On the contrary, it is strongly implied that they did not. (3) It is manifestly implied that *they* were baptized because *she* believed."

Dr. Alexander's statement of the argument is that generally employed by debatants; that of Dr. Barnes the one most common among preachers and teachers who have no opponent before them. In reference to the former it is sufficient to say, that "the repeated mention of whole households as baptized" affords not the slightest evidence in favor of infant baptism, unless it can be proved that in at least *one* of these households there were *infants*. It there were infants in one, this would establish the presumption that there might be in some others. But until there is proof that there were infants in some of them, it may be inferred that the absence of infants was the very circumstance which led to the immersion of the whole family. Indeed, a fair induction of such cases fully justifies this inference in reference to Lydia's case. There is positive proof that there were no infants in any other family whose immersion is mentioned in the New Testament. There were none in the household of Cornelius; for they all spoke in tongues, and believed. There were none in that of the jailer; for they all believed and rejoiced in the Lord. None in the houshold of Stephanas; for they "addicted themselves to the ministry of the saints."* Now, inasmuch as one of the peculiarities of all households who were immersed, of whom we know the facts, was the absence of infants, we are justified in the conclusion, no evidence to the contrary appearing, that this was also a peculiarity of Lydia's household. The argument, therefore, as stated by Dr. Alexander, is not only inconclusive, but, when properly viewed, establishes a presumption quite the reverse.

The argument, as stated by Dr. Barnes, is based entirely upon the *silence* of the Scriptures. He says: "*Her* believing is particularly mentioned;" but "it is not intimated that *they* believed. On the contrary, it is strongly implied that they did not." Now, if the mere silence of Luke in reference to their faith implies strongly that they did not believe, his silence in reference to Lydia's *repentance* implies as strongly that she did not repent. In some cases of conversion, the repentance of the parties is "particularly mentioned." "It is not intimated" that Lydia repented; therefore, says the logic of Dr. Barnes, "there is a strong presumptive proof that this was an instance of" *baptism without repentance*. If men are allowed thus to prove what is Scripture doctrine, by what the Scriptures *do not mention*, there is no end to the doctrines and practices which the Bible may be made to defend. If Dr. Barnes were compelled to meet the argument in reference to Lydia's repentance, he would do it very easily, and, in so doing, would refute his own in reference to the baptism of her children. He would show that we know that Lydia repented, because

* Compare 1 Cor. i: 16 and xvi: 15.

none but those who repented were admitted to baptism on other occasions. Just so, we know that all baptized on this occasion believed, because none but believers were baptized on other occasions. Not till he can prove, from other statements of the Scriptures, that persons were baptized by the apostles without faith, can he establish the presumption that these parties were not believers, simply because their faith is not mentioned.

Dr. Barnes concludes his note on this case, by saying, "It is just such an account as would now be given of a household or family that were baptized on the faith of the parent." This is true. But it is equally true, that it is just such an account as would now be given of a household or family that were baptized without an infant among them. The presence, therefore, of one or more infants, which is essential to the argument, remains absolutely without proof.

The mere absence of proof is not the worst feature of the pedobaptist assumptions in this case. For the assumption that infants were here baptized depends upon five other assumptions, the falsity of either of which would vitiate the whole argument. It is assumed, *First*, That some of the household were baptized without faith. *Second*, That Lydia was, or had been, a married woman. *Third*, That she had children. *Fourth*, That one or more of her children were infants. *Fifth*, That her infant children were so young as to necessarily be brought with her from Thyatira to Philippi. Now, so long as it remains possible that all the parties baptized were believers; or that Lydia was a maiden; or that she was a married woman or widow without children; or that her children were of a responsible age; or that her younger children were left at home in Thyatira when she came to Philippi to sell her purple cloths; so long as any one of these hypotheses can *possibly* be true, so long will it be *impossible* to prove an instance of infant baptism in her household.

One more suggestion is necessary to a full statement of the argument in this case. When Lydia invited Paul's company to lodge in her house, they were backward about complying, as is evident from the remark that "she *constrained* us." Now there can be no probable reason assigned for this reluctance, but the fact that it was *her* house, and the brethren felt it a matter of delicacy to be the guests of a *woman*. To the full extent of the probability of this supposition, which is hightened by the fact that she calls the house her own, is it probable that she was an unmarried woman, and, therefore, *improbable* that she had infant children. Thus we find that all the known facts in the case are adverse to the argument in favor of infant baptism.

16–18. We are next introduced to an incident which led to a decided change in the fortunes of Paul and Silas. (16) "*And it came to pass, as we were going to prayer, there met us a certain female servant, having a spirit of divination, who brought her masters much gain by soothsaying.* (17) *The same followed Paul and us, and cried out, saying, These men are servants of the most high God, who show us the way of salvation.* (18) *She did this for many days. But Paul, being much grieved, turned and said to the spirit, I command you, in the name of Jesus Christ, to come out of her. And he came out the same hour.*" Demons exhibited a knowledge of the person of Jesus, and the mission of himself and the apostles, which seems not to have been derived from preaching This was a superhuman knowledge. But there is no evidence known to me that they could foretell future events, though it was believed by the heathen generally that they could. It was the prevalent confidence in the vaticinations of persons possessed by them that enabled this girl to bring her owners much gain.

If Paul had reasoned as many do at the present day, he would have been glad that this girl followed him with such a proclamation. It was the very thing of which he was trying to convince the people of Philippi, who already had confidence in the demoniac. Why, then, was he not rejoiced at so powerful co-operation, instead of being grieved, and shutting the mouth of an apparent friend? It must be because he saw the matter in a far different light from that in which it appears to those advocates of "spirit rappings," who exult in them as affording strong confirmation to the gospel.

The course pursued by Paul was the same with that of Jesus, who invariably stopped the mouths of demons when they attempted to testify to his claims. The propriety of this course will be apparent upon observing: *First*, That to have permitted demons to testify for the truth would have convinced the people that there was an alliance between them and the preachers. *Second*, This supposed alliance would have caused all the good repute of Jesus and the apostles to reflect upon the demons, and all the evil repute of demons to reflect upon them. It was an ingenious effort of the devil to ally himself with Jesus Christ, in order the more effectually to defeat his purposes. If Christ and the apostles had given countenance to demons while telling the truth, they could have used their indorsement to gain credence when telling a lie; and thus, believers would have been left to the mercy of seducing spirits, fulfilling, with the apparent sanction of Christ, the prophesy of Paul that, "In the latter times men shall depart from the faith, giving heed to seducing spirits and teachings of demons, speaking lies in disguise, having the conscience seared with a hot iron."* To guard against this result, it was necessary to exorcise all demons who ventured to speak in favor of the truth.

In the present instance, Paul could not pursue the settled course of the apostles, without greatly depreciating the value of the slave; and doubtless it was an extreme reluctance to interference with the rights of property which induced him to submit to the annoyance for so many days. At length, seeing no other means of relief, he cast the demon out, and, in doing so, framed the exorcising sentence in such a way as to indicate an antagonism between the demon and Jesus Christ; saying, "*In the name of Jesus Christ* I command you to come out of her." The immediate obedience of the spirit demonstrated the authority of the name by which Paul spoke, and thus the very attempt of the devil to gain an apparent alliance with Jesus through this demon was made the occasion of demonstrating the divine power of the latter.

19–21. (19) "*Then her masters, seeing that the hope of their gain was gone, seized Paul and Silas and dragged them into the market-place to the rulers,* (20) *and leading him forward to the magistrates, they said,*

* 1 Tim. iv: 1, 2.

ACTS XVI: 21-25.

These men, being Jews, do exceedingly trouble our city, (21) *and are announcing customs which it is unlawful for us, being Romans, to receive or to observe."* In this accusation, the real cause of complaint was concealed, for several reasons: *First,* The disinterested multitude would naturally sympathize with the girl who had been restored to her mind, rather than with the masters who had made her misfortune a source of profit. *Second,* To have made prominent the fact that Paul, by a word, had expelled the demon, would have made an impression favorable to him and his cause. But the Jews and their religion were particularly obnoxious to the Romans, and hence, when the accusation was made by men of wealth and influence, that these men, "*being Jews,*" were introducing customs contrary to the religion and laws of Rome, it was easy to excite the populace against them.

22–24. (22) "*And the multitude rose up against them, and the magistrates, having torn off their garments, commanded to beat them with rods.* (23) *And having laid many stripes upon them, they cast them into prison, charging the jailer to keep them safely;* (24) *who, having received such a commandment, thrust them into the inner prison, and made their feet fast in the stocks.*" It appears that the magistrates gave them no opportunity to defend themselves, but simply yielded to the clamor of the multitude, in utter disregard of all the forms of justice. It was that same miserable truckling to the passions of a mob, whom they ought to have ruled into sobriety and reason, which has stamped with infamy the name of Pontius Pilate.

25. The condition of the two brethren, as night drew on, was miserable to a degree scarcely conceivable. Besides the physical pain of sitting in a dark dungeon, with their backs bleeding from the scourge, and their feet fastened in the stocks to prevent even the relief which a change of position might afford, their minds were racked with a sense of the deep injustice done them; with the reflection that such was the return they met at the hands of men for whom they had sacrificed their all on earth, and their present reward for faithful service of the Lord; and with the most mournful anticipations of their future fate. Most men, under such circumstances, would have been wild with rage against their persecutors, unconcerned for the fate of an unfriendly world, and full of doubts as to the protecting favor of God. But in the darkest and bitterest hour of their sufferings, these faithful disciples brought forth the richest fruits of their faith and piety. (25) "*But at midnight Paul and Silas prayed and sang praises to God, and the prisoners heard them.*" Men do not pray when they are enraged, nor when they are hopeless. The soul must recover from the turmoil of violent passion, before it can offer thoughtful prayer. But still greater composure is necessary to induce a disposition to engage in singing. One in deep distress may be soothed by the music of other voices, but is not inclined to join in the song himself. That Paul and Silas prayed at midnight is the clearest evidence that the tempest of their feelings, which must, at the whipping-post, and when first thrust within the dungeon and fastened in the stocks, have driven away all sober thought, and smothered all utterance, had by this time subsided. And that, after praying, they "sang praises to God," shows how quickly the soothing effects of prayer had still further calmed and cheered their

spirits. The song they sang was not a plaintive strain, suited to the sorrows of the lonely prisoner; but it swelled up in those firm and animated tones which are suited to the praises of God. How rich the treasures of faith and hope which can thus cheer the gloom of a midnight dungeon, and calm the spirit of the bleeding prisoner of Jesus Christ!

26. The song of the apostles was a strange sound to the other prisoners, but one most welcome to heaven; and God, who appeared almost to have forsaken his servants, came to their relief in a manner peculiar to himself, yet most surprising to all within the prison. (26) *"And suddenly there was a great earthquake, so that the foundations of the prison were shaken, and immediately all the doors were opened, and every one's bonds were loosed."* The prisoners were all awake when this occurred, having been awakened by the singing, and must instinctively have connected the phenomenon with those midnight singers.

27. The jailer seems not to have heard the singing, but was awakened by the motion of the earthquake, the slamming of the doors, and the clanking of the fetters which fell from the hands of the prisoners. (27) *"And the jailer, awaking out of sleep, and seeing the prison-doors open, drew his sword, and was about to kill himself, supposing that the prisoners had fled."* It was not so dark as to prevent him from seeing, to some extent, what had taken place. He supposed that the prisoners had, as a matter of course, all rushed out through the open doors. He knew that the penalty, under the Roman law, for allowing prisoners to escape, was death; and that peculiar code of honor among the Romans, which made them prefer to die by their own hands, rather than by that of an enemy or an executioner, drove him to this attempt at suicide.

28. He had already planted the hilt of his sword upon the floor, and was about to cast himself upon the point of it, when Paul, who must now have left his dungeon, saw what he was doing, and arrested his mad purpose. (28) *"But Paul cried, with a loud voice, saying, Do yourself no harm, for we are all here."* Reassured by this statement, and by the calmness of the tone in which it was uttered, he drew back from the leap he was about to make into eternity.

29, 30. As soon as he could collect his senses, he recollected that the calm speaker who had called to him had been preaching salvation in the name of the God of Israel; and he immediately perceived that the earthquake, the miraculous opening of doors, and the unlocking of chains and handcuffs were connected with him and his companion. In an instant he recognizes the divine authority, and, glancing into the black eternity from which he had suddenly been rescued, his own salvation, rather than the safety of his prisoners, at once absorbs his thoughts. (29) *"Then he called for a light, and sprang in, and came trembling, and fell down before Paul and Silas; (30) and led them out, and said, Sirs, what must I do to be saved?"* That he asked this question proves that he had some conception of the salvation of which Paul had been preaching; and that he trembled, and fell at their feet, shows that he was overwhelmed with a sense of danger, and painfully anxious to escape from it. At sunset, when coldly thrusting the bleeding apostles into the dungeon, he cared but little for this question. In the midst of life and health, when all goes well with us, we may thrust this awful question from us; but when we come within an inch of death, like the jailer at midnight hanging over the point of his own sword, it rushes in upon the soul like a lava torrent, and burns out all other thoughts.

30, 31. Leading the brethren into his family apartment, he received a full and satisfactory answer to his question. (30) *"They said, Believe on the Lord Jesus Christ, and you shall be saved, and your house.* (31) *And they spake the word of the Lord to him and to all who were in his house."* Those who advocate the doctrine of justification by faith only, appeal with great confidence to this answer of the apostle, as proof of that doctrine. We can not enter upon the merits of this doctrine, except as it is affected by this and other passages in Acts.

To state the argument in its strongest form, it would stand thus: In answer to the question, What shall I do to be saved? *one* thing is commanded to be *done:* " *Believe on the Lord Jesus Christ;*" and *one* thing is promised: " *You shall be saved."* Now, then, Paul could not have made this promise on this one condition, unless he knew that *all* who believe on the Lord Jesus are saved. No less than the universal proposition that *all* who believe shall be saved, would justify the conclusion that if the *jailer* believed, *he* would be saved. Paul, then, assumes this universal proposition, and, therefore, it must be true. But there are some who believe, and are consequently saved, who have never been *immersed;* therefore, immersion does not constitute a part of what we must do to be saved.

The fallacy of this very plausible argument is to be found in the ambiguous usage of the term *believe.* This ambiguity does not arise from the fact that there are different *kinds* of faith; but from the fact that the term is sometimes used abstractly, and sometimes to include the repentance and obedience which properly result from faith. Whatever is affirmed of faith *only* must necessarily contemplate it in the former sense. But in that sense it can not secure justification, as is proved by the force of those passages which treat of it in this sense. John, in his gospel, says: "Among the chief rulers many *believed* on him; but because of the Pharisees they did not confess him, lest they should be put out of the synagogue: for they loved the praise of men more than the praise of God."[*] James also says: "As the body without faith is dead, so faith *without works* is dead also."[†] In these passages faith is considered separately from the works which should follow it, and is declared to be *dead,* or inoperative.

Now, the statement of Paul to the jailer is not, that if he would believe on the Lord Jesus Christ with a *dead* faith, or a faith so weak as to be overpowered by worldly motives, he should be saved; but he evidently contemplates a *living* faith—a faith which leads to immediate and hearty obedience. In this usage of the term it is true that not only the jailer, but every other believer may be promised, " Believe on the Lord Jesus, and thou shalt be saved." Yet it is equally true that the salvation does not result from the faith only; and that it is not enjoyed until the faith brings forth the contemplated obedience. If faith without works is dead, then it remains dead as long as it remains without works. It thus remains until the believer is immersed, if he

[*] John xii: 42, 43.   [†] James ii: 21.

proceed according to apostolic example; therefore, faith without immersion is dead. Paul acted upon this principle in the case before us. For, after telling him, in the comprehensive sense of the term believe, that if he would believe on the Lord Jesus he should be saved, he immediately gives him more specific instruction, and *immerses* him the same hour of the night.* Those who argue that the jailer obtained pardon by faith alone, leave the jail too soon. If they would remain one hour longer, they would see him immersed for the remission of his sins, and *rejoicing* in the knowledge of pardon *after* his immersion, not before it.†

There is another aspect of this answer to the jailer which must not be passed by; for it confirms what we have already said, and at the same time harmonizes this with other inspired answers to the same question. To Saul, who was a penitent believer, and sent to Ananias to learn what he should do, the latter replied: "Arise and be immersed and wash away your sins." To the Jews on Pentecost, who had faith, but faith *only*, Peter commands: "Repent and be immersed, every one of you, in the name of Jesus Christ, for the remission of sins." But to the jailer, who was a heathen, Paul commands, "*Believe* on the Lord Jesus Christ;" and intending more fully to develop the manner in which his faith should be manifested, promises, "and you shall be saved." Thus each answer is adapted to the exact religious state of the party to whom it is addressed, requiring first that which is to be done first, and enjoining to be done only that which had not been done.

The conduct of the jailer in prostrating himself before Paul and Silas, and crying out, "What shall I do to be saved?" shows that he already believed them to be messengers from God, and understood that their message had reference to the salvation of men. But there is no evidence that his faith or his information extended beyond this. Having commanded him to believe on the Lord Jesus Christ, it was necessary to put within his reach the means of faith; and this Paul proceeds to do by preaching "the word of the Lord to him and to all who were in his house."

33, 34. The preaching, as would be expected under circumstances so favorable, had the desired effect both upon the jailer and his household. (33) "*And he took them the same hour of the night, and washed their stripes, and was immersed, he and all his, immediately.* (34) *And having led them into his house, he set food before them, and rejoiced, believing in God with all his house.*"

Those pedobaptist writers who claim the example of the apostles in favor of affusion and infant baptism attempt to find support for these practices in this case of conversion. Their argument for affusion depends entirely upon the assumption that the baptism was performed within the prison. If this assumption were admitted, it would prove nothing in favor of affusion so long as it is possible that there were conveniences for immersion within the prison. But the assumption is in direct conflict with the facts in the case. The facts are briefly as follows: *First*, When the jailer was about to commit suicide, Paul saw him, which shows that he was then outside of his dun

* See verse 33, below. ‡ Verse 34.

geon, in the more open part of the prison. *Second*, Hearing Paul's voice, the jailer sprang into the prison, and "*led them out*"—not out of the *dungeon*, but out of the *prison*. *Third*, Being now out of the prison, "they spoke the word of the Lord to him and to all who were in his house." While speaking, then, they were in the house, and not in the prison. *Fourth*, "He took them and washed their stripes, and was baptized." The verb *took*, in this connection, implies the *removal* of the parties to some other spot for the washing and baptizing. Whether to some other part of the house, or out of the house, it does not determine. But, *fifth*, when the baptizing was concluded, "he *led them into* his house," which shows that, before it was done, he had *taken them out of* the house. Between the moment at which he took them out of the house and the moment he brought them into it, the baptizing was done. But they would not, at this hour of the night, have gone out, unless there was some necessity for it, which the demands of affusion could not supply. The circumstance, though not in itself a proof of immersion, affords strong circumstantial evidence in its favor, and is suggestive of that river on the banks of which Lydia first heard the gospel, and in which she was immersed.

It has been suggested that the party could not have passed through the gates of the city at this hour of the night; but there is no evidence that Philippi was a walled town. Again, it is sometimes objected, that the jailer had no right to take his prisoners outside the jail; and that Paul and Silas showed, by their conduct on the next morning, that they would not go out without the consent of the authorities.* But this is to assume that the jailer would rather obey men than God, and that Paul and Silas were so punctilious about their personal dignity that they would refuse to immerse a penitent sinner through fear of compromising it. Such assumptions are certainly too absurd to be entertained when once observed; but, even if we cling to them, they can not set aside the fact, so clearly established above, that the jailer did lead them out of the prison.

As for the assumption that infants were baptized here, we have already observed, in commenting on Lydia's conversion, that it is precluded by the fact that all the household believed. "He rejoiced, *believing* in God *with all his house.*" Moreover, Paul and Silas spoke the Word to "*all* who were in the house," yet they certainly did not preach to infants. As there were no infants in the house while hearing, and none while subsequently believing and rejoicing, there could be none at the intermediate baptizing.

Before dismissing this case of conversion, which is the last we will consider in detail in the course of this work, we propose a brief review of its leading features, that we may trace its essential uniformity with those already considered. The influence which first took effect upon him was that of the earthquake, and the attendant opening of the prison-doors. This produced a feeling of alarm and heathenish desperation. It awakened within him no religious thought or emotions until the voice of Paul had recalled all that he had known of the apostolic preaching, when he instantly perceived that the miracle had been wrought by the God whom Paul and Silas preached. The proper

* Verse 37.

effect of miraculous attestation of a messenger of God is next apparent in his rushing forward, falling before them, and exclaiming, "Sirs, what must I do to be saved?" He is now a believer in the divine mission of the apostles, but not yet a believer in Jesus Christ. Whatever he hears from these men, however, he is ready to receive as God's truth. He hears from them the "word of the Lord," and the next we see, he is washing from the neglected stripes of the prisoners the clotted blood, and submitting to immersion. That he was immersed proves that he was both a believer and a penitent. *After* immersion, he rejoices. The case exhibits the same essential features which we have found in all others; the same word of the Lord spoken and attested by miraculous evidence; the same faith in the Lord Jesus Christ, followed by repentance, and the same immersion, followed by the same rejoicing. Thus we trace a perfect uniformity in the apostolic procedure, and in the experience of their converts.

35, 36. When the magistrates gave orders for the imprisonment of Paul and Silas, it would naturally be supposed that they intended to make some further inquiry into the charges preferred against them. But we are told, (35) *"When it was day, the magistrates sent the officers, saying, Release those men.* (36) *The jailer told Paul these words, The magistrates have sent word that you be released. Now, therefore, depart, and go in peace."* This order was given without any further developments known to the magistrates, at least so far as we are informed, and shows that they had only imprisoned the brethren, as they had scourged them, to gratify the mob; and now that the clamor of the mob had ceased, they had no further motive to detain them.

37–39. To be thus released from prison, as though they had simply suffered the penalty due them, would be a suspicious circumstance to follow the missionaries to other cities; and, fortunately, the means of escaping it were at hand. (37) *"But Paul said to them, They have beaten us publicly, uncondemned, being Romans, and have cast us into prison; and do they now cast us out privately ? No. But let them come themselves, and lead us out.* (38) *The officers told these words to the magistrates, and when they heard that they were Romans, they were alarmed.* (39) *And they came, and entreated them, and led them out, and asked them to depart out of the city."* If the fact of their having been scourged and imprisoned *should* follow them to other cities, it would do them no harm, provided it were also known that the magistrates had acknowledged the injustice done them, by going in person to the prison, and giving them an honorable discharge.

As it was a capital crime, under the Roman law, to scourge a Roman citizen, and Paul and Silas both enjoyed the rights of citizenship, they had the magistrates in their power, and could dictate terms to them. The terms were promptly complied with; for men who can be induced to pervert justice by the clamor of an unthinking mob will nearly always prove cowardly and sycophantic when their crimes are exposed, and justice is likely to overtake them. By making complaint to the proper authorities, Paul might have procured their punishment; but he had been taught not to resent evil, and was himself in the habit of teaching his brethren, "Avenge not yourselves, but rather give place unto wrath; for it is written, Vengeance is mine; I will repay, saith

ACTS XVI: 40; XVII: 1-3.

the Lord."* His conduct, on this occasion, happily illustrates this precept. If he had appealed to the Roman authorities for the punishment of his tormentors, he would have been *avenging himself* in the most effectual method. But to yield, as he did, this privilege, was to leave vengeance in the hands of God, to whom it belongs. By this course Paul gained the approbation of God, and the admiration of posterity, while justice lost nothing; for the unresenting demeanor of the apostle "heaped coals of fire on their heads," and the Judge of all the earth held their deeds in remembrance. The incident justifies Christians in making use of civil laws to protect themselves, but not to inflict punishment on their enemies.

40. When they were discharged, they took their own time to comply with the polite request of the magistrates. (40) *"Then they went out of the prison, and went into the house of Lydia; and having seen the brethren, and exhorted them, they departed."* Who these "brethren" were, besides Luke and Timothy, we can not tell; but the presumption is, that they were others who had been immersed during their stay in the city.

XVII: 1. Luke now drops the pronoun of the first person, in which he has spoken of the apostolic company since they left Troas, and resumes the third person, which shows that he remained in Philippi after the departure of Paul and Silas. He also speaks of these two brethren as if they constituted the whole company, until they are about to leave Berea, when Timothy is again mentioned.† This leads to the presumption that Timothy remained with Luke, to still further instruct and organize the infant congregation in Philippi. Leaving the cause thus guarded behind them, Paul and Silas seek another field of labor. (1) *"And having passed through Amphipolis and Apollonia, they went into Thessalonica, where was the synagogue of the Jews."* The distance from Philippi to Amphipolis was thirty-three miles; from Amphipolis to Apollonia, thirty miles; and from Apollonia to Thessalonica, thirty-seven miles; making just one hundred miles to the next city which the apostles undertook to evangelize. The whole of this distance was over one of those celebrated military roads built by the Romans, and elegantly paved with flag-stones.‡

At Philippi there was no synagogue, and the swift passage of Paul and Silas through Amphipolis and Apollonia indicates that there was none in either of those cities; hence the synagogue in Thessalonica was the only one in a large district of country, for which reason it is styled *"the* synagogue of the Jews." The existence of a synagogue in a Gentile city was always an indication of a considerable Jewish population. Thessalonica, on account of its commercial importance, was then, and continues to be, under its modern name Salonica, a great resort for Jews.|| It was a knowledge of this fact, no doubt, which hastened Paul to this city, anticipating, through the synagogue, a more favorable introduction to the people than he had enjoyed at Philippi.

2, 3. (2) *"And according to Paul's custom, he went in to them, and for three Sabbath-days disputed with them from the Scriptures,* (3) *opening*

---
* Rom. xii: 19.   † Acts xvii: 14.
‡ Life and Ep., vol. 1, pp. 317, 318. || Life and Ep., vol. 1, p. 325.

them, and setting forth that it was necessary that the Christ should suffer, and arise from the dead, and that this Jesus whom I preach to you is the Christ." This was certainly a well-chosen course of argument. One of the chief objections which the Jews urged against Jesus during his life was his humble and unpretending position in society, which was inconsistent, in their estimation, with his claims to the Messiahship. And since his resurrection, the preaching of the Christ as crucified was, to the mass of the Jews, a scandal, because it appeared an impeachment of the prophets to proclaim the despised and crucified Jesus as the glorious Messiah whose coming they had predicted. But Paul begins his argument with the Thessalonian Jews, by showing that the writings of the prophets themselves made it necessary that the Messiah "should suffer and arise from the dead." Having demonstrated this proposition, it was an easy task to show that "this Jesus whom I preach to you is the Christ." It was well known that he had suffered death, and Paul had abundant means of proving that he had risen again. This proof was not confined to his own testimony, as an eye-witness of his glory, though we may well suppose that he made use of this, as he did on subsequent occasions.* But he gave ocular demonstration of the living and divine power of Jesus, by working miracles in his name. This we learn from his first epistle to the Church in this city, in which he says: "Our gospel came to you not in word only, but also in power, and in the Holy Spirit, and in much assurance; as you know what manner of men we were among you for your sake."† The power of the Holy Spirit, working miracles before them, gave an assurance of the resurrection and glory of him in whose name they were wrought, which the "word only" of all the men on earth could not give. Without such attestation, the word of man in reference to the affairs of heaven has no claim upon our confidence; but with it, it has a power which can not be resisted without resisting God.

This course of argument and proof occupied three successive Sabbaths. During the intervening weeks the two brethren carefully avoided every thing which might raise a suspicion that they were governed by selfish motives. They asked no man in the city for even their daily bread.‡ They received some contributions to their necessities from the brethren in Philippi,‖ but the amount was so scanty as to still leave them under the necessity of "laboring night and day."§

4. The effect of arguments and demonstrations so conclusive, accompanied by a private life so irreproachable, was quite decisive. (4) "*Some of them believed, and adhered to Paul and Silas; of the devout Greeks a great multitude, and of the chief women not a few.*" In this description the parties are distributed with great exactness. The expression "some of them" refers to the Jews, and indicates but a small number. Of the "devout Greeks," who were such Gentiles as had learned to worship God according to Jewish example, there was a "great multitude," and not a few of the "chief women," who were also Gentiles. The great majority of the converts, therefore, were Gentiles; and Paul afterward addresses them as such, saying, "You turned to God from idols, to serve the living and true God."¶

---

* Chapters xxii and xxvi. † 1 Thes. i: 5. ‡ 1 Thes. ii: 9.
‖ Phil. iv: 16. § 1 Thes. ii: 9. ¶ 1 Thes. i: 9.

5-9. Such a movement among the devout Gentiles, whose presence at the synagogue worship was a source of pride to the Jews, was exceedingly mortifying to those Jews who obstinately remained in unbelief. Their number and popular influence in Thessalonica enabled them to give serious trouble to Paul and Silas. (5) "*But the unbelieving Jews, being full of zeal, collected certain wicked men of the idle class, and raising a mob, set the city in an uproar. And rushing to the house of Jason, they sought to bring them out to the people.* (6) *But not finding them, they dragged Jason and certain brethren before the city rulers, crying out, These men, who have turned the world upside down, have come hither also;* (7) *whom Jason has received; and they are all acting contrary to the decrees of Cæsar, saying that there is another king, Jesus.* (8) *And they troubled the people and the city rulers, when they heard these things;* (9) *and having taken security of Jason and the others, they released them.*"

In the accusation preferred by the Jews there were two specifications, each one of which had some truth in it. Nearly everywhere that Paul and Silas had preached, there had been some public disturbance, which was in some way attributable to their preaching. But their accusers were at fault in throwing the censure on the wrong party. The fact that angry excitement follows the preaching of a certain man, or set of men, is no proof, either in that day or this, that the preaching is improper, either in matter or manner. When men are willing to receive the truth, and to reject all error, the preaching of the gospel can have none but peaceful and happy effects. But otherwise, it still brings "not peace, but a sword,"* and is the "savor of death unto death."† The apostolic method was to fearlessly preach the truth, and leave the consequences with God and the people.

The other specification, that the brethren acted contrary to the decrees of Cæsar, saying that there was another king, Jesus, shows that Paul, while opposing the Jewish idea that the Messiah was to be an earthly prince, had not failed to represent him as a king. He represented him, indeed, as the "King of kings, and Lord of lords." But the accusation contained a willful perversion of his language; for these Jews knew very well, as their predecessors before the bar of Pilate knew, that Jesus claimed to be no rival of Cæsar. If he had, they would have been better pleased with him than they were.

One reason why the Gentiles and city rulers were so readily excited by this accusation was the fact that the Jews had then but recently been banished from Rome, as we learn from a statement below in reference to Priscilla and Aquila.‡ The unbelieving Jews in Thessalonica, anxious to prove their own loyalty, adroitly directed public odium toward the *Christian* Jews, as the real disturbers of the public peace, and enemies of Cæsar.

10. Such was the state of feeling in the city that Paul and Silas saw no prospect of accomplishing good by further efforts, while the attempt would have been hazardous to the lives of brethren. (10) "*Then the brethren immediately sent away Paul and Silas by night, to Berea; who, when they arrived, went into the synagogue of the Jews.*"

* Matt. x: 34. † 2 Cor. ii: 16. ‡ Acts xviii: 2.

This city lies about sixty miles south-west of Thessalonica. It contains, at the present day, a population of fifteen or twenty thousand, and was, doubtless, still more populous then.* Here again the apostles find a synagogue, and make it the starting point of their labors.

11. We have now, at last, the pleasure of seeing one Jewish community listen to the truth and examine it like rational beings. (11) "*Now these were more noble-minded than those in Thessalonica, who received the word with all readiness of mind, searching the Scriptures daily to see if these things were so.*" Their conduct can not be too highly commended, nor too closely imitated. The great sin of the Jews was a refusal to examine, candidly and patiently, the claims of the gospel. Having fallen into error by their traditions, they resisted, with passion and uproar, every effort that was made to give them additional light, or to expose their errors. Their folly has been constantly re-enacted by religious partisans of subsequent ages, so that the progress of truth, since the dark ages of papal superstition, has been hedged up, at every onward movement, by men who conceived that they were doing God service in keeping his truth from the people. If such men live and die in the neglect of any duty, their ignorance of it will be so far from excusing them that it will constitute one of their chief sins, and secure to them more certain and more severe condemnation. There is no greater insult to the majesty of heaven than to stop our ears when God speaks, or to close our eyes against the light which he causes to shine around us. The cause of Christ, as it stands professed in the world, will never cease to be disgraced by such exhibitions of sin and folly, until all who pretend to be disciples adopt the course pursued by these Jews of Berea; search the Scriptures, upon the presentation of every thing claiming to be God's truth, and "see whether these things are so." Unless the word of God can mislead us, to follow *implicitly* where it leads can never be unacceptable to its Author.

12. If the claims of Jesus are false, an honest and thorough investigation of them is the best way to prove them so. If they are true, such an investigation will be certain to convince us and to bless us. With the Bereans, the logical result of a daily investigation is stated thus: (12) "*Therefore, many of them, and not a few of the honorable men and women who were Greeks, believed.*" It was not here, as in Thessalonica, that "*some* of them" and "a great *multitude* of Greeks" believed; but it was "*many* of them," and "not a *few* of the Greeks." That they believed, is distinctly attributed to the fact that they "searched the Scriptures;" showing again, that faith is produced by the word of God.

13, 14. There seemed to be no serious obstacle to the gospel in Berea, and the disciples may have begun to flatter themselves with the hope that the whole city would turn to the Lord, when an unexpected enemy sprung upon them from the rear. (13) "*But when the Jews of Thessalonica knew that the word of God was preached by Paul in Berea, they came thither also, and stirred up the people.* (14) *Then the brethren immediately sent Paul away, to go as if to the sea; but Silas and Timothy remained there.*" There was always sufficient material

* Life and Ep., vol. 1, pp. 339-341.

for a mob, in the rude heathen population of a city as large as Berea, and there was always sufficient appearance of antagonism between the gospel as preached by Paul, and the laws and customs of the heathen, to enable designing men to excite the masses against it. Hence the easy success of these embittered enemies from Thessalonica, who, in addition to other considerations, could ask if Bereans would tolerate men who had been compelled to fly by night from Thessalonica.

The statement that the brethren sent Paul away to "go *as if* to the sea," certainly implies some disguise of his real purpose. The only supposition answerable to the phraseology employed is, that he started in the direction of the sea, and then turned, so as to pursue the land route to Athens,* which was the next field of labor. Mr. Howson, who insists that he went by sea, does not display his usual ability in arguing the question.† Paul once traveled from Corinth to Berea by land,‡ and why not now from Berea through Athens to Corinth? The fact that it was the more tedious and less usual route, being two hundred and fifty miles overland, is a good reason why he should have chosen it the more certainly to elude pursuit.

Whether by land or by sea, the apostle now leaves Macedonia, and starts out for another province of ancient Greece. He has planted Churches in three important cities of Macedonia. Of these, Thessalonica occupied the central position, with Philippi one hundred miles to the north-east, and Berea sixty miles to the south-west. Each of these becomes a radiating center, from which the light of truth might shine into the surrounding darkness. We have the testimony of Paul himself, that from at least one of them the light shone with great intensity. He writes to the Thessalonians: "From you has sounded out the word of the Lord, not only in Macedonia and Achaia, but also in every place your faith toward God is spread abroad, so that we have no need to say any thing."‖ There was no need of Paul's voice at any more than central points, when he could leave behind him congregations such as this. No doubt much of their zeal and fidelity were owing to the fostering care of such men as Silas and Timothy, and Luke, whom the apostle occasionally left behind him.

15–17. (15) *"Now they who conducted Paul led him to Athens; and having received a commandment to Silas and Timothy that they should come to him as quickly as possible, they departed.* (16) *And while he was waiting for them in Athens, his spirit was roused within him, when he saw the city given to idolatry.* (17) *Therefore, he disputed in the synagogue with the Jews and the devout persons, and in the market-place daily with those who happened to be there."*

In the ancient world there were two distinct species of civilization, both of which had reached their highest excellence in the days of the apostles. One was the result of human philosophy; the other, of a divine revelation. The chief center of the former was the city of Athens; of the latter, the city of Jerusalem. If we compare them, either as respects the moral character of the people brought respectively under their influence, or with reference to their preparation for

---

* See Olshausen and others on the passage. † Life and Ep., vol. 1, p. 342. *Note.*
‡ Acts xx: 3, 4. ‖ 1 Thes. i: 8.

a perfect religion, we shall find the advantage in favor of the latter. Fifteen hundred years before, God had placed the Jews under the influence of revelation, and left the other nations of the earth to "walk in their own ways." By a severe discipline, continued through many centuries, the former had been elevated above the idolatry in which they were sunk at the beginning, and which still prevailed over all other nations. They presented, therefore, a degree of purity in private morals which stands unrivaled in ancient history previous to the advent of Christ. On the other hand, the most elegant of the heathen nations were exhibiting, in their social life, a complete exhaustion of the catalogue of base and beastly things of which men and women could be guilty.* In Athens, where flourished the most profound philosophy, the most glowing eloquence, the most fervid poetry, and the most refined art which the world has ever seen, there was the most complete and studied abandonment to every vice which passion could prompt or imagination invent.

The contrast in reference to the preparation of the two peoples to receive the gospel of Christ is equally striking. In the center of Jewish civilization the gospel had now been preached, and many thousands had embraced it. It had spread rapidly through the surrounding country; and even in distant lands, wherever there was a Jewish synagogue, with a company of Gentiles, who, by Jewish influence, had been rescued from the degradation of their kindred, it had been gladly received by thousands of devout men and honorable women. But nowhere had its triumphs penetrated far into the benighted masses outside of Jewish influence. The struggle now about to take place in the city of Athens is to demonstrate still further, by contrast, how valuable "a schoolmaster to bring us to Christ" had been the law and the prophets.

Walking along the streets of a city whose fame had been familiar to him from childhood, and seeing, in the temples and statues on every hand, and the constant processions of people going to and from the places of worship, evidence that "the city was given to idolatry;" though a lonely stranger, who might have been awed into silence by the magnificence around him, Paul felt his soul aroused to make one mighty struggle for the triumph, even here, of the humble gospel which he preached. His first effort, as usual, was in the Jewish synagogue. But there seem to have been none among the Jews or devout Gentiles there to receive the truth. The pride of human philosophy, and the debasement of refined idolatry had overpowered the influence of the law and the prophets, so that he fails of his usual success. He does not, however, despair. Having access to no other formal assembly, he goes upon the streets, and places of public concourse, and discourses to "those who happened to be there."

18. By efforts so persistent he succeeded in attracting some attention from the idle throng, but it was of a character, at first, not very flattering. (18) *"Then certain of the Epicurean and Stoic philosophers encountered him, and some said, What will this babbler say? And others, He seems to be a proclaimer of foreign demons; because he preached to them Jesus and the resurrection."* The persistency with which he sought the

* See Romans 1: 22–32.

attention of every one he met suggested the epithet "*babbler*," and the prominence in his arguments of the name of Jesus and the resurrection suggested to the inattentive hearers that these were two foreign demons whom he was trying to make known to them.

The two classes of philosophers whom he encountered were the antipodes of each other, and the practical philosophy of each was antipodal to the doctrine of Paul. The Stoics taught that the true philosophy of life was a total indifference to both the sorrows and pleasures of the world; while the Epicureans sought relief from life's sorrows in the studied pursuit of its pleasures.* In opposition to the former, Paul taught that we should weep with those who weep, and rejoice with those who rejoice; and in opposition to the latter, that we should *deny* ourselves in reference to all ungodliness and worldly lusts.

19–21. Notwithstanding the contempt with which Paul was regarded by some of his hearers, he succeeded in arresting the serious attention of a few. (19) "*And they took him and led him to the Areopagus, saying, Can we know what this new doctrine is, of which you speak?* (20) *For you are bringing some strange things to our ears. We wish to know, therefore, what these things mean.* (21) *For all the Athenians, and the strangers dwelling there, spent their time in nothing else than telling or hearing something new.*" The Areopagus was a rocky eminence, ascended by a flight of stone steps cut in the solid rock, on the summit of which were seats in the open air, where the judges, called Areopagites, held court for the trial of criminals, and of grave religious questions. The informal character of the proceedings on this occasion shows that it was not this court which had summoned Paul, but that those who were interested in hearing him selected this as a suitable place for the purpose. This is further evident from the note of explanation here appended by Luke, that the Athenians, and strangers dwelling there, spent their time in nothing else than telling and hearing something new. It was more from curiosity, therefore, that they desired to hear him, than because they really expected to be benefited by what they would hear.

22–31. After persevering, but necessarily disconnected conversational efforts on the streets, Paul has now an audience assembled for the special purpose of hearing him, and may present his theme in a more formal manner. He has now not an audience of Jews and proselytes, but an assembly of demon-worshipers. He can not, therefore, open the Scriptures, and begin by speaking of the long-expected Messiah. The Scriptures, and even the God who gave them, are to them unknown. Before he can preach Jesus to them, as the Son of God, he must introduce to them a true conception of God himself. It was this consideration which made the following speech of Paul so different from all others recorded in Acts. We will first hear the whole discourse, and then examine the different parts in their connection with one another.

(22) "*Then Paul stood up in the midst of the Areopagus, and said: Men of Athens, I perceive that in every respect you are devout worshipers of the demons.* (23) *For as I passed along, and observed the objects of your worship, I found an altar with this inscription,* TO THE UNKNOWN

---

* For a more complete account of these two sects, see Life and Ep., vol. 1, pp. 366–370.

GOD. *Whom, therefore, you worship without knowing him, him I announce to you.* (24) *The God who made the world, and all things which are in it, being Lord of heaven and earth, dwells not in temples made with hands.* (25) *Neither is he served by the hands of men, as though he needed any thing, for it is he who gives to all men life and breath and all things,* (26) *and has made from one blood all nations of men, to dwell upon the whole face of the earth, having determined their prearranged periods, and the boundaries of their habitations,* (27) *that they should seek the Lord, if haply they might feel after him and find him, although he is not far from each one of us.* (28) *For in him we live, and move, and have our being; as also some of your own poets have said,* '*For we are also his offspring.*' (29) *Being, then, the offspring of God, we ought not to think that the Deity is similar to gold or silver, or stone graven by the art and device of man.* (30) *Now the times of this ignorance God has overlooked; but now he commands all men everywhere to repent,* (31) *because he has appointed a day in which he will judge the world in righteousness by a man whom he has appointed, of which he has given assurance to all by raising him from the dead.*"

The excellence of an argumentative discourse is measured by the degree of adaptation to the exact mental condition of the audience, and the conclusiveness with which every position is established. It would be difficult to conceive how this discourse could be improved in either of these particulars.

The audience were worshipers of demons, or dead men deified. Nearly all their gods were supposed to have once lived on the earth. They regarded it, therefore, as an excellent trait of character to be scrupulous in all the observances of demon worship. Paul's first remark was not that they were "too superstitious,"* nor that they were "very religious;"† though both of these would have been true. But the term he employs, δεισεδαιμονεστίρους, from δειδω *to fear*, and δαιμων a *demon*, means *demon-fearing*, or *given to the worship of demons*. This was the exact truth in the case, and the audience received the statement of it as a compliment. The second remark is introduced as a specification under the first: "For, as I passed along and observed the objects of your worship, I found an altar with this inscription, TO THE UNKNOWN GOD." After erecting altars to all the *known* gods, so that a Roman satirist‡ said it was easier to find a *god* in Athens than a *man*, they had extended their worship even to such as might be in existence without their knowledge. No specification could have been made to more strikingly exemplify their devotion to demon worship. The commentators have suggested many hypotheses by which to account, historically, for the erection of this altar, all of which are purely conjectural. It is sufficient to know, what the text itself reveals, that its erection resulted from an extreme desire to render due worship to all the gods, both known and unknown.

Having spoken in this conciliatory style, both of their worship in general, and of this altar in particular, Paul next excites their curiosity, by telling them that he came to make *known* to them that very God whom they had already worshiped without knowing him. They had, by this inscription, already confessed that there was, or might

---

* Common version.   † Bloomfield and others.   ‡ Petronius. Life and Ep., 1, p. 363.

be a God to them unknown; hence they could not complain that he should attempt to introduce a new God to their acquaintance. They had also rendered homage to such a God while they knew him not; hence they could not consistently refuse to do so after he should be revealed to them. Thus far the course of the apostle's remarks was not only conciliatory, but calculated, and intended, to bind the audience in advance to the propositions and conclusions yet to be developed.

He next introduces the God to whom he refers as *the* God who made the world, and all things in it, and who is Lord of both heaven and earth. That there was such a God, he assumes; but the assumption was granted by a part of his audience, the Stoics, and the Epicureans found it difficult to account to themselves for the fact that the world *was* made, without admitting that there was a God who made it. He endeavors to give them a just conception of this God, by presenting several points of contrast between him and the gods with whom they were familiar. The first of these is, that, unlike them, "He does not dwell in temples made with hands." All around the spot where he stood were temples in which the gods made their abode, and to which the people were compelled to resort in order to communicate with them. But that the God who made heaven and earth does not dwell in temples made by human hands, he argued from the fact that he was "*Lord* of heaven and earth;" which implies that he could not be confined within limits so narrow. This was enough to establish his superiority to all other gods in power and majesty.

The next point of contrast presented has reference to the services rendered the gods. His hearers had been in the habit of presenting meat offerings and drink offerings in the temples, under the superstitious belief that they were devoured by the gods. But Paul tells them that the unknown God "is not served by the hands of men as though he needed any thing; for it is he who gives to all men life and breath and all things, and has made from one blood all nations of men," and appointed beforehand their periods, and the boundaries of their habitations. These facts demonstrate his entire independence of human ministrations, and exhibit, in a most striking manner, the dependence of men upon him. They not only sustain the point of contrast presented by Paul, but they involve an assumption of the most special providence of God. By special providence, we mean providence in reference to individual persons and things. If God gives to *all* men life and breath and *all* things, he acts with reference to each individual man, to each individual breath that each man breathes, and to each particular thing going to make up *all* the things which he gives them. Again, if God appoints beforehand the "*periods*" of the nation, (by which I understand all the great eras in their history,) and the "boundaries of their habitations," he certainly directs the movements of individual men; for the movements of nations depend upon the movements of the individual men of whom they are composed. Sometimes, indeed, the movements of one man, as of Christopher Columbus, determine the settlement of continents, and the destiny of mighty nations. In view of these facts, we must admit the most special and minute providence of God in all the affairs of earth. It would never, perhaps, have been doubted, but for the philosophical difficulty of reconciling it with the free agency of men, and of discriminating between it and the working of miracles. This difficulty, however, affords no rational ground for such a doubt, for the *method* of God's agency in human affairs is above human comprehension. To doubt the reality of an assumed fact, the nature of which is confessedly above our comprehension, because we know not how to reconcile it with other known facts, is equivalent to confessing our ignorance at one moment, and denying it the next. It were wiser to conclude, that, if we could only comprehend that which is now incomprehensible, the difficulty would vanish. While the uneducated swain is ignorant of the law of gravitation, he can not understand how the world can turn over without spilling the water out of his well; but the moment he apprehends this law the difficulty disappears.

The incidental statement that God made from *one blood* all the nations of men, is an inspired assertion of the unity of the race, and accords with the Mosaic history. To deny it because we find some difficulty in reconciling it with the present diversity in the types of men, is another instance of the fallacy just exposed. It is to deny an assertion of the Scriptures, not because of something we know, but of something we do not know. We do not know, with certainty, what caused so great diversity among the races of men, and, because of this ignorance, we deny their common paternity. Such a denial could not be justified, unless we knew all the facts which have transpired in human history. But much the larger portion of human history is unwritten and unknown; and, at the same time, we are dependent, for all we do know of the first half of it, upon the word of God. The only rational course, therefore, which is left to us, is to receive its statements in their obvious import as the truth of history.

In arguing this last proposition, Paul interweaves with his proof a statement of God's purpose concerning the nations, "that they should seek the Lord, if haply they might feel after him, and find him." He here has reference to those nations who were without revelation; and means, I think, that one purpose of leaving them in that condition was to make a trial of their ability, without the aid of revelation, to seek and feel after the Lord so as to find him. It resulted in demonstrating what Paul afterward asserted, that "the world by wisdom knew not God," and that, therefore, "it pleased God, by the foolishness of preaching, to save those who believe."*

From this reference to the efforts of men to find God, a natural association of thought led the speaker to assert the omnipresence of God: "Although he is not far from each one of us; for in him we live, and move, and have our being; as also some of your own poets have said, For we are also his offspring." The connection of thought in this passage is this: We are his offspring, as your own poets teach, and this is sufficient proof that he is still about us; for he certainly would not abandon the offspring whom he has begotten.

From the conclusion that we are the offspring of God, Paul advances to the third point of contrast between him and the gods around him: "Being, then, the *offspring* of God, *we* ought not to think that the Deity

* 1 Cor 1: 21.

is similar to gold, or silver, or stone, graven by the art and device of man." This was a strong appeal to the self-respect of his hearers. To acknowledge that they were the offspring of God, and at the same time admit that he was similar to a carved piece of metal, or marble, was to degrade themselves by degrading their origin.

The argument by which he revealed to them the God who had been unknown is now completed. He has exhibited the uselessness of all the splendid temples around him, by showing that the true God dwells not in them, and that he is the God who made the earth and the heavens and all conceivable things. He has proved the folly of all their acts of worship, by showing that the real God has no need of any thing, but that all men are dependent on him for life and breath and all things. He has exhibited the foreknowledge; the providence, general and special; the omnipresence, and the universal parentage of this God; and has made them feel disgusted at the idea of worshiping, as their creator, any thing similar to metal or marble shaped by human hands. Thus their temples, their services, and their images are all degraded to their proper level, while the grandeur and glory and paternity of the true God are exalted before them.

The speaker next advances to unfold to his hearers their fearful responsibility to the God now revealed to them. The times of ignorance, in which they had built these temples and carved these images, he tells them that God had *overlooked*; that is, to use his own language on another occasion, he had "suffered the nations to walk in their own ways."* "But now, he commands all men everywhere to repent; because he has appointed a day in which he will judge the world in righteousness, by a man whom he has appointed, of which he has given assurance to all by raising him from the dead." This was evidently not designed for the concluding paragraph of the speech, but was a brief statement of the appointment of Jesus as judge of the living and the dead, preparatory to introducing him fully to the audience. But here his discourse was interrupted, and brought abruptly to a close.

32, 33. (32) "*And when they heard of a resurrection of the dead, some mocked; but others said, We will hear you again concerning this matter.* (33) *So Paul departed from among them.*" There are two strange features in the conduct of this audience. *First*, That they listened so patiently while Paul was demonstrating the folly of all their idolatrous worship, which we would expect them to defend with zeal. *Second*, That they should interrupt him with mockery when he spoke of a resurrection from the dead, which we would have expected them to welcome as a most happy relief from the gloom which shrouded their thoughts of death. But the former is accounted for by the prevailing infidelity among philosophic minds in reference to the popular worship, rendering formal and heartless with them a service which was still performed by the masses with devoutness and sincerity. Their repugnance to the thought of a resurrection originated not in a preference for the gloomy future into which they were compelled to look, but in a fondness for that philosophy by which they had concluded that death was an eternal sleep. Their pride of opinion had crushed

* Acts xiv: 16.

the better instincts of their nature, and led them to mock at the hope of a future life, which has been the dearest of all hopes to the chief part of mankind. Thus the devotees of human philosophy, instead of being led by it to a knowledge of the truth, were deceived into the forfeiture of a blessed hope, which has been enjoyed by ruder nations, amid all their ignorance and superstition.

34. Although his discourse terminated amid the mockery of a portion of his audience, the apostle's effort was not altogether fruitless. (34) *"But certain men followed him and believed; among whom were Dionysius the Areopagite, and a woman named Damaris, and others with them."* We find, however, no subsequent trace of a Church in Athens within the period of apostolic history, and these names are not elsewhere mentioned. We are constrained, therefore, to the conclusion, that the cold philosophy and polished heathenism of this city had too far corrupted its inhabitants to admit of their turning to Christ, until some providential changes should prepare the way.

XVIII: 1. Having met with so little encouragement in the literary capital of Greece, the apostle next resorts to its chief commercial emporium. (1) *"After these things Paul departed from Athens, and went to Corinth."* This city was situated on the isthmus which connects the Peloponnesus with Attica. Through the Saronic Gulf and Ægean Sea on the east, it had direct communication with all the great Asiatic cities, and with Rome and the west through the Gulf of Corinth and the Adriatic. It was, therefore, a place of great commercial advantages; and, at the time of Paul's visit, was the chief city of all Greece. Its advantages for trade had attracted the large Jewish population which the apostle found there.

2, 3. Paul entered this large city a stranger, alone, and penniless. What little means he had brought with him from Macedonia was exhausted, and his first attention was directed to the supply of his daily wants. He knew what it was to suffer "hunger and thirst;"* but he had been taught to look to heaven and pray, "Give us this day our daily bread." A kind Providence found him lodging and means of livelihood. (2) *"And having found a certain Jew named Aquila, born in Pontus, and Priscilla his wife, lately come from Italy because Claudius had commanded all the Jews to depart from Rome, he went to them,* (3) *and because he was of the same trade, he remained with them, and worked; for they were tent-makers by trade."* To be thus under the necessity of laboring as a journeyman tent-maker was certainly a most discouraging condition for one about to evangelize a proud and opulent city. From the calm and unimpassioned style in which Luke proceeds with the narrative, we might imagine that Paul's feelings were callous to the influence of such circumstances. But his own pen, which often reveals emotions that were not known to Luke, gives a far different representation of his feelings. Writing to the Corinthians after long years had passed away, and all transient emotions had been forgotten, he says, "I was with you in weakness, and in fear, and in much trembling.† Though keenly sensitive to all the distressing influences which surrounded him, he had, withal, so strong confidence in the power of truth, and so gloried in the very humility of the gospel, that he never

---

* 2 Cor. xi: 27.   † 1 Cor. ii: 3.

despaired. The companionship of two such spirits as Aquila and Priscilla afterward proved to be,. was, doubtless, a source of great encouragement to him.

4, 5. Notwithstanding all the discouragements of his situation, he devoted the Sabbaths, and whatever portion of the week his manual labor would permit, to the great work. (4) "*But he discoursed every Sabbath in the synagogue, and persuaded both Jews and Greeks.* (5) *And when Silas and Timothy came down from Macedonia, Paul was pressed in spirit, and testified to the Jews that Jesus is the Christ.*" It will be recollected by the reader, that Silas and Timothy, whose arrival is here mentioned, had tarried in Berea, and that Paul had sent back word to them, by the brethren who conducted him to Athens, to rejoin him as soon as possible.* He had also "waited for them in Athens,"† before his speech in the Areopagus. We would suppose, from Luke's narrative, that they failed to overtake him there, and now first rejoined him in Corinth. But Paul supplies an incident in the First Epistle to the Thessalonians, which corrects this supposition. He says: "When we could no longer forbear, we thought it good to be left *alone* in *Athens*, and *sent Timothy* to establish you and to comfort you concerning your faith."‡ This shows that Timothy, at least, had actually rejoined him in Athens, and had been sent back to learn the condition of the congregation in Thessalonica. His present arrival in Corinth, therefore, was not from his original stay in Berea; but from a recent visit to Thessalonica. Probably Silas had remained till now in Berea.

The arrival of Silas and Timothy brings us to a new period in the life of Paul, the period of his letter-writing. We have already made some use of his epistles to throw light upon the somewhat elliptical narrative before us; but we shall henceforth have them as cotemporary documents, and will be able to fill up from them many blanks in Paul's personal history. The First Epistle to the Thessalonians was written from Corinth soon after the arrival of Timothy, as is proved by the concurrence of the two facts, that, on the return of Silas and Timothy, as seen in the text just quoted, they found Paul in Corinth, and that, in the epistle itself, Paul speaks of their arrival as having just taken place at the time of writing.‖ Several statements in this epistle throw additional light upon the state of Paul's feelings during his first labors in Corinth. He was not only "pressed in spirit," as stated by Luke, "in weakness, in fear, and in much trembling," as he himself says to the Corinthians;§ but he was racked with uncontrollable anxiety concerning the brethren in Thessalonica, for whom he would have been willing to sacrifice his own life, and who were now suffering the severest persecution.¶ The good report brought from them by Silas and Timothy gave him much joy, but it was joy in the midst of distress. He says: "When Timothy came to us from you, and brought us good tidings of your faith and love, and that you have remembrance of us always, desiring greatly to see us, as we also to see you, therefore, brethren, we were comforted over you in all our *affliction and distress* by your faith: for now we live, if you stand fast in the Lord."** It was, therefore, with a zeal newly kindled from almost

---

* Acts xvii: 14, 15. † Acts xvii: 16. ‡ 1 Thes. iii: 1, 2. ‖ 1 Thes. iii: 6.
‡ 1 Cor. ii: 3. ¶ 1 Thes. ii: 8, 14–16. ** 1 Thes. iii: 6–8.

utter despair, by the good report from Thessalonica and the arrival of his fellow-laborers, that he now so "earnestly testified to the Jews that Jesus is the Christ."

6, 7. The increase of Paul's earnestness was responded to by an increased virulence in the opposition of the unbelieving Jews. (6) *"But when they resisted and blasphemed, he shook his raiment, and said to them, Your blood be upon your own head; I am clean. Henceforth I will go to the Gentiles.* (7) *And he departed thence, and went into the house of a man named Justus, a worshiper of God, whose house was adjacent to the synagogue."* When they began to resist his preaching with passion and violent imprecations, he could no longer hope to do them good, and to press the subject further upon them would be to cast pearls before swine. Upon leaving the synagogue, he was not driven into the streets for a meeting-place; but, as was usually the case, while he was urging, with so little success, the claims of Jesus upon the Jews, at least one Gentile, who had learned to worship the true God, heard him more favorably, and offered him the use of his private dwelling, which stood close by. Justus was not yet a disciple, but, as suits the meaning of his name, he was disposed to see *justice* done to the persecuted apostle.

8. Although he left the synagogue in apparent discomfiture, he was not without fruits of his labors there. (8) *"But Crispus, the chief ruler of the synagogue, believed on the Lord, with all his house; and many of the Corinthians, hearing, believed and were immersed."* It was very seldom that men of high position in the Jewish synagogues were induced to obey the gospel. It is greatly to the credit of Crispus, therefore, that he was among the first in Corinth to take this position, and this, too, at the moment when the opposition and blasphemy of the other Jews were most intense. He must have been a man of great independence of spirit and goodness of heart—the right kind of a man to form the nucleus for a congregation of disciples.

The conversion of these Corinthians is not detailed so fully as that of the eunuch, of Saul, or of Cornelius, yet enough is said to show that it was essentially the same process. "Many of the Corinthians, hearing, believed, and were immersed." They heard what Paul preached, "that Jesus is the Christ." This, then, is what they believed. That they repented of their sins is implied in the fact that they turned to the Lord by being immersed. To hear the gospel preached, to believe that Jesus is the Christ, and to be immersed, was the entire process of their conversion, briefly expressed.

9, 10. Although his success, when about leaving the synagogue, must have been a source of some comfort to Paul, an incident occurred just at this period, which shows that he was far from being relieved, as yet, from the "weakness, and fear, and much trembling" which had oppressed him. (9) *"Then the Lord said to Paul in a vision by night, Be not afraid; but speak, and be not silent;* (10) *for I am with you, and no man shall assail you to hurt you. For I have many people in this city."* The Lord never appeared by a vision to comfort his servants, except when they needed comfort. The words "Be not afraid' imply that he was alarmed, and the assurance that no one should hurt him implies that his alarm had reference to his personal safety. His very success had, doubtless, fired his opponents to fiercer opposition, and his recent sufferings at Philippi seemed about to be repeated. But, at the darkest hour of his night of sorrow, the light of hope suddenly dawned upon him, and he was strengthened with the assurance that many in the city would yet obey the Lord.

In the declaration, "I have many people in this city," the Lord called persons who were then unbelievers, and perhaps idolaters, his people. This would *accord* with the Calvinistic idea that God's people are a certain definite number whom he has selected, many of whom are yet unconverted. But it can not prove this doctrine, because it admits of rational explanation upon another hypothesis. He knew that these people would yet believe and obey the gospel, and he could, therefore, with all propriety of speech, call them his by anticipation. Such is no doubt the true idea.

An expression similar to this occurs in the eighteenth chapter of Revelations, where the angel, announcing the downfall of the mystic Babylon, cries: "Come out of her, *my people*, that you be not partakers of her sins, and that you receive not of her plagues." It has been argued, from this, that God has a people in the apostasy, who are already accepted as his own. But the language, like the statement, "I have many people in this city," may be used simply in anticipation. The most that can be argued from it, is that he knew a people would *come out* of Babylon whom he could accept, and that he called them his people on account of that fact.

11. Under the assurance given by the Lord in the vision, Paul was encouraged to continue his labors. (11) "*Then he continued there a year and six months, teaching among them the word of God.*" Instead of the more usual expression, "*preaching* the word of God," we have here "*teaching* the word of God." This change of phraseology is not without a purpose. It indicates that Paul's labor, during this period, consisted not so much in proclaiming the great facts of the gospel, as in *teaching* his hearers the practical precepts of the Word. He was executing the latter part of the commission as recorded by Matthew: "Teaching them to observe and do all that I have commanded you."

12, 13. The next paragraph introduces an incident which occurred within this period of eighteen months, and which is worthy of special notice, because of several peculiarities not common to the scenes of apostolic suffering. (12) "*While Gallio was proconsul of Achaia, the Jews, with one accord, rose up against Paul and led him to the judgment-seat,* (13) *saying, This man is persuading men to worship God contrary to the law.*" Here we have the same charge, in form, which was preferred against Paul at Philippi and Thessalonica, causing all the trouble which befell him in those cities.* But the charge, in those instances, was preferred by Greeks, with reference to the Roman law; while, in the present, the Jews had the boldness to prefer it in their own name, with reference to their own law. This fact indicates a degree of confidence in their own influence which we have not seen exhibited by the Jews in any other Gentile city.

14–16. In this case, however, they had to deal with a man of far different character from the magistrates of Philippi, or the city rulers

* Acts xvi: 20–23; xvii: 5–10.

of Thessalonica. Gallio was a brother of Seneca, the famous Roman moralist, who describes him as a man of admirable integrity, amiable and popular.* Such was the character which he exhibited on this occasion. Instead of yielding to popular clamor, as did so many provincial and municipal officers, before whom the apostles were arraigned, he examined carefully the accusation, and seeing that it had reference, not to any infraction of the Roman law, but to questions in regard to their own law, he determined at once to dismiss the case. (14) *"But when Paul was about to open his mouth, Gallio said to the Jews, If it were a matter of injustice or wicked recklessness, Jews, it would be reasonable that I should bear with you.* (15) *But since it is a question concerning a doctrine and words, and your own law, do you see to it; for I do not intend to be a judge of these matters.* (16) *And he drove them from the judgment-seat.*" This is the only instance, in all the persecutions of Paul, in which his accusers were dealt with summarily and justly. The incident reflects great credit upon Gallio.

17. Prompt and energetic vindication of the right, on the part of a public functionary, will nearly always meet the approbation of the masses, and will sometimes even turn the tide of popular prejudice. Whether the disinterested public were favorable or unfavorable to Paul before the decision, we are not informed; but when the case was dismissed, the spectators were highly gratified at the result. (17) *" Then all the Greeks seized Sosthenes, the chief ruler of the synagogue, and beat him before the judgment-seat; and Gallio cared for none of these things."* For once, the heart of the unconverted multitude was with the apostle, and so indignant were they at the unprovoked attempt to injure him, that when it was fully exposed, they visited upon the head of the chief persecutor the very beating which he had laid up for Paul. Sosthenes was most probably the successor of Crispus, as chief ruler of the synagogue, and may have been selected for that position on account of his zeal in opposing the course which Crispus had pursued. The beating which the Greeks gave him was a riotous proceeding, which Gallio, in strict discharge of his duty, should have suppressed. That he did not do so, and that Luke says, "Gallio cared for none of these things," has been generally understood to indicate an easy and yielding disposition, which was averse to the strict enforcement of law. This, however, is inconsistent with the promptness of his vindication of Paul, and his indignant dismissal of the accusers. I would rather understand it as indicating a secret delight at seeing the tables so handsomely turned upon the persecutors, prompting him to let pass unnoticed a riot, which, under other circumstances, he would have rebuked severely. The rage and disappointment of the Jews must have been intense; but the rough handling which their leaders experienced admonished them to keep quiet for a time.

18. This incident occurred some time previous to the close of the eighteen months of Paul's stay in Corinth, as we learn from the next verse. (18) *"Now Paul, having still remained for many days, bade the brethren farewell, and sailed into Syria, and with him Priscilla and Aquila, having sheared his head in Cenchrea; for he had a vow."* It is after the

---

* Life and Ep., vol. 1, p. 418, and note.

ACTS XVIII: 18.

arraignment before Gallio, and previous to his departure from Corinth, that we best locate the date of the Second Epistle to the Thessalonians. That it was written in Corinth is determined chiefly by a comparison of its contents with those of the First Epistle. The congregation was still suffering from the same persecution mentioned in the First Epistle,* and there was still among them some improper excitement in reference to the second coming of the Lord.† Both these circumstances indicate that it was written shortly after the first; as soon, perhaps, as Paul could hear from them after their reception of the first. That it was after the arraignment before Gallio, is sufficiently evident, I think, from the absence of those indications of distress in the mind of the writer which abound in the First Epistle. He did not enjoy this comparative peace of mind until after the persecutions of the Jews culminated and terminated in the scene before Gallio's judgment-seat. Many eminent commentators have contended that it was Aquila, and not Paul, who sheared his head at Cenchrea. The main argument by which they defend this position is based upon the fact that the name of Aquila is placed after that of his wife Priscilla, and next to the participle κειράμενος, *having sheared*, for the very purpose of indicating that the act was performed by him.‡ Others, who insist that it was Paul, reply that the order of the names is not conclusive, inasmuch as they occur in this order in three out of the five times that they are mentioned together in the New Testament.‖ My own opinion is that it was Paul, and my chief reason for so thinking is this: the term Paul is the leading subject of the sentence, to which all the verbs and participles must be referred, unless there is some grammatical necessity for detaching one or more of them, and referring them to another subject. Priscilla and Aquila are subjects of the verb sailed understood: "Paul sailed into Syria, and with him (*sailed*) Priscilla and Aquila." But if it was intended also to refer the act of shearing to Aquila, the English would require the relative and verb instead of the participle: "with him Priscilla and Aquila *who had sheared* his head," instead of "Priscilla and Aquila, *having* sheared his head." The Greek, in order to express this idea, would also have required the *article* or *relative* after Aquila. In the absence of such a modification of the construction, we must refer the terms κειράμενος, *having shaved*, and εἶχε, *had*, to the leading subject of the sentence, with which agree all the other verbs, προσμείνας *tarried*, ἀποταξάμενος *took leave of* and ἐξέπει *sailed away*. The objection that Paul could not have taken such a vow consistently with his position in reference to the law of Moses, is fallacious in two respects. *First*, It assumes a degree of freedom from legal observances on the part of Paul which his conduct on subsequent occasions shows that he had not attained.§ *Second*, It assumes, without authority, that this vow was one peculiar to the law, which it would be improper for Christians to observe. The vow of the Nazarite would certainly be improper now, because it required the offering of sacrifices at its termination.¶ But this was

---
* Compare 2 Thes. iii: 9, with 1 Thes. ii: 14–16; iii: 1–4.
† Compare 2 Thes. ii: 1–3 with 1 Thes. iv: 13; v: 3.
‡ See Bloomfield and Howson.
‖ Acts xviii: 26; Rom. xvi: 3; 1 Cor. xvi: 19; 2 Tim. iv: 19; also, Hackett and Olshausen. § See Com. xxi: 24. ¶ See Com. xxi: 24.

not that vow, seeing the hair was sheared in Cenchrea; whereas the Nazarite's hair could be sheared only at the temple in Jerusalem.* What the exact nature of the vow was, we have now no means of determining. The only practical value of this incident arises from its bearing upon present practice. But this is altogether independent of the question whether it was Paul or Aquila who had the vow. If we admit it was Aquila, the presence of Paul, and the approbation indicated by his silence, gives to it the apostolic sanction. We conclude, therefore, that disciples would be guilty of no impropriety in making vows, and allowing the hair to grow until the vow is performed. But it must not be inferred, from this conclusion, that we are at liberty to make *foolish* or *wicked* vows, which would be better broken than kept.

19–22. Embarking at Cenchrea, which was the eastern port of Corinth, on a voyage for Syria, the frequent commercial intercourse between Corinth and Ephesus† very naturally caused the vessel to touch at the latter city, which was the destination of Priscilla and Aquila. (19) "*And he went to Ephesus, and left them there. He himself went into the synagogue and discoursed to the Jews.* (20) *They requested him to remain longer with them, but he did not consent,* (21) *but bade them farewell, saying, I must by all means keep the coming feast in Jerusalem; but I will return to you, God willing.* (22) *And he set sail for Ephesus; and having gone down to Cæsarea, he went up and saluted the Church, and went down to Antioch.*" The context plainly implies that the Church which he "went up and saluted" was that in Jerusalem, and not, as some have supposed, that in Cæsarea; for it had just been said that he must reach Jerusalem, and the statement that he "went up," especially as it occurs after reaching Cæsarea, implies that he went up where he had intended to go. The final termination of his journey, however, was not Jerusalem, but Antioch, whence he had started with Silas on his second missionary tour. The two missionaries had gone through Syria and Cilicia; had revisited Derbe, Lystra, and Iconium; and had taken a circuit through Phrygia, Galatia, and Mysia, to Troas on the Archipelago. Thence they had sailed into Europe, and had made known the gospel throughout Macedonia and Achaia, planting Churches in the principal cities. Setting sail on their return, Paul had left an appointment in Ephesus, where he had formerly been forbidden by the Spirit to preach the Word;‡ had revisited Jerusalem, and was now at the end of his circuit, once more to gladden the hearts of the brethren who had "commended him to the favor of God," by rehearsing all that God had done with him, and that he had opened still wider "the door of faith to the Gentiles." Whether Silas had returned with him we are not informed. What changes had taken place in Antioch during his absence is equally unknown. The historian has his eye upon stirring events just ahead in Ephesus, and hastens all the movements of the narrative to bring us back to that city.

23. In accordance with this plan, he gives but a brief glance at the apostle's stay in Antioch, and the first part of his third missionary tour. (23) "*Having spent some time there, he departed, passing through*

---

* See Com. xxi: 24.   † Life and Ep., vol. 1, p. 423.   ‡ Acts xvi: 6.

ACTS XVIII: 24–26.

the district of Galatia, and Phrygia, in order, confirming all the disciples." The historian now leaves Paul in the obscurity of this journey among the Churches, and anticipates his arrival in Ephesus, by noticing some events there, which were, in the providence of God, opening the way for his hitherto forbidden labors in that city.

24–26. (24) "*Now a certain Jew named Apollos, born in Alexandria, an eloquent man, and mighty in the Scriptures, came to Ephesus. (25) This man was instructed in the way of the Lord, and, being fervent in spirit, he spoke and taught accurately the things concerning the Lord, understanding only the immersion of John. (26) He began to speak boldly in the synagogue. But Aquila and Priscilla, having heard him, took him and expounded to him the way of the Lord more accurately.*" The distinguished position which Apollos acquired, after this, in the Church at Corinth, and the familiarity of his name among disciples of all subsequent ages, renders it a matter of some interest to acquire an accurate conception of his personal endowments and his subsequent history. The former are set forth in the two statements, that he was "eloquent," and that he was "mighty in the Scriptures." The gift of eloquence is a natural endowment, but culture is necessary to its effective development. That he was an Alexandrian by birth gives assurance that he was not wanting in the most thorough culture; for Alexandria, being the chief point of contact between Greek and Jewish literature, was the chief seat of Hebrew learning in that and some subsequent generations. The Alexandrian Jews, who constituted a large element in the population of that city, were noted for their wealth and their learning.

That he was "mighty in the Scriptures," shows that he had been educated to a thorough knowledge of the word of God. The apostles, being inspired, and able to speak with miracle-confirmed authority, were not entirely dependent upon purely scriptural proofs. But he, being uninspired, was entirely dependent upon the use of the prophesies and types of the Old Testament, in proof of the Messiahship. In a day when a knowledge of the word of God had to be acquired from manuscripts, and in which the art of reading was acquired by only a few, it was no ordinary endowment to be familiar with the Scriptures. Such an attainment is rare, even in this day of printed Bibles, and among preachers who *profess* to devote their lives chiefly to the study of the Bible. Indeed, the amount of clerical ignorance now extant would astonish the masses of men, if they only had the means of detecting it.

What were the exact attainments of this distinguished man in reference to the gospel is a question of some difficulty, though in reference to it there is a very general agreement among commentators. It is generally agreed that he understood no more of the gospel than was taught by John the Immerser; and of this the statement that he understood only the immersion of John is considered sufficient proof. But 1 confess myself unable to reconcile this supposition with two other statements of the historian, equally designed to give us his religious status. The first is the statement that he was "*instructed* in the *way* of the Lord;" and the second, that he "taught *accurately* the things concerning the Lord." That the term Lord refers to the Lord Jesus Christ can not be doubted by one who considers Luke's style, and observes the connection of thought in the passage. But for Luke to say, at this late period, that a man was instructed in the way of the Lord and taught it accurately, certainly implies a better knowledge of the gospel than was possessed by John; for he preached him as one yet to come, and knew nothing of his death, burial, or resurrection. The two expressions combined would, if unqualified, convey the idea that he understood and taught the gospel correctly, according to the apostolic standard. They are qualified, however, by the statement that he "understood only the *immersion* of John." This is the only limitation expressed, and therefore we should grant him all the knowledge which this limitation will allow. Whatever a man must lack, then, of a thorough knowledge of the gospel, who knows no *immersion* but that of John, we must grant that Apollos lacked; yet the other things of the Lord he taught accurately. His ignorance had reference to the points of distinction between John's immersion and that of the apostles, which were chiefly these, that John did not promise the Holy Spirit to those who were immersed, and did not immerse into the name of the Father, and of the Son, and of the Holy Spirit. Whatever confusion of thought upon kindred topics is necessarily involved in ignorance of these two things, Apollos must also have been subject to; but we are not authorized to extend his ignorance any further than this. On these points he was instructed by Priscilla and Aquila, and was then able to teach the things concerning the Lord *more* accurately. There is no evidence whatever that he was reimmersed.*

27, 28. For some reason unexplained, Apollos concluded to leave Ephesus, and visit the Churches planted by Paul in Achaia. (27) "*And when he desired to cross into Achaia, the brethren wrote, urging the disciples to receive him. When he arrived, he afforded much aid to those who through favor had believed:* (28) *for he powerfully and thoroughly convinced the Jews in public, clearly showing by the Scriptures that Jesus is the Christ.*" This is the earliest mention of letters of commendation among the disciples. It shows that they were employed simply to make known the bearer to strange brethren, and commend him to their fellowship.

The parties to whom Apollos afforded much aid were not, as some have contended, "those who believed through *his gift;*"† for the term χαρις is never used in the sense of either a spiritual or a natural gift. Neither, for the same reason, can we render the clause, "he aided *through his gift* those who believed."‡ *Favor* is the true meaning of the original term, and it stands connected in the sentence with the participle rendered *believed.* If there were any incongruity in the idea of believing through favor, we might, with Bloomfield, connect it with the verb, and render the clause "he afforded much aid, through favor, to those who believed." But though this is the only instance in which parties are said to have believed through the favor of God, it is true of all disciples; for the favor of God both supplies the object of faith, and brings before men the evidence which produces faith. Luke's own collocation of the words, therefore, should guide us, and it rules us to the rendering, "he afforded much aid to those who through favor had believed."

* See further, Com. xix: 1-7.   † Olshausen.   ‡ See Bloomfield.

Apollos mightily convinced the *Jews* in Achaia; whereas Paul's converts had been mostly among the Gentiles. This was, no doubt, owing to the peculiarity of his endowments, giving him access to some minds which were inaccessible to Paul. A variety of talents and acquirements among preachers is still necessary to the success of the gospel among the immense variety of the minds and characters which make up human society.

XIX: 1-7. Having sketched briefly the visit of Apollos to Ephesus, and thus prepared the way for an account of Paul's labors in the same city, the historian now reaches the point for which he had so hurriedly passed over the apostle's journey from Antioch through Galatia and Phrygia and around to Ephesus.* The appointment which he left in Ephesus, as he passed through on his way to Jerusalem,† is now to be fulfilled. (1) *"Now while Apollos was in Corinth, Paul, having passed through the upper districts, came to Ephesus, and finding certain disciples,* (2) *said to them, Have you received the Holy Spirit since you believed?* *But they said to him, We have not so much as heard that the Holy Spirit is given.* (3) *He said to them, Into what, then, were you immersed?* *They said, Into John's immersion.* (4) *Then Paul said, John indeed immersed with the immersion of repentance, saying to the people that they should believe on him who would come after him, that is, on the Christ Jesus.* (5) *And when they heard this they were immersed into the name of the Lord Jesus.* (6) *And when Paul laid hands on them, the Holy Spirit came upon them, and they spoke with tongues and prophesied.* (7) *All the men were about twelve."*

This passage is valuable chiefly because it shows how the apostles dealt with parties who, at that time, were immersed with John's immersion. This, no doubt, was Luke's object in introducing it. In order to understand the case, it is necessary to keep distinctly in view the facts stated of the parties previous to and subsequent to their immersion by Paul. They are called *disciples,* and were known as such when Paul found them; for it is said "he found certain disciples." They were disciples, not of John, but of Jesus; for the uniform currency of the term disciple, throughout Acts, requires us to so understand it. This is further evident from Paul's question, "Have you received the Holy Spirit since you *believed?*" The term believed evidently refers to Jesus as its object. They were known, then, as disciples of Jesus, and were so recognized by Paul.

Up to the moment of his conversation with them, Paul knew nothing of any irregularity in their obedience; for this was made known, to his surprise, during the conversation. When, therefore, he asked the question, "Have you received the Holy Spirit since you believed?" he could not have referred to that gift of the Spirit which all disciples receive; for he would take this for granted, from the fact that they were disciples. He must, then, have had reference to the miraculous gift, which some disciples did not receive.

It is inconceivable that these disciples were ignorant of the existence of the Holy Spirit, hence a literal rendering of their reply, "We have not so much as heard that there is a Holy Spirit," would convey a false idea. The supplement *given* is necessary to complete the sense,

* Acts xviii: 23. † Acts xviii: 21.

as it is in John vii: 39, where it is said, "The Holy Spirit was not yet, because Jesus was not yet risen." The term *given* must be supplied, in the latter case, in order to avoid the denial of the existence of the Spirit previous to the resurrection; and, in the former, to avoid the declaration of an ignorance on the part of these men inconsistent with the fact that they were disciples.

This answer at once revealed to Paul that there was some irregularity in their religious history; for no one could be properly discipled without learning that the Holy Spirit was to be given. He at once perceived, too, that the irregularity must have been connected with their immersion; for he inquires, "Into what, then, were you immersed?" If the gift of the Spirit had no connection with immersion, this inquiry would have been inapposite, and Paul would not have propounded it. But the apostles taught as Peter did on the day of Pentecost, when he said, "Repent and be immersed, every one of you, in the name of Jesus Christ, for the remission of sins, and you shall *receive the gift of the Holy Spirit.*" It is only on the supposition that Paul knew this to be the universal teaching of rightly-informed brethren, that he inferred something wrong about their immersion, from their ignorance of the gift of the Holy Spirit. This supposition, however, which is a necessary, not an optional one, makes the whole matter very plain. Paul's first question had reference to the miraculous gift of the Spirit; but when they said they knew not that the Holy Spirit was given, he saw that they were ignorant of even the ordinary gift, which is promised to all who repent and are immersed, and that they were immersed without proper instruction.

Their reply, that they were immersed into John's immersion, relieved the case of all obscurity, and Paul then understood it perfectly. He explained, that John's immersion was one of repentance, to be *followed* by faith in the Messiah when he should come. Those immersed by him believed that the Messiah was coming; but they did not, until *after* their immersion, believe that *Jesus* was the Messiah, nor did they have a promise of the Holy Spirit. They were not, therefore, immersed into the name of Jesus, or that of the Holy Spirit. This is further evident from the fact that Paul commanded these twelve to be "immersed into the name of the Lord Jesus," which the authority of the commission requires us to understand as equivalent to the expression, "into the name of the Father, and of the Son, and of the Holy Spirit." These points of defect, however, were not peculiar to the immersion of these twelve, but attached also to that of the twelve apostles, the hundred and twenty disciples, and the five hundred who saw Jesus together in Galilee after the resurrection,* none of whom were reimmersed. What, then, led to the immersion of these parties? If their immersion had taken place, like that of all these others just named, while John's immersion was still an existing institution, no reason could be given for their reimmersion. This, then, forces us to the conclusion that they had been immersed with John's immersion after it had ceased to be administered by divine authority. Apollos had been recently preaching this obsolete immersion in Ephesus, and these persons may have been immersed by him. If so, they submitted

* 1 Cor. xv: 6.

ACTS XIX: 8-12.

to an institution which had been abrogated more than twenty years, and this was the defect which led to their reimmersion. The general conclusion, from all the premises, is this: that persons who were immersed with John's immersion, while it was in lawful existence, were received into the Church of Christ without reimmersion. But persons who were thus immersed, after the introduction of apostolic immersion, were reimmersed. The reason why Apollos was not reimmersed as well as the twelve, was, doubtless, because, like the apostles and the other original disciples, he was immersed during the ministry of John.

8-12. It is worthy of note that Paul commenced his labors in Ephesus by rectifying what he found wrong in the few disciples already there, before he undertook to add to their number. It is an example worthy of imitation to the full extent that may be found practicable. When he had accomplished this, he was prepared to grapple with the Jewish and pagan errors which pervaded the community. (8) *"Then he went into the synagogue, and spoke boldly for about three months, discussing and persuading the things concerning the kingdom of God. (9) But when some were hardened and unbelieving, and spoke evil of the way before the multitude, he departed from them and separated the disciples, discussing daily in the school of one Tyrannus. (10) This continued for two years, so that all who dwelt in Asia heard the word of the Lord Jesus, both Jews and Greeks. (11) And God worked unusual miracles by the hands of Paul, (12) so that handkerchiefs or aprons were carried from his person to the sick, and the diseases departed from them, and the wicked spirits went out of them."* This scene in the Jewish synagogue is quite uniform in its details, with others which we have noticed. Here is the same earnest argument and persuasion upon the one invariable theme; the same increasing obstinacy and evil speaking on the part of the unbelieving Jews, and the same final separation of Paul and the few who believed, from the synagogue and the majority who controlled it. As the private house of Justus had been his retreat in Corinth, the schoolhouse of Tyrannus was his resort in Ephesus. Such incidents have their counterpart in the history of all men who have attempted, from that day to this, to correct the religious teachings of their cotemporaries. All such attempts are regarded by prevailing religious parties as troublesome innovations, and the houses erected for public worship are often closed against them. But such petty annoyances are not sufficient now, as they were not then, to suppress the truth. Paul, in the school-house of Tyrannus, had access to the ears of many who would never have entered a synagogue, and who were conciliated by the very fact that it was the *Jews* who persecuted him. This circumstance gained him a favorable hearing from the Greeks, while the unusual miracles wrought gave overwhelming attestation to the words he spoke.

13-17. It is difficult to imagine how men could witness miracles so astonishing and not acknowledge the presence of divine power. We would suppose that even atheism would be confounded in the presence of such manifestations, and that the most hardened sinner would tremble. How deep the depravity, then, of men, even Jews by birth and education, who *would* see in them nothing but the tricks of a skillful and designing magician. Simon the sorcerer had offered to purchase this power with money, and Bar-jesus had sought to convince Sergius Paulus that it was a cheat; but the former was made to tremble under the withering rebuke of Peter, and the latter had been smitten with blindness by the power which he reviled. A similar display of human depravity, followed by a castigation equally severe, occurred in connection with the unusual miracles just mentioned. (13) "*Then certain of the wandering Jewish exorcists undertook to call the name of the Lord Jesus over those who had wicked spirits, saying, We adjure you by the Jesus whom Paul preaches.* (14) *And they were seven sons of Sceva, a Jewish high priest, who did this.* (15) *But the wicked spirit answered and said, Jesus I know, and Paul I am acquainted with; but who are you?* (16) *And the man in whom the wicked spirit was, leaped upon them, and overcame them, and prevailed against them, so that they fled, naked and wounded, out of the house.* (17) *And this became known to all the Jews and Greeks dwelling in Ephesus, and fear fell upon them all, and the name of the Lord Jesus was magnified.*" Nothing is more mortifying, or better calculated to provoke the contempt of the community, than the unexpected exposure of mysterious pretensions such as were assumed by these exorcists. The spirit was enraged at their insulting pretensions, and doubtless enjoyed the joke of exposing them. The seven resisted until they were stripped and wounded, when they fled, presenting a very ludicrous aspect as they passed along the streets. While all Ephesus was laughing at them, it was remembered that the spirit acknowledged the authority of Jesus, and of Paul, and that a licentious use of the name of Jesus was the cause of all their trouble. The mirth awakened by the event was soon changed into reverence for the name of Jesus, which they now saw was not, as the exorcists had pretended, a mere conjurer's talisman.

18–20. The exposure of the seven exorcists reflected discredit upon all the pretenders to magic in Ephesus, while the name of Jesus was magnified. The effects upon the public mind were immense and astonishing. (18) "*Then many of those who believed came and confessed and declared their practices.* (19) *And many of those who practiced curious arts, brought together their books, and burned them before all. And they counted the value of them, and found it fifty thousand pieces of silver.* (20) *So mightily did the word of God grow and prevail.*"

The believers who "came and confessed and declared their practices," had not, till now, realized the impropriety of those arts, which their heathen education had taught them to regard with reverence. That others, who were not yet disciples, did the same thing, and even burned up their books, is a striking proof of the fear that fell upon them all. The pieces of silver in which the value of the books was computed were doubtless the Attic didrachma; for it was a Greek city, and this was the most common silver coin among the Greeks. It was worth fifteen cents of Federal money, and the value of all the books was seven thousand five hundred dollars; a sufficient indication of the extent to which these arts prevailed, and of the number and value of the books written in explanation of them. This whole account is in full accordance with the profane history of Ephesus, which

ACTS XIX: 21, 22.

represents it as the chief center of magic arts in the whole Roman empire.*

21, 22. The conclusion of the preceding events brought Paul to a period of comparative quiet, in which he began to think of leaving Ephesus. (21) "*When these things were accomplished, Paul purposed in spirit to pass through Macedonia and Achaia, and go to Jerusalem, saying, After I have been there, I must also see Rome.* (22) *So he sent into Macedonia two of those who were ministering to him, Timothy and Erastus; but he himself stayed in Asia for a season.*"

It is supposed by some that, previous to this period, Paul had made a short visit to Corinth, and returned again to Ephesus. This supposition is based upon expressions in the Second Epistle to the Corinthians, which are understood to imply such a visit. I regard the evidence, however, as insufficient for a safe conclusion, and will, therefore, treat the narrative as though no such visit had taken place. The reader who is curious to investigate the question should refer to Mr. Howson on the affirmative,† and Paley on the negative.‡

The First Epistle to the Corinthians was written from Ephesus, as we learn from the remark, (chapter xvi: 8,) "I will tarry in Ephesus until Pentecost; for a great and effectual door is opened to me, and there are many adversaries." It was also during the present visit that it was written, for, during his first visit, he did not *tarry* at all.‖ The exact date of the epistle is best fixed within the period covered by the words "he himself stayed in Asia for a season;" for it was then that "a great and effectual door" was first opened to him. Other evidences of the date concur with these, and are fully stated by Mr. Howson.§

This is not really the first epistle Paul wrote to the Corinthians; for in it he speaks of another, which he had previously written, upon the subject of fornication. He says: "I wrote to you in an epistle not to keep company with fornicators."¶ This is all we know of the subject-matter of the epistle, which is lost; and perhaps it was for the reason that it treated of this subject alone, and in a less detailed method than does the epistle now called the first, that it was not preserved with the other two.

Subsequent to the date of the lost epistle, some members of the household of Chloe had brought him information of great disorders and corruption in the Church in Corinth.** He learned that the congregation was distracted by party strife;†† that fornication, and even incest, were still tolerated by them;‡‡ that some of them were engaged in litigation before the civil courts;‖‖ that his own apostolic authority was called in question;§§ that their women, contrary to the prevailing rules of modesty, took part in the worship with unvailed faces;¶¶ that some confusion and strife had arisen in reference to the spiritual gifts among them;*** that some among them were even denying the resurrection;††† and that the Lord's supper was profaned by feasting and drunkenness.‡‡‡ Besides all this, he had received a letter from them calling for information in reference to marriage and

* See Life and Ep., vol. 2, p. 21. † Ib. p. 26. ‡ Horæ Paulinæ on 2 Cor. xiii: 1.
‖ Acts xviii: 19, 20. § Vol. 2, p. 33. ¶ 1 Cor. v: 9–13.
** 1 Cor. i: 11. †† 1 Cor. ch. i, ii, iii. ‡‡ 1 Cor. ch. v.
‖‖ 1 Cor. ch. vi. §§ 1 Cor. ch. iv and ix. ¶¶ 1 Cor. xi: 1–16.
*** 1 Cor. ch. xii, xiii, xiv. ††† 1 Cor. xv: 12. ‡‡‡ 1 Cor. xi: 17–34.

divorce, and the eating of meats offered to idols.* To answer their questions, and to correct and rebuke these disorders, was the object of the epistle. The temper in which it is written appears calm and stern; yet it is not conceivable that Paul could hear of corruptions so gross in a Church which had cost him so much labor and anxiety, without intense pain. Though no such feeling was allowed to manifest itself in the epistle, he was constrained, afterward, to confess it, and say to them, "Out of *much affliction and anguish of heart,* I wrote to you, with *many tears.*"† It was, therefore, with a heart full of anguish in reference to some results of his past labors, but buoyed up by the opening of a wide and effectual door in his present field, that he sent Timothy and Erastus into Macedonia, but remained himself in Asia for a season.

23–27. (23) "*Now, about that period, there arose no small stir concerning that way.* (24) *For a certain man named Demetrius, a silversmith, brought no little employment to the artisans by making silver shrines of Diana.* (25) *Calling them together, and the workmen employed about such things, he said, Men, you understand that by this employment we have our wealth.* (26) *And you see and hear that not only at Ephesus, but in almost the whole of Asia, this Paul, by his persuasion, has turned away a great multitude, saying that they are not gods which are made with hands;* (27) *and not only is this our business in danger of coming into contempt, but also the temple of the great goddess Diana will be despised, and the majesty of her whom all Asia and the world worships will be destroyed.*" This is the most truthful and candid of all the speeches ever uttered against Paul. The charge that he had said these were not gods which were made with hands, was literally true, and free from exaggeration. The appeals, too, by which he sought to stir up the passions of his hearers, were candid; for he appeals directly to their pecuniary interest, which was suffering; to their veneration for the temple, which was counted one of the seven wonders of the world and to their reverence for the goddess who was the chief object of their worship. The statement of the effects already produced by Paul's preaching throughout the city and the province, endangering their whole system of idolatry, was equally truthful. Whether he is entitled to the same degree of credit in reference to the *motive* which prompted him, is more doubtful; for the fact that the class of men in Ephesus who had the greatest *pecuniary* interest in the worship of Diana were the first to defend her sinking cause, is a suspicious circumstance, especially when we remember that these artisans had better reason than any others to know that the pieces of silver which they had molded and polished with their own hands were not gods. It appears to have been a corrupt determination to save their traffic at all hazards, which made them ignore the evidence of their own senses, and rendered them impervious to the arguments and demonstrations of Paul.

28, 29. The prospect of pecuniary ruin enraged the artisans, while their veneration for the goddess suggested the best theme on which to give vent to their wrath before the people. (28) *And when they heard this they were full of wrath, and cried out, saying, Great is Diana of the*

---

* 1 Cor. vii : 1 ; viii : 1. † 2 Cor. ii : 4.

Ephesians. (29) *And the whole city was filled with confusion; and having caught Gaius and Aristarchus, Macedonians, Paul's companions in travel, they rushed with one accord into the theater."* The outcry, "Great is Diana of the Ephesians," awakened the old enthusiasm of all the idolaters who heard it, and the tone of rage with which it was uttered, suggesting some assault upon the honor of the goddess, threw the gathering mob into a frenzy. It was a kind providence in reference to Paul, that he happened to be out of their reach. Not finding him, they seize his companions, and rushing into the theater, where criminals were sometimes exposed to wild beasts, they are about to take the part of the wild beasts themselves. What was the fate of Gaius and Aristarchus is not here stated, though both names occur afterward in the history, and probably designate the same individuals.*

30, 31. When Paul heard the tumult, and knew that his companions had been dragged within the theater, he could but suppose that they were being torn to pieces. This thought alone was intensely harrowing to his feelings; but it was still more so to know that they were suffering in his stead. He could not endure to remain inactive at such a crisis, but resolved to die with them. (30) *"But Paul, having determined to go in to the people, the disciples would not permit him;* (31) *and some of the Asiarchs,† also, who were his friends, sent to him and entreated him not to trust himself within the theater."* By such means he was restrained from his desperate purpose, after having fully made up his mind to die. The desperation to which he was driven he afterward describes to the Corinthians in this touching language: "We would not have you ignorant, brethren, of our trouble which came to us in Asia, that we were exceedingly pressed down beyond our strength, so that we despaired even of life: but we had within ourselves the sentence of death, that we should not trust in ourselves, but in God who raises the dead."‡ Giving up all hope of life, as he started toward the theater, and trusting in Him who raises the dead, when the tumult had subsided, and he was assured of safety, he felt much as if he had been raised from the dead. He therefore says, in the same connection, "Who delivered me from so grievous a death, and is delivering, in whom I trust that he will even yet deliver us: you also helping by prayer for us, that for the gift bestowed on us by means of many persons, thanks may be given by many on our behalf."‖

32–34. Leaving the apostle, for a time, in the cloud of sorrow which we will find still enveloping him when we meet him again, we turn to witness the proceedings within the theater. (32) *"Now some were crying one thing and some another; for the assembly was confused, and the greater part knew not on what account they had come together.* (33) *And they put forward Alexander out of the crowd, the Jews urging him forward. And Alexander, waving his hand, wished to make a defense to the people.* (34) *But knowing that he was a Jew, all with one voice, for about two hours, cried out, Great is Diana of the Ephesians."* There were two reasons why the Jews should feel some anxiety to defend themselves before this mob. *First,* It was well known in Ephesus that

---
* Acts xx: 4; xxvii: 2.
† This was the title of officials chosen to preside over the annual games in the province of Asia.—HOWSON, ii: 83.   ‡ 2 Cor. i: 8, 9.   ‖ 2 Cor. i: 10, 11.

they were as much opposed to idols and idol-worship as were the disciples. *Second*, The fact that the apostle and many of his brethren were Jews, naturally attracted toward all the Jews the hatred which had been aroused against them. A courageous and manly adherence to their own principles would have prompted them to share with the disciples the obloquy of their common position; but they were endeavoring to persuade the multitude that Paul and his party should not be identified with themselves. The cowardly trick was perceived by the multitude, as soon as they perceived that it was a Jew who was trying to address them, and they gave it the rebuke it deserved by refusing to hear him.

35–41. The rage of an excited multitude, unless it find some new fuel to keep up the flame, will naturally subside in a few hours. While it is at its hight, it becomes only the more furious the more it is opposed; but when it begins to subside, frequently a few well-chosen words are sufficient to restore quiet. Acting upon this principle, the city authorities had not, thus far, interfered with the mob; but when they were exhausted by long-continued vociferation, the following well-timed and well-worded speech was addressed to them. (35) *"But the public clerk, having quieted the people, said, Men of Ephesus, what man is there who does not know that the city of Ephesus is a worshiper of the great goddess Diana, and of the image which fell down from Jupiter?* (36) *Seeing, then, that these things can not be spoken against, you ought to be quieted, and do nothing rashly.* (37) *For you have brought hither these men, who are neither robbers of temples nor blasphemers of your goddess.* (38) *If, then, Demetrius, and the artisans who are with him, have a complaint against any one, the courts are open, and there are proconsuls; let them accuse one another.* (39) *But if you are making inquiry concerning other matters, it shall be determined in a lawful assembly.* (40) *For we are in danger of being called to account for this day's tumult, there being no cause for which we will be able to give an account of this concourse.* (41) *And having spoken thus, he dismissed the assembly."*

This is evidently the speech of a man well skilled in the management of popular assemblies, and, doubtless, its happy adaptation to the circumstances is what suggested to Luke the propriety of preserving it. It is probable that the speaker, like the Asiarchs who interfered to keep Paul out of danger, was a friend to the apostle, and a man of too much intelligence to receive with blind credulity the popular delusion in reference to the temple and image of Diana. The speech, indeed, has a ring of insincerity about it, indicating that the speaker was merely humoring the popular superstition for the special purpose before him. Upon this hypothesis the speech appears the more ingenious. The confident assumption that the divine honors bestowed on their goddess, and the belief that her image fell from heaven, were so well known that no man would call them in question, was soothing to their excited feelings; and the remark that the unquestionable certainty of these facts ought to make them feel entirely composed on the subject, brought them, by a happy turn of thought, to the very composure which he desired, and which they fancied was the result of a triumphant vindication of their cause. Advancing, then, to the case of the disciples, like a trained advocate, he ignores the real charge against them, that of denying that they are gods which are made with hands, and declares that they are neither *temple robbers*, nor *revilers* of their *goddess*. Then, as for the men who had excited them to this disturbance, the proconsular courts were the proper place for complaints like theirs, and they had no right to *disturb the people* with such matters. Finally, he gives them a gentle hint as to the unlawfulness of their assemblage, and the probability that they would be called to account for it by the Roman authorities. This last remark had special force with the majority, who, according to Luke, "knew not on what account they had come together;" and the whole speech was well aimed toward the result which followed, the dispersion of the mob. The city authorities had reason to congratulate themselves that so fierce a mob had been so successfully controlled, and the disciples could but be thankful to God that they had escaped so well.

XX: 1. (1) *"After the tumult had ceased, Paul called to him the disciples, and bade them farewell, and departed to go into Macedonia."* Thus ended the long-continued labors of the apostle in Ephesus. The "great and effectual door," which he saw open before him but a few weeks previous, had now been suddenly closed; and the "many adversaries," for the noble purpose of resisting whom he had resolved to remain in Ephesus till Pentecost,* had prevailed against him. He had accomplished much in the city and province, but there seemed now a terrible reaction among the people in favor of their time-honored idolatry, threatening to crush out the results of his long and arduous labors. When the disciples, whom he had taught and warned with tears, both publicly and from house to house, for the space of three years,† were gathered around him for the last time, and he was about to leave them in a great furnace of affliction, no tongue can tell the bitterness of the final farewell. All was dark behind him, and all forbidding before him; for he turns his face toward that shore across the Ægean, where he had been welcomed before with stripes and imprisonment. No attempt is made, either by Luke or himself, to describe his feelings, until he reached Troas, where he was to embark for Macedonia, and where he expected to meet Titus returning from Corinth. At this point, a remark of his own gives us a clear insight to the pent-up sorrows of his heart. He writes to the Corinthians: "When I came to Troas for the gospel of Christ, and a door was opened to me by the Lord, I had *no rest* in my spirit, because I found not my brother Titus; but took leave of them, and came away into Macedonia."‡ We have followed this suffering apostle through many disheartening scenes, and will yet follow him through many more; but only on this occasion do we find his heart so sink within him that he can not preach the gospel, though a door is opened to him by the Lord. He had hoped that the weight of sorrow which was pressing him down above his strength to bear,‖ would be relieved by the sympathy of the beloved Titus, and the good news that he might bring from Corinth; but the pang of disappointment added the last ounce to the weight which crushed his spirit, and he rushed on, blinded with tears, in the course by which Titus was coming. A heart so strong to endure, when once crushed, can not readily resume its wonted buoyancy. Even after the

* 1 Cor. xvi: 8, 9. † Verse 31. ‡ 2 Cor. ii: 12, 13. ‖ 2 Cor. 1: 8.

sea was between him and Ephesus, and he was once more among the disciples of Macedonia, he is still constrained to confess, "When we had come into Macedonia, our flesh had no rest, but we were afflicted on every side; without were fightings; within were fears."* Finally, however, the long-expected Titus arrived with good news from Corinth, and thus the Lord, who never forgets his servants in affliction, brought comfort to the overburdened heart of Paul, and enabled him to change the tone of the second letter to the Corinthians, and express himself in these words: "Nevertheless, God, who is the comforter of those who are lowly, comforted us by the coming of Titus, and not by his coming only, but by the consolation with which he was comforted in you, telling us your earnest desire, your mourning, your fervent mind toward me, so that I rejoiced the more."†

But the news brought by Titus was not all of a cheering kind. He told of the good effects of the former epistle; that the majority of the Church had repented of their evil practices; that they had excluded the incestuous man;‡ and that they were forward in their preparation for a large contribution to the poor saints in Judea.|| But he also brought word that Paul had some bitter personal enemies in the Church, who were endeavoring to injure his reputation, and subvert his apostolic authority.§ For the purpose of counteracting the influence of these ministers of Satan,¶ encouraging the faithful brethren in their renewed zeal, and presenting to them all many solemn and touching reflections suggested by his own afflictions, he addressed them the epistle known as the Second to the Corinthians, and dispatched it by the hands of Titus and two other brethren, whose names are not mentioned.**

That we are right in assuming this as the date of this epistle, is easily established. For, *First*, He refers, in the epistle, to having recently come from Asia into Macedonia,†† which he had now done according to the history. *Second*, He wrote from Macedonia, when about to start from that province to Corinth.‡‡ But he was never in Macedonia previous to this, except when there was as yet no Church in Corinth, and he was never here afterward on his way from Asia to Corinth.

2, 3. The career of the apostle for the next few months is not given in detail, but the whole is condensed into this brief statement: (2) "*And when he had gone through those parts, and had given them much exhortation, he went into Greece;* (3) *and having spent three months there, he resolved to return through Macedonia, because a plot was laid against him by the Jews as he was about to set sail for Syria.*" Several events transpired in the interval thus hurriedly passed over, a knowledge of which is accessible through epistles written at the time, and which we shall briefly consider.

When Paul and Barnabas were in Jerusalem on the mission from the Church in Antioch, as recorded in the fifteenth chapter of Acts, it was formally agreed, among the apostles then present, that Peter, James, and John should labor chiefly among the Jews, and Paul and

---
* 2 Cor. vii: 5. † 2 Cor. vii: 5–12. ‡ 2 Cor. ii: 5–11. | 2 Cor. ix: 1, 2.
§ See 2 Cor. x, xii, *passim.* ¶ Ib. xi: 13–15. ** Ib. viii: 16–24.
†† Ib. i: 8: vii: 5. ‡‡ Ib. viii: 3, 4; xii: 14; xiii: 1.

Barnabas among the Gentiles. It was stipulated, however, that the latter should assist in providing for the poor in Judea. "This," says Paul, "I was also forward to do."* In accordance with this agreement, we find that he was now urging a general collection in the Churches of Macedonia and Achaia for this purpose.† The Churches in Achaia, indeed, were ready for the contribution a whole year before this, and Paul had written to them in the First Epistle to the Corinthians, "Upon the first day of the week, let each of you lay by him in store, as God has prospered him, that there be no collections when I come."‡ For prudential considerations, such as prompted him so often to labor without remuneration from the Churches, he was not willing to be himself the bearer of this gift, although the Churches in Macedonia had entreated him to do so.|| He at first, indeed, had not fully intended to go to Jerusalem in connection with it; but had said to the Churches, "Whomsoever you will approve by letters, them will I *send* to take your gift to Jerusalem; and if it be proper that I should go also, they shall go with me."§ The importance of the mission, however, grew more momentous as time advanced, so that he resolved to go himself, and the enterprise became a subject of most absorbing interest.

The circumstance which led to this result was the increasing alienation between the Jews and the Gentiles within the Church. The decree of the apostles and inspired brethren in Jerusalem, though it had given great comfort to the Church in Antioch, where the controversy first became rife,¶ and had done good everywhere that it was carried,** had not succeeded in entirely quelling the pride and arrogance of the judaizing teachers. They had persisted in their schismatical efforts, until there was now a wide-spread disaffection between the parties, threatening to rend the whole Church into two hostile bodies. By this influence the Churches in Galatia had become almost entirely alienated from Paul, for whom they once would have been willing to pluck out their own eyes, and were being rapidly led back under bondage to the law of Moses.†† The Church in Rome, at the opposite extremity of the territory which had been evangelized, was also disturbed by factions, the Jews insisting that justification was by works of law, and that the distinctions of meats and holy days should be perpetuated.‡‡ Such danger to the cause could but be to Paul a source of inexpressible anxiety; and while it was imminent he concentrated all his energies to its aversion.

Already engaged in a general collection among Churches composed chiefly of Gentiles, for the benefit of Jewish saints in Judea, and knowing the tendency of a kind action to win back alienated affections, he pushes the work forward with renewed industry, for the accomplishment of this good end. He presents this motive to the Corinthians, in the following words: "For the ministration of this service not only supplies the *wants* of the saints, but also *superabounds* to God, by means of many *thanksgivings*, (they *glorifying* God, through the proof supplied by this ministration of your subjection to the gospel of Jesus Christ

* Gal. i: 6-10. † 2 Cor. i: 1; viii: 1-15. ‡ 1 Cor. xvi: 2; ix: 1, 2.
| 2 Cor. viii: 4. § 1 Cor. xvi: 3, 4. ¶ See Com. xv: 30-35.
** See Com. xvi: 4, 5. †† Comp. Gal. i: 6; iv: 15, 16; iv: 10-21; v: 1.
‡‡ Rom., chapters iii, iv, v, and xiv.

which you have confessed, and of the liberality of your fellowship for them and for all,) and by their *prayers* in your behalf, having a *great affection* for you on account of the exceeding favor of God which is in you."* He here expresses as great confidence in the good result of the enterprise, as if it were already accomplished, and the Jews were already overflowing with affection to the Gentiles, and offering many thanksgivings and prayers to God in their behalf. Thus he felt while stimulating the liberality of the brethren; but when the collections were all made in the Churches, and he was about to start from Corinth to Jerusalem with it, his anxiety was most intense, and he began to fear that the alienation of the Jews was so great that they would not accept the gift, and thus the breach he was trying to close would be opened wider. We know this by the almost painful earnestness with which he calls upon the brethren at Rome to pray with him for the success of his efforts. He says: "Now I *beseech* you, brethren, for the *Lord Jesus Christ's sake*, and for the *love of the Spirit*, that you *strive* together with me in *prayer* to God for me, that I may be *delivered* from the *disobedient* in Judea, and that my service which I have for Jerusalem may be *accepted by the saints.*"† If he called thus earnestly for the prayers of the distant Church at Rome, how much more must he have enlisted those of the Churches in Achaia and Macedonia, who were immediately concerned in the enterprise itself! We have here the spectacle of a man who was regarded with suspicion, if not with positive dislike, by a large portion of his brethren, securing from others who were involved with him in the same reproach, a self-denying contribution for the temporal wants of the disaffected party; and, then, fearing lest their disaffection was so great as to lead them to reject the gift—a fear which would cause most men to withhold it entirely—he calls upon all the donors to unite in persistent prayer that it might not be rejected. The object of it all, too, was to gain no selfish ends, but to win back the alienated affections of brethren, and to preserve the unity of the body of Christ. No nobler instance of disinterested benevolence can be found in the history of men. The prosecution of the enterprise, as we will hereafter see, was in keeping with the magnanimity of its inception. But before we consider it further, we must briefly notice some kindred facts.

For the same grand purpose which prompted the great collection, Paul wrote, during his three months' stay in Corinth, the two epistles to the Galatians and the Romans. This we have already assumed in our references to them as cotemporaneous with the collection. The most conclusive evidence for assigning to them this date may be briefly stated as follows: In the epistle to the Romans, Paul expressly states that he was about to start for Jerusalem with the contribution which had been collected.‡ But this could have been said only toward the close of his present stay in Corinth. Moreover, Gaius, who lived in Corinth, was his host at the time of writing to the Romans;‖ and Phœbe, of the Corinthian seaport Cenchrea, was the bearer of the epistle.§ As for Galatians, it contains a reference to Paul's *first* visit to them, implying that he had been there a second time. His

* 2 Cor. ix: 12-14.   † Rom. xv: 30, 31.   ‡ Rom. xv: 25, 26.
‖ Comp. Rom. xvi: 23, 1 Cor. i: 14.   § Rom. xvi: 1.

ACTS XX: 4-6. 245

words are: "You know that it was on account of sickness that I preached the gospel to you at the first."* It was written, then, after his second visit. But this leaves the date very indefinite, and there are no other notes of time within the epistle itself to fix it more definitely. There is, however, a close correspondence in subject-matter between it and the epistle to the Romans, indicating that they were written under the same condition of affairs, and about the same time. This, in the absence of conflicting evidence, is considered conclusive.† It is not certain which of the two was written first, but, as in Romans Paul speaks of his departure for Jerusalem as about to take place, it is more probable that Galatians was written previous to this. In both, the apostle contends by authority and by argument against the destructive teaching of the judaizing party, striving, by this means, to put them to silence at the same time that he was aiming, by a noble act of self-denial, to win back their good-will, both to himself and to the Gentiles, whose cause he had espoused.

Having dispatched these two epistles, and collected about him the messengers of the various Churches, the apostle was about to start for Syria by water, when, as the text last quoted affirms, he learned that a plot was laid against him by the Jews, which determined him to change his course. This plot was probably an arrangement to waylay him on the road to Cenchrea, and perhaps both rob and murder him. Having timely notice of the danger, "he determined to return through Macedonia," and started by another road.

4, 5. (4) "*And there accompanied him, as far as Asia, Sopater of Berea; Aristarchus and Secundus of Thessalonica; Gaius of Derbe, and Timothy; and Tychicus and Trophimus of Asia.* (5) *These, going before, waited for us at Troas.*" This sentence brings us again into company with two familiar companions of Paul, from whom we have been parted for some time. The name of Timothy has not occurred in the history before, since he was dispatched with Erastus from Ephesus into Macedonia.‡ He had, however, joined company again with Paul while the latter was in Macedonia, as we learn from the fact that his name appears in the salutation of the Second Epistle to the Corinthians.∥ Luke, the other party here introduced, has not been an eye-witness of the scenes he was describing since the scourging of Paul and Silas in Philippi. His significant *we* and *us* were discontinued then,§ and are not resumed until he says, in this verse, "These, going before, waited for *us* at Troas." The probability is, that he had resided in that city during the whole of this period, and now, as Paul was passing through on his way to Jerusalem, he once more joined the company. During his absence the narrative has been very hurried and elliptical. We shall now, for a time, find it circumstantial in the extreme.

6. The delay of Paul at Philippi may be well accounted for by the strong affection which he bore toward the congregation there, and his present expectation that he would see their faces in the flesh no more.¶ ·(6) "*And we, after the days of unleavened bread, sailed away from Philippi, and came to them in Troas in five days, where we remained*

* Gal. iv: 13. † See the argument more fully stated, Life and Ep., vol. 2, p. 135.
‡ Acts xix: 22. ∥ 2 Cor. i: 1. § Acts xvi: 16, 17. ¶ Comp. verse 25.

seven days." The "days of unleavened bread" here mentioned remind us that it had been nearly one year since the close of Paul's labors in Ephesus; for he was awaiting the approach of Pentecost when the mob was aroused by Demetrius.* He probably left there between the Passover and Pentecost, and as the Passover had now returned again, the time he had spent in his tour through Macedonia and Achaia and back to Philippi must have occupied ten or eleven months.

The voyage from Philippi to Troas occupied, as here stated, five days, though, on a former occasion, they had sailed from Troas and reached Philippi in two days.† The delay on this trip is suggestive of adverse winds.

The brethren who had preceded Paul and Luke to Troas had already spent there the five days occupied by the latter on the journey, and a portion of the seven days of unleavened bread which they spent in Philippi. The seven additional days now spent there by the whole company, making an aggregate of more than two weeks, gave sufficient time to accomplish much in a community where a door was already opened by the Lord.‡

7. The last period of seven days included and was terminated by the Lord's day. (7) "*And on the first day of the week, when the disciples came together to break the loaf, Paul discoursed to them, about to depart on the next day, and continued his discourse till midnight.*" This passage indicates both the day of the week in which the disciples broke the loaf, and the prime object of their meeting on that day. It shows that the loaf was broken on the first day of the week; and we have no apostolic precedent for breaking it on any other day.

The disciples came together on that day, even though Paul and Luke and Timothy, and all the brethren who had come from Greece, were present, not primarily to hear one or more of them discourse, but "*to break the loaf.*" Such is the distinct statement of the historian. That such was an established custom in the Churches is implied in a rebuke administered by Paul to the Church at Corinth, in which he says: "When you come together into one place, it is not to eat the Lord's supper."‖ Now, for this they would not have deserved censure, had it not been that to eat the Lord's supper was the proper object of their assemblage. These facts are sufficient to establish the conclusion that the main object of the Lord's-day meetings was to to break the loaf.

This conclusion will be of service to us in seeking to determine the frequency with which the loaf was broken. If the prime object of the Lord's-day meeting was to celebrate the Lord's supper, then all the evidence we have of the custom of meeting every Lord's day is equally conclusive in reference to the weekly observance of the Lord's supper. But the former custom is universally admitted by Christians of the present day, and therefore there should be no dispute in reference to the latter.

It must, in candor, be admitted, that there is no express statement in the New Testament that the disciples broke the loaf every Lord's day; neither is it stated that they *met* every Lord's day. Yet the

---

* 1 Cor. xvi: 8.   † Acts xvi: 11, 12.   ‡ Com., verse 1.   ‖ 1 Cor. xi: 20.

ACTS XX: 7.

question, how often shall the congregation meet together to break the loaf, is one which can not be avoided, but must be settled practically in some way. The different religious parties have hitherto agreed upon a common principle of action, which is, that each may settle the question according to its own judgment of what is most profitable and expedient. This principle, if applied by congregations instead of parties, is a safe one in reference to matters upon which we have no means of knowing the divine will, or the apostolic custom. But when we can determine, with even a good degree of probability, an apostolic custom, our own judgment should yield to it. So all parties have reasoned in reference to the Lord's day. The intimations contained in the New Testament, together with the universal custom known to have existed in the Churches during the age succeeding that of the apostles, has been decided by them all as sufficient to establish the divine authority of the religious observance of the Lord's day; and yet they have not consented to the weekly observance of the Lord's supper, the proof of which is precisely the same.

As a practical issue between the advocates of weekly communion and their opponents, the question really has reference to the *comparative weight* of evidence in favor of this practice, and of monthly, quarterly, or yearly communion. When it is thus presented, no one can long hesitate as to the conclusion; for in favor of either of the intervals last mentioned there is not the least evidence, either in the New Testament, or in the uninspired history of the Churches. On the other hand, it is the universal testimony of antiquity that the Churches of the second century broke the loaf every Lord's day, and considered it a custom of apostolic appointment. Now it can not be doubted that the apostolic Churches had some regular interval at which to celebrate this institution, and seeing that all the evidence there is in the case is in favor of a weekly celebration, there is no room for a reasonable doubt that this was the interval which they adopted.

It is very generally admitted, even among parties who do not observe the practice themselves, that the apostolic Churches broke the loaf weekly; but it is still made a question whether, in the absence of an express commandment, this example is binding upon us. This question is likely to be determined differently by two different classes of men. Those who are disposed to follow chiefly the guide of their own judgment, or of their denominational customs, will feel little influenced by such a precedent. But to those who are determined that the very slightest indication of the divine will shall govern them, the question must present itself in this way: "We are commanded to do this in memory of Jesus. We are not told, in definite terms, how often it shall be done; but we find that the apostles established the custom of meeting every Lord's day for this purpose. This is an inspired precedent, and with it we must comply. We can come to no other conclusion without assuming an ability to judge of this matter with more wisdom than did the apostle."

We return to the meeting in Troas. The extreme length of Paul's discourse on this occasion is in striking contrast with the brevity of his other speeches, as reported by Luke. It is to be accounted for by the anxiety of the apostle, in bidding them a final farewell, to leave the brethren as well guarded as possible against the temptations which awaited them.

8–10. The long and solemn discourse was interrupted at midnight, by an incident which caused great alarm, and some confusion, in the audience. (8) "*Now there were many lamps in the upper chamber where we were assembled;* (9) *and there sat in the window a certain young man named Eutychus, who was borne down by deep sleep: and as Paul was discoursing a very long time, borne down with sleep, he fell from the third story down, and was taken up dead.* (10) *But Paul went down, and fell upon him, and embraced him, and said, Be not troubled, for his life is in him.*" It is assumed, by some writers, that the young man was not really dead, and Paul's remark, "his life is in him," is adduced in proof of the assumption.* If this remark had been made when Paul first saw him, it might, with propriety, be so understood; but as it was made after he had fallen upon him, and embraced him, actions evidently designed to restore him, it should be understood as only a modest way of declaring that he had restored him to life.

11. The alarm produced by the death of Eutychus, the astonishing display of divine power in his restoration to life, and the stillness of the midnight hour in which it all transpired, could but add greatly to the solemnity which already pervaded the audience. Their feelings were too deeply wrought upon to think of sleep, and the meeting was still protracted. They returned to the upper chamber, where the lights were still burning, and the elements of the Lord's supper remained as yet undistributed. Paul, notwithstanding the length and earnestness of his discourse, was still unexhausted. (11) "*And having gone up, and broken the loaf, and eaten it, he conversed yet a long time, even till daybreak, and so he departed.*" Thus the whole night was spent in religious discourse and conversation, interrupted, at midnight, by a death and a resurrection, and this followed by the celebration of the Lord's death, which brings the hope of a better resurrection. The whole scene concluded at daybreak, in one of those touching farewells, in which the pain of parting and the hope of meeting to part no more, struggle so tearfully for the mastery of the soul. It was a night long to be remembered by those who were there, and will yet be a theme of much conversation in eternity.

It is a question of some curiosity whether it was at daybreak on Sunday morning or Monday morning, that this assembly was dismissed. They were assembled in the early part of the night, yet the time of their assembling was included in the "first day of the week." If the brethren in Troas were accustomed to begin and close the day at midnight, according to the Greek custom, it must have been Sunday night when they met. But if they reckoned according to the Jewish method, which began and closed the day with sunset, then they must have met on what we call *Saturday* night; for in this case the whole of that night would belong to the first day of the week, and *Sunday* night to the second day. It is supposed, by many commentators, that the Greek method prevailed, and that they met Sunday night; but, with Mr. Howson, I am constrained to the other opinion; a con-

* Olshausen.

clusive proof of which I find in the fact, that if the meeting was on Sunday night, then the loaf was broken on Monday morning; for it was broken after midnight. There can be no doubt of this fact, unless we understand the breaking of the loaf, mentioned in the eleventh verse, as referring to a common meal. But this is inadmissible; for, having stated, (verse 7,) that they came together to break the loaf, and now stating, for the first time, that Paul did break the loaf, we must conclude that by the same expression Luke means the same thing. To the objection that Paul alone is said to have broken and eaten the bread, I answer, that this would be a very natural expression to indicate that Paul officiated at the table; but, on the other hand, if it was a common meal, it would be strange that he alone should eat, especially to the exclusion of his traveling companions, who were going to start as early in the morning as he did. I conclude, therefore, that the brethren met on the night after the Jewish Sabbath, which was still observed as a day of rest by all of them who were Jews or Jewish proselytes, and considering this the beginning of the first day of the week, spent it in the manner above described. On Sunday morning Paul and his companions resumed their journey, being constrained, no doubt, by the movements of the ship, which had already been in the harbor of Troas seven days. His example does not justify traveling on the Lord's day, except under similar constraint, and upon a mission as purely religious as that which was taking him to Jerusalem.

12. Recurring again to the incident concerning Eutychus, in order to state more particularly the gratification which the brethren felt at his recovery, Luke here remarks: (12) "*And they brought the young man alive, and were not a little comforted.*" The close connection of this remark with the departure of Paul and his company, and its disconnection from the statement concerning the resumption of the meeting, indicate that it refers to their bringing him away from the meeting.

13. Paul and his whole company departed at an early hour in the morning, the meeting breaking up at daybreak for this purpose. But their routes for the day were different. (13) "*We went forward to the ship, and sailed for Assos, intending there to take in Paul; for so he had appointed, intending himself to go on foot.*" The coasting voyage of the ship around Cape Lectum to Assos was about forty miles, while the distance across was only twenty.* This would enable Paul to reach that point on foot about as soon as the ship could sail there with favorable winds. His motive in choosing to walk this distance, and to go alone, has been a subject of various conjectures. But the deep gloom which shrouded his feelings, caused by prophetic warnings of great dangers ahead; by the critical state of the Churches everywhere; and by the final farewell which he was giving to Churches which he had planted and nourished, naturally prompted him to seek solitude for a time. On shipboard solitude was impossible, and while in port there was always a group of disciples or a whole congregation claiming his attention. His only opportunity, therefore, during the whole voyage, for solitary reflection, such as the soul longs for amid trials

* Life and Ep., vol. 2, p. 208.

like his, was to seize this occasion for a lonely journey on foot. Amid the more stirring scenes of the apostle's life, while announcing, with oracular authority the will of God, and confirming his words by miraculous demonstrations, we are apt to lose our human sympathy for the man, in our admiration for the apostle. But when we contemplate him under circumstances like the present, worn down by the sleepless labors of the whole night; burdened in spirit too heavily for even the society of sympathizing friends; and yet, with all his weariness, choosing a long day's journey on foot, that he might indulge to satiety the gloom which oppressed him, we are so much reminded of our own seasons of affliction, as to feel, with great distinctness, the human tie which binds our hearts to his. No ardent laborer in the vineyard of the Lord but feels his soul at times ready to sink beneath its load of anxiety and disappointment, and finds no comfort except in allowing the very excess of sorrow to waste itself away amid silence and solitude. In such hours it will do us good to walk with Paul through this lonely journey, and remember how much suffering has been endured by greater and better men than we.

14–16. The ship and the footman arrived together. (14) *"And when he met us at Assos, we took him on board and went to Mitylene.* (15) *Sailing thence, the next day we arrived opposite Chios. In another day we came to Samos, and remaining all night at Trogyllium, on the following day we went to Miletus;* (16) *for Paul had determined to sail by Ephesus, so that he might not spend time in Asia; for he was hastening, if it were possible for him, to be in Jerusalem on the day of Pentecost."* If the ship had been under Paul's control, he could have spent at Ephesus the time which was spent at Miletus, without delaying his arrival in Jerusalem. The fact, therefore, that he avoided Ephesus, to keep from losing time, shows that the vessel was not under his control, but that a visit to Ephesus would have required him to leave the ship that he was on, and take passage on some other bound for that port. This might have caused delay, and the uncertainty of meeting at Ephesus a vessel bound for Syria might have protracted the delay too long to reach Jerusalem in the time desired. The mention of the matter by Luke shows that Paul felt some inclination to revisit Ephesus, that he might witness the present results of his protracted labors there. The day of Pentecost, however, furnished the only occasion which he could expect before fall,* on which the Jews would be generally congregated in Jerusalem, and he desired to be there to distribute the contribution for the poor without visiting the rural districts individually for that purpose. We will yet see that he made the journey in time for the feast.

17. His desire to see the brethren in Ephesus was gratified, in part, by a short delay of the vessel in the harbor of Miletus. (17) *"But from Miletus he sent to Ephesus, and called for the elders of the Church."* The distance was about thirty miles.† He might have gone up himself but for some uncertainty about the movements of the vessel, which was probably waiting for some expected ship to come into port before proceeding. If he had missed the vessel, it

---

* At the feast of Tabernacles.   † Life and Ep., vol. 2, p. 214.

ACTS XX: 18-21.

would have defeated his purpose of attending the feast; whereas, if the elders should get down too late, they would suffer only the inconvenience of the walk.

18-21. The interview with these elders may be regarded as a type of all the meetings and partings which took place on this journey, and was, probably, described with minuteness on this account. (18) *"And when they had come to him, he said to them, You well know from the day in which I first came into Asia, after what manner I was with you all the time,* (19) *serving the Lord with all humility and many tears and trials which befell me by the plots of the Jews;* (20) *that I have kept back nothing that was profitable, but have declared it to you, and taught you both publicly and from house to house,* (21) *testifying to both Jews and Greeks repentance toward God, and faith in our Lord Jesus Christ."* The order in which the terms repentance and faith occur in this last sentence, and in some other passages,* has been urged as proof that repentance occurs before faith in the order of mental operations. But this is a most fallacious source of reasoning. From it we might argue that sanctification precedes faith, because Paul addresses the Thessalonians as having been chosen to salvation "through sanctification of spirit and the belief of the truth;"† or that the confession precedes faith, because Paul says: "If thou shalt confess with thy mouth the Lord Jesus, and believe in thy heart that God has raised him from the dead, thou shalt be saved."‡ The order of the words describing two actions proves nothing in reference to the order of their occurrence, except when it is made evident that it was the writer's intention to indicate the order of occurrence. No such intention is manifest here.

The purpose of the sentence in question is to state the two leading topics on which he had testified among the Ephesians, and the order in which they are mentioned was suggested by the nature of the case. All the Jews in Ephesus and all the Gentiles who attended the synagogue worship already believed in God, before Paul preached to them concerning Jesus. It was also necessary that all the heathen should learn to believe in God, before hearing the gospel of the *Son* of God. Moreover, they might be induced to repent toward God, as they had all been taught that they must do, before they believed that Jesus was the Son of God. Repentance toward God, bringing men to an honest and candid state of mind, was a most excellent preparation for faith in Jesus Christ. This was the design of John's ministry. He prepared them for the reception of Jesus Christ, by calling them to repentance before God. Paul also attempted to make known the true God to the Athenians, and told them that God had "commanded all men everywhere to repent," before he introduced to them the name of Jesus. This, however, is far from being proof of repentance before faith in the ordinary sense of the expression, which requires not repentance toward *God* before faith in *Christ*, but repentance toward *God* before *faith in God*.

That a man can repent toward a God in whose existence he does not believe, is not assumed by any party; but all grant that some degree or species of faith must precede repentance, while the prevailing

---
* Mark i: 15. † 2 Thes. ii: 13. ‡ Rom. x: 9.

Protestant parties contend that *saving* faith, as it is styled, must follow repentance. The mistake which they commit arises from a misconception of the nature of both faith and repentance. Regarding repentance as simply *sorrow for sin*, and faith as a *yielding up of the will to Christ*, they very readily reach the conclusion that the former must precede the latter. But in this conception the sorrow for sin which produces repentance is mistaken for repentance itself; while the yielding up of the will to Christ, which is really repentance,* is mistaken for faith. Repentance, therefore, really covers all the ground usually assigned to both repentance and saving faith, leaving no room for faith to arise after it.

A correct definition of faith is equally inconsistent with this conception. It is "confidence as to things hoped for, conviction as to things not seen."† It can exist, in this its fullest sense, only when its object is both unseen and a subject of hope. When the object is not a subject of hope, as in the faith that the worlds were framed by the word of God,‡ the faith is merely a conviction as to something not seen. But Jesus the Christ, the prime object of the Christian's faith, is both unseen, and the being upon whom all our hopes depend. Faith in him, therefore, is both "confidence as to things hoped for, and conviction as to things not seen." But it is impossible for me to repent of the sins which I have committed against Christ before I am *convinced* in reference to his Messiahship, and have confidence in reference to the things which he has promised. It is, therefore, impossible for repentance to precede faith, in reference to him. On the contrary, faith, or conviction that he is the Christ, and confidence in reference to what he has promised, is the chief means of leading men to repentance; although it is still true, that deists, such as modern Jews, and some others who believe in God but reject Christ, might be induced to repent toward *God* before they believe in *Christ*.

We may further remark, that, in the scriptural distribution of our conception of the divine nature, God is the proper object of repentance, and Jesus Christ of faith. To believe that Jesus is the Christ is *the* faith; but repentance is not thus limited; it has reference to *God*, independent of the distinction between Father and Son. It is this thought which suggested the connection of the term repentance with the name of God, and faith with that of Christ.

22–27. The apostle next reveals to these brethren the cause of that deep sorrow which we have seen brooding over his spirit even before his departure from Corinth. (22) "*And now, behold, I go bound in spirit to Jerusalem, not knowing the things which shall befall me there,* (23) *except that the Holy Spirit testifies in every city, saying, that bonds and afflictions await me.* (24) *But none of these things move me, neither do I hold my life dear to myself, so that I may finish my course with joy, and the ministry which I have received of the Lord Jesus, to testify the gospel of the favor of God.* (25) *And now, behold, I know that you all, among whom I have gone preaching the kingdom of God, will see my face no more.* (26) *Wherefore, I call you to witness this day, that I am pure from the blood of all;* (27) *for I have kept back nothing from declaring to you the whole counsel of God.*"

* See Com. iii : 19. † Heb. xi : 1. ‡ Heb. xi : 3.

ACTS XX: 28-38.

28-35. Having thus eloquently expressed himself in reference to his past fidelity and his present devotion, he gives them a prophetic warning in reference to trials which yet awaited them, and places his own example minutely before them for imitation. (28) "*Take heed, therefore, to yourselves, and to all the flock in which the Holy Spirit has placed you as overseers, to be shepherds to the Church of the Lord, which he has purchased through his own blood.* (29) *For I know this, that after my departure, fierce wolves will enter in among you, not sparing the flock.* (30) *Also from among yourselves men will arise, speaking perverse things, to draw away disciples after them.* (31) *Therefore, watch; remembering that by night and by day, for three years, I ceased not to warn each one with tears.* (32) *And now, brethren, I commend you to God and to the word of his favor, which is able to build you up, and to give you an inheritance among all the sanctified.* (33) *I have coveted no man's gold, or silver, or apparel.* (34) *You yourselves know that these hands have ministered to my necessities, and to those who were with me.* (35) *In all things I have shown you, that so laboring, you should support the weak, and should remember the words of the Lord Jesus, that he himself said, It is more blessed to give than to receive.*" It was a fearful responsibility which rested on the shoulders of these men, to watch as shepherds for the flock, and realize that only by fidelity like that of Paul, could they be free from the blood of them all. In leaving them to this work, he directs their thoughts to the only power sufficient to strengthen them to perform it, by commending them to *God* and to his *Word*, assuring them that the Word was able to build them up, and give them inheritance among the sanctified. This is another among many proofs which we have seen of the confidence of the apostles in the sufficiency and power of the word of God.

The closing admonition has reference to relief of the needy, and to the discharge of their duty, even if it were necessary for them to struggle hard to make their own bread and meat, remembering that it is more blessed to give than to receive. In this, also, he could appeal to his own example, saying, "You yourselves know that these hands," holding them out to them, "have ministered to my necessities, and to those who were with me." Thus he warns and admonishes these elders, in a speech of inimitable pathos, which is recorded by Luke that it might bear the same lesson to elders of Churches everywhere, teaching that no less than apostolic zeal and self-sacrifice are expected of them.

36-38. When these solemn and touching words were concluded, the apostle was ready to re-embark upon the vessel about to weigh anchor in the harbor, and the final farewell must be spoken. (36) "*And when he had thus spoken, he kneeled down, and prayed with them all;* (37) *and they all wept much, and fell upon Paul's neck, and kissed him,* (38) *sorrowing most of all for the word which he had spoken, that they should see his face no more. And they conducted him to the ship.*" It would be difficult to imagine a more touching scene. The tears of women and of children are sometimes shallow; but when full-grown men, men of gray hairs, who have been hardened to endurance by the bitter struggles of life, are seen to weep like children, and to fall upon one another's necks, we have the deepest expression of grief ever witnessed on earth. Such, however, is not the sorrow of this world. When the strong man of the world is overwhelmed with grief, he seeks for solitude, and his heart grows harder while it is breaking. But the sorrow of the man of faith is softening and purifying. It binds the afflicted in closer sympathy with one another and with God, while it is sanctified by prayer. It is painful, but it is not altogether unwelcome. It is a sorrow which we are willing to feel again, and which we love to remember. The history of the Church is full of scenes like this. When the paths of many pilgrims meet, and they mingle together, for a few days, their prayers, their songs of praise, their counsels, and their tears, the hour of parting is like a repetition of this scene on the sea-shore at Miletus. Tears, and heavings of the breast, which tell of grief and love and hope all struggling together in the soul; the parting hand and fond embrace; the blessing of God invoked, but not expressed; the sad turning away to duties which the soul feels for the moment too weak to perform—these are all familiar to the servants of God, and are remembered as tokens of those hours when, most of all, the joys of heaven seem to triumph over the sorrows of earth.

If Paul had been parting from these brethren under happy anticipations for them both, the sorrow of neither party could have been so great. But, added to the pain of a final parting was the gloom of their own uncertain future, and the terrible and undefined afflictions which certainly awaited him. There is not, in the history of our race, apart from the sufferings of the Son of God, a nobler instance of self-sacrifice than is presented by Paul on this journey. He had already, twelve months before this, recounted a catalogue of sufferings more abundant than had fallen to the lot of any other man. He had been often in prison, and often on the verge of death. From the Jews he had five times received forty stripes save one, and had three times been beaten with rods. Once he was stoned, and left on the ground, supposed to be dead. He had suffered shipwreck three times, and spent a day and a night struggling in the waters of the great deep. In his many journeys, he had been exposed to perils by water, by robbers, by his own countrymen, by the heathen; in the city, in the wilderness, in the sea, and among false brethren. He had suffered from weariness and painfulness and wakefulness. He had endured hunger and thirst, and had known what it was to be cold for want of sufficient clothing. Besides all these things, which were without, he had been and was still bearing a burden not less painful in the care of all the Churches.* And besides even all this, was that thorn in the flesh, the messenger of Satan to buffet him, which was so irritating and humiliating that he had three times prayed the Lord to take it from him.† These sufferings we would think enough for the portion of one man; and we would suppose that his scarred‡ and enfeebled frame would be permitted to pass the remainder of its days in quiet. Yet here we find him on his way to Jerusalem, engaged in a mission of mercy, but warned by the voice of prophesy that bonds and afflictions still awaited him. Most men would have said: I have suffered enough. The success of my present enterprise is doubtful, at best, and it is certain to bring me once more into prison, and into untold afflictions. I will, therefore, remain where I am, amid brethren who love me, and

* 2 Cor. xi: 23-28.   † 2 Cor. xii: 7-9.   ‡ Gal. vi: 17.

ACTS XXI: 1-6.

strive to end my days in peace. Such may have been the feelings of the Ephesian elders, as they clung tearfully around him; but how grandly the hero lifts himself above all such human weakness, while he exclaims: "None of these things move me, neither do I hold my life dear to myself, so that I may finish my course with joy, and the ministry which I have received of the Lord Jesus, to testify the gospel of the favor of God." When parting forever from such a man, they well might weep, and stand mute upon the shore till the white sails of his vessel grew dim in the distance, ere they turned in loneliness to the toils and dangers which they were now to encounter without the presence or counsel of their great teacher. We are not permitted to return with them to Ephesus, and listen to their sorrowful conversation by the way; but must follow that receding vessel, and witness the bonds and afflictions which await its most noted passenger.

XXI: 1-3. The vessel proceeded by a coasting voyage along the southern shore of Asia Minor. (1) *"And it came to pass, when we had separated from them, and set sail, that we ran with a straight course and came to Cos; and the next day to Rhodes, and thence to Patara. (2) And finding a ship going across to Phenicia, we embarked and set sail. (3) Passing in sight of Cyprus, and leaving it to the left, we sailed to Syria, and landed at Tyre, for there the ship was to unload her cargo."* The change of vessels at Patara must have been occasioned by the fact that the one in which they had hitherto sailed was not bound for a Phenician port. That the new vessel is said to be *going across* to Phenicia, and that it left Cyprus on the *left*, is an indication that the other was going to cling still further to the coast of Asia Minor, and was probably bound for Antioch.

4. The time employed by the sailors in putting out freight, and taking on board a fresh cargo, gave Paul another opportunity for communing with brethren on shore. (4) *"And having found the disciples, we remained there seven days. They told Paul, through the Spirit, not to go up to Jerusalem."* Here Paul met a repetition of those prophetic warnings which had already cast a gloom over his feelings, and so much alarmed were the brethren at the prospects before him, that they entreated him to go no further. We are not to understand that these *entreaties* were dictated by the Spirit; for this would have made it Paul's duty to desist from his purpose; but the statement means that they were enabled to advise him not to go, by knowing, through the Spirit, what awaited him. The knowledge was supernatural; the advice was the result of their own judgment.

5, 6. When the seven days had passed, including, most likely, a Lord's day, in which the disciples came together to break bread, another scene of painful parting occurred, like that at Miletus. (5) *"And it came to pass that when we completed those days, we departed and went our way, they all, with their wives and children, conducting us forward till we were out of the city. And we kneeled down on the shore and prayed. (6) And bidding each other farewell, we went on board the ship, and they returned home."* Unlike the scene at Miletus, the sorrow of manly hearts was here accompanied by the tenderness of female sympathy and the tears of children. The tears of the company were bitter, but they were sanctified and made a blessing to each heart, by prayer.

Thus, though all before the apostle, during this journey, was darkness and danger, all around him and behind him was earnest prayer to God in his behalf. Borne forward upon the current of such devotion, he was able to breast the storm, and defy all the powers of earth and hell.

7. The journey by water was soon completed, and the remainder of the distance was performed on foot. (7) *"And from Tyre we went down to Ptolemais, completing the voyage, and saluted the brethren, and remained with them one day."* If the vessel had been going forward to Cæsarea without delay, they had better have continued on board than to have traveled the distance of thirty or forty miles to that city on foot.* We conclude, therefore, that the vessel either intended lying in port for awhile, or did not intend to touch at Cæsarea.

The fact that Paul found brethren in Tyre and Ptolemais on the coast of Phenicia, where he had never preached before, reminds us once more of the dispersion of the Church in Jerusalem, and the fact that "they who were scattered abroad upon the persecution which arose about Stephen, traveled as far as Phenicia, speaking the Word to none but the Jews."†

8, 9. The single day spent with the brethren in Ptolemais was sufficient for the solemn admonitions which Paul was leaving with all the Churches, and for another painful farewell. (8) *"And the next day we departed, and went to Cæsarea. And entering into the house of Philip the evangelist, who was one of the seven, we abode with him.* (9) *Now he had four daughters, who were virgins, and who prophesied."* When we parted from Philip, after the immersion of the eunuch, he had prosecuted an evangelizing tour through Azotus and the intermediate cities, to Cæsarea.‡ It was probably while he was engaged in this tour that Peter had come to Cæsarea, and immersed the family and friends of Cornelius. When Philip arrived, he found the nucleus of a Church, and here we still find him, after a lapse of more than twenty years. He seems never to have returned to Jerusalem, to resume his position as a deacon of that Church, but accepted the providential arrangement by which he was thrown out into a wider field of usefulness, and thenceforward was known as Philip the evangelist. That he had four maiden daughters, who had the gift of prophesy, indicates the strict religious training which he had given to his family.

10–14. During the interval spent with the family of Philip, another, and the last of the prophetic warnings which Paul encountered on this journey was given, causing a scene of sorrow similar to those at Miletus and Tyre. (10) *"And while we were remaining several days, there came down from Jerusalem a certain prophet named Agabus;* (11) *and he came to us, and took Paul's girdle, and bound his own hands and feet, and said, Thus says the Holy Spirit: So shall the Jews in Jerusalem bind the man who owns this girdle, and shall deliver him into the hands of the Gentiles.* (12) *And when we heard this, both we and they of that place besought him not to go up to Jerusalem.* (13) *But Paul answered, What do you mean by weeping and breaking my heart? For I am ready not only to be bound, but also to die in Jerusalem, for the name of the Lord Jesus.* (14) *And when he would not be persuaded, we held our peace, saying, The will of the Lord be done."*

---

* Life and Ep., vol. 2, p. 232.   † Acts xi: 19.   ‡ Acts viii: 40.

Agabus was the same prophet who went from Jerusalem to Antioch, and announced the famine which caused the mission of Paul and Barnabas into Judea with a contribution for the poor.* It was a singular coincidence that the same man should now meet him, after the lapse of so many years, when entering Judea on a similar mission, and warn him of his own personal danger. The dramatic manner in which his prophesy was delivered gave Paul a more distinct conception of the afflictions which awaited him. If his traveling companions had hitherto been silent when brethren were entreating him to desist from the journey, as is implied in the narrative, their courage now failed them, and they joined in the entreaties of the brethren in Cæsarea. The fearfulness of his prospects was a sufficient trial to his own courage, when he enjoyed at least the silent sympathy of his chosen companions; but when they deserted him, and threw the weight of their influence upon the weight already too heavy for him, the effect was crushing to his heart, though the steadfastness of his purpose was not shaken. The duty imposed upon him by the fearful condition of the Church at large was paramount to all personal considerations, and he felt willing to be bound and to die in his efforts to maintain the honor of the name of the Lord Jesus by preserving the unity of his body. Upon this declaration of his sublime self-devotion, the brethren felt unable to offer another objection, and gave expression to their reluctant resignation by the remark, "The will of the Lord be done."

15, 16. (15) "*And after those days, we packed up our baggage, and went up to Jerusalem.* (16) *Some of the disciples from Cæsarea went with us, conducting us to one Mnason, a Cyprian, and an old disciple, with whom we should lodge.*" The journey had been accomplished in time for the feast of Pentecost. This is made to appear by enumerating the days spent on the journey from Philippi. Leaving that city immediately after the days of unleavened bread, which was seven days after the Passover, he reached Troas in five days, where he spent seven.† Four days were occupied in the passage from Troas to Miletus.‡ Two are sufficient to allow for the stay at Miletus.|| In three he sailed from Miletus to Patara, which place he left the same day he reached it;§ and two more days, with favorable weather, would take him to Tyre.¶ There he spent seven days, and three in the journey thence to Cæsarea.** Allowing two days more for the journey from Cæsarea to Jerusalem, we have enumerated only forty-two of the forty-nine days intervening between the Passover and Pentecost, leaving seven for the stay at the house of Philip. That the feast of Pentecost did transpire immediately after his arrival in Jerusalem, is indicated by the immense multitude of Jews then assembled there, and the presence of some from the province of Asia, who had known Paul in Ephesus.†† Nothing but the annual feasts brought together in Jerusalem the Jews from distant provinces.

17. The period which had been looked forward to for months with prayerful anxiety had now arrived, and Paul was to know, without further delay, whether or not the service which he had for Jerusalem would be accepted by the saints.‡‡ To his unspeakable relief, the

---
* Acts xi: 27–30.   † Acts xx: 6.   ‡ Acts xx: 13–15. || Com. xx: 17.   § Acts xxi: 1–2.
¶ Life and Ep , vol. 2, p. 227.   ** Acts xxi: 4–8.   †† Acts xxi: 27.   ‡‡ Rom. xv: 31.

historian was able to say, (17) "*Now when we were come to Jerusalem, the brethren received us gladly.*" If Luke had given any account of the contribution Paul was bringing, we should have expected him to say something more definite about its reception than is implied in this remark. But, as he saw fit to omit all mention of the enterprise, we are at liberty to infer, from the glad reception given to the messengers, that the gift they bore was also welcome. The main object of Paul's visit and of his prayers was now accomplished. He had finished this much of his course and his ministry with joy, and his heart was relieved from its chief anxiety. Whether the Lord would now accept his prayer for deliverance from the disobedient in Jerusalem, he felt to be a matter of minor importance.

18–26. After the general statement that they were gladly received by the brethren, Luke proceeds to state more in detail what followed. (18) "*And on the day following, Paul went in with us to James, and all the elders were present.* (19) *And having saluted them, he related particularly what God had done among the Gentiles through his ministry.* (20) *When they heard it, they glorified the Lord, and said to him, You see, brother, how many myriads of Jews there are who believe, and they are all zealous for the law.* (21) *Now they have heard concerning you, that you teach all the Jews who are among the Gentiles apostasy from Moses, telling them not to circumcise their children, nor to walk according to the customs.* (22) *What, then, is it? The multitude must by all means come together; for they will hear that you have come.* (23) *Do this, therefore, which we tell you. We have here four men who have a vow upon them.* (24) *Take them, and purify yourself with them, and bear the expenses for them, in order that they may shear their heads, and all may know that those things of which they have heard concerning you are nothing; but that you yourself also walk orderly and keep the law.* (25) *But as respects the Gentiles who have believed, we have already written, having decided that they observe no such thing, only that they keep themselves from things offered to idols, and from blood, and from things strangled, and from fornication.* (26) *Then Paul took the men, and the next day went with them into the temple purified, announcing the fulfilling of the days of purification, when an offering should be offered for each one of them.*"

This I confess to be the most difficult passage in Acts to fully understand, and to reconcile with the teaching of Paul on the subject of the Mosaic law. We shall have the exact state of the question before our minds, by inquiring, *first*, What was the exact position of the Jerusalem brethren in reference to the law? *second*, What had Paul actually taught upon the subject? and, *third*, How can the course pursued by both be reconciled to the mature apostolic teaching?

First: It is stated, in this speech, of which James was doubtless the author, that the disciples about Jerusalem were "all zealous for the law." They recognized the authority of Moses as still binding; for they complained that Paul taught "apostasy from Moses." The specifications of this apostasy were, *first*, neglect of circumcision; *second*, abandonment of "the customs." By "the customs" are meant those imposed by the law, among which, as seen in their proposition to Paul, were the Nazarite vows, with their burnt-offerings, sin-offerings, and meat-offerings;* and, as seen in Paul's epistles, abstinence from unclean meats, and the observance of Sabbath-days, holy days, new moons, and Sabbatic years.†

Second. Our inquiry into Paul's teaching on the subject must have separate reference to what he had taught before this time, and what he taught subsequently. None of his oral teachings on the subject are preserved by Luke, hence we are dependent for a knowledge of his present teaching upon those of his epistles which were written previous to this time. In none of the specifications above enumerated did he fully agree with his Jewish brethren. True, he granted the perpetuity of circumcision; yet not because he acknowledged with them the continued authority of the law, but because of the covenant with Abraham which preceded the law.‡ As for the law, he taught that it had been "a schoolmaster to lead us to Christ, that we might be justified by faith, but after faith is come, we are *no longer under* the schoolmaster;"‖ that, "now we are *delivered* from the law, being *dead* to that in which we were held;" that we are "become *dead* to the law by the body of Christ."§ In repudiating the authority of the law, he necessarily repudiated all *obligation* to observe "the customs." In reference to all these, he afterward said to the Colossians, that God had "*blotted out* the handwriting of *ordinances* which was against us, which was contrary to us, and *took it out of the way,* nailing it to the cross." "Let no man, therefore, judge you in food or in drink, or in respect of a holy day, or of the new moon, or of Sabbaths; which are a shadow of things to come, but the body is Christ."¶ While thus repudiating the *obligation* to observe the ordinances, he admitted the *innocence* of their observance, and forbade any breach of fellowship on account of it, laying down in reference to them all, this rule: "Let not him who eats, despise him who eats not; and let not him who eats not, judge him who eats."** In reference, therefore, to *meats* and *days,* he and the judaizers agreed that the Jews might observe them; but they differed as to the *ground* of this conclusion: the latter affirming that it was a matter of duty; the former holding that it was a matter of indifference.

Thus far we have omitted special mention of one custom, because its importance demands for it a separate consideration. We refer to sacrifices. It is evident, from the transaction before us, as observed above, that James and the brethren in Jerusalem regarded the offering of sacrifices as at least innocent; for they approved the course of the four Nazarites, and urged Paul to join with them in the service, though it required them to offer sacrifices, and even *sin-offerings.* They could not, indeed, very well avoid this opinion, since they admitted the continued authority of the Mosaic law. Though disagreeing with them as to the ground of their opinion, as in reference to the other customs, Paul evidently admitted the opinion itself, for he adopted their advice, and paid the expense of the sacrifices which the four Nazarites offered.

Third. The commentators uniformly agree that Paul was right, and that the rites observed on this occasion are to be referred to that class which are indifferent, and in reference to which Paul acted upon

---

* Num. vi: 13–17.   † Rom. xiv; Gal. iv: 9, 10; Col. ii: 16, 17.   ‡ See Com. xvi: 3.
‖ Gal. iii: 24, 25.   § Rom. vii: 4–6.   ¶ Col. ii: 14, 17.   ** Rom. xiv: 1–6.

the principle of being a Jew to the Jew, that he might win the Jew.* This would not be objectionable, if the proceeding had reference merely to meats and drinks, holy days, etc., to which it appears to be confined in their view; for all these were indifferent then, and are not less so at the present day. Who would say that it would now be sinful to abstain from certain meats, and observe certain days as holy? But it is far different with bloody sacrifices. If disciples, either Jewish or Gentile, should now assemble in Jerusalem, construct an altar, appoint a priesthood, and offer sin-offerings, they could but be regarded as apostates from Christ. But why should it be regarded as a crime now, if it was innocent then?

The truth is, that, up to this time, Paul had written nothing which directly conflicted with the service of the altar, and he did not yet understand the subject correctly. His mind, and those of all the brethren, were as yet in much the same condition on this subject that they were before the conversion of Cornelius, in reference to the reception of the uncircumcised into the Church. If we admit that the proposition above quoted from Galatians, affirming that "we are no longer under the law," was, when fully understood, inconsistent with the continuance of sacrifice, we make his case only the more like Peter's in regard to the Gentiles; for he announced propositions, on Pentecost, which were inconsistent with his subsequent course, until he was made to better understand the force of his own words. Peter finally discovered that he was wrong in that matter, and Paul at length discovered that he was wrong in his connection with the offerings of these Nazarites. Some years later, the whole question concerning the Aaronic priesthood and animal sacrifices was thrust more distinctly upon his mind, and the Holy Spirit made to him a more distinct revelation of the truth upon the subject, and caused him to develop it to the Churches, in Ephesians, Colossians, and especially in Hebrews. In the last-named epistle, written during his imprisonment in Rome, he exhibited the utter inefficiency of animal sacrifices; the sacrifice of Christ, once for all, as the only sufficient sin-offering; and the abrogation of the Aaronic priesthood by that of Christ, who was now the only high priest and mediator between God and man. After these developments, he could not, for any earthly consideration, have repeated the transaction with the Nazarites; for it would have been to insult the great High Priest over the house of God, by presenting, before a human priest, an offering which could not take away sin, and which would proclaim the insufficiency of the blood of the atonement. We conclude, therefore, that the procedure described in the text was inconsistent with the truth as finally developed by the apostles, but not with so much of it as was then understood by Paul. This conclusion presents but another proof that the Holy Spirit, in leading the apostles "into all the truth," did so by a gradual development running through a series of years.†

When Paul finally was enabled to understand and develop the whole truth on this subject, no doubt the opinions and prejudices of the more liberal class of Jewish disciples yielded to his clear and conclusive

---

* Bloomfield, Olshausen, Neander, Hackett, Howson, etc.
† See Com. x: 9–23; xi: 1–18.

arguments. But, doubtless, some still clung to the obsolete and unlawful service of the temple, assisting the unbelieving Jews to perpetuate it. Then came in the necessity for the destruction of their temple and city, so that it should be impossible for them to longer offer sacrifices which had been superseded. The destruction of the temple was not the *legal* termination of the Mosaic ritual; for it ceased to be legal with the death of Christ;* but this brought to an end its illegal continuance.

Before we dismiss this passage there are two more points claiming a moment's attention. First, the justness of the accusation which the brethren had heard against Paul. He had certainly taught the Jews that they were no longer *under* the law, and that "the customs" were no longer *binding*, and this was, in one sense, "apostasy from Moses." But he had not, as he was charged, taught them to *abandon* the customs; for he had insisted that they were innocent; and, in reference to circumcision, he had given no ground of offense whatever. Hence the charge, as understood by those who preferred it, was false; and it was with the utmost propriety that Paul consented to disabuse their minds, though the means he adopted for that purpose was improper.

The last point claiming attention is the nature of the purification which Paul underwent. The statement which we have rendered, he "purified himself with them," is understood, by some commentators, to mean that he took part in their vow of abstinence.† But for this meaning of the term, ἁγνίζω, there is no authority in the New Testament; everywhere else it means to *purify*, and Paul's own statement to Felix, that "they found me *purified* in the temple,"‡ in which he speaks of the same event, and uses the same word, is conclusive as to its meaning here. It will be remembered that no Jew who, like Paul, had been mingling with Gentiles, and disregarding the ceremonial cleanness of the law, was permitted to enter the inner court of the temple without being *purified*. This purification he must have undergone, and there is no evidence that he underwent any other. But it is said he purified himself "with them," which shows that they, too, were unclean. Now, when a Nazarite became unclean within the period of his vow, it was necessary that he should *purify* himself, *shear his head* on the *seventh* day after, and on the *eighth* day bring certain offerings. Then he lost the days of his vow which had preceded the uncleanness, and had to begin the count anew from the day that the offering was presented. This is fully stated in the sixth chapter of Numbers, where the law of the Nazarite is prescribed. Such was the condition of these Nazarites, as is further proved by the notice given of the "days of purification," and the mention, in the next verse below, of "*the seven* days," as of a period well known. Nazarites had no purification to perform except when they became *unclean* during their vow; and there was no period of *seven days* connected with their vow, except in the instance just mentioned. In this instance, as the head was to be sheared on the seventh day, and the offerings presented on the eighth, there were just seven whole days employed. Paul's part was to give notice to the priest of the beginning of these days, and to

---

* Eph. ii: 14-16; Col. ii: 14.   † Bloomfield, Olshausen.   ‡ Acts xxiv: 18.

pay the expenses of the offerings; but he had to purify himself before he went in for this purpose.

27–30. (27) "*Now when the seven days were about to be completed, the Jews from Asia, seeing him in the temple, aroused the whole multitude, and laid hands on him,* (28) *crying out, Men of Israel, help ! This is the man who teaches all men everywhere against the people and the law and this place, and has even brought Greeks into the temple, and polluted this holy place.* (29) *For they had previously seen Trophimus the Ephesian in the city with him, whom they thought Paul had brought into the temple.* (30) *And the whole city was moved, and the people ran together, and seizing Paul, dragged him out of the temple ; and the doors were immediately closed.*" If Paul's own brethren in Jerusalem had become prejudiced against him on account of his teaching in reference to the law, it is not surprising that the hatred of the unbelieving Jews toward him should be intense. Their treasured wrath was like a magazine, ready to explode the moment a match should be applied; and to charge him with *defiling* the holy place, which they believed that he had already *reviled* in every nation, was enough to produce the explosion. It is not the custom of mobs to investigate the charges heaped upon their victims; hence, without knowing or caring to know, whether he had really brought Trophimus into the temple, they seized him and dragged him out into the court of the Gentiles. The doors of the inner court were closed, to prevent the defilement of that holy place by the blood which was likely to be shed.

31–34. For the second time in his history the Roman authorities came to Paul's rescue from the hands of his countrymen. *(31) "*And as they were seeking to kill him, word came to the chiliarch†* *of the cohort that all Jerusalem was in an uproar,* (32) *who immediately took soldiers and centurions, and ran down upon them. And when they saw the chiliarch and the soldiers, they quit striking Paul.* (33) *Then the chiliarch drew near and seized him, and commanded him to be bound with two chains, and inquired who he was, and what he had done.* (34) *But some of the multitude cried out one thing, and some another ; and not being able to know the certainty on account of the tumult, he commanded him to be led into the castle.*" The inability of the mob to agree upon any charge against him shows the precipitancy with which they had rushed upon him, while the multiplicity of charges which they vociferated shows the intensity of their hatred. The chiliarch was indifferent through total ignorance of the case, and desired to act prudently; hence he determined to protect the prisoner, and hold him for examination under more favorable circumstances.

35–39. It was but a short distance to the castle of Antonia, which overlooked the temple inclosure, and was connected with it by a stairway. Thither the apostle was rapidly borne, the mob pressing after him. (35) "*And when he was on the stairs, he was borne by the soldiers, on account of the violence of the multitude.* (36) *For the crowd of people followed, crying out, Away with him !* (37) *And when he was about to be led into the castle, Paul said to the chiliarch, May I say something to you ? He said, Do you understand Greek ?* (38) *Are you not that*

---

* The first was in Corinth, before Gallio. Com. xviii: 14–16.
† Captain of a thousand.

ACTS XXI: 39, 40; XXII: 1-16.

Egyptian, who formerly made an insurrection, and led out into the wilderness four thousand Assassins? (39) Paul said, *I am a Jew, of Tarsus, in Cilicia; a citizen of no unknown city; and I beseech you, permit me to speak to the people.*" This conversation shows that the chiliarch was utterly ignorant of the character and history of his prisoner. The best conclusion he could form from the confused outcries of the mob was the one indicated in the question just quoted. When he learned that he was a Jew, he was still more perplexed concerning the rage of the people, and not less astonished at the coolness displayed by Paul. In the hope of learning something more definite, he at once gave him liberty to speak, and stood by, an interested hearer.

40. "*And when he gave him permission, Paul, standing upon the stairs, waved his hand to the people. And when there was general silence, he spoke to them in the Hebrew dialect, saying,*

XXII: 1, 2. (1) "*Men, brethren, and fathers, hear my defense, which I now make to you.* (2) *And when they heard that he spoke to them in the Hebrew dialect, they kept the greater quiet.*" It is happily remarked by Mr. Howson, that, had he spoken in Greek, the majority of his hearers would have understood him; but, "the sound of the holy tongue in that holy place fell like a calm upon the troubled waters." It was a mark of respect for Jewish nationality which they were not prepared to expect from Paul; and the result was, that the silence, which was only general at the waving of his hand, became universal at the utterance of his first sentence.

3-16. (3) "*And he said, I myself am a Jew; born in Tarsus of Cilicia, yet brought up in this city at the feet of Gamaliel, educated according to the strictest doctrine of the law of our fathers, and was zealous toward God as you all are this day.* (4) *I persecuted this way, even to death; binding and delivering into prisons both men and women;* (5) *as the high priest and the whole body of the elders are my witnesses: from whom, also, I received letters to the brethren, and went to Damascus, to bring those who were there bound to Jerusalem, that they might be punished.* (6) *But it came to pass, as I journeyed and was drawing near to Damascus, about noon, a great light from heaven suddenly flashed around me.* (7) *I fell to the ground, and heard a voice saying to me, Saul, Saul, why do you persecute me?* (8) *And I answered, Who art thou, Lord? He said to me, I am Jesus the Nazarene, whom you persecute.* (9) *Now, they who were with me saw the light, and were afraid; but they heard not the voice of him who spoke to me.* (10) *And I said, Lord, what shall I do? And the Lord said to me, Arise, and go into Damascus, and there it shall be told thee concerning all things which are appointed for thee to do.* (11) *And, as I could not see for the glory of that light, I was led by the hand by those who were with me, and went into Damascus.* (12) *And one Ananias, a pious man according to the law, well spoken of by all the Jews who dwelt there,* (13) *came to me, and stood, and said to me, Brother Saul, look up. And that moment I looked up upon him.* (14) *And he said, The God of our fathers has chosen you to know his will, and to see the Just One, and to hear the voice of his mouth.* (15) *For you shall be a witness for him to all men, of what you have seen and heard.* (16) *And now, why do you tarry? Arise, and be immersed, and wash away your sins, calling on the name of the Lord.*" Such portions of this speech as are necessary to a full understanding of Paul's conversion, we have considered in commenting on the ninth chapter. The words of Ananias, "Arise and be immersed," probably demand a moment's additional notice, on account of the use which has been made of them by many pedobaptist writers and speakers of an inferior grade. It is urged that the words should be rendered, "Standing up, be baptized;" and that they indicate that Paul was baptized on the spot, without leaving the house. We might admit the rendering without granting the conclusion; for the command to be baptized required him to do whatever was necessary to that act. If the act was immersion, it required him to go where it could be performed, however great the distance, and the words are entirely consistent with that idea. If he was to be immersed, he must, of necessity, arise from his prostrate or sitting position for that purpose. If he was to be sprinkled, he might as well have remained, as candidates for that ceremony now commonly do, upon his knees.

17–21. After this brief account of his course of persecution and his conversion, he advances to the events which occurred upon his return to Jerusalem, and which led to that peculiar ministry that had excited the hatred of his hearers. (17) *"And it came to pass, when I returned to Jerusalem, and was praying in the temple, that I was in a trance, (18) and saw him saying to me, Make haste, and depart quickly out of Jerusalem, for they will not receive your testimony concerning me. (19) And I said, Lord, they know that I was imprisoning and beating in every synagogue those who believe on thee, (20) and when the blood of thy witness, Stephen, was shed, I myself was standing by, and consenting to his death, and guarding the raiment of those who slew him. (21) And he said to me, Depart, for I will send you far hence to the Gentiles."*

By allowing Paul to speak, Lysias expected to learn something about the charges against him, supposing that he would address himself immediately and strictly to a defense. What must have been his surprise, then, to hear him, after asking the people to hear his defense, proceed with a narrative, the bearing of which upon the case was so obscure? It must be confessed that the speech afforded very little of the light that he was seeking; and even to men who are better prepared to understand it than he, it is still a source of astonishment. Here is a man in the hands of a heathen soldiery, with a prison-door opening behind him, and before him a mob thirsting for his blood, whom to appease would save him from prison, and, perhaps, from death, yet appearing to be utterly oblivious of the danger which surrounded him, and though permitted to speak, making not the slightest effort to obtain release. He could most truthfully have denied bringing Greeks into the temple, or speaking improperly of the people, the law, or that holy place; but he was so far elevated above all selfish considerations, that he desired no vindication of himself not involving a vindication of the cause he was pleading. He saw before him a deluded multitude rushing blindly to destruction, and though they were thirsting for his own blood, he pitied them, and resolved to give them light. Under the smart of the bruises they had inflicted on him, and amid their wild outcries, he remembered

ACTS XXII: 22-29.

when he once took part in similar mobs, and the blood of Stephen rose up before his vision. This enabled him to excuse their rage, and, as the vision of Christ glorified, which he had witnessed on the road to Damascus, had changed him from a persecutor to a disciple, he resolved to try its effect upon them. He did not altogether miscalculate its power; for they listened to the whole account of his conversion with profound attention. The narrative demonstrated the divine authority of Jesus, and enabled Paul to assume, as a basis for his further argument, that it was proper to do whatever he might command. He then proceeds to account for his going to the Gentiles. It was not my own choice, for I desired to stay in Jerusalem. But the Lord commanded me in a vision to leave the city. I even remonstrated against his decision, when he peremptorily commanded, "Depart, for I will send you far hence to the Gentiles."

22-24. When he reached this point in his discourse, he appeared to the mob about to *vindicate* the course which they condemned as criminal, instead of *apologizing* for it, and their rage was renewed. (22) "*Now they heard him up to this word, then raised their voices and said, Away with such a fellow from the earth! For it is not fit that he should live.* (23) *And as they were shouting, and tossing up their garments, and casting dust into the air,* (24) *the chiliarch commanded him to be led into the castle, saying that he should be examined by scourging, in order that he might know on what account they cried out so against him.*" The idea of scourging a man who is assailed by a mob, to make him confess the cause for which he is assailed, is most abhorrent to all proper sense of justice, yet it prevailed in the most enlightened heathen nations of antiquity. Rome, it is true, exempted from its effects all who enjoyed the rights of citizenship; but the existence of such a distinction, in a matter in which all human beings should have equal rights, is a further proof of their ignorance of the true principles of public justice. To the enlightening and rectifying influence of Christianity, modern nations are indebted for many happy changes in jurisprudence.

25-29. When Paul was led within the castle, the executioner made immediate preparation for his cruel work. (25) "*And as he was bending him forward with the straps,** *Paul said to the centurion, who was standing by, Is it lawful for you to scourge a man who is a Roman, and uncondemned?* (26) *When the centurion heard this, he went and told the chiliarch, saying, Take heed what you are about to do, for this man is a Roman.* (27) *Then the chiliarch came and said to him, Tell me, are you a Roman?* *And he said, Yes.* (28) *And the chiliarch answered, With a great sum I obtained this citizenship. And Paul said, But I was born so.* (29) *Then they who were about to examine him immediately departed from him; and the chiliarch was alarmed, when he knew that he was a Roman, and that he had bound him.*" Previous to applying the scourge, the victim was bent forward upon a reclining post, to which he was bound by straps. It was this binding which caused the alarm of the chiliarch, and not the binding of his arms with chains. The latter was legal, and hence Paul remained so bound,† but the former was illegal. It was just at the critical moment,

---
* For the correctness of this rendering see Bloomfield, *in loco*. † Acts xxii: 30; xxvi: 29.

when he was bent forward upon the post, and the straps were being adjusted, that the quiet assertion of citizenship caused his release, and struck terror into the heart of the officer. Notwithstanding this exemption was extended only to a favored few, we can but admire the majesty of a law, which, in a remote province, and within the walls of a prison, suddenly released a prisoner from the whipping-post, by the simple declaration, "I am a Roman citizen!"

30. Lysias was disposed to do his duty, but he experienced great difficulty in deciding what it was. He had first inquired of the mob; had then heard a speech from Paul; and had now gone as far as he dared toward the trial by scourging; yet he knew nothing more about the charges against his prisoner than he did at first. He determined to make one more effort. (30) *" On the next day, desiring to know the certainty as to what he was accused of by the Jews, he released him from his bonds, and commanded the high priests and the whole Sanhedrim to come together, and brought Paul down, and placed him before them."*

XXIII: 1, 2. No sooner had the prisoner and the Sanhedrim come face to face, than the chiliarch must have perceived that he was again to be disappointed in his efforts to understand the case; for, instead of preferring formal charges against Paul, the proceedings were opened by calling upon him to defend himself. (1) *" Then Paul, looking earnestly on the Sanhedrim, said: I have lived in all good conscience before God until this day. (2) Then the high priest Ananias commanded those who stood by him, to smite him in the mouth."* No doubt the blow was as prompt as the word. The interruption was as unexpected as it was exasperating.

3-5. For once in the history of his persecutions, the provocation was too great for Paul, and found vent in a burst of anger. (3) *" Then said Paul to him, God shall smite thee, thou whitewashed wall. And do you sit to judge me according to the law, and command me to be smitten contrary to the law? (4) But those who were standing by said, Do you revile God's high priest? (5) Paul said, I did not know, brethren, that he was the high priest; for it is written, Thou shalt not speak evil of the ruler of thy people."* The flash of anger was but momentary. No sooner were the words spoken than his habitual self-control regained its ascendency. He frankly admits that he had done wrong, but excuses himself by the fact that he knew not that it was the high priest. If he had been disposed to further excuse himself, by urging that the high priest deserved all he had said of him, his plea would have been true, but insufficient. For how can we return good for evil, if we return to men their deserts? It were well if his example should be imitated by all disciples who meet with injustice at the hands of their rulers.

6-10. The presence in which Paul stood was not unfamiliar to him. He doubtless remembered the faces of many in the Sanhedrim, and was intimately acquainted with the party feelings which often distracted their councils, and which had been known to stain the streets of Jerusalem with blood.* Seeing that they were determined not to do him justice, he resolved to take advantage of their party feuds in order to secure his own safety. (6) *" But when Paul knew that one*

* Raphall, Post Biblical History of the Jews, vol. 2. p. 132.

part were Sadducees, and the other Pharisees, he cried out in the Sanhedrim, Brethren, I am a Pharisee, the son of a Pharisee. Concerning the hope of the resurrection of the dead I am called in question. (7) And when he had said this, there arose a dissension between the Pharisees and the Sadducees, and the multitude was divided. (8) For the Sadducees say there is no resurrection, nor angel, nor spirit. But the Pharisees confess both. (9) And there arose a great outcry; and the scribes, who were of the Pharisees' party, arose and contended, saying, We find no evil in this man. And if an angel or a spirit has spoken to him, let us not fight against God. (10) And there being a great dissension, the chiliarch, fearing that Paul would be torn in pieces by them, commanded the soldiers to go down and take him by force from their midst, and lead him into the castle." It will be observed, that in stating the difference between the two parties, Luke uses the term *both* when the reference is to three specifications, viz.: resurrection, angel, and spirit. This arose, no doubt, from the fact that the three specifications are really combined in two, as the existence of angels or spirits involves but the one question of the existence of purely spiritual beings.

Under ordinary circumstances, it is not probable that so violent a dissension could have been so easily excited. The circumstance is indicative of an unusual exasperation of the parties just preceding this event. Such a state of things, combined with the complete agreement declared by Paul with the Pharisees on the points at issue, naturally inclined them to favor his release. He declared this agreement in strong terms, asserting not only that he was a Pharisee, but the son of a Pharisee, and that it was for *the* hope peculiar to the party that he was arraigned as a criminal. They saw that the establishment of his doctrine would certainly be the ruin of the opposing sect, and losing sight, for a moment, of its effects upon their own party; forgetting, too, the ill-founded charge against Paul, in reference to the law and the temple, they declared that they could find no fault in the man. Perhaps, also, the awkward position they were in with reference to the proof of those charges rendered them somewhat willing to find an excuse for admitting his innocence. But the slightest hint, on their part, of his innocence, was sufficient to arouse the Sadducees, because they saw that it was prompted chiefly by hatred to themselves. On the part of the Sadducees, the two most violent passions to which they were subject, hatred toward the disciples and jealousy toward the Pharisees, combined to swell the uproar which broke up the deliberations of the assembly. Paul was near being a victim to the storm which he had raised, when the Roman soldiery came to his rescue. Lysias was once more disappointed in his efforts to learn the truth about his case, and must have been in greater perplexity than ever, as he commanded the soldiers to lead him back into the castle.

11. If we had some epistle from Paul's pen, written at this time, it would tell of great distress and despondency; for such a state of mind is clearly indicated by an event which now transpired. (11) *"And the night following, the Lord stood by him and said, Take courage, Paul, for as you have testified concerning me in Jerusalem, so you must also testify in Rome."* It is not to be presumed that this

personal appearance of the Lord to encourage him occurred when it was not needed, or when encouragement could be supplied in an ordinary way. It is quite certain, therefore, that Paul's spirit was greatly burdened that night. The long-dreaded bonds and afflictions, which had hung like a dark cloud before him on his journey from Corinth to Jerusalem, had now at last fallen upon him. Thus far, since his arrest, he may have been cheered by the hope that the fervent prayers of himself and many brethren, which, in anticipation of these calamities, had been urged at the throne of favor for months past, would prove effectual for his deliverance, and for the realization of his long-cherished desire to visit Rome.* But his speeches before the mob and the Sanhedrim had only exasperated his enemies, who were now, more than ever, intent upon his destruction; and his jailer, though disposed to do justice, knew not what to do but to keep him in prison. In whatever direction he could look, prison walls or a bloody grave stood before him, and hedged up his way, either to Rome or to any other field of future usefulness. But just at the proper moment to save him from despair, the solemn assurance is given, that his long-continued prayers would yet be answered, and he should preach the Word in Rome as he had done in Jerusalem. In tracing the fulfillment of this promise, we shall witness a remarkable illustration of the workings of providence in answer to prayer.

12–16. The light did not immediately dawn upon his prospects, but the darkness continued for a while to grow deeper. (12) *"And when it was day some of the Jews made a conspiracy, and bound themselves under a curse, saying that they would neither eat nor drink until they had killed Paul. (13) And there were more than forty who made this agreement. (14) They went to the high priests and elders, and said, We have bound ourselves under a great curse, that we will eat nothing till we have killed Paul. (15) Now then, do you, with the Sanhedrim, notify the chiliarch to bring him down to you to-morrow, as though you would inquire more accurately concerning him, and we, before he comes near, are ready to slay him. (16) But the son of Paul's sister heard of their lying in wait, and came and entered into the castle, and told Paul."* It is difficult for a conspiracy of this kind, requiring the consultation of so many persons, to be concocted and executed with perfect secrecy. Especially is it so when the intended victim is one about whom the whole community is, at the time, intensely excited. It is not at all surprising, therefore, that some of Paul's many friends heard of it, and that his nephew undertook the dangerous task of communicating it to him. He at once saw, that, notwithstanding the assurance of safety given the night before, the danger of his situation was more alarming than ever. The chiliarch could not well refuse to grant so reasonable a request; and if it be granted, his doom is sealed. If the Pharisees who had befriended him in the Sanhedrim had not become indifferent to his fate, they had been outwitted, so that the Sadducees were about to make the request in the name of the whole Sanhedrim without consulting them.

17–22. A moment's reflection was sufficient to show Paul that his

* Rom. xv: 30–32.

only hope of safety was in the chiliarch, and, therefore, he at once had the facts communicated to him. (17) "*Then Paul called to him one of the centurions, and said, Lead this young man to the chiliarch; for he has something to tell him.* (18) *He then took him and led him to the chiliarch, and said, The prisoner, Paul, called me to him and requested me to lead this young man to you, who has something to say to you.* (19) *The chiliarch took him by the hand, and drawing aside in private, asked him, What is it that you have to tell me?* (20) *And he said, The Jews have agreed to request you that you bring down Paul into the Sanhedrim tomorrow, as though they would inquire more accurately concerning him.* (21) *But do not be persuaded by them; for there lie in wait for him more than forty men of them, who have bound themselves under a curse neither to eat nor drink until they have slain him. And they are now prepared, expecting a promise from you.* (22) *Then the chiliarch dismissed the young man, charging him to tell no one that you have made known these things to me.*" The injunction of secrecy was prompted in part by a desire for the young man's safety; but chiefly by an unwillingness that the Jews should know the real cause of the step he was about to take. If they should discover that their machinations could influence his policy, they might be emboldened to give him further trouble.

23–30. There were at least three lines of policy between which the chiliarch could have chosen. If he had been disposed to gratify the Jews, he might have given Paul up to their malice, without probability of being known to his superiors as accessory to the murder. If he had preferred to defy their power, and display his own, he might have sent him down to the Sanhedrim under a strong guard. Or if he desired to protect Paul, yet to avoid giving unnecessary offense to the Jews, he might send him away that night before their request was laid before him. It reflects credit upon his character that he chose the course which both justice and prudence dictated. (23) "*And he called to him two of the centurions, and said, Make ready two hundred soldiers, and seventy horsemen, and two hundred spearmen, to go to Cæsarea at the third hour of the night,* (24) *and provide beasts, in order that they may mount Paul and take him to Felix the governor.* (25) *And he wrote a letter in this form:* (26) *Claudius Lysias to the most excellent governor Felix, greeting.* (27) *This man was seized by the Jews, and was about to be killed by them, when I came with the soldiery and rescued him, having learned that he was a Roman.* (28) *And desiring to know the cause for which they accused him, I led him down into their Sanhedrim,* (29) *and found him accused concerning questions of their law, but having nothing laid to his charge worthy of death or of bonds.* (30) *And it being disclosed to me that a plot against the man was about to be executed by the Jews, I immediately sent him to you, commanding his accusers to say before you what they have against him. Farewell.*" But for one misrepresentation in this letter, there would be nothing discreditable to Lysias in this whole affair. He had acted like a just and prudent man in managing a difficult case; but in reporting to his superior, he so states the facts as to give himself credit to which he was not entitled. He states that his first rescue of Paul was prompted by the fact that he was a Roman citizen; whereas, in truth, he knew nothing of Paul's citizenship till after he had seized him and had prepared to scourge him. Thus a motive was claimed which was not real, and a fault which he had committed was suppressed. When we remember, however, that it is a common fault with military commanders to make the most favorable reports of their achievements, we are not disposed to give Lysias a low rank among his compeers for veracity.

The statement that he had commanded Paul's accusers to say before Felix what they had against him, was not strictly true; for, at the time of writing, he had given no such command. But it was not intended to deceive the governor; for he intended to issue the order before the letter could be received. When this order was issued, the Jews were bitterly disappointed, and the forty conspirators had a prospect of a good long fast. They naturally felt some ill-will toward Lysias, as we shall see manifested hereafter,* for snatching their victim out of their hands.

The letter also shows, that though Lysias could not understand the exact nature of the charges against Paul, he knew that they had reference to the Jewish law, and was satisfied that what they accused him of was not worthy either of death or of imprisonment. Under this conviction, if he had not been constrained to send him away for safety, he would, probably, have released him.

31–35. (31) "*Then the soldiers, according to what was commanded them, took Paul and conducted him by night to Antipatris,* (32) *and, on the next day, they returned to the castle, leaving the horsemen to go forward with him.* (33) *They went to Cæsarea, delivered the epistle to the governor, and presented Paul before him.* (34) *And when the governor read the epistle, he asked of what province he was, and, learning that he was from Cicilia,* (35) *he said, I will hear you when your accusers are also come. And he commanded him to be kept under guard in Herod's palace.*" This was a palace erected by Herod the Great, who built Caesarea.†

When the troops guarding Paul had passed beyond the immediate vicinity of Jerusalem, there was no further use for the powerful force of infantry; hence the return of the four hundred soldiers and spearmen. The distinction between these two classes is, that those called *soldiers* belonged to the regular Roman legions, while the spearmen were light-armed troops attached to the legions.

This incident in Paul's history has been made to bear a part in the controversy as to whether military service is compatible with Christianity. It is urged that Paul could not consistently accept the services of an army of four hundred and seventy men to protect his life from a Jewish mob, unless he acknowledged the rightfulness of military service. But the facts in the case are not suitable to the argument. He did not, in the exercise of his freedom, voluntarily call for military interference; but the military had already interfered, without consulting his wishes, and taken violent possession of him; and his request was, that they should exercise the power which they had chosen to assume, for his safety rather than for his destruction. If a man were confined within the den of a gang of robbers, he might, with all propriety, request them to keep him out of the reach of another gang who were seeking his life. Such a request would be no

* Acts xxiv: 7.   † Jos. Ant. xv: 3, 6.

more an indorsement of highway robbery than Paul's request, expressed through his nephew, was an indorsement of military service. There is not an instance on record in which the apostles ever called for military interference in their times of suffering and persecution.

XXIV: 1. When the Jews were commanded by Lysias to present their accusation before Felix, though disappointed in their first plot, they still hoped to accomplish his destruction, and made no delay in following up the prosecution. (1) "*Now, after five days, Ananias the high priest, with the elders and a certain orator named Tertullus, came down, and informed the governor against Paul.*" It is most natural to count these five days from the time that Paul left Jerusalem, as that was the date at which the Jews were informed by Lysias of the transfer of the case.

2-9. The orator, Tertullus, was employed to plead the case before Felix, and the high priest and elders appeared as witnesses. (2) "*And when he was called, Tertullus began to accuse him, saying:* (3) *Seeing that by you we have attained to great tranquillity, and a prosperous administration is effected for this nation by your foresight, in every respect and in every place, we accept it, most excellent Felix, with all thankfulness.* (4) *But that I may not delay you too long, I entreat you to hear us, in your clemency, a few words.* (5) *For we have found this man a pest, exciting sedition among all the Jews throughout the world, and a ringleader of the sect of the Nazarenes.* (6) *He also attempted to profane the temple; when we seized him, and wished to judge him according to our own law.* (7) *But Lysias the chiliarch came, and with great violence snatched him out of our hands,* (8) *and commanded his accusers to come before you. From him you yourself may be able, by examination, to obtain knowledge of all these things of which we accuse him.* (9) *And the Jews assented, saying that these things were so.*" The complimentary words with which this speech is introduced were not undeserved by Felix; for he had restored tranquillity to the country, when it was disturbed, first by hordes of robbers; afterward by organized bands of Assassins, and, more recently, by that Egyptian for whom Lysias at first mistook Paul.* In suppressing all these disturbances, his administration had been prosperous.

The accusation against Paul, sustained by the testimony of the Jews, contained three specifications. It charged him, *first*, with exciting the Jews to sedition; *second*, with being the ringleader of the sect of Nazarenes; *third*, with profaning the temple. Tertullus also took occasion to vent his indignation against Lysias, for interfering by violence, as he falsely alleged against him, with the judicial proceedings of the Sanhedrim. Finally, he asserts that Felix would be able, if he would examine Lysias, to gain from his lips a knowledge of all of which they were now informing him.

10-21. (10) "*Then Paul answered, (the governor nodding to him to speak): Knowing that you have been for many years a judge for this nation, I do the more cheerfully defend myself:* (11) *for you are able to know that there are not more than twelve days since I went up to worship in Jerusalem.* (12) *And neither in the temple, nor in the synagogues, nor about the*

* Jos. Ant. B. 20, ch. viii: par. 5. Wars, B. 13.

city, did they find me disputing with any one, or exciting sedition among the multitude; (13) *neither are they able to prove the things of which they accuse me.* (14) *But this I confess to you, that according to the way which they call a sect, I so worship the God of my fathers, believing all things which are in the law, and those written by the prophets,* (15) *having hope toward God, which they themselves also entertain, that there is to be a resurrection of the dead, both of the just and the unjust.* (16) *And in this do I exercise myself to have always a conscience void of offense toward God and man.* (17) *Now after many years, I came to present alms to my nation, and offerings,* (18) *in the midst of which, certain Jews from Asia found me in the temple, purified, not with a multitude, nor with tumult.* (19) *They ought to be here before you and accuse me, if they have any thing against me.* (20) *Or let these themselves say if they found any wrong in me when I was standing before the Sanhedrim,* (21) *except in reference to this one sentence which I uttered when standing among them, Concerning the resurrection of the dead, I am called in question by you this day."*

This speech contains a distinct reply to each specification made by Tertullus. In answer to the charge of stirring up sedition, he shows first, that it had been only twelve days since he went up to Jerusalem. As it had now been five days since he left there, and he had been in prison one day previous to leaving, his previous stay there could have been only six days, which would have afforded no suffcient time for stirring up sedition. Moreover, they could not prove that he was engaged even in disputation with any one, in the temple, in the synagogues, or in any part of the city. As to being a ringleader of the sect of the Nazarenes, he frankly confesses that he belongs to what they call a sect: yet he believes all the law and the prophets, hopes for a resurrection of the dead, and is habitually struggling to lead a conscientious life. Finally, in reference to the charge of profaning the temple, implying disrespect for the Jewish people, he declares that the very object of his visit to Jerusalem was to bear alms to the people; and that when the Jews from Asia seized him in the temple, he was purified, and engaged about alms-giving, and the offerings of the temple. In conclusion, he notes the significant fact, that those who first seized him, and knew what he was doing, were not there to testify; while he challenges those who were present to state a single act of his that was wrong, unless it were the very heinous offense of declaring that he believed, with the great mass of the Jews, in the resurrection of the dead. This last point was made, and presented in the ironical form which it bears, in order to show Felix that it was party jealousy which instigated his Sadducee prosecutors.

22. His defense, though he had no witnesses present to prove his statements, had the desired effect upon Felix. (22) *"And when Felix heard these things, knowing more accurately concerning that way, he put them off, and said, When Lysias the chiliarch comes down, I will thoroughly examine the matters between you."* In this decision he took Tertullus at his word; for he had already said that he could learn all about the affair by examining Lysias. But the decision is attributed to his "knowing more accurately concerning that way," showing that he had come to the same conclusion with Lysias, that Paul was

ACTS XXIV: 23-27.

accused merely about questions of the Jewish law,* and not of crime against Roman law.

23. When the Jews were dismissed, if Felix had possessed a strict regard for justice, he would have released Paul. As it was, he only relaxed the rigor of his previous confinement. (23) *"And he commanded the centurion that Paul should be guarded, but have relaxation, and to forbid none of his friends to minister to him or visit him."* His confinement was now the least rigorous which was considered compatible with safe-keeping. He was under what was called the military custody, being placed in charge of a soldier, whose left arm was chained to Paul's right, and who was responsible with his own life for the safety of his prisoner. The guards were relieved at regular intervals, and the "relaxation" allowed Paul was, probably, an occasional release from the chain.†

24. *"Now, after some days. Felix came, with his wife Drusilla, who was a Jewess, and sent for Paul, and heard him concerning the faith in Christ."* Drusilla, according to Josephus, was a daughter of Herod Agrippa, whose persecutions of the apostles, and miserable death, we have considered in commenting on the twelfth chapter. She was a woman of remarkable beauty, the lawful wife of Azizus, king of Emesa, but was now living in adulterous intercourse with Felix.‡ Concerning Felix, Tacitus testifies, that "with every kind of cruelty and lust, he exercised the authority of a king with the temper of a slave."||

25. Under the summons to speak concerning the faith in Christ, Paul was at liberty to choose the special topic of discourse, and did so with direct reference to the character of his hearers. (25) *"And as he reasoned concerning righteousness and temperance, and judgment to come, Felix, being full of fear, answered, Go your way for this time, and when I have a convenient season, I will call for you."* The common version, "Felix trembled," may be true, but it is claiming more for the effect of Paul's discourse than is asserted by Luke. He was "filled with fear," which shows that Paul addressed him on these appropriate topics, not in a spirit of bravado, but in that earnest and solemn strain which alone can penetrate the heart. This feeling was the beginning necessary to a change of life; but lust and ambition smothered the kindling fires of conscience, and the common excuse of alarmed but impenitent sinners was urged to get rid of the too faithful monitor. It is a sad warning to all who thus procrastinate, that to neither Felix nor Drusilla did the season ever come which they thought convenient to listen to such preaching. Felix was soon dismissed in disgrace from his office; and Drusilla, with a son by Felix, perished in that eruption of Mount Vesuvius which ingulfed the cities of Pompeii and Herculaneum.§

26, 27. True to the character which Tacitus attributes to Felix, Luke adds that (26) *"Hoping also that money would be given to him by Paul, so that he would release him, he therefore sent for him the oftener, and conversed with him. (27) But after two years Felix received Portius Festus as a successor; and wishing to do the Jews a favor, Felix left*

---

* Comp. xxiii: 29. † Life and Ep., vol. 2, p. 288. ‡ Ant. xx: 17.
|| Hist., B. v, ch. 9. § Jos. Ant. xx: 17.

Paul bound." Having learned, from Paul's own lips, that he had been up to Jerusalem to bear alms from distant Churches to the poor, and knowing something, perhaps, of the general liberality of the disciples toward one another, he could have no doubt, judging them according to the usage of the age, that they would be willing to purchase Paul's freedom at a high price. That it was not done, shows that the disciples had too elevated a standard of morality to buy from a corrupt judge release from even unjust and protracted imprisonment.

These two years, if we judge from the silence of history, were the most inactive of Paul's career. There are no epistles which bear this date; and though his friends and brethren had free access to him, we have no recorded effects of their interviews with him. The only moments in which he emerges into our view, from the obscurity of his prison, are those in which he appeared before his judges. We shall, on this account, contemplate his conduct on these occasions with the deeper interest.

XXV: 1–5. The long imprisonment of Paul seems not in the least to have moderated the hatred of his enemies; but upon the change of governorship they renewed their efforts for his destruction. (1) *"Now when Festus had come into the province, after three days he went up from Cæsarea to Jerusalem.* (2) *And the high priest and the chief men of the Jews informed him against Paul, and besought him,* (3) *requesting as a favor against him, that he would send for him to Jerusalem, preparing an ambush to kill him on the way.* (4) *But Festus answered that Paul should be kept in Cæsarea, and that he himself would shortly depart thither.* (5) *Let the influential men among you, said he, go down with me, and if there is any thing wrong in this man, accuse him."* He further told them, as we learn from his speech to Agrippa,* that it was contrary to Roman law to condemn a man to death before he had an opportunity for defense, face to face with his accusers. All this shows that Festus was, at this time, disposed to see justice done. He, of course, knew nothing of the plot to waylay Paul: for they kept this purpose concealed, while they professed another.

6–8. He made no delay in granting them the promised hearing. (6) *"And when he had remained among them not more than ten days, he went down to Cæsarea, and the next day sat upon his judgment-seat, and commanded Paul to be brought.* (7) *And when he arrived, the Jews who had come down from Jerusalem stood around, bringing many and heavy charges against Paul, which they were not able to prove:* (8) *while he answered in defense, Neither against the law of the Jews, nor against the temple, nor against Cæsar have I at all offended."* The specifications embraced in this defense are the same as in the defense against the speech of Tertullus before Felix, showing that the charges were still the same. Being a "ringleader of the sect of Nazarenes" was his sin against the law; the false imputation of taking Greeks into the temple, his sin against that holy place; and the excitement of sedition among the Jews, his sin against Cæsar. In the last specification, reference was had to the mobs which the Jews were in the habit of exciting against him, whose crimes were thus charged upon him.

* Verse 16.

9. The accusers not being able to prove their charges, and the prisoner having plead not guilty to each specification, he should have been unconditionally released. But Festus, notwithstanding the fairness of his answer to their demands in Jerusalem, was now disposed to yield to the clamor of the Jews. (9) *But Festus, wishing to do the Jews a favor, answered Paul and said, Are you willing to go up to Jerusalem, there to be judged concerning these things before me?"* It is possible that Festus still knew nothing of the plot to murder Paul by the roadside; but he knew that the Jews desired his death, and he here exhibited a willingness to give them the opportunity which they desired.

10, 11. The purpose of the Jews was well understood by Paul. He remembered the purpose of the similar request preferred before Claudius Lysias, and perceived that his only safety was in frustrating their present attempt. Fortunately, the very imprisonment which exposed him to danger also furnished the means of his safety. (10) *Then Paul said, I am standing at Cæsar's judgment-seat, where I ought to be judged. To the Jews I have done no wrong, as you yourself very well know.* (11) *If I am a wrong-doer, and have committed any thing worthy of death, I refuse not to die. But if there is nothing in these things of which they accuse me, no man is able to deliver me up to them. I APPEAL TO CÆSAR."* This appeal every Roman citizen had the right to make, and it required a transfer of the case to the imperial court in Rome. The statement. "I stand at Cæsar's judgment-seat," was intended to justify him in refusing to be taken for trial away from Cæsarea, which was the appointed capital of the province where the courts were properly held.

His appeal to Cæsar, like his communication to Lysias, which secured his rescue in Jerusalem, is claimed as a sanction of military power. But, like that, it is only a demand made upon the military power which was holding him in unjust confinement, not to add to this injustice the crime of yielding him up to assassination. It is not an appeal from a free man to military power for protection; neither was there any necessity for the use of violence in granting his request on either occasion.

12. This appeal put an end to the trial, as it did to the murderous hopes of Paul's enemies. (12) *" Then Festus, having conferred with his council, answered, You have appealed to Cæsar ; to Cæsar you shall go."* The conference with his advisers was probably in reference to Paul's right to make the appeal; for he would hardly have dared, if the right was unquestioned, to hesitate about allowing it. His answer indicates some irritation under the severe rebuke of Paul's last speech.

13. The custom of extending congratulations to men newly inducted into high office, which has prevailed in every age of the world, led to the next important incidents of Paul's confinement in Cæsarea. (13) *" Now when some days had passed, King Agrippa and Bernice came to Cæsarea to salute Festus."* This Agrippa was the son of the Herod who murdered the Apostle James. He was, at this time, king of Chalcis, but afterward of Galilee.* Bernice was his sister. She had been married to her uncle, Herod, former king of Chalcis, but he had died, and she was still a widow. She afterward married Polemo, king of

* Jos. Ant. xx: 7, 1; and 8, 4.

Cilicia.* Like nearly all the Herod family, both male and female, she was licentious and ambitious. But she and Agrippa, being Jews by birth, were better able to understand Paul's case than Festus.

14–21. Festus knew that the charges against Paul had reference to the Jewish law; but he still had not a sufficient understanding of the case to report it intelligibly to the emperor, as he now had to do, under Paul's appeal. He determined, therefore, to obtain the benefit of Agrippa's more familiar acquaintance with Jewish affairs. (14) *"And when they had passed many days there, Festus set forth before the king the facts concerning Paul, saying, There is a certain man left a prisoner by Felix, (15) concerning whom, when I was in Jerusalem, the high priests and elders of the Jews informed me, demanding judgment against him. (16) To whom I answered, that it is not the custom of the Romans to deliver any man up to death before the accused has the accusers face to face, and has an opportunity for defense concerning the accusation. (17) Then they came hither, and I, making no delay, sat on the judgment-seat the next day, and commanded the man to be brought: (18) concerning whom, when the accusers stood up, they brought no charge of such things as I supposed. (19) But they had against him certain questions concerning their own demon-worship, and concerning a certain Jesus who had died, whom Paul affirmed to be alive. (20) And I, being perplexed in the dispute about this matter, asked if he wished to go to Jerusalem, and there be judged concerning these things. (21) But Paul made an appeal to be kept for the examination of Augustus, and I commanded him to be kept till I shall send him to Cæsar."* From this speech it appears that the perplexity of Festus was not so much in reference to the main issue between the Jews and Paul, as in reference to the bearing which the case had upon Roman law. He discovered that the main issue between the parties had reference to that "Jesus who had died, and whom Paul affirmed to be alive." This Jesus being claimed by Paul as an object of worship, he supposed it was an instance of that demon-worship, or worship of dead men deified, which was common among the Greeks and Romans. It is for this reason that he characterizes all their charges against him as "certain questions concerning their *demon-worship.*" By overlooking the exact mental status of the speaker, and the etymological force of the term δεισιδαιμονία, commentators have failed to give it the proper meaning both here and in chapter xvii: 22.

22. It is not probable that this was the first time that Agrippa had heard either of Paul or of Jesus. No doubt he had heard much of both, and had some curiosity to hear more. The singular circumstances which now surrounded Paul added much to his curiosity, and afforded the means of gratifying it. (22) *"Then Agrippa said to Festus, I wish to hear the man myself. To-morrow, said he, you shall hear him."*

23–27. (23) *" On the next day, therefore, Agrippa and Bernice having come with much pomp, and entered into the audience-chamber, with the chiliarchs and the prominent men of the city, at the command of Festus Paul was brought forth. (24) Then Festus said, King Agrippa, and all men who are here present with us, you see the man concerning whom all the multitude of the Jews have dealt with me, both in Jerusalem and here,*

* Jos. Ant. xix: 9, 1; xx: 7, 3.

crying out that he ought not to live any longer. (25) *Now I perceived that he had done nothing worthy of death; but he himself having appealed to Cæsar, I determined to send him,* (26) *concerning whom I have nothing certain to write to my lord. Wherefore, I have brought him before you, and especially before thee, King Agrippa, that, after examination had, I may have something to write.* (27) *For it seems to me unreasonable to send a prisoner, and not to designate the charges against him."* Festus belonged to one peculiar class of men, who found it difficult to decide how to treat Christians. The bigoted Jews, whose national prejudices were assailed by the new preachers, were prompt to decide that "they ought not to live any longer." The blind devotees of heathen worship, like those in Philippi and Ephesus, were of the same opinion; especially when the new doctrine came into conflict with their worldly interests. The firm friend of impartial justice, such as Gallio, could easily see that they were unjustly persecuted. But to the skeptical politician, like Festus, who regarded all religion as a mere superstitious homage paid to dead heroes, and who aimed to so administer government as to be popular with the most powerful class of his subjects, it was a more difficult question. He saw clearly that Paul was guilty of nothing worthy of death or of bonds; therefore, he would not consent that the Jews should kill him; yet he was equally unwilling to offend them by releasing him. He was incapable, from his worldly and selfish nature, of appreciating Paul's noble devotion to the good of humanity, and equally unable to understand the enmity of the Jews toward him. He must now, of necessity, send him to the emperor, but he confessed that he had no good reason to give the emperor for doing so, and was about to do an unreasonable act. In this predicament it was quite natural that he should call for the advice of Agrippa.

XXVI: 1–3. Festus having stated the case, and the assembly being in waiting, the king assumed the presidency of the assembly. (1) *" Then Agrippa said to Paul, You are permitted to speak for yourself. Then Paul stretched forth his hand, and offered his defense:* (2) *I think myself happy, King Agrippa, because I shall defend myself this day before you, touching all the things of which I am accused by the Jews;* (3) *especially as you are acquainted with all the customs and questions among the Jews. Wherefore, I beseech you to hear me patiently."* It must have been his left hand which he stretched forth as he began this exordium, for his right was chained to the soldier who guarded him.* The compliment to Agrippa for his acquaintance with Jewish customs and controversies was not undeserved.† It afforded Paul unfeigned gratification to know, that, after so many efforts to make himself understood by such men as Lysias, Felix, and Festus, he was at length in the presence of one who could fully understand and appreciate his cause.

4–8. After the exordium, he proceeds to state, first, his original position among the Jews, and to show that he was still true to the chief doctrine which he then taught. (4) *" My manner of life from my youth, which was from the beginning among my own nation in Jerusalem, all the Jews know,* (5) *who knew me from the beginning, if they were willing to*

---

* Verse 29.   † Life and Ep., vol. 2, p. 294.

testify, that, according to the strictest sect of our religion, I lived a Pharisee. (6) *Even now, it is for the hope of the promise made by God to the fathers, that I stand here to be judged;* (7) *to which promise our twelve tribes, by earnest worshiping night and day, hope to attain. Concerning this hope, King Agrippa, I am accused by the Jews.* (8) *What! Is it judged a thing incredible among you, that God should raise the dead?*" The Pharisees were the least likely of all the Jewish sects to be unfaithful to Jewish institutions. It was, therefore, much in Paul's favor that he was able to call even his enemies to witness that from his youth he had lived in the strict discipline of that sect. It was yet more so, to say that he was still a firm believer in the leading doctrine of the party, and to reiterate the assertion made on two former occasions, that it was on account of the hope of a resurrection that he was accused.* This was not the avowed cause, but it was the real cause of their accusations; for the assumption that *Christ* had risen from the dead was the ground-work of all Jewish opposition and persecution. He interprets *the promise* made by God to the fathers, by which he doubtless means the promise, "In thee and in thy seed shall all the families of the earth be blessed," as referring to the resurrection, because that is the consummation of all the blessings of the gospel. He exposes the inconsistency of his enemies by observing, that it was even *Jews* who were accusing him of crime in demonstrating this great hope so cherished by the twelve tribes. Then, turning from Agrippa to the whole multitude,† he asks, with an air of astonishment, if they really deem it an incredible thing that God should raise the dead. If not, why should he be accused of crime for declaring that it had been done?

9-11. To still further illustrate his former standing among the Pharisees, he describes his original relation toward the cause of Christ. (9) "*I thought with myself that I ought to do many things contrary to the name of Jesus, the Nazarene,* (10) *which I also did in Jerusalem. Many of the saints I shut up in prison, having received authority from the high priests; and when they were put to death, I gave my vote against them.* (11) *And in all the synagogues I punished them often, compelling them to blaspheme; and being exceedingly mad against them, I persecuted them even to foreign cities.*" With such a record as this, there was no room to suspect him of any such bias as would render him an easy or a willing convert to Christ. On the contrary, it must have appeared to Agrippa, and the whole audience, most astonishing that such a change could take place. Their curiosity to know what produced the change must have been intense, and he proceeds to gratify it.

12-18. (12) "*Whereupon, as I was going to Damascus, with authority and commission from the high priests,* (13) *at midday, O King, I saw in the way a light from heaven, above the brightness of the sun, shining around me and those who were journeying with me.* (14) *And when we had all fallen to the earth, I heard a voice speaking to me, and saying, in the Hebrew dialect, Saul, Saul, why do you persecute me? It is hard for you to kick against the goads.* (15) *And I said, Who art thou, Lord? And he said, I am Jesus, whom you persecute.* (16) *But rise and stand*

---

* Before the Sanhedrim and before Felix.
† Observe the plural number of the pronoun "you." Verse 8.

upon your feet; for I have appeared to you for this purpose, to choose you for a minister and a witness of the things which you have seen, and of those in which I will appear to you; (17) delivering you from the people and the Gentiles, to whom I now send you (18) to open their eyes, to turn them from darkness to light, and from the power of Satan to God, that they may receive remission of sins, and inheritance among the sanctified by faith in me." On the supposition that Paul here spoke the truth, Agrippa saw that no prophet of old, not even Moses himself, had a more authoritative or unquestionable commission than he. Moreover, the same facts, if true, demonstrated, irresistibly, the resurrection and glorification of Jesus. As to the truth of the narrative, its essential features consisted in facts about which Paul could not be mistaken, and his unparalleled suffering, for more than twenty years, together with the chain even now upon his arm, bore incontestible evidence of his sincerity. But being an honest witness, and the facts such that he could not be mistaken, the facts themselves must be real. It is difficult to conceive what stronger evidence the audience could have had in favor of Jesus, or what more triumphant vindication of the change which had taken place in Paul.

19–21. By these facts the speaker proceeds to justify his change of position, and his subsequent career. (19) "*Whereupon, King Agrippa, I was not disobedient to the heavenly vision;* (20) *but announced, first to those in Damascus, then in Jerusalem, and in all the country of Judea, and to the Gentiles, that they should repent and turn to God, and do works suitable to repentance.* (21) *On account of these things the Jews seized me in the temple, and attempted to kill me.*" This is a more detailed statement of the cause of Jewish enmity, which had been more briefly expressed by the statement that it was concerning the hope of the resurrection that he was accused.

22, 23. That the Jews had not succeeded, with all their mobs, and conspiracies, and corruption of rulers, in destroying his life, was a matter of astonishment, and Agrippa might well admit that it was owing to the protecting providence of God. (22) "*Having, however, obtained help from God, I have stood until this day, testifying both to small and great, saying nothing else than those things which Moses and the prophets did say should be,* (23) *that the Christ should suffer, and that he first, by his resurrection from the dead, should show light to the people and to the Gentiles.*" Here he assumes that, instead of dishonoring Moses, he and his brethren alone were teaching the things which both Moses and the prophets had foretold; that it was required, by their writings, that the Messiah should suffer and rise from the dead.

By the statement that Christ *first* showed light to the people and the Gentiles by his resurrection, he must mean that he was the first to bring the subject into clear light, by an actual resurrection to glory; for there had already been some light upon it, as is proved by Paul's previous statement in reference to *the hope* to which the twelve tribes had been, in all their worship, seeking to attain.

24. At this point in his speech, Paul was interrupted by Festus. It was a very strange speech in the ears of that dissolute heathen. It presented to him a man who from his youth had lived in strict devo-

tion to a religion whose chief characteristic was the hope of a resurrection from the dead; who had once persecuted to death his present friends, but had been induced to change his course by a vision from heaven; and who, from that moment, had been enduring stripes, imprisonment, and constant exposure to death, in his efforts to inspire men with his own hope of a resurrection. Such a career he could not reconcile with those maxims of ease or of ambition which he regarded as the highest rule of life. Moreover, he saw this strange man, when called to answer to accusations of crime, appear to forget himself, and attempt to convert his judges rather than to defend himself. There was a magnanimity of soul displayed in both the past and the present of his career, which was above the comprehension of the sensuous politician, and which he could not reconcile with sound reason. He seems to have forgotten where he was, and the decorum of the occasion, so deeply was he absorbed in listening to and thinking of Paul. (24) *"And as he offered these things in his defense, Festus cried, with a loud voice, Paul, you are beside yourself. Much learning has made you mad."*

25. Paul saw at once, from the tone and manner of Festus, as well as from the admission of his great learning, that the charge of insanity was not intended as an insult; but that it was the sudden outburst of a conviction which had just seized the mind of the perplexed and astonished governor. His answer, therefore, was most respectful. (25) *"But he said, I am not mad, most noble Festus, but speak forth words of truth and soberness."* He saw, however, that Festus was beyond the reach of conviction; for a man who could see in the foregoing portion of this speech only the ravings of a madman, could not easily be reached by the argument, or touched by the pathos of the gospel.

26, 27. In Agrippa Paul had a very different hearer. His Jewish education enabled him to appreciate Paul's arguments, and to see repeated, in that noble self-sacrifice which was an enigma to Festus, the heroism of the old prophets. As Paul turned away from Festus and fixed his eye upon the king, he saw the advantage which he had over his feelings, and determined to press it to the utmost. He continues: (26) *"For the king understands concerning these things, to whom also I speak with freedom: for I am persuaded that none of these things are hidden from him; for this thing was not done in a corner. (27) King Agrippa, do you believe the prophets? I know that you believe."*

28. With matchless skill the apostle had brought his proofs to bear upon his principal hearer, and with the boldness which only those can feel who are determined upon success, he pressed this direct appeal so unexpectedly, that the king, like Festus, was surprised into a full expression of his feelings. (28) *"Then Agrippa said to Paul, You almost persuade me to be a Christian."* Under ordinary circumstances, such a confession would have struck the auditory with astonishment. But under the force of Paul's speech, there could not have been a generous soul present that did not sympathize with Agrippa's sentiment.

29. Paul's reply, for propriety of wording and magnanimity of sentiment, is not excelled in all the records of extemporaneous response: (29) *"And Paul said, I could pray to God, that not only you, but all who*

I was ,nt this day, were both almost and altogether* *such as I am, except these bonds.*" It was not till he came to express a good wish for his hearers and his jailers, a wish for that blessedness which he himself enjoyed, that he seemed to think again of himself, and remember that he was in chains.

30–32. The course of remark and the feeling of the audience had now reached that painful crisis in which it was necessary either to yield at once to the power of persuasion, or to break up the interview. Unfortunately for the audience, and especially for Agrippa, the latter alternative was chosen. The heart that beats beneath a royal robe is too deeply encased in worldly cares to often or seriously entertain the claims of such a religion as that of Jesus. A spurious religion, which shifts its demands to suit the rank of its devotees, has been acceptable to the great men of the nations, because it helps to soothe an aching conscience, and is often useful in controlling the ignorant masses; but men of rank and power are seldom willing to become altogether such as was the Apostle Paul. They turn away from too close a pressure of the truth, as did Paul's royal auditory. (30) "*When he had said these things, the king rose up, and the governor, and Bernice, ana those seated with them;* (31) *and when they had gone aside, they conversed with one another, saying, This man has done nothing worthy of death or of bonds.* (32) *And Agrippa said to Festus, This man might have been set at liberty, if he had not appealed to Cæsar.*" The decision that he had done nothing worthy of death or of bonds was the judgment of the whole company, while Agrippa went further, and said that he ought, by right, to be set at liberty. If Festus had decided thus honestly before Paul made his appeal, he would have been released; but as the appeal had now been made, to Cæsar he must go. Whether Festus now knew any better than before what to write to Cæsar, Luke leaves to the imagination of the reader.

XXVII: 1, 2. Not long after the interview with Agrippa, Paul saw an immediate prospect of departing upon his long-purposed voyage to Rome. The answer to his prayers was about to be realized, and the promise made him by night in the prison of Claudius Lysias, that he should yet testify of Jesus in Rome as he had done in Jerusalem, was about to be fulfilled. This was being accomplished, not by any direct divine interference, but by a providential combination of circumstances. The machinations of the Jews, the corruption of Felix, the indecision of Festus, the prudence of Paul, and the Roman statute

* The majority of recent critics condemn the rendering of ἐν ὀλίγῳ in Agrippa's remark, and Paul's response, by *almost*, and of ἐν πολλῷ by *altogether;* and render the two thus: "In a *little time* you persuade me to become a Christian." "I could pray to God, that *both in a little and in much time*, you were such as I am," etc., (Hackett.) They understand Agrippa as speaking ironically, and twitting Paul for supposing him to be an easy convert. It must be admitted that the usage of these two Greek phrases is favorable to this rendering; but Bloomfield shows that they do not necessarily require it. On the other hand, the rendering proposed involves Paul's reply in an inconsistency of phraseology: for how could Agrippa become such as he *both* in a little time *and* in *much* time? If, to avoid this difficulty, we render, with Conybeare, (Life and Ep. *in loco,*) "*whether* soon or late," we force the conjunction καὶ into a sense which is not authorized. It must be admitted that there are philological difficulties in both the common version of the passage, and all that are proposed as substitutes, and it is not easy to decide in which the difficulties are the greatest. But I think the connection of thought and of circumstances are clearly such as I have represented above, and this determines me in favor of the common version.

in behalf of citizens, had all most strangely, yet most naturally, combined to fulfill a promise of God made in answer to prayer. (1) *"And when it was determined that we should sail into Italy, they delivered Paul and certain other prisoners to a centurion of the Augustan cohort, named Julius.* (2) *And embarking on a ship of Adramyttium, we put to sea, intending to sail to places along the coast of Asia, Aristarchus, a Macedonian of Thessalonica, being with us."* Here, again, we find the significant *"we"* of Luke, showing that he was again in Paul's company. The last time we met with this term was upon the arrival of the apostolic company in Jerusalem.* He had probably not been far from Paul during the two years of imprisonment in Cæsarea, and was now permitted to accompany him to Rome. Aristarchus was also a voluntary companion of the prisoner, as we infer from the manner in which his name is mentioned. There were, however, other prisoners on board.†

As the ship belonged to Adramyttium, which is on the coast of Mysia, it was now homeward bound, and was not expected to take the prisoners further than its own destination. But as they were about to touch at several "places along the coast of Asia," they could calculate upon falling in with some vessel bound for Rome.

3. The apostolic company are now fairly launched upon their voyage, the details of which constitute a peculiar and most interesting passage in sacred history.. (3) *"And the next day we landed at Sidon: and Julius, treating Paul humanely, permitted him to go to the friends, and partake of their kindness."* Here we learn that Paul found friends, who were, doubtless, brethren, in the city of Sidon. Thus we find that both the Phenician cities, Tyre and Sidon, to whose wickedness the Savior once so significantly alluded, had, ere now, received the gospel. With the brethren in the former place Paul had spent a week on his voyage to Jerusalem, and now the beginning of another voyage, not much less mournful, is cheered by the hospitality of those in the latter.

4. *"And having put to sea from that place, we sailed under the lee of Cyprus, because the winds were contrary."* As the proper course of the ship was westward, the contrary wind must have come from that quarter. With a favorable wind she would have passed to the south of Cyprus; but in tacking to make headway against a contrary wind, they necessarily passed to the east and north-east of that island, leaving it on the left. An additional reason for taking this tack may have been a desire to take advantage of a current which flows westward along the southern shore of Asia Minor, as far as the Archipelago, and greatly favors the progress of westward-bound vessels.‡

5, 6. Passing around the north-east point of Cyprus, the vessel entered the open sea to the south of Cilicia and Pamphylia. (5) *"And when we had sailed across the sea along Cilicia and Pamphylia, we came to Myra, a city of Lycia.* (6) *There the centurion found a ship of Alexandria, sailing for Italy, and put us on board of it."* Thus, according to expectation, they fell in with a vessel bound for Italy, and left the

---
* Acts xxi: 17, 18. † Verse 42.
‡ For the nautical information connected with this voyage not found in the text, I am indebted to Mr. Howson's most exhaustive chapter on the subject, Life and Ep., vol. 2, chap. xxiii.

ship of Adramyttium. Their new vessel was one of the many grain ships which supplied Rome with bread from the granaries of Egypt.* She was a vessel of good size, accommodating, on this voyage, two hundred and seventy-six passengers.† She had, probably, undertaken to sail direct from Alexandria to Rome; but the same contrary winds which had thus far retarded the progress of the other vessel had compelled her to sail far to the northward of the direct route.

7-8. The wind was still contrary when they left Myra. (7) *"And having sailed slowly many days, we reached Cnidus with difficulty, the wind not favoring us, and sailed under the lee of Crete, over against Salmone; (8) and coasting along it with difficulty, we came into a place called Fair Havens, near which was the city of Lasea."* From Myra to the island of Cnidus is only one hundred and thirty miles; hence it *must* have been slow sailing to be "many days" reaching that place. From that island their course to Cape Salmone, which was the most eastern point of the island of Crete, was a little to the west of south. The wind, to turn them this much out of their course, could have been but little, if any, north of west. The lee of Crete, under which they sailed, was the southern shore, which but partially protected them from the wind, rendering it difficult to keep near the shore until they reached the harbor called Fair Havens. This was about half way the length of the island.

9-12. The voyage, thus far, had been so tedious that winter was approaching, and it was deemed unsafe to attempt to complete it before spring. It became a question, however, whether they would spend the winter where they were, or seek a more desirable winter haven. (9) *"Much time having now elapsed, and navigation being already unsafe, because the fast had already passed, Paul admonished them,* (10) *saying, Sirs, I perceive that this voyage will be with violence and much loss, not only of the cargo and the ship, but also of our lives.* (11) *But the centurion believed the master and the owner of the ship rather than the things which were spoken by Paul.* (12) *And the harbor being inconvenient to winter in, the majority advised to depart thence, so as, if possible, to reach Phœnix, and spend the winter there, a harbor of Crete looking to the south-west and north-west."* Paul's advice to the mariners was the beginning of an activity in behalf of the ship and crew which forms the chief matter of interest in the remainder of the voyage. We will yet see how nearly his prediction was fulfilled. He did not claim for it the authority of inspiration, and, therefore, we should not claim it for him; but he had some experience at sea, and expressed the result of his own judgment. It was quite natural, however, that the centurion, who seems to have had control of the matter, should put more confidence in the judgment of the owner and the master than in his. He had not yet learned to appreciate his prisoner as he did subsequently.

The description given of the harbor of Phœnix has occasioned some perplexity to commentators. As the wind was blowing from north of west, a harbor "looking to the north-west and south-west," *from the shore*, would be entirely exposed to the weather; whereas this description is given to show that it was a safe harbor in which to spend the winter. Mr. Howson is undoubtedly right in assuming that Luke

* Verse 38. † Verse 37.

supposes the beholder to be looking from the water, where a vessel would lie at anchor, toward the inclosing shore, and means that to him the harbor would look to the north-west and the south-west. Such a harbor would be safe against any wind in the quadrant from southwest to north-west, and was precisely such as was needed at that time.

13. The harbor called Fair Havens lay on the east side of Cape Matala, which they would have to round in order to reach Phœnix; but it could not be rounded in the face of a north-west wind, hence they had to wait for the wind to change. (13) "*Now when the south wind blew moderately, thinking they had gained their purpose, they weighed anchor, and sailed close by the shore of Crete.*" They felt that all was secure, and even had their boat swinging astern, as they tacked slowly along the smooth sea under a gentle southern breeze. It was a deceitful lull, the prelude to unexpected disasters.

14-17. (14) "*But not long after, a tempestuous wind, called Euroclydon, struck against her,* (15) *and the ship being seized by it, and unable to face the wind, we gave up and were driven by it.* (16) *And running under the lee of an island called Clauda, with difficulty we were able to secure the boat.* (17) *When they had taken it up, they used helps, undergirding the ship. And fearing lest they should fall into the Syrtis,* they lowered the sail, and so were driven.*" It was just as they were rounding Cape Matala, and expected to be borne by the southern wind directly to Phœnix, that they were whirled away by this tempest. The direction from Crete to Clauda is south-west; the wind, therefore, must have been from the north-east. This is indicated by the name Euroclydon, which Bloomfield translates "*the wave-stirring easter.*" Such a wind, varying from north-east to south-east, is said still to prevail in those seas.

While passing under the lee of Clauda, the island checked the violence of the storm, and enabled them to take some precautions which were impossible in the open sea. The first of these was to "secure the boat," which had thus far drifted astern, and was likely to be dashed in pieces. The second was to undergird the ship, a process called *frapping* in modern style, which consists in passing heavy cables under the hull, and fastening them securely on the deck, to prevent the timbers from parting under the force of the waves. The third precaution was to lower the sails, so as to prevent the vessel being driven too rapidly before the wind.

18-20. (18) "*And being exceedingly tempest-tossed, the next day we lightened the vessel,* (19) *and on the third day, with our own hands we cast out the tackling of the ship.* (20) *And as neither the sun nor the stars appeared for many days, and no small tempest lay on us, at last all hope that we should be saved was taken away.*" The sailors now began to realize the truth of Paul's prediction about the character of the voyage, and they were prepared to listen to him with more respect when he addressed to them the following speech:

21-26. (21) "*Now, after long abstinence, Paul stood in the midst of them, and said, Sirs, you should have hearkened to me, and not have sailed from Crete, and gained this harm and loss.* (22) *And now, I exhort you to be of good cheer; for there will be no loss of life among you, except of the ship.* (23) *For there stood by me this night an angel of*

---

* An extensive sand-bank to the north of Africa, still known as the Syrtis.

ACTS XXVII: 24-32.

God, whose I am and whom I serve, (24) *saying, Fear not, Paul; you must be brought before Cæsar: and behold, God has given you all those who are sailing with you.* (25) *Wherefore, sirs, be of good cheer; for I believe God, that it will be even as it was told me.* (26) *But we must fall upon a certain island.*" Paul's former prediction was already fulfilled in part, and they all believed that it was about to be in full. His reference to it was designed both to rebuke them for not heeding it, and to remind them of its correctness. His present prediction conflicted with the former in reference to loss of life; but their lives had been so completely despaired of, that they were not disposed to find fault with the former prediction, even in this particular. The present, however, was certainly spoken upon divine authority; and if we suppose the former to have been also, then the security of all their lives may be regarded as a boon granted to Paul in answer to prayers offered subsequent to the first prediction. That their safety was in some sense owing to him, is evident from the words, "God has *given to you* all those who are sailing with you."

27-29. Notwithstanding the assurance of final safety, their danger, for a time, became more imminent. (27) "*And when the fourteenth night was come, as we were driven along in the Adriatic Sea, about midnight the sailors supposed that they were drawing near to some land;* (28) *and having sounded, they found it twenty fathoms. And going a little further, they sounded again, and found it fifteen fathoms.* (29) *Then fearing lest they should fall upon breakers, they cast four anchors out of the stern, and wished for day.*" From this time till day-break, the ship lay with her bow to the shore, where the waves were dashing fearfully over hidden rocks; and was held back from inevitable destruction only by the four anchors cast astern. It was a period of fearful suspense, rendered hideous by the darkness of the night and the raging of the storm. They "wished for day," but they knew not whether it would bring relief, or only render them more certain of destruction.

30-32. Under circumstances like these, both the nobler and the baser traits of human character have fair opportunity to exhibit themselves. The strong and skillful have often been known to save themselves without concern for the more helpless; while, at times, the utmost magnanimity has been displayed by the few. Both traits of character were exhibited here; one by the sailors, the other by Paul. (30) "*Now the sailors were seeking to escape from the ship, and letting down the boat into the sea, under pretense of casting anchors out from the bow;* (31) *when Paul said to the centurion and the soldiers, Unless these remain in the ship you can not be saved.* (32) *Then the soldiers cut off the ropes of the boat, and let her fall off.*" Here we see that while the sailors, who alone could have any hope of steering the vessel safe to land, were selfishly leaving the passengers to their fate, and the soldiers were so paralyzed with fear as not to discover their design, Paul was perfectly self-possessed, and was watching for the safety of all. He had an assurance from God that no lives would be lost, yet he was just as watchful as though no such promise had been given; and he assured the soldiers that they would not be saved if the sailors were permitted to leave the vessel. We have here a happy illustration of the manner in which God's decrees and human free agency harmonize to produce a given result. It was a decree of God that the passengers and crew should be saved, and it was certain to be accomplished; but the voluntary watchfulness of Paul, and the desire of self-preservation on the part of the soldiers, were contingencies on which the result depended, and which contributed to it. In determining, therefore, that a thing shall be done, or declaring that it will be done, God anticipates the *voluntary* action of parties concerned, and only interferes, by miracles, where such action would fail of the contemplated result. In the matter of salvation, we should act as Paul did in this case: be as watchful and laborious as though God had promised us no assistance, yet as confident of divine assistance as though all were dependent on it alone.

33-36. In a time of extreme danger like the present, a man who is able to maintain complete self-possession has great control over those who are alarmed. Paul had already displayed his coolness and watchfulness to the soldiers, and had outgeneraled the sailors; consequently he became at once the leading spirit in the whole ship's company. During the entire inactivity of the crew, while swinging at anchor and waiting for daylight, he endeavored to impart his own calmness to them all. (33) "*Now while day was coming on, Paul besought them all to take some food; saying, This is the fourteenth day that you have been waiting, and continued fasting, having taken nothing.* (34) *Wherefore, I beseech you to take some food; for this is for your preservation; for not a hair shall fall from the head of any of you.* (35) *And when he had thus spoken, he took a loaf and returned thanks to God before all, and broke it, and began to eat.* (36) *Then all were of good cheer, and they also took some food.*" Here, again, th apostle assures them that no harm shall befall them, yet in the same breath urges them to eat heartily, as a precaution for their safety. Their safety, though certain, was still dependent upon their exertions, and, in order that they might have strength for the labor before them, it was necessary that they should break their long and exhausting fast. The remark that they had taken no food for fourteen days must be interpreted in the light of the circumstances. It is not a remark of Luke addressed to his readers, but one of Paul, addressed to his hearers. If they had taken any food at all during the time, which they certainly did, unless they were sustained by a miracle, they could but understand him as merely expressing, in strong terms, their severe abstinence. Such was undoubtedly his meaning. If Luke had been describing the fact in his own words instead of Paul's, perhaps he would have stated it to us with some qualifications.

The cheerfulness of Paul, as he gave thanks to God, broke the loaf, and began to eat, inspired them all with new courage. As their excitement subsided, their appetites returned; and a hearty meal, which generally smooths a rough temper, and acts as a sedative upon all mental excitement, completed the restoration of general cheerfulness, and prepared them to undertake, with alacrity, the work yet to be done.

37-38. The gathering of the whole ship's company to partake of this meal seems to have suggested to the historian to mention, here, the number of persons on board. (37) "*Now all the souls in the ship were two hundred and seventy-six.* (38) *And when they had eaten enough, they lightened the ship, casting the wheat into the sea."* This was all done between the time of eating and daylight, and was no inconsiderable labor. It was designed to lessen the draught of the vessel, so that when run ashore she might float into the shallow water.

39–41. All was now done that could be, until daylight should reveal the nature of the shore ahead. (39) *"And when it was day they did not recognize the land. But they discovered a certain inlet having a sandy shore, into which they determined, if it were possible, to thrust the ship. (40) And having cut away the anchors, they abandoned them to the sea; at the same time loosing the rudder-bands, and hoisting the foresail to the wind, they held toward the shore. (41) And falling into a place between two seas, they ran the ship aground; and the bow sticking fast, remained immovable; but the stern was broken by the violence of the waves."* At every point, except the one to which the vessel was steered, the shore was rocky; for this point was selected because it had a sandy shore. It required some seamanship to land where they did. While lying at anchor, the rudders, which were merely paddle-rudders, one at each side of the stern, had been lashed up, to prevent them from fouling with the four anchor-cables also astern. These were loosed to guide the vessel; and the foresail was unfurled to give the vessel the impetus necessary to a successful use of the rudders. By a skillful use of both she was steered clear of the rocks, and stranded on the sandy beach. Here "two seas met;" that is, the waves from two different points met each other, and spent their combined force upon the stern of the vessel, and she was rapidly going to pieces.

42. At this critical juncture there was exhibited by the soldiers an instance of depravity even greater than that of the sailors the night before. They owed their present prospect of safety to the watchfulness of Paul, yet they felt no apparent gratitude to him, and while hoping to escape themselves, they were regardless of the lives of himself and the other prisoners. (42) *"Now the purpose of the soldiers was, that they would kill the prisoners, lest any of them should swim out and escape."* Such is the depravity of human nature, when void of religious truth, and trained to the cruelties of war.

43, 44. But God had a purpose and a promise to fulfill, which did not admit of such a disposition of the prisoners, and the more cultivated nature of the centurion was the means of saving them. The incidents of the voyage had made an impression upon his mind most favorable to Paul, and he would not ignore the gratitude which he owed him. (43) *"But the centurion, determined to save Paul, kept them from their purpose, and commanded those who could swim to cast themselves out and go first to land; (44) and the remainder, some on boards, and some on fragments of the ship. And thus it came to pass that all escaped safe to land."* Paul's last prediction was literally fulfilled, and his fellow-prisoners owed their lives to the centurion's partiality for him.

XXVIII: 1, 2. (1) *"And after they had escaped, they knew that the island was called Melita. (2) Now the barbarians showed us no little philanthropy: for they kindled a fire, on account of the rain that was falling, and on account of the cold, and brought us all to it."* In calling the islanders barbarians, Luke adopts the style of the Greeks, by whom all nations were styled barbarians except themselves. The term had not the same sense of reproach which it bears now; yet those to whom it was applied were regarded as comparatively uncivilized. Their kindness to the shipwrecked strangers was true philanthropy, being prompted by the simple fact that they were men in distress. It was a most timely relief to the drenched and chilled and exhausted voyagers.

3-6. While they were endeavoring to make themselves comfortable around the fire, an incident occurred which had an important bearing upon the future welfare of the travelers. (3) *"Now Paul, having gathered a bundle of sticks, and laid them on the fire, a viper came out from the heat, and fastened on his hand. (4) And when the barbarians saw the beast hanging from his hand, they said one to another, No doubt this man is a murderer; whom, though he has escaped from the sea, Justice permits not to live. (5) Then he shook off the beast into the fire, and suffered no harm. (6) But they were waiting for him to swell up, or suddenly fall down dead. And when they had waited a great while, and saw that no harm came to him, they turned about, and said that he was a god."* This scene is like that at Lystra reversed. There the people first took Paul for a god, and afterward stoned him. Here they first suppose him to be a murderer, and then a god. Their bad opinion of him had not been based upon the mere fact that he was bitten by a serpent, for they knew that innocent men were liable to the same misfortune, but by the occurrence of this incident in so close connection with his safe escape from an almost hopeless shipwreck. The fact that he was a prisoner helped them to the conclusion that he had committed murder, and was now receiving a just retribution in a violent death. They attributed his punishment to the goddess of justice, using the Greek term Δίκη, the name of that goddess. When, after watching a long time, they found that the bite, so fatal to other men, had no effect on him, their heathen education led them irresistibly to the conclusion that he was a god.

It is almost universally conceded that the island here called Melita is the modern Malta, which lies directly south of Sicily. The evidence for this conclusion is fully summed up by Mr. Howson, to whom the inquisitive reader is referred.*

7. The admiration awakened by this event among the rude populace finally led to a more comfortable entertainment of the ship's company. (7) *"In the regions around that place were the estates of the chief man of the island, Publius by name, who received us and entertained us courteously three days."* This "chief man" is supposed to have been the Roman governor of the island. It was an instance of distinguished hospitality, to entertain for three days, with food and lodging, two hundred and seventy-six strangers.

8-10. But no man ever loses by such hospitality, especially if it be extended to a servant of God. Publius was not without a reward for his kindness. (8) *"And it came to pass that the father of Publius lay afflicted with fever and dysentery; to whom Paul went in, and having prayed, laid his hands upon him, and healed him. (9) When this was done, others also in the island who had diseases came and were healed.*

* Life and Ep., vol. 2, pp. 341-346.

(10) *And they honored us highly, and when we were departing, loaded us with such things as we needed."* The voyagers had lost every thing in the shipwreck, yet, through the services of Paul, they had lacked nothing during their stay on the island, and were now about to leave it with all the necessaries for the remainder of the voyage, supplied free of cost. At the beginning of the voyage Paul was one of the most unobserved of all the passengers; but he had gradually become the chief dependence of the whole company, and had acquired an ascendency over every mind. Much of this was due to his inspiration; yet native force of character and superior talent, place them where you will, will elevate their possessor to distinction and authority. Especially will this be true in times of danger and difficulty.

We can not suppose that Paul healed diseases so generally among the islanders, without mentioning the name of Jesus. On the contrary, though Luke makes no mention of it, we can not doubt that, from the palace of the governor to the remotest hamlet of the island, the name and power of Jesus were fully proclaimed during the three months of the apostle's stay.

11–14. (11) *"Now after three months we set sail in a ship of Alexandria, which had wintered in the island, whose emblem was Castor and Pollux.* (12) *And landing at Syracuse, we remained there three days.* (13) *Thence, taking an indirect course, we arrived at Rhegium. And after one day, a south wind sprang up, and we went the next day to Puteoli.* (14) *Finding brethren there, we were entreated to remain with them seven days; and so we went to Rome."* Castor and Pollux were represented, in Greek mythology, as sons of Jupiter, and the patron deities of sailors. Their images, carved or painted on the prow, served the purpose of distinguishing this vessel, as do the names painted upon ships and steamboats at the present day. The ship would now be called the Castor and Pollux.

Syracuse, the famous capital of Sicily, where they remained three days, was directly in their route, and the delay was probably for the purposes of trade. From this place to Rhegium they were again troubled with unfavorable winds, as is evident from their sailing by an "indirect course," and the mention of a south wind springing up the second day after they reached this port. The south wind was directly in their course, and they sailed rapidly before it to Puteoli, accomplishing a distance of one hundred and eighty miles* on the next day after they started.

It was, doubtless, an unexpected pleasure to Paul to find brethren in Puteoli, and equally unexpected to them to have the great apostle to the Gentiles in their midst. The request that he should remain with them *seven* days indicates a desire to have him present at their Lord's-day meeting. It is suggestive of a season of religious intercourse, terminated by the day on which the disciples came together to break the loaf. The ship had reached her final port; for Puteoli, situated on the northern side of the Bay of Naples, was the chief landing-place for vessels engaged in the trade between Rome and Egypt.† The remainder of the journey was to be performed on foot, and there was nothing to prevent Paul's delay with the brethren, except the will of the centu-

* Life and Ep., vol. 2, p. 349. † Life and Ep., vol. 2, p. 350–353.

rion, who was under too great obligations to him to refuse any reasonable request.

15. The delay of seven days was long enough for news to reach the brethren in Rome, that Paul was in Puteoli on his way to their city. (15) *"And the brethren, having heard from that place concerning us, came out to meet us as far as Appii Forum and Three Taverns. When Paul saw them he thanked God and took courage."* The two places here mentioned were about ten miles apart,* and it was doubtless two different companies who met them, having left Rome at different times. One party had come about forty miles, to Appii Forum, and the other about thirty, to the places called Tres Tabernæ, or Three Taverns.† Such a mark of respect extended to him in his bonds was highly gratifying, and no wonder that he "thanked God and took courage."

16. Finally, the gates of "the eternal city," as it was proudly styled, were entered. The prisoners were at the end of their long journey, and soon learned the disposition to be made of them for the time being. (16) *"And when we came into Rome, the centurion delivered the prisoners to the Prætorian Prefect; but Paul was permitted to dwell by himself, with the soldier who guarded him."* The Prætorian Prefect was commander of the imperial guards, and had custody of all persons to be tried before the emperor.‡ It was probably the influence of Julius, the centurion, in his favor, which obtained for Paul the distinguished privilege of living in his own rented house, with only a single guard.

Paul had now accomplished a journey which he had contemplated for many years, and had met with some of the brethren whom he had called upon two years and a half ago, to strive together with him in prayer to God that he might come to them with joy, by the will of God, and with them be refreshed.‖ God had twice promised him that he should visit Rome,§ and now, the promise was fulfilled, and his prayers were answered. But how different his entrance into the imperial city from what he had fondly hoped! Instead of coming in a free man, to appear in the synagogue, and in the forum, for the name of Jesus, he is marched in between files of soldiers, reported to the authorities as a prisoner sent up for trial, and kept night and day under a military guard. How poor his prospect for evangelizing the vast population! If Paul the tent-maker, a penniless stranger, had commenced his labors in the commercial emporium of Greece, "in weakness, and in fear and in much trembling," how shall Paul the *prisoner*, with all the suspicion of crime which attaches to such a situation, begin the work of salvation in the capital of the whole world? The prospect was sufficiently disheartening; but he had one consolation which he did not enjoy in Corinth. He was not a stranger here; but was well known to all the brethren, who had heard his Epistle to the Romans read in the Lord's-day meetings, and who were eager to form his personal acquaintance. He had already thanked God and taken courage, when some of them had met him on the way, and now he was emboldened, by their sympathy, to send forth even from his prison-walls a voice of warning to the vast multitudes around him.

17–20. He made no delay in beginning his work; and his first ap-

---

* Life and Ep., vol. 2, p. 360.   † Hackett.   ‡ Life and Ep., vol. 2, p. 364.
‖ Rom. xv: 30–32.   § Acts xxiii· 11; xxvii: 24.

peal, according to his uniform custom, was addressed to his own kinsmen according to the flesh. (17) "*And it came to pass, after three days, that he called together the chief men of the Jews; and when they had come together, he said to them, Brethren, I have done nothing against the people, or the customs of the fathers; yet I was delivered a prisoner from Jerusalem into the hands of the Romans;* (18) *who, having examined me, were disposed to release me, because there was no cause of death in me.* (19) *But the Jews opposing it, I was compelled to appeal to Cæsar; not that I had any thing of which to accuse my nation.* (20) *For this cause I have requested to see you and speak to you. For it is on account of the hope of Israel that I am bound with this chain.*" The propriety of this interview, and of the individual statements in the speech, is quite obvious. It might have been supposed, from the fact that he was accused by the Jews, that he had been guilty of some crime; and from his appeal to Cæsar, that he intended to prefer charges against his accusers. The fact that the Romans would have released him but for the opposition of the Jews, was much in his favor on the first point; and on the latter, his own disavowal was sufficient. His closing remark, that it was for the hope of Israel that he was bound with a chain, was well calculated to enlist their sympathies; for it was no uncommon thing for Jews to be persecuted.

21, 22. The response of the Jews was candid and becoming. (21) "*And they said to him, We have neither received letters from Judea concerning you, nor has any of the brethren who have come reported or spoken any evil concerning you.* (22) *But we think it proper to hear from you what you think; though concerning this sect, it is known to us that it is everywhere spoken against.*" It is rather surprising that they had heard nothing of the exciting scenes of Paul's life in the last two years; but it often thus happens that events pass almost unnoticed by a living generation, which are destined, in subsequent ages, to figure as the leading events of history. By hearing *nothing*, however, they had heard nothing prejudicial to him, except that the *sect* of which he was an advocate had a bad reputation. If they had acted on the principle which often governs predominant religious parties, this would have been sufficient to turn away their ears. Doubtless, they *had* acted somewhat on this principle toward the preachers of the gospel who had preceded Paul in Rome; but the direct personal appeal which he made to them, and the conciliatory manner and matter of his address, induced them to think proper to hear what he thought. In these words, they gave good expression to an important rule of conduct; for, however a party who attempts to show us the truth may be spoken against, it is always proper to hear them before pronouncing sentence against them.

23, 24. Before the Jews took leave of Paul, they made arrangements for a formal and deliberate hearing of what he thought. (23) "*And having appointed him a day, there came to him into his lodging a greater number, to whom he expounded and testified the kingdom of God, persuading them concerning Jesus, both from the law of Moses and the prophets, from morning till evening.* (24) *Some believed the things which were spoken, and some believed not.*" Sufficient time was occupied to place the whole subject before them, and to support each separate proposition with suitable evidence. The result was such a division of sentiment as almost uniformly attended the preaching of the gospel.

25–28. From what follows, we have reason to suppose that the unbelieving party gave some unbecoming expression to their sentiments. (25) *"And disagreeing among themselves, they dispersed, Paul saying one word: Well did the Holy Spirit speak through Isaiah the prophet to our fathers,* (26) *saying, Go to this people and say, With hearing you will hear and will not understand, and seeing, you will see and not perceive;* (27) *for the heart of this people has become gross, and their ears are dull of hearing, and their eyes they have closed; lest they should see with their eyes, and hear with their ears, and understand with their heart, and should turn, and I should heal them.* (28) *Be it known to you, therefore, that the salvation of God is sent to the Gentiles, and they will hear it."* The purpose of henceforth turning to the Gentiles, implied in the last remark, indicates that far the larger portion of his hearers rejected the gospel.

The quotation from Isaiah furnishes the true explanation of the failure of the gospel to effect the salvation of all who hear it fully proclaimed. The theory that the human soul must be regenerated by an immediate influence of the Holy Spirit, or that the Spirit must impart a special force to the Word in individual cases, before the gospel can be received, is an attempt to explain this matter; but it is not consistent with the explanation here given by Paul. Upon those theories, when a part of Paul's hearers went away unbelievers, the reason was that *they* had not enjoyed a divine influence which was granted to the *others*. On Paul's theory, however, the Lord had done as much for the one party as for the other; and the reason why one party were not believers was because, unlike the others, their ears were dull of hearing, and their eyes were closed. Neither was this condition superinduced without their own volition; for they are expressly charged with *closing their own eyes*. As they closed them *voluntarily*, they *could* have kept them open. Had they done so, it is implied that the process would have been reversed. They would have *seen* the truth; seeing it to be truth, they would have given it a respectful *hearing;* hearing, they would have *understood* it, and would have turned to the Lord that they might be healed. This was precisely the experience of the party who believed. They had themselves once been gross of heart and dull of hearing, and had closed their eyes against the truth as presented by previous preachers in Rome; but now they *opened* their eyes to what Paul presented, and the consequence was, they turned to the Lord. We conclude, therefore, that the power of the gospel is sufficient for the conversion of all who will see and hear. For this reason, it is sent to all in the same words; all who hear enjoy the same divine influence, and those only are lost who willfully refuse to hear the truth, or obstinately resist it. In this arrangement there is no respect of persons with God, nor can any man attribute his final ruin to a withholding of saving influences on the part of the Holy Spirit.

29. Notwithstanding the principal part of Paul's visitors went away unbelievers, they could not at once cast the subject off from their at-

tention. Luke follows them, as they went away, with this remark: (29) "*And when he said these things, the Jews departed, having much disputation among themselves.*"

30, 31. The narrative is now brought abruptly to a close, by the following statement: (30) "*Now Paul remained in his own hired house two whole years, and received all who came in to him,* (31) *preaching the kingdom of God, and teaching the things concerning the Lord Jesus Christ with all freedom of speech, no one forbidding.*" Here, again, Luke observes the distinction between *preaching* and *teaching*. Originating in the apostolic commission, which was the starting point of Acts, it has been preserved throughout the narrative, and now appears at its close.

The liberty granted Paul, of living in a rented house with the soldier who guarded him, enabled him to pursue these labors to the utmost advantage possible for one in military confinement. The brethren needed no invitation to visit him and hear his *teaching;* while their influence, actively exerted, was sufficient to bring in a large number of persons to hear his *preaching.*

The results of these efforts Luke does not see fit to enumerate; nor does he gratify the natural curiosity of the reader by continuing to its final close the biography of Paul. He leaves him at the end of two years' imprisonment, without even informing us whether he was then released. True, the remark that he "remained in his own hired house two whole years, and received those who came to him," seems to imply a *change* after that time; but it might have been a change to closer confinement, so far as is indicated by this remark.

It is probable that the narrative was brought to a close here, partly because the composition of it was concluded just at this time. The two years of comparative inactivity which Luke enjoyed while a companion of the prisoner Paul afforded a good opportunity for writing it, and it is quite certain that the last paragraph was not written till the close of this period.

But, independent of this consideration, the leading purpose of the narrative itself rendered this a most fitting point at which to bring it to a close. Having started out to show the manner in which the apostles and evangelists executed their commission, he had now led his readers from Jerusalem through Judea, Samaria, the provinces of Asia Minor, the islands of the Mediterranean, Macedonia, and Achaia, to the imperial city of Rome; and leaving the principal laborer here, still engaged in "preaching the kingdom of God, and teaching the things concerning the Lord Jesus Christ," his purpose is accomplished, and the narrative closes.

A commentary on Acts, strictly confined to the subject-matter of the text, would here be brought to a close. But as it has been a part of our purpose to give somewhat more fullness to the biography of Paul, by introducing information derived from other inspired sources, we have yet a few paragraphs to pen. Fortunately, the intense curiosity awakened by the closing chapters in reference to the further career of the apostle may, in some degree, be gratified. This curiosity directs itself chiefly to two questions suggested by the later portion of the history: *first,* what were the results to the cause of his long-wished-for visit to Rome? *second*, what was the result of his appeal to Caesar?

In reference to the first question, we have already remarked, that his entrance into Rome was far different from what he had fondly hoped, and he could not reasonably expect to accomplish much while confined with a chain, and resting under the suspicion of being deservedly in confinement. But we have already seen that he continued to preach and teach for two years, and we learn something of the extent and success of his labors from epistles which he wrote during this period. Ephesians, Colossians, and Philemon were the earliest of these epistles, being written at one time, and forwarded, the former two by Tychicus,* and the last by Onesimus,† the two messengers traveling together. In the two former there are indications of great anxiety in reference to the success of his efforts, and intimations of serious obstacles in the way. He exhorts the brethren to pray for him, that a door of utterance might be opened to him, and that he might have boldness to speak the gospel as it ought to be spoken.‡ This request shows that there were some obstructions to the proclamation of the truth, and that they were such as were calculated to check the boldness of his utterance.

Notwithstanding these obstructions, the last of the three letters above named reveals some success which had already rewarded his labors. Out of the very dregs of the dissolute and corrupt society of the metropolis, a Greek‖ slave, who had run away from his master, a convert of Paul's in Asia Minor,§ had, by some means, been induced to visit the apostle and hear the gospel. It proved the power of God to free him from a bondage far worse than that from which he had fled. After he became a disciple, Paul found him profitable to him for the ministry;¶ being of service, no doubt, in bringing within the sound of the gospel many of his former companions. For this reason he had a strong desire to retain him as an assistant; but having no right to do so without the consent of Philemon, his master, and being unwilling to enjoin by authority upon the latter the obvious duty of liberating a slave capable of so great usefulness, he sent him home to his master, with an epistle, in which he delicately intimates his wishes in the premises, but leaves the whole subject to his own sense of propriety.** Sending him home without the means to recompense his master for any thing of which he had defrauded him, Paul promises to pay the sum, if any, out of his own purse.†† Thus his preaching had begun to take effect upon the most hopeless class of the city population, at a time when he was urging distant congregations to pray that God would open to him a door of utterance.

But, eventually, in answer to these prayers, a door of utterance was thrown open far wider than he had reason to expect. In the Epistle to the Philippians, written at a later period, when he was expecting his trial and release,‡‡ he says: "I wish you to understand, brethren, that the things which have happened to me have fallen out rather to the *furtherance* of the gospel, so that my bonds in Christ are made manifest

---
* Ep. vi: 21; Col. iv: 7–9.
‖ So his name indicates.
** Phil. 8–16.
† Phil. 10–12.
§ Phil. 19.
†† Phil. 18, 19.
‡ Ep. vi: 18, 19; Col. iv: 2–4
¶ Phil. 11–13.
‡‡ Phil. i: 19–27.

in all the palace, and in all other places, and many brethren in the Lord, growing confident by my bonds, are much more bold to speak the word without fear."* From his prison, the Lord had opened a door of utterance into the imperial palace itself; so that Paul the prisoner had an audience whose ears would have been wholly inaccessible to Paul the unfettered apostle. His discourse before the emperor, if we may judge by that before Agrippa, must have awakened new thoughts and emotions in the Roman court; and what awakened new interest there could not be long in spreading to "all other places." The Lord had led him by a strange method to Rome, and surrounded him with many discouragements; but his purpose was now unfolded, and Paul saw in the result, as it affected both the disciples and the community at large, a wisdom which before had been inscrutable. He had now demonstrated what he had once written to the Romans, that he was not ashamed of the gospel of Christ, and was ready to preach it even in Rome; for he had preached it to both the proudest and the poorest of the population, and that with a chain upon his arm.

No two years of Paul's life were better filled with earnest labor than these two spent in his Roman prison. Besides the oral efforts just referred to, and the epistles to Ephesians, Colossians, Philemon, and Philippians, he is supposed, also, near the close of this period, to have written Hebrews, the most profound, next to Romans, of all his productions. He was not alone in his toil and danger, but was constantly surrounded by some of those noble brethren who were so ardently attached to his person. Timothy joins with him in the opening salutation of Colossians, Philemon, and Philippians. Aristarchus and Epaphras were his fellow-prisoners;† Mark, who once forsook him and Barnabas, and went not with them to the work, was now with him;‡ Demas, who afterward forsook him, "having loved this present world,"‖ was as yet by his side;§ and Luke, the beloved physician, who shared the perils of his voyage from Cæsarea, continued to relieve the dreariness of his imprisonment,¶ and indited the last paragraph of Acts, as we conjecture, just as the two years expired.

The question as to the result of Paul's appeal to Cæsar is not settled by direct scriptural evidence, yet it is determined, to the satisfaction of nearly all the commentators, that he was released at the end of the two years mentioned by Luke. The evidence on which this conclusion is based consists partly in the unanimous testimony of the earliest Christian writers after the apostles, and partly in the difficulty of fixing a date for the epistles to Timothy and Titus without this supposition. There are events mentioned in these epistles, for which no place can be found in the preceding history; such as his leaving Timothy in Ephesus, to counteract the influence of false teachers, while he went into Macedonia;** his leaving Titus in Crete, to set in order the things that were wanting there, and to ordain elders;†† his visit to Miletus, when he left Trophimus there sick;‡‡ and to Nicopolis, where he spent the winter.‖‖ The argument drawn from both these sources is very fully and satisfactorily stated by Mr. Howson, to whom the more inquisitive reader is referred.§§

---

* Phil. i: 12–14. † Col. iv: 10; Phil. 23. ‡ Col. iv: 10. ‖ 2 Tim. iv: 10.
§ Col. iv: 14. ¶ Col. iv: 14. ** 1 Tim. i: 3. †† Titus i: 5.
‡‡ 2 Tim. iv: 20. ‖‖ Titus iii: 12. §§ Vol. 2, chap. xxvii.

On the supposition of his release, the subsequent known facts are best arranged as follows: He first fulfilled the purpose so confidently expressed to the Philippians of visiting them again;* and next took advantage of the lodging which he had directed Philemon to prepare for him at Colosse.† While in Asia, he would scarcely pass by the city of Ephesus; but it is after a short visit to Spain, that we locate that visit, at the conclusion of which he left Timothy there and went into Macedonia.‡ It was contrary to the expectation once entertained by Paul, that he was once more greeted by the brethren in Ephesus; for he had bidden them farewell four years ago with the conviction that they would see his face no more.‖ Leaving Timothy in Ephesus, and going to Macedonia, he wrote back to him the First Epistle to Timothy,§ in which he expressed a hope of rejoining him soon at Ephesus.¶ This he most likely did, as he soon after visited Crete, in company with Titus; and the most usual route from Macedonia to this island was by way of Ephesus. Having made a short visit in Crete, he left Titus there, to "set in order the things which were wanting, and ordain elders in every city."** Shortly after leaving the island, he wrote the Epistle to Titus. He was then on his way to Nicopolis, a city of Epirus, where he expected to spend the winter.†† On the way he had passed through Miletus, where he left Trophimus sick; and Corinth, where he left Erastus.‡‡ Whether he spent the whole winter in Nicopolis, or was imprisoned again before spring, is not certainly known; but the next that we know of him, he was a prisoner in Rome the second time, as is indicated in his Second Epistle to Timothy. From this epistle we learn several interesting particulars of his last imprisonment, and of the beginning of his final trial. His situation was more alarming, and he was attended by fewer friends than before. Demas forsook him, through love of this world, and went to Thessalonica; Crescens, for some reason unexplained, went to Galatia, and Titus to Dalmatia.‖‖ Tychicus he had sent to Ephesus.§§ Luke, alone, of all his former fellow-laborers, was with him, though he was expecting Timothy to soon rejoin him, and bring Mark with him.¶¶

At the time of writing, he had passed through the first stage of his trial, and was awaiting the second. The want of human sympathy which he had felt in his prison was realized still more intensely during his trial. He says: "At my first answer, no man stood with me, but all forsook me. I pray God that it may not be laid to their charge."*** Even Luke, who dared to visit him in his prison, and remain with him when others fled, shrunk from the fearful position of standing by his side in the presence of Nero. But the venerable man of God, though deserted in his most trying hour by human friends, was able to say, "Notwithstanding, the Lord stood with me, and strengthened me, that by me the preaching might be fully known, and that all the Gentiles might hear; and I was delivered out of the mouth of the lion."††† Thus again had he fearlessly and fully vindicated his preaching in the presence of the imperial court, and passed, a second time, through

* Phil. ii : 24. † Phil. 22. ‡ Life and Ep., vol. 2, p. 447. ‖ Acts xx : 25.
§ 1 Tim. i : 3. ¶ 1 Tim. iii : 14. ** Titus i : 5. †† Titus iii : 12.
‡‡ 2 Tim. iv : 20. ‖‖ 2 Tim. iv : 10. §§ 2 Tim. iv : 12. ¶¶ 2 Tim. iv · 11.
*** 2 Tim. iv : 16. ††† 2 Tim. iv : 17.

the fiery ordeal, without personal injury. The declaration that he was delivered out of the mouth of the lion is an allusion to the case of Daniel, of which his own reminded him. But there was another stage of his trial yet before him, and from this he had reason to anticipate the most fatal results. From all the indications in view, he was induced to write to Timothy, "I am now ready to be offered, and the time of my departure is at hand."* He had some years before declared, "I hold not my life dear to myself, so that I may finish my course with joy, and the ministry which I have received of the Lord Jesus, to testify the gospel of the favor of God." Now, he was about to yield up his life, and upon looking back over the course he had run, and the ministry with which he had been intrusted, the conditions specified were completely fulfilled. With all confidence he is able to say, "I have fought a good fight, I have finished my course, I have kept the faith." † All who have followed his course with us in these pages can bear testimony to this declaration, and, after glancing back with him over the long series of stripes, imprisonment, and exhausting toil through which he had passed, can enter into the feeling of relief and joy with which he looked forward and exclaimed, "Henceforth there is laid up for me a crown of righteousness, which the Lord, the righteous judge, will give to me at that day; and not to me only, but to all them also who love his appearing."‡ Like a mariner on a long voyage, whose bark had been tossed by many waves, and shrouded in the gloom of many a storm, his soul was cheered, at last, by a view of the desired haven close at hand. He is still, however, beaten by the storm, and one more dark billow is yet to roll over him, ere he rests upon the calm waters within the haven. Here the curtain of inspired history closes over him, and the last sound we hear is his own shout of triumph as he braces himself for the last struggle. It only remains for the earliest uninspired history of the Church to confirm his own anticipations, by testifying that his trial finally resulted in a sentence of death, and that he was beheaded outside the gates of Rome, in the last year of the reign of Nero, A. D. 68.|| We bid him adieu till the resurrection morning, well pleased that the course of the narrative on which we have commented has been so directed as to keep us for so long a time in his company.

* 2 Tim. iv: 6.   † 2 Tim. iv: 7.   ‡ 2 Tim. iv: 8. || Life and Ep., vol. 2, p. 487.

THE END.